DICTIONARY OF RETAILING

DICTIONARY OF RETAILING

YOGINDER SINGH

2007

CYBER TECH PUBLICATIONS
4264/3 Ansari Road, Daryaganj, New Delhi - 110 002

Dictionary of Retailing

First Edition 2007

Published by G.S. Rawat
For Cyber Tech Publications
4264/3, Ansari Road, Daryaganj, New Delhi - 110 002
E-mail : cybertechpublishers@yahoo.com
Phone : 011-23244078,
Fax : 011-23280028

Printed at
Tanwar Offset Press, Moujpur, # 9810878184

A

A 1 Condition Best or first-class condition.

AAAI See *Affiliated Advertising Agencies International (AAAI)*

Abandonment A transpportation term referring to cargo damaged in transit on a public carrier and refused at its destination.

ABATE To decrease or reduce a money obligation.

ABC Analysis The technique is used for planning and control purposes. Items are listed by sales volume and classified into three categories: A) those that account for the largest percent of sales and must be stocked at all times; B) those that account for medium levels of sales; and C) those that account for the lowest level of sales. Lower levels of stock may be maintained for the B and C categories.

Absolute Sale An agreement between a buyer and a seller in which the parties agree that there will be no conditions or restrictions affecting the transaction.

Absolute Advantage A trade theory model used to demonstrate the advantages of nation specialisation and subsequent trade. The position of a nation in international marketing is greatly enhanced if it is the sole producer of a product or can produce the product more cheaply and efficiently than any other nation. If, instead of producing all products within its own borders the nation produces only those goods for which it has an advantage and trades with another country having the advantage in another product, both trading partners will benefit.

Absolute Product Failure A product to recoup in the marketplace, the investment made in its development, production and marketing.

Absolute Sale An agreement between a buyer and a seller in which both parties agree that there will be no conditions or restrictions affecting the sales transaction.

Absolute Thresholds This is important to marketers seeking to discover means of differentiating their product in the marketplace as well as those seeking to create effective advertising messages. The basic premise is that people no longer consciously sense stimuli above or below certain limits. See also *just noticeable difference.*

Accents In fashion merchandising, accents are the particular points of emphasis used by the designer to give the style a point-of-view.

Acceptance (1) A writte promise to pay, as in a promissory note. (2) Favorable recepton of a product by the consuming public.

Acceptance Fashion A fashion which has received favorable reception 'in th marketplace.

Accelerated Purchase A sales promotion goal achieved when consumers or channel members purchase the product before the time they would have normally bought.

Acceptable Price Range This includes those prices that buyers are willing to pay for goods or services.

Acceptance. (1) A written promise to pay, as in a promissory note. (2) Favourable reception of a product, brand or line of products by the consuming public.

Acceptance Sampling In quality control, the use of statistical sampling to determine the quality of produced goods and materials. A representative number of items is checked from each lot. The results are used to determine the acceptability of the entire lot. Acceptance sampling is part of a manufacturing firm's inspection process. See also *quality control.*

Accessible Site A site for a retail establishment that may easily be reached by customers and employees. The driving time and/or distance to the site is short and the store's parking area is easy to enter and leave.

Accessories (1) Items used to complete a fashion look, such as handbags, scarves, jewelry, hats, gloves, and shoes. (2) In general, anysubordinate item that adds to the usefulness or attractivenss of the principal item, such as camera lenses or automible mud flaps.

Accessory Equipment Products, usually movable, having a lower cost and shorter life span than installed equipment and which are not incorporated into the finished manufactured product (*e.g.*, tools and office equipment). Although accessory equipments is often charged to the capital budget, it may be treated as an expense item in some organisations.

Acid Test Ratio A financial ration which indicates teh ability of a firm to meet its current obligations, thus summarizing the firm's financial position at a given moment in time. Teh formula is:

$$\frac{\text{Cahs + Receivables + Marketable securities}}{\text{Total current liabilities}}$$

A ration of 1 to 1 is usually considered satisfactor. If the ratio is 2 or more, a minimum risk is presumably indicated. Also known as the "quick" ratio.

Account In Marketing, an account is generally taken to mean a customer with whom the marketer does business.

Account Classification The categorisation of a salesperson's customers into groups, based on criteria such as potential sales, for the purpose of developing a sales call plan. Comment: The classification scheme reflects the relative attractiveness of the various customers and is used to direct sales effort.

Account Executive In advertising, an executive who serves as a liaison between an advertiser and its advertising agency, and who coordinates all aspects of the agency's work on behalf of its client. The account executive oversees and directs the planning in, research, copywriting, art work, media selection, ad production, sales promotion, public relations and accounting functions of the advertising agency.

Account Group The members of the various advertising agency functional departments (such as account management, creative, media planning, research, traffic, etc.) who are assigned to work on an ongoing basis on the projects related to a particular agency clients.

Account Opener In bank marketing an account opener is a gift or premium given to a depositor by the bank as an incentive to open a new account or add to an existing account.

Accounting The (AICPA) Committee on Terminology has defined accounting as: "the art of recording, classifying and summarizing in a significant manner and in terms of money, transactions and evens which are in part at least, of a financial character and interpreting the results thereof."

Acquisition 1. (product development definition) The acquiring by one firm of another firms's technology (process, facility or material) product rights (trademarks) or entire businesses in order to increase its total sales. The acquisition may be related to the firm's current business (*e.g.*, the acquisition of a competitor, a supplier or a buyer) or may be unrelated (*e.g.*, the acquisition of an entirely different business). Acquisition is a method of expanding one's product offering by means other than internal development. Any combination that forms one company from two or more previously existing companies is known as a merger.

2. (strategic marketing definition) The acquiring by one firm of other technology (process, facility or material) product rights (trademarks) or entire businesses in order to increase its total sales. The acquisition may be related to the firm's current business (*e.g.*, the acquisition of a competitor, a supplier or a buyer) or may be unrelated (*e.g.*, the acquisition of an entirely new business). Acquisition is a method of expanding one's product offering by means other than internal development. Any combination that forms one company from two or more previously existing companies is known as a merger.

Acquisition Budget Funds to be used in acquiring customers through sales promotion activities and advertising.

Acquisition Cost Any of the expenses associated with obtaining inventory through either manufacturing or buying the product. For the manufacturer, all the costs associated with beginning production are considered acquisition costs (raw materials, new plants or equipment etc.). For retailers and wholesalers, acquisition costs are the expenses for record keeping and handling the paperwork for each order, thus influencing the *reorder point (ROP)* and the *economic order quantity (EOQ)*.

Acquisition Value The buyers' perceptions of the relative worth of a product or service to them. It is formally defined as the subjectively weighted difference between the most a buyer would be willing to pay for the item less the actual price of the item.

Acronym Aword formed from the first letters of te words in a name or phrase

Active Buyer In direct marketing, any customer whose last purchase was made within the last 12 months. Also called actives and active customers.

Active Member In direct marketing, particularly in such operations as book and record clubs, any member who is currently fulfilling the original commitment or who has already fulfilled that commitment and has made additional purchases in the last 12 months. The member has either paid a fee (on a 6-month, annual or lifetime basis etc.) for the right to receive information about and/or actually purchase items or has committed himself/herself to make a minimum number of purchases during a particular period of time by virtue of goods and/or services already received.

Active Subscriber A customer who has committed himself/herself to receive regular delivery of magazines, books, stamps, or other goods and/or services for a period of time currently in effect.

Activities, Interests and Opinions (AIO) A measurable series of psychographic variables involving the interests and beliefs of consumers.

Activity Based Costing A cost accounting system that ties actual costs to the direct performance and value of activities. Costs are not allocated based on a formula, but are traced and charged to specific activities.

Ad Valorem Duty A tax on imports laid in the form of a percentage ofthe value of th eproperty.

Adaptation The ability of both individuals and organisations to respond to the surrounding environment, including both opportunities and threats.

Adaptation Pricing Policy A pricing for the rest of the world of adapting home country prices to local competitive and market circumstances. It is also known as polycentric pricing policy.

Adaptive Behaviour Theory A theory of evolutionary change in which firms most capable of adapting to changing conditions in the market-place are seen as having the best chance of survival.

Adaptive Planning An iterative process framework for organising myriad information flows, analyses, issues and opinions that coalesee into strategic decisions. There are four stages to this process: (1) situation assessment—the analysis of internal and environmental factors that influence business performance, combined with a comparison of past performance relative to objectives and expectations, (2) strategic thinking—identification of key issues that have a major impact on performance and the generation of creative strategic options for dealing with each issue, (3) decision making—selection of strategic thrust, choices of options and allocation of resources in light of mutually acceptable objectives and (4) implementation—ongoing activities that translate strategic decisions into specific programmes, projects and near-term functional action plans. The process is iterative because the implementation phase will eventually be followed by a revised situation assessment.

Adaptive Product Also called adapted product, this market entry acquires its uniqueness by variation on another, more pioneering product. The degree of adaption is more than trivial (to avoid being an emulative product or "me -too" product) but it varies greatly in significance.

Adaptive Selling An approach to personal selling in which selling behaviours are altered during the sales interaction or across customer interactions, based on information about the nature of the selling situation.

Add-on Sales (1) Additional charge purchases made before all previous purchases have been paid in full. (2) In sales, additional purchases of related merchandise made at the suggestion of th esalesperson.

Additions to Retail Percentage Total price changes as a percentage of original price.

$$\text{Addition to retail percentage} = \frac{\text{New Price} - \text{original price}}{\text{Original price}}$$

Additional Markdown Afurther decrease in an itm's selling price beyond the original markdown.

Additional Markup An increase in the original retail price of goods due toerrors in origianl pricing or to increases in their market value.

Adjusted Balance Method A method by which retailers calculate the balance in a charge account upon which a service charge is to be assessed. Under the adjusted balance method, charges are made after payments made during the billing period have been subtracted from the outstanding balance. See also *previous balance method and average daily balance method.*

Adjusted Retail Book Value An endign retail bookvalue correctedto reflectstock shortages andoverages.

$$\text{Adjusted retail} = \frac{\text{Ending retail book value} - \text{stock}}{\text{shortage} + \text{stock overages}}$$

Administered Distribution System See *administered vertical marketing system*

Administered Marketing Network See *administered vertical marketing system*

Administered Pricing Prices may be set or administered, by the manufacturer or other marketing channel members. The seller may hold this set price steady over a period of time, but unless the firm sells directly to the ultimate consumer, other channel members may make the set price difficult to hold. For example, wholesalers selling to discount outlets will tend to bring down the price set by the manufacturer. Most firms do administer prices; all firms engaged in monopolistic competition do.

Administered Vertical Marketing System A vertical marketing system in which the channel members, while retaining much of their autonomy, are informally coordinated in their marketing activities by the dominant member of the channel. Dominance is achieved through the exercise of political or economic power rather than throughout right ownership.

Administrative Control A term applied to studies relying on questionnaires and referring to the speed, cost and control of the replies afforded by the mode of administration.

Adopter Categories Persons or firms that adopt an innovation are often classified into five groups according to the sequence of their adoption of it: (1) Innovators (the first 2 to 5 percent); (2) Early adopters (the next 10 to 15 per cent); (3) Early majority (the next 35 per cent); (4) Late majority (the next 35 per cent); (5) Laggards (the final 5 to 10 per cent). The numbers are percents of the total number of actual adopters, not of the total adopter categories (the number of persons or firms in the marketplace). There is wide disagreement on the exact portion in each category.

Adoption Curve A distribution curve which graphically represents the diffusion of an innovation as various groups adopt new products. The curve illustrates new products. The curve illustrates the number of adopters who have purchased a new product or service during each time period beginning with the launch date. It takes the shape of a normal statistical distribution in that a small number of people adopt the innovation when it first becomes available and this rate of adoption increases until 50% of the potential users have tried it After this point has been reached, the number of individuals adopting the product within each time period decreases until there are no potential adopters who have not yet tried the innovation. An alternative method of representing the same process is the diffusion curve, an *S*-shaped curve which results from plotting the cumulative number of adopters against time. See also *diffusion process*.

Adoption Process (1) A decision-making activity entered into by consumers when they are confronted by new products or services. It entails a number of stages: awareness, interest, evaluation, trial and finally, if the product is purchased, adoption. Post adoption confirmation, *i.e.,* the decision to purchase the product or service on a regular basis in the future, is sometimes treated as a part of the process. Also known as the buying decision-making process and the consumer's decision process. (2) In fashion merchandising, the adoption process is the diffusion of styles and trends from their point of origin; *e.g.,* from a particular social class, to other classes or segments of society. See also *diffusion process.*

Adoption Process Segmentation Variables The stages that a consumer must pass through in the process of becoming a regular user of a product or service. These stages include awareness, interest, evaluation, trial and adoption. For a new or unconventional product or service (such as home banking by computer). See also *adoption process.*

Advance Dating The practice of setting a specific future date, after shipment and after the invoice date, when the terms of sale become applicable. For example, under the terms "2/10, net 30 as of March 1," a 2% discount will be made for payment within 10 days and the net payment period will be calculated from March 1, regardless of the shipping and/or invoice dates. Advance dating is sometimes used to allow for transportation of merchandise and sometimes to encourage orders in advance of the normal buying season. See also *seasonal dating.*

Advance Order An order placed well in advance of the desired time of shipment. This practice generallyenables a buyer to obtain a lower price for the goods since he has given the manufacturer business during slack periods.

Advanced Sales Training Ongoing or continuing training for sales personnel, sometimes intended as a refresher course, but more often providing more sophisticated and problem-oriented sales training is much more concerned with strategies and skills in consultive selling system selling, and sales negotiation than in sales force indoctrination training. See also *sales training.*

Advertised Brand A brand that is owned by an organization (usually a manufacturer) that uses a marketing strategy usually involving a substantial advertising. An advertised brand is a consumer product, though it need not be and is contrasted with a private brand, which is not normally advertised heavily.

Advertisement Any announcement or persuasive message placed in the mass media in paid or donated time or space by an identified individual, company or organisation.

Advertiser An individual, firm or other organisation that originates or sponsors an advertisement or advertising campaign. The advertiser, whether the client of an advertising agency or the producer of in-house advertising, may be a political candidate, a manufacturer, a retail organi-sation, a wholesaler, an association or public service organisation, etc.

Advertising The paid non-personal communication of a message intended to sell or promote a product, service, person, idea, or issue. The sponsor of the message is almost always identified. The media employed to transmit advertising include newspapers, magazines, television, radio, direct mail, etc. The goal of advertising, which may be regarded as a marketing tool, is to persuade, remind or inform the target audience. There are, basically, only two types of advertising: institutional or corporate advertising and product or brand advertising. Both are a part of the promotion process, which, in turn, forms the marketing communication system. See also *institutional advertising* and *product advertising*.

Advertising Agency An independent organisation equipped to provide all phases of advertising for its clients. The agency prepares and places advertisements, and may perform related research and promotional activities. In a full-line agency these services are paid primarily by commissions from the media that carry the advertising (a percentage of the dollar value of the media they purchase for a client). For example, if an agency purchases $100,000 worth of space in a particular magazine, the magazine bills the agency for $85,000 and the agency bills the client for the full $100,000, keeping the difference to cover costs and profits. The agency typically consists of a group of experts on various phases of advertising. Most large advertising agencies have at least four departments: (1) research— which collects data on customers; (2) creative—

which prepares and produces copy and art; (3) media—which selects the vehicles for the ads and buys the time and/or space; and (4) account management—which serves as a liaison between the client and the agency. Agencies often specialize in the type of goods they handle (such as consumer goods, industrial goods, international business, services, etc.). See also *a la carte agency and boutique agency*, which are specialised types of advertising agencies that provide other than full service.

Advertising Allowance A sum of money paid by a manufacturer or producer to a reseller (usually a retailer) to compensate the reseller for the cost of locally advertising the producer's product. Such advertising is most generally aimed at the ultimate consumer and is developed at the local level in support of a particular product, line or brand. Also known as coop money. See also *cooperative advertising* and *promotional allowance*.

Advertising Appropriation The total amount of money allocated for an organisation's advertising program during a specific time period. The appropriation may be based on a percentage of past or projected sales, calculated according to the cost of the task at hand or a combination of the two.

Advertising Budget The decision about how much money should be spent for advertising during a specific time period in order to accomplish the specific objectives of a client. This decision also involves the allocation of specific amounts of the total advertising appropriation to various media, creative approaches, times of the year and to the production costs involved in preparing the advertising messages for placement in the various media.

Advertising Campaign A planned advertising effort which extends over a period of time and which is designed to promote a particular product or service. The advertising campaign involves setting objectives, determining an advertising budget, positioning the product, deciding on a message, selecting the appropriate media and measuring the campaign's effectiveness.

Advertising Claim A statement made in advertising about the benefits, characteristics and/or performance of a product or service designed to persuade the customer to make a purchase.

Advertising Contract A contractual agreement between an advertiser and the operator of any form of advertising media for the purchase of specified types of advertising time or space.

Advertising Copy The verbal or written component of advertising messages.

Advertising Council A nonprofit organisation in the United States composed of advertisers, advertising agencies, and advertising media whose purpose is to organise and carry out public service advertising. The Council selects particular public service organisations to support, identifies volunteer advertising agencies to create advertising campaigns for each selected public service organisation and coordinates the distribution of the advertising materials to the advertising media, which donate time or space in which to disseminate each campaign to the public.

Advertising Effectiveness An evaluation of the extent to which a specific advertisement or advertising campaign meets the objectives specified by the client. There is a wide variety of approaches to evaluation, including inquiry tests, recall tests and market tests. The measurement approaches include recall of ads and advertising themes, attitudes toward the advertising, persuasiveness and impact on actual sales levels.

Advertising Goals Those specific purposes which underlie an advertisement or advertising campaign. Most advertising has as its goal the stimulation (within a particular time frame) of some specific and immediate activity on the part of the consumer. See also *advertising objectives*.

Advertising Idea The theme or concept that serves as the organising thought for an advertisement. Ideas are used to dramatize the product-related information conveyed in advertising.

Advertising Manager In business organisations, the employee responsible for supervising the development of advertising for the firm. Also reviews and approves ads which are ready to be placed in the media. See also *advertising sales manager*.

Advertising Media All of the channels employed by advertisers to reach their audiences and convey their sales messages. Advertising media include print media (such as newspapers and magazines), broadcast media (radio and television), outdoor (such as billboards), transit (such as car cards and posters in stations) and point-of-purchase displays.

Advertising Models Large numbers of models have been used to assist in making advertising decisions. Econometric and other market models, as well as decision calculus models such as ADBUDG, have been used in the determination of advertising budgets. Media selection and scheduling models have included linear and nonlinear programming-type models, such as MEDIAC and decision calculus models. Few models, such as Aaker's ADMOD (1975), have been designed to deal simultaneously with budget, copy and media allocation decisions.

Advertising Objectives The communication and sales objectives assigned to advertising, which flow from prior decisions regarding the product's target market, target position and marketing mix. Advertising objectives may inform persuade or remind. If they inform, they may tell about a new product or service, suggest new uses for the product, correct false impressions about the product or service, announce price changes, build the company's image or reduce consumer fears. If intended to persuade, the advertising objectives may be to build brand preference, to encourage brand switching or to simply persuade the customer to purchase the product or service. Finally, if its advertising is intended to remind, the objectives may be to inform the customers as to where the product or service may be purchased and to remind them that it may be needed at a later date. See also *advertising goals*.

Advertising Penetration The percentage of the target market that remembers a significant portion of the advertising message conveyed by an advertised campaign.

Advertising Platform The main issues or selling points an advertiser wishes to include in an advertising campaign.

Advertising Sales Manager The employee of a media organisation (newspaper, magazine, television network, etc.) responsible for selling advertising space or time to prospective advertisers.

In the broadcast media more commonly called a sales manager. See also *advertising manager*.

Advertising Sales-Response Curve The graphic representation of the relationship between advertising expenditures on the horizontal axis and the results in sales on the vertical axis. The usual assumption is that sales will increase as advertising expenditures increase.

Advertising Specialities Items of little value (pencils, key rings, ash trays, etc.) which carry the name of the firm or product, its picture, logo etc., and which are used as giveaways. The objective of such advertising is to create goodwill.

Advertising Strategy A statement prepared by the advertiser (often in association with an advertising agency) setting for the (1) competitive frame, (2) target market and (3) message argument to be used in an advertising campaign for a specific product or service.

Advertising Substantiation The documentation by means of tests or other evidence of product performance claims made in advertising. Federal Trade Commission decisions indicate that it is a deceptive and/or unfair practice for advertisers to fail to possess reasonable documentation for product performance claims made in advertising messages before the claims are disseminated to the public.

Advisor A descriptive model explaining the level of marketing communication expenditures for industrial products. Two of the more important explanatory variables are the size of the product market (*i.e.,* dollar sales in the previous year) and the number of potential customers that the marketing effort is to reach.

Advocacy Advertising Advertising whose objective is to support a particular belief or course of action on the part of its audience. It is designed to induce or discourage certain specific forms of activity with regard to controversial subjects. See also *cause marketing* and *cause-related marketing.*

Advocate Channel A personal communication channel consisting of company salespeople contracting buyers in the target market.

Affect (1) (consumer behaviour definition) The feelings a person has toward an attitude object such as a brand, advertisement, salesperson etc. Affect is growing in importance in attempts to understand and predict consumer behaviour. (2) (consumer behaviour definition) The affective responses include states such as emotions, specific feelings, and moods that vary in level of intensity and arousal.

Affective Component In attitude research, particularly in the tripartite view or structural approach, the affective component is the individual's overall feelings of like or dislike about a service, product or similar object. It is the emotional component of attitude formation. See also *attitude*.

Affective Conflict A state of conflict that exists when a channel member feels stress, frustration, tension or hostility toward another channel member.

Affiliated Store A store operated as a unit of a voluntary group or franchise group. Also it may be a store controlled by another store but operated under a separate name.

Affiliative Group Any reference group such as the family, church, school, etc. to which an individual actually belongs.

Affinities A tendency for similar or complementary retail stores to be located in close proximity to one another. For example, furniture stores in a city may be located in close proximity to one another in order to facilitate consumer comparison shopping.

Affirmative Disclosure A procedure adopted by the Federal Trade Commission in its attempt to regulate advertising. The procedure stipulates that if the information contained in an advertisement is considered insufficient by the commission, it may require a company to disclose some of the limitations of its product or service within its subsequent advertising. This is done so that the consumer may judge the product's (or service's) negative as well as positive attributes.

After Market The aggregate demand for parts and service which follows the sale of a product such as an automobile or computer.

After Sales Support The services offered by the selling firm after the sale has been made to promote goodwill, ensure customer satisfaction and develop customer loyalty. Comment: This requires a salesperson to monitor order processing; to ensure proper installation and initial use of products; and to provide maintenance, repair services and information on the care and use of products.

Agency Cost The dollar reduction in welfare experienced by the principal due to the inherent nature of the agency relationship with management.

Agency of Record (AOR) An advertising agency assigned specific media buying responsibilities by a client.

Agency Theory A theory of the firm that seeks to explain corporate activities as arising out of the natural conflicts between the principals (stockholders) and agents (managers) of a firm.

Agent In a broad business sense an agent is stone who acts as an intermediary between two parties for the purpose of facilitating trade. For more restricted uses of the term see also *agent middleman, manufacturer's agent*, and *selling agent*.

Agent Middleman A wholesaling middleman (sometimes called an agent wholesaler or simply an agent) who, acting as a market intermediary, performs a number of wholesaling functions without taking title to the goods he sells and frequently without taking physical possession of the goods. The agent middleman is highly specialised and has and extensive knowledge of the market in which he operates. His principal function is to render assistance in the passing of title to goods from one party to another. Included under the term agent middleman are selling agent, manufacture's agent, broker , commission merchant and auction company.

Agents and Brokers Independent middlemen (intermediaries) who do not take title to the goods they handle, but do actively negotiate the purchase or sale of goods for their clients.

Aggregate Monetary Demand The total planned expenditure (within and economy) by consumers, firms, government and foreigners on goods and services which are produced within that economy. Indirect taxes and import components are deducted before calculating the aggregate monetary demand.

Aggregation A concept of market segmentation that assumes that most consumers are alike. Retailers adhering to the concept focus on common dimensions of the market rather than uniqueness and the strategy is to focus on the broadest possible number of buyers by an appeal to universal product themes. Reliance is on mass distri-bution, mass advertising and a universal theme of low price.

Aging 1. In retailing, the length of time merchandise has been in stock. 2. For certain products such as tobacco, liquor, and cheese, aging is part of the curing process.

Agribusiness The business functions related to agriculture. Agribusiness includes farming as well as the processing of food and other agricultural products, the manufacture of farm equipment and the production of ancillary farm goods such as fertilisers.

AIDA An approach to understanding how advertising and selling supposedly work. The assumption is that the consumer passes through several steps in the influence process. First, Attention must be developed, to be followed by Interest, Desire and finally Action as called for in the message. Another, but similar, scheme was developed by Lavidge and Steiner in 1961, later to be dubbed the AIDA: Hierarchy of Effects Model by Palda in 1966. This approach involves the hierarchy of effects: awareness, knowledge, liking, preference, conviction and finally purchase in that order. Note the similarity to the adoption process.

AIO Inventory In psychographic research, a method used to determine consumers' activities, interests and opinion (AIO) by means of a life-style measurement survey.

Air Freight The use of airplanes for transporting goods. Because air freight rates are more expensive than truck or freight rates, this mode of shipping is usually reserved for situations in which speed is essential and or distant markets must be reached. It is a particularly effective means of shipping perishables (such as fresh fish or flowers) and high-value, low bulk items (such as jewellery). The cost of air freight may also be justified when it leads to decreases in inventory levels, the number of ware-houses required and packaging costs. See also *air freight decision tool.*

Airport-to-Airport Shipping Transportation of merchandise from one airport to another by an air carrier.

Air Truck A coordinated mode of shipping goods which involves the combined use of air freight and truck freight. Its ease of use is made possible through containerisation.

All the Traffic Will Bear See *profit maximisation objective.*

All-You Can-Afford Budgeting An approach to the advertising budget that establishes the amount to be spent on advertising as the funds remaining after all other necessary expenditures and investments have been covered in the comprehensive budget for the business or organisation.

All-You-Can-Afford Technique A method of developing a promotional budget in which all non-promotional marketing expenses are budgeted first and remaining funds allocated to promotional purposes.

Allocation The process by which large, homogeneous inventories are broken down into smaller lots as the goods get closer to the final market. Allocation may involve several levels of middleman, each handling increasingly smaller quantities. Retailers complete the process by selling individual items to the individual consumer. Allocation helps to alleviate the discrepancy of quantity. Also called *bulk-breaking, sorting out* and *dispersion.*

Allowance A reduction from list or invoice price made by a manufacturer, wholesaler or retailer in return for the performance of certain services or activities on the part of the customer or to compensate the customer for some other reason. For example, advertising and promotional allowances compensate wholesalers and retailers for the expenses incurred in promoting a product locally. Cost allowances compensate the customer for such problems as goods delivered late or damaged. Trade-in allowances compensate the customer for old equipment turned in when new equipment is purchased. See also discount, a similar form of price reduction and specific forms of allowance, such as *cost allowance, trade-in allowance, promotional allowance, advertising allowance* and *trade discount.*

Alphanumeric A contraction of the words "alphabetic" and "numeric."

The term applies to any code or coding system that provides for letters, numbers, and special symbols (such as punctuation marks). These codes are often machine processable and may enable the user to use a computer for such functions as inventory control. Sometimes called alphameric.

Alteration Cost The net cost of altering goods for customers for repair of items in stock. The cost includes labour, supplies and all expenses, including costs for this service when purchased outside the store.

Alteration Room A section run in conjunction with one or more selling departments, that alters merchandise to customers' wishes, especially for men's and women's apparel.

American Telemarketing Association (ATA) An association of telephone marketing businesses and related firms, based in Glenview, Illinois. The association seeks to promote the use of telephone sales and to improve the industry's public image. ATA publishes a quarterly newsletter and an annual *Membership Roster*. It also provides a speakers bureau, seminars, library and educational standards for university courses.

Analog Approach A method of trade area analysis that is also known as the similar store or mapping approach. The analysis is divided into four steps: (1) describing the current trade areas by using a technique known as customer spotting; (2) plotting the customer on a map; (3) defining the primary trade zone, secondary trade zone and tertiary trade zone; and (4) matching the characteristics of stores in the trade areas with a potential new store to estimate its sales potential

Analytic Hierarchy Process (AHP) A three-step process for making resource allocation decisions. First, the organisation's objectives, sub-objectives and strategies are organized hierarchically Next, the decision maker evaluates, in a pairwise fashion, each of the elements in a particular stratum of the hierarchy with respect to its importance in accomplishing each of the elements of the next-higher stratum. Finally, a model is applied to these pairwise judgements that produces a set of importance (or priority) weights for each element of each stratum in the hierarchy (Wind and Saaty 1980). Areas of application in marketing include the product portfolio decision, selection of new products to develop and generation and evaluation of various marketing mix strategies.

Analytical Marketing System (AMS) One of four subsystems of a company's marketing information system (MIS), which consists of a statistical bank and a model bank for analysing marketing data and problems. The statistical bank is essentially a collection of statistical procedures or routines which may be used to extract meaningful information from data. These procedures include routines for calculating averages, measuring dispersion, and cross tabulation of the data. The researcher may also use the multivariate statistical techniques contained in the statistical bank to uncover relationships in the data. Those include multiple regression analysis, discriminate analysis, factor analysis, and cluster analysis. The model bank on the other hand, is a collection of models used by marketers to make marketing decisions. The bank includes models for new product sales forecasting, site selection, sales-call planning, media mix, and marketing mix budgeting. The models may be descriptive, verbal, graphic, or mathematical. See also *marketing information system (MIS)* and *model.*

Anchor Store A large and well-known retail operation located in a shopping centre and serving as an attracting force to draw consumers to the cėntre.

Anchoring Effect The result when buyers make comparisons of prices or products against a reference price or reference product. The result of this comparison is usually weighted toward the anchor, creating an anchor bias, the anchoring effect.

Ancillary Service 1. (physical distribution definition) A service offering provided by model operators in addition to basic transportation services. The provision of such services typically includes sorting, storing product prior to delivery, marking or tagging the product and collecting rate shipment. 2. (retailing definition). The service such as layaway, gift wrap, credit and others not directly related to the actual sale of a specific product within the store. Some of these services are charged for and some are not.

AnticipationA discount in addition to the cash discount if a bill is paid prior to the expiration of the cash discount period, usually at the rate of 6 percent per annum—*e.g.*, at this rate, for 60 days prepayment, which is 1/6 of an interest year, the anticipation ratio would be 1 percent of the facc amount.

Anti-competitive Leasing Arrangement A lease that limits the type and amount of competition a particular retailer faces within a trading area or shopping center.

Anti-dumping Duties The penalty duties on goods that have been declared in violation of antidumping laws. The duties that take the form of special additional import charges equal to the dumping margin.

Anti-dumping Laws The laws passed by a host government to protect local industries from dumping.

Anti-dumping Tariff A tax levied against imported goods which are being dumped (sold at prices below those in the home market) on the domestic market. See also *countervailing duty.*

Approach The first few minutes of the contact between a salesperson and a potential customer. Approach is the stage in the sales presentation which is designed to gain and hold the prospect's attention. It includes the following these steps: (1) salesperson introduces himself/herself to the prospect; (2) salesperson "sells" himself/herself, the product and the company to the prospect; (3) salesperson gets and holds the prospect's attention and interest. During the approach, the salesperson draws out the prospect to determine his/her needs. This information will later be used to convince the prospect of the advantages of the salesperson's product or service. There are many different approaches, including the benefit approach (which emphasises the benefit to the prospect of doing business with the salesperson), the curiosity approach (in which the salesperson bases his/her presentation on the prospect's curiosity and interest), the dramatic approach (an eye-opening show or demonstration which often involves the prospect) and the factual approach (which uses an interesting fact about the product or service to capture the prospect's attention). See also the names of specific approaches.

Approach, Sales The initial stage in a sales interaction. Comment:

The objectives of the approach are securing approval for the sales call, getting the prospect's attention and interest and building rapport with the prospect.

Approval Sale A sale subject to later approval or selection, the customer having unlimited return privileges.

Approved Vendor List A list of suppliers with whom purchasing agents are allowed to close contracts.

Apron A form attached to an invoice or copy of purchase order in retail stores, containing details to check before payment. It is sometimes called a rider.

Arbitrage The simultaneous purchase and sale of the same commodity or security in two different markets in an attempt to profit from price differences in the two markets.

Arbitrary Allocation See arbitrary approach

Arbitrary Approach A method for allocating a firm's promotional budget in which the amount spent on promotion for a particular time period is the result of deriving an executive decision rather than from scientific analysis. Also known as arbitrary allocation.

Arbitration In negotiations, the process by which both parties to a dispute agree to submit the dispute to a third party for a binding decision.

Arcade Shopping Centre An enclosed shopping area with a number of stores in lanes under archways and with one roof overhead.

Area of Dominant Influence (ADI) The geographic area surrounding a city in which the broadcasting stations based in that city account for a greater share of the listening or viewing households than do broadcasting stations based in other nearby cities.

Area Sampling A method of probability sampling in which the stratified sample is made on the basis of geography rather than by demographics or other population characteristics. Geographic areas (such as city blocks) serve as the segments or primary units. The researcher divides the population first by mutually exclusive geographic areas and then draws a sample of the groups to interview. This method of obtaining a random sample is most useful when population lists are unavailable. See also *sampling, probability sampling* and *random sampling.*

Arm's Length Policy A practice in transfer pricing in which the home or parent company charges foreign subsidiaries the same price it charges firms who are not part of the organisation.

Arrival of Goods (AOG) This is applicable to the cash discount period, indicating that the discount will be granted if payment is made within the number of days specified, calculated from the time the goods arrive at the destination. It is used for the purpose of accommodating distantly located customers. The net payment period. however, is computed from the time of shipment.

Art In advertising, Art is the illustration appearing inan advertisement (photographs, drawings, charts, graphs, etc.) as well as the layout of the visual components of the ad.

Art Director A person possessing good taste who is skilled in the visualization of advertising ideas.

Articles of Partnership A legal document that covers all items agreed upon by the partners in a business and which each partner has signed.

Articulated Railcar An extended rail chassis that can haul up to ten containers on a single flexible unit. This reduces the weight and the time required to interchange railcars.

Artificial Intelligence (AI) An area of computer science concerned with designing smart computer systems. AI systems exhibit the characteristics generally associated with inteligence in human learning, reasoning and solving problems.

Artificial Trading Area That geographic area specified by a firm as the territory in which it will conduct its business.

Artwork Any illustration (including design elements, drawing, painting, photography) used in the production of print advertising. The term is often used in the short form *art.*

Asch Phenomenon Named after a study conducted by S.E. Asch (published 1958) in which he demonstrated the influence groups have upon individual choice making. He found that if individuals can determine the expectations of the group to which they belong they tend to adhere to those expectations in making purchase decisions.

Aspirational Group Any group to which an individual would like to belong (such as a little leaguer wishing to become a professional baseball player). For marketing, the implication is that the desire to emulate the chosen group influences consumer buying decisions. The little leaguer will want to eat the "breakfast of champions," the media student will aspire to a Mechedes, the secretary seeking promotion to a management position will "dress for success," etc.

Assembling The process of developing an inventory of homogeneous products, such as agricultural produce, from the small lots of a number of small producers so that they may be handled economically further along the marketing channel. Goods so accumulated may be shipped and sold in larger lots and thus benefit from such factors as lower shipped rates (in carload or truckload quantities). Goods are brought to collection points by the individual small producers and collected by an agent middleman known as an assembler. Assemblers seldom take title to the goods they handle. Also called accumulating or concentration.

Assessor A model for predicting the market share of a new frequently purchased product using pretest market information. Perceptions and preferences of potential customers are measured via interview and a simulated shopping experience conducted at a central location. The prediction is based on the sample participants' reaction to advertising (exposure to advertisements for several brands), estimated level of product trial (based on the simulated shopping experience), estimated repeat purchase level (via follow-up interview) and brand preference judgements (Silk and Urban 1978). Evidence on the model's predictive validity has been reported by Urban and Katz (1983).

Asset The Financial Accounting Standards Board (FASB) has defined an asset as a "probable future economic benefit obtained or controlled by a particular enterprise as a result of past transaction" (1979). Simply stated, an asset is any item owned (such as cash, receivables, inventory, equipment, land, buildings and goodwill) whether tangible or intangible.

Asset Conversion A means of internally financing a firm's projects by liquidating one form of asset to employ elsewhere within the firm or repay a liability.

Asset Turnover The Financial ratio whichresultsfromdividing a compans et sales for the accounting period by its average assets during he same perod. Ameans of examining the company's operations over a period of time.

$$\text{Asset turnover} = \frac{\text{Net sales}}{\text{Average assets during the accounting period}}$$

Asset Turnover Ratio The ratio of net sales to total assets.

$$\text{Asset turnover} = \frac{\text{Net sales during the period}}{\text{Average assets during the period}}$$

Assigned Mailing Date In direct marketing, the date on which a list user must mail a particular purchased list, by virtue of a prior agreement between the list owner and the user. The user may not mail that list on any other date except with the specific authorization of the list owner.

Assignment (1) The transfer of claim, right, property, etc. (2) The legal paper authorising this transfer.

Associated Buying Office A type of resident buying office that is cooperatively maintained in a central market by a group of noncompeting independent stores. It is controlled and financed by the stores, each store paying a prorated share of the office expenses.

Association Advertising A form of horizontal cooperative advertising performed by trade associations (such as the Florida Citrus Growers Association) to promote primary demand for a class of products (such as Florida oranges). See also *cooperative advertising*

Association Advertising Format A type of advertisement that conveys its message by establishing a relationship between an event, an activity, or an image and the product being promoted. For example an ad using this format would seek to transfer the excitement generated by skydiving to a product such as beer. Distinct from association advertising which is a form of horizontal cooperative advertising.

Association of Direct Marketing Agencies (ADMA) A professional organisation of firms engaged in multi-media direct marketing. ADMA sponsors seminars and workshops. Its headquarters are in Brookline, Massachusetts.

Assorting The process of developing a heterogeneous inventory of products for the convenience of customers. This function is usually performed by wholesalers or retailers in order to supply an assortment of products such as hardware, drugs, grocery items, etc. The convenience factor may motivate sellers to stock related items, not directly associated with their principal line of goods. For example, a lawn mower dealer may sell grass seed and other related gardening items.

Assortment (1) A mix of similar and/or complementary products designed to provide benefits to a specific market. (2) In retailing, the range of choice within a particular classification of goods, such as style, color, size and price.

Atmospherics The environmental factors consciously designed to create a certain mood, develop a particular image and/or stimulate sales. These factors include layout, architecture, colour scheme and other sensory stimuli. In retail stores, atmospherics are used to develop an image, draw customers and increase the probability that customers will mark purchases. In other environments, such as banks and offices, atmospherics may be used to inspire confidence. In sum, atmospherics are a form of nonpersonal communication. See also *ambiance*.

Atomistic Competition A condition in the marketplace in which there are so many competitors that no one seller can influence the price of the product or commodity they all make or produce. This condition exists in farm commodity production and in the women's ready-to-wear industry.

Attention The process by which a consumer selects information in the environment to interpret. Also, it is the point at which a consumer becomes aware or conscious of particular stimuli in the environment..

Attitude A person's knowledge and positive or negative cognitive evaluations about an object such as a product or service. Attitudes are learned, enduring and made up of three components: (1) knowledge; (2) affect; and (3) action tendency. Knowledge, the cognitive component of attitude, is usually expressed as a belief. For example, "I believe whole grain breads are nutritionally superior to white bread." The consumer's overall feeling toward the product is called affect or the affective component. For example, "I prefer whole grain bread to white bread." The action tendency, or behavioural component is the consumer's readiness to act on his/her beliefs and feelings. For example, "I will buy whole grain bread on my next shopping trip." The more favourable a consumer's attitude to a product, the more likely he/she is to use and purchase the product or service. Marketers are, therefore, interested in changing negative attitudes as well as reinforcing the positive attitudes of satisfied customers. The enduring aspect of attitude enables the consumer to behave in a fairly consistent way toward similar objects without having to interpret and react to every object in a fresh way.

Attitude Scale A measurement tool used to determine the intensity of a subject's feelings toward a product or other object. Subjects respond to a series of adjectives, phrases or sentences about the product by checking whether they "strongly agree, agree, have no opinion, disagree or strongly disagree" with each statement. Researchers then tally the answers to get an indication of the strength of consumer opinions.

Attraction Model A market share model that predicts a particular brand's market share as the quotient of that brand's "attraction" divided by the sum of the "attraction" level for all brands in the market. The attraction levels for all brands in the market. The attraction level for a brand is often in turn expressed as a function of customer characteristics, the marketing mix and the competitive environment. Conditions under which an attraction model can be expected to hold have been described by Bell, Keeney and Little (1975).

Attribute Mapping In new product planning, a statistical means of analysing a market in an effort to find openings for new products. Existing products are positioned on a chart called an attribute space with each position being determined by the product's characteristics. Open spaces indicate gaps into which new products may be introduced. Also known as market position analysis.

Attribution Theory A theory or group of several theories, stemming from Heider's (1958) belief in the importance of understanding individual's "naive theories" of causality. Attribution theory assumes that individuals attempt to understand their environments in an analytical fashion, arriving at explanations of causality through a fairly logical process. Kelly (1967, 1972) provided an influential elaboration of the process by which individuals infer causality. Based on this, attribution theory suggests that individuals make inferences of causality based on the extent to which events covary across individuals, situations and cover time.

Auction A market in which goods are sold to the highest bidder. The auction usually is well publicised in advance or held at specific times well known in the trade. Exchange is effected in accordance with definite rules, with sales made to the highest bidder.

Auction Company An agent middleman selling by the auction method; *i.e.,* customers may examine the product before engaging in competitive bidding for its purchase. Commonly employed in the sale of agricultural products, such as fruit, tobacco, livestock, etc. The auction company receives a commission from the seller of the merchandise based on the final sales price. Also known as auction houses.

Audience (1) The total number of individuals reached by an advertisement or other promotion. For example, the number of viewers seeing a particular television commercial or seeing a particular print advertisement in a magazine or newspaper. (2) The target group at which a promotional message is aimed. For example, marketers may gear their advertisements to appeal to a particular segments of the population, such as "puppies." Also called target audience. See also *receiver*.

Audience Accumulation The total number of different persons or households exposed to a media vehicle or to a particular advertising campaign during a specified period of time.

Audience Composite See *audience profile*

Audience Duplication The total number of persons or households exposed more than once to the same media vehicle or to a particular advertising campaign during a specified period of time.

Audience Profile The characteristics of the audience reached by an advertising medium (print or broadcast) or a particular station, newspaper, or magazine etc. It includes both demographic and psychographic characteristics. Generally presented as a percentage figure which may be compared to the population as a whole. Also known as audience comp, audience composite and audience composition.

Audience Share The percentage of the total listening or viewing audience, *i.e.,* those with their sets actually turned on which are tuned to a particular program at a specific time.

Audience Study Survey research aimed at learning who the audience is for an advertising medium and how it reacts to the advertising message.

Audimeter An electronic monitoring device used to measure the time periods during which a television set is being used and the specific channel to which it is tuned at each moment.

Audit An examination of a firm's accounting records and the evidence in support of its correctness. The audit may be internal or external. The internal audit is performed in-house by employees of the firm. It involves a review of the firm's business records, reports, financial statements, etc. to verify their accuracy and confirmity to the organisation's policies. The external audit, on the other hand, is conducted by a certified public accountant or other auditor employed by an independent outside accounting firm. The purpose of the external audit is to verify the record's compliance with generally accepted accounting principles (GAAP). The annual reports of publicly held firms contain the external auditor's evaluation of the firm's accounting techniques and the accuracy of its financial documentation. See also *marketing audit.*

Audit Bureau of Circulations (ABC) An organisation sponsored by advertisers, advertising agencies and print media publishers that verifies the audience circulation figures claimed by newspapers and magazines.

Audited Sales The reconciliation of daily cash and charge sales against the recorded total on the sales registers. This reconciliation is accomplished in a back office procedure at the end of the day.

Auditing (Post and Pre) Transportation freight bills are checked to assure billing accuracy. *Preauditing* determines the proper rate and charges prior to payment of a freight bill. *Postauditing* makes the same determination after payment.

Augmented Product The core product together with its attendant benefits and services.

Authority. The power or right to give orders or commands, take actions, make decisions and to expect obedience. See also *market division of authority*.

Authorisation A process by which credit sales are approved either through a telephone system from the selling floor to the credit office or by an automated system tied into a point-of-sale system.

Authorised Dealer A dealer who has a contractual agreement (similar to a franchise) to sell the products of a particular manufacturer. The authorised dealer generally has the rights to the distribution of these products within a particular trading area.

Automated Guided Vehicle System (AGVS) A materials handling system that does not require a driver. The AGVS is automatically routed and positioned at destination by an optical or magnetic guidance system.

Automated Storage and Retrieval Equipment (ASAR) An automated unit load handling system using high-rise, structured steel vertical racks that improves materials handling productivity, provides maximum storage density per square foot of floor space, and minimises the direct labour required for handling.

Automated Teller Machine (ATM) A machine that allows use of special cards by consumers to make deposits, withdraw cash or transfer funds among accounts via electronic funds transfer.

Automated Warehouse A warehouse which is controlled by a central computer and which utilises sophisticated electronic materials handling systems. Automated warehouses require far fewer employees than traditional warehouses, thus reducing labour 'costs. They tend to be single-storied structures. The computer reads orders and directs equipment such as lift trucks and electric hoists to gather the goods. The computer then moves the goods to the loading docks and issues invoices. Automated warehouses are gradually replacing older, less efficient, multi-storied warehouses. They tend to have a lower incidence of employee injuries, pilferage, and breakage. Inventory control is also improved.

Automatic Checkout Machine (ACM) A system whereby customers have the opportunity to check themselves out of a store by scanning their purchases with the point-of-sale system, entering their customer identification card, and receiving clearance to exit the store.

Automatic Merchandising Machine Operator An establishment primarily engaged in the retail sales of products by means of automatic merchandising units, also referred to as vending machines.

Automatic Reorder The reorder of staple merchandise on the basis of predetermined minimum stock and specified reorder quantities without the intervention of the buyer except for periodic revision and reorder quantities. This can be handled manually by reorder clerks or automatically by computer methods.

Automatic Reordering A system whereby supplies of staple merchandise are monitored and when they have been reduced to a predetermined minimum a reorder procedure is activated.

Automatic Selling The retail sale of goods or services through coin or currency-operated machines activated by the ultimate consumer-buyer.

Automatic Stabilisers Those aspects of government partici-pation in the marketplace (through both expenditures and taxation) which serve to counteract trends in economic activity without necessitating policy changes. Un-employment benefits, for example, prevent incomes from falling as fast as they normally would in a recession, thus helping to stabilise the economy.

Automatic Vending A form of non-store, non-personal retailing of goods and services through coin operated, self-service machines. Merchandise most commonly sold by this method includes cigarettes, candy, soft drinks and hot beverages. Services provided by automatic vending machines include telephone calls via pay phones and banking services via automatic tellers.

Automation Any system or method in which many of the processes automatic all performed or controlled by self-operating machinery, electronic devices, etc.

Autonomic Decision Making A pattern of decision making within a family in which an equal number of decisions are made individually by each spouse.

Autonomous Operation Achieved by branch stores as they grow larger, develop more autonomy in operation, and are treated on "equal stores" basis with flagship (downtown) store.

Auxiliary Dimensions of a Product Features of a product, other than the product itself, which add to the product's attractiveness, usefulness and consumer appeal. For example, packaging, warranties, repair services, and brand names are all examples of auxiliary dimensions of a product which may influence the consumer to select it over other products or other brands of the same product.

Available Market The available market for a product or service consists of all the potential customers who can afford the product or service, who have access to it and who have exhibited an interest in using or owning it.

Average Cost The total cost of doing business divided by the quantity of goods either produced or sold. See also *cost, cost-plus pricing, average field cost* and *average variable cost.*

Average Cost Per Unit Total cost, i.e., the sum of fixed costs and variable costs at a given level of output, divided by the number of units.

Average Collection Period of Receivables The financial ratio which results from dividing the number of days in one year (365) by the *receivables turnover.*

$$\text{Average Collection period of receivables} = \frac{365}{\text{Receivables turnover}}$$

Average Revenue The total revenue (income generated by sales, etc.) divided by the quantity of goods required to produce that revenue. The average revenue line is the demand curve facing the firm. See also *revenue.*

Average Daily Balance Method A method by which retailers calculate the balancein a charge accountuponwhich a service charge is to be assessed. Under the average daily balance method the customer's balance for each day of the billing period is added up and then divided by the number of days inteh period. Tehresultignfigure is used as abasis for comptign the srvice charge. See also *adjusted balance method and previous balance method.*

Average Gross Sales The dollar amout of allsales divided by the number of transactons that produced those sales. Thisis designed to give the retailer an approximate picture of the "normal" dollar figure per sale.

$$\text{Average gross sales} = \frac{\text{All (gross) sales}}{\text{Number of transactions of salescheks}}$$

Average Inventory of Item That amount which represents the midpoint between highest and lowest inventory levels.

Awareness The initial stage in the consumer adoption process during which the buyer becomes aware of the product but has gathered little information about it.

B

Back Haul Reshipping freight over therute it has just completed.

Back Order An order, or part of an order, to be shipped at a later date.

Backdoor Selling Practice by a wholesaler of selling to consumes while representing himself as a supplier to retailers only.

Backing Activities Those stoe operations which do not involve direct contact with the customer. They may be carried out by sales people or by employees expressly hired to perform to the task.

Backup Order Merchanidise retained by manufacturer and available to buyer for quick shipment in the event of subsequent need.

Backward Integration Efforts on the part of a firm to buy or gain control of its supplier companies. For example, a large retail organisation may own its own manufacturing facilities and operate its own distribution system.

Backward Invention A product planning strategy in international marketing in which firms doing business in developing countries modify (and sometimes simplify) their products so that they may be more appealing in the domestic market. For example, water pumps ordinarily powered by electricity may be modified so that they are compatible with local power sources.

Bait Advertising An alluring but insincere offer to sell whereby the advertiser does not intend to sell the advertised product at the advertised price; the purpose is to increase customer traffic. It is also called bait and switch advertising.

Bait and Switch Merchandising Promoting a product at a very low price for the purpose of luring customers into the store. The retailer has not intenton of selling the advertised product, but attempts to switch the customer to a more expensive item.

Bait and Switch Advertising The advertising of a product or service at an unusually low price with an intention to switch the customer to a higher priced item when the customer comes to the store to buy the advertised item. This practice is illegal if customers find it difficult or impossible to buy the advertised item.

Bait and Switch Pricing See *bait and switch merchandising*

Bait Pricing See *bait and switch merchandising*

Balance of Payments In international trade, the balance of payments is the sum of all transactions between a country and its trading partners. Such transactions include merchandise trade, travel, income on investments, military expenditures, foreign aid and flow of capital funds.

Balance of Trade The relationship between the values of a country's imports and its exports. A trade deficit exists when imports exceed exports. A trade surplus exists when exports exceed imports. See also *balance of payments*.

Balance Sheet A classified financial statement showing a firm's assets, liabilities and net worth (*i.e.*, owner's or stockholder's equity) at a particular moment in time.

Balance Sheet Method An approach used by salespeople to gain commitment from a buyer by asking the buyer to think of the pros and cons of various alternatives. It is often referred to as the Ben Franklin method.

Balanced Stock An assortment of merchadise with sufficient breadth and depth to meet demand of target customers while maintaining a reasonable investment in inventory. Also called model stock or ideal stock.

Balanced Tenancy The relationship between type and number of stores in a shopping centre and the needs of the centre's customers.

Banded Pack Related items offered at retail, which are held together by a tape or plastic film strip and are sold as a unit.

For example, a can of shaving cream and a razor sold together in this manner constitute a banded pack. Also called a factory pack.

Banded Premium See *on-pack premium*

Bankruptcy The state or condition of being unable to pay one's debts. The debtor may be an individual or corporation and the bankruptcy proceeding may be voluntary (initiated by the debtor) or involuntary (intimated by creditors).

Banner A series of cross tabulations between a criterion or dependent variable and several, sometimes many, explanatory variables in a single table.

Bar Code An information technology application that uniquely identifies various aspects of product's characteristics as well as additional information regarding delivery and handling instructions. The information is read by scanning devices and greatly increases the speed accuracy and productivity of the distribution process.

Bargain Basement The lower level of a department store devoted to selling merchandise that has been marked down in upsetairs departments, or merchandise not represented in upstairs depatments at all. Appeals to customers most concerned with low price.

Bargain Square An arrangement of four tables in the form of a square upon which sale merchandise has been arranged.

Bargain Store A store in which low price is the most important consideration. Often deals in large job lots and distress merchandise. Bargain stores often have large quantities of specific items,but narrow assortments.

Barriers to Competition The economic, legal, technical, psychological or other factors that reduce competitive rivalry below the level that would otherwise occur naturally. Barriers include branding, advertising, patents, entry restrictions, tariffs and quotas. Product differentiation is a barrier to competition.

Barriers to Entry The economic, legal, psychological, technical and other forces that limit access to markets and hence reduce the threat of new competition.

Barter The direct exchange of goods or services between the parties involved in a commercial transaction without money being employed. In international marketing barter is regarded as a type of countertrade.

Basic Low Stock The lowest level of inventory judged permissible for an item. It indicates a conception of the smallest number of units that could be on hand without losing sales at the lowest sales period of the year or season.

Basic Stock List One method for developing an assortment plan,the basic stock list is composed largely of staple items and for this reason is more specific than the model stock plan which is also used for developing assortment plans. Included on the basic stock lit will be the name of the item, brand identification, physical description, cost and retail price, and other information which precisely identifies the merchandise. See also *model stock plan*.

Basic Stock Method of Inventory A planning method whereby the value of beginning of monthstock may be calculated. Used as a tool planning basic monthly stoks of merchandise. Basic stock = Average stock for seasn – Average monthly sales

$$\text{BOM} = \text{Sales} + \frac{\text{Net \$ sales}}{\text{Stock turnover}} - \frac{\text{NET \$ sales}}{\text{No. of months}}$$

Basic Trading Centre A term used by the Rand McNally company to designate cities which serve as centres for shopping goods purchases for a significant surrounding areas as well as for their own population.

Basing-Point Pricing A pricing strategy in which the cost of goods has two components: (1) their cost at the point of production plus (2) the cost of transporting them from a designated center (the basing point), which may be different from the point of manufacture. Basing-point pricing allows the producer to charge all customers in the same area identical transportation costs regardless of the actual distance the goods are shipped.

Battle of the Brands The competitive struggle at the retail level between national brands on the one hand and middleman and retailer brands on the other. More recently, generic or "no-name" products have joined the competition.

Bayesian Probability A probability based on a person's subjective or personal judgements and experience.

Behavioural Analysis A sales management evaluation and control method for monitoring sales force performance. A behavioural analysis involves evaluating the actual behaviour of salespeople as well as their ultimate performance in terms of sales volume. Examples of behavioural analysis include self-rating scales, supervisor ratings and field observations.

Behaviourism In an advertising context, an application of the stimulus-response theory of learning in which a stimulus (an advertising message) is repeated often enough to produce the desired response (the purchase of a product or service).

Belief A thought or understanding held by a person about a thing or occurrence

Below-the-Market Strategy See *pricing below the market*

Benefit Approach A technique used by salespersons in the first few minutes of contact with a prospect. The salesperson attempts to focus the prospect's thoughts directly on the benefit to be derived from the good or service being sold. The benefit should be concrete and specific, such as a monetary savings. See also *approach*.

Benefit Market Segmentation A market segmentation technique which attempts to identify the benefits consumers seek in a product or class of products and divide the consumer market accordingly. For example, in the market for women's shoes, customers may seek comfort, high fashion, durability, practicality, versatility, etc. Market researchers have found, in general, that consumers usually want a combination of benefits, but stress one or more when making a purchase decision. Benefit market segmentation is also useful in uncovering opportunities for new products.

Benefit Segmentation The process of grouping consumers into market segments on the basis of the desirable consequences sought from the product. For example, the toothpaste market may include one segment seeking cosmetic benefits such as white teeth and another seeking health benefits such as decay prevention.

Best Buy An item which is of high usuality and, at the same time, competitivel priced in relation to other retailers. A lower than normal markup may be taken to achieve a price advantage.

Best Seller An item which consistently sells rapidly through a season or year at full price.

Best Selling Price Lines Those lines of merchandise, thoughrelativelyfew in number, which produce a large proportion of a store's sales.

Beta Binomial Model A probability mixture model commonly used to represent pattern of brand choice behaviour or media exposure patterns. The model assumes that each individual's behaviour follows a Bernoulli process. That is, an individual performs some behaviour of interest (*e.g.*, buying a brand of interest) with probability (*e.g.*, occasion on which purchase is made from the product category of interest). The number of times that the behaviour of interest is exhibited, out of a given number of opportunities, has the binomial distribution for any individual. The model further assumes that the probability values *p* vary across individuals according to a beta distribution (Greene 1982; Massy, Montgomery and Morrison 1970). A generalisation of this model to represent choice among more than two items is termed the Dirichlet multinomial model. These models are used to predict future brand choice or media exposure patterns based on individual's past behaviour.

Better Business Bureau A voluntary, non-profit organisation dedicated to promoting ethical practices in the conduct of business.

Bid (1) An offer to buy, as in a public auction. (2) An offer to perform a task or supply goods made by a vendor at a price which he feels will be competitive and acceptable to the buyer. See also *sealed bid and open bid.*

Bidding An invitation to potential suppliers to submit their offers and a price for a particular opportunity. A closed bid is formal, written and sealed and usually all closed bids are opened and reviewed at the same time, with the contract being awarded to the lowest bidder who meets the specifications. An open bid is usually more informal and is used when specific requirements are hard to rigidly define or when products vary substantially.

Big-Early, Little-Late Method A method of developing media advertising schedules in which the beginning of the campaign is regarded as most significant and thus allocated the largest amount of money.

Bill of Exchange A unconditional order in writing addressed by one person (the drawer) to another (the drawee), signed by the person giving it, requiring the person to whom it is addressed to pay on demand or at a fixed or determinable future time, a sum certain in money to, or to the order of a specified person or to bearer.

Bill of Lading 1. (global marketing definition) A vital document in international trade that is required to establish legal ownership and facilitate financial transactions. The bill of lading serves the following purposes: (1) as a contract for shipment between the carrier for shipment; (2) as a receipt from the carrier for shipment; and (3) as a certificate of ownership or title to the goods. 2. (physical distribution definition) The basic document in the purchase of transportation service. It describes commodities and quantities shipped as well as the terms and conditions of carrier liability. Current law allows the bill of lading to be electronically generated and transmitted.

Bill of Materials (BOM) An assessment of the combination of assemblies, subassemblies, parts and materials needed to support planned production as detailed in the materials requirement plan.

Billed Cost The price appearing on a vendor's bill before deducting cash discounts, but after deducting any trade discounts and quantity discounts from the list price.

Bird Dog An individual who, for a fee, provides sales leads to a salesperson. The individual also is called a spotter.

Birdyback A coordinated transportation arrangement in which both air and ground modes of transportation are used. For example, goods would be shipped partly by aeroplane and partly by truck.

Black Box A term used by marketing researchers to describe the consumer's mind and to indicate that what goes on inside that mind is largely hidden from the researcher's view.

Black Market Trade in products, commodities, currencies etc. which is in violation of the law; *e.g.*, tax laws, regulations governing rates of exchange, price ceilings, etc.

Blanket Order A pre-season order placed with a vendor to be delivered in a number of later shipments. Quantities and styles may be specified, but detailed instructions regarding colour, size, *etc.* may be included in subsequent orders.

Bleed Advertisement The print ads or brochures for which the colour graphics and/or artwork extends to the edge of the page. Such pages have no unprinted margins or borders and are usually sold at a premium price.

Block Plan A store layout plan that delineates the actual sizes, shapes and locations of all store components.

Blocked Currency A currency regulated by its government in a manner that precludes it being taken out of the country or converted to other currencies.

Blue Laws State and local laws which prohibit retail stores from operating on Sundays or which restrict the Sunday sale of certain products; *e.g.*, beer and liquor. Although on religious grounds, its effect is to reduce time competition between large and small retailers.

Blueline A print of an ad, brochure or other advertising materials produced on photosensitive paper (hence the blue colour). It is used to confirm the location of all artwork, headlines, graphics and text components before printing.

Blunder An error that arises when editing, coding, key punching or tabulating the data.

BMA See *Bak Marketing Association (BMA)*

Body Language The nonverbal signals communicated in sales interactions through facial expressions, arms, legs and hands.

Boiler Room A facility from which telephone salespeople make solicitations.

Bona Fide Sale A transaction in which the seller acts in good faith regarding the terms of the sale.

Bonded Warehouse A form of public warehouse which stores imported goods or other goods on which a tax must be paid prior to the release of the products for sale (such as cigarettes and alcoholic beverages). See also *public warehouse.*

Bonus Money in addition to regular salary and commissions paid to employees in recognition of special services performed or for holidays, etc.

Bonus Pack A promotional package in which the customer is offered more than the regular amount for the regular price.

Book Inventory A perpetual system of inventory maintained by adding the value of incoming goods to the value of previous inventory and then subtracting the value of sales, markdowns and discounts.

Book Value per Share of Common Stock The financial ration which results when the total stockholders' equity less the preferred stockholdrs' equity is divided by the number of common stock shares out standing. An indication of a company's financial position at a givn point in time.

$$\text{Book value per share of common stock} = \frac{\text{Total shareholders' equity} - \text{Preferred stock holders' equity}}{\text{\# of shares of commonstock outstanding}}$$

Booking The act of order-taking, especially for delivery at a later date. Frequently the amount of production is based on the booking of advance orders.

Boomerang Method A method used by salespeople to respond to customer objections by turning the objection into a reason for acting immediately.

Boston Consulting Group Matrix A method of evaluating a company's product offerings and marketing opportunities developed by the Boston Consulting Group. Products are classified as stars, cash cows, question marks or dogs and assigned to a space in the four box matrix (the Boston Box). Appropriate strategies may then be developed for the company's entire product portfolio.

Bottom Line An accounting term commonly used to express profit or loss.

Bottom-up Planning Planning initiated by employees near the bottom of the organizational ladder. Unit objectives and the resources required to attain them are set forth and subsequently transmitted up the organisation for evaluation and approval at the decision-making level.

Bottom-up Theory A theory of fashion adoption in which young, lower-income persons are seen as the innovators of new styles. Fashion then spreads upward through the various social classes, although in order of adoption the next group may be members of the confident, secure, upper class. The new fashion is then likely to spread widely throughout the population.

Bounce Back Offer A coupon or other selling device included in a customer ordered product, premium, refund or other package that attempts to sell more of the same or another product to the recipient.

Boundary Spanning A concept describing job tasks or responsibilities beyond the traditional managerial area. Boundary spanning can be internal to the firm (extending beyond traditional organisation departments) or external to the firm (crossing between channel members).

Boutique From the French word meaning "little shop," a boutique may be a small specialty store or an area within a larger store. Emphasis is on merchandise selected for a specific customer, presented in an attractive and unified manner and accompanied by individualised attention on the part of the sales staff.

Boutique Agency An advertising agency that specialises in writing and designing advertising material and thus focuses on the creative and art aspects of the advertising campaign. Unlike larger, full-service agencies, boutique agencies charge on a per-job basis. Also known as a creative boutique.

Boutique Merchandising A form of store organisation in which related merchandise from a number of departments is brought together in one shop to meet special customer demand.

Boutique Store Layout A form of retail store layout pattern that brings together complete offerings from one vendor or for one use in one section as opposed to having the items in separate departments. For example, a tennis boutique in a department store will feature rackets, balls, shoes and tennis outfits..

Box-Jenkins Method A method for forecasting sales that relies on procedures for identifying models that best fit a set of time series data and statistical tests to examine the adequacy of the fitted models, where the models, consist of a combination of autoregressive and moving average terms.

Box Store a no-frills, qarehouse-type store which often displays merchandise on or in its shipping carton.

Bracket Creep The movement of consumers to higher and higher income tax brackets during periods of inflation regardless of the lack of any real increase in income. This phenomenon is less serious since the 1986 tax reform, which greatly reduced the number of tax brackets.

Brainstorming A group method of problem solving, used in product concept generation. It is sometimes thought to be an open, free-wheeling idea session, but more correctly is a specific procedure developed by Alex Osborn, with precise rules of session conduct. Now it has many modifications in format of use, each variation with its own name.

Branch A geographically detached unit of a firm which is still an integral part of the business. Branches of companies frequently restrict their activities to the selling function.

Branch House An establishment maintained by a manufacturer, separate from the headquarters establishment and used primarily for the purpose of stocking, selling, delivering and servicing the manufacturer's product.

Branch House Wholesaler A national, regional or sectional wholesaler who operates a number of variously located establishments to provide better customer service in all parts of the territory covered. It differs from a chain wholesaler in that each branch is closely supervised as an extension of the main wholesale house.

Branching Question A technique used to direct respondents to different places in a questionnaire based on their spouse to the question at hand.

Branch Store In department or other large stores, the smaller retail units owned and operated by the parent store and generally located in the suburbs or in metropolitan area shopping centres.

Brand A trade name or symbol which gives a product an identity—distinguishing it in the marketplace as the product of a particular manufacturer or distributor.

Brand Choice Models These stochastic models of individual brand choice focus on the brand that will be purchased on a particular purchase occasion, given that a purchase event will occur. This type of model includes Bernoulli processes and Markov models. Models in this category vary in their treatment of population heterogeneity, purchase event feedback and exogenous market factors.

Brand Contacts Any information-bearing experience that a customer or prospect has with the brand, the product category or the sponsoring organisation that relates to the marketer's product or service.

Brand Development Index (BDI) A measure of the extent to which the sales of products in a market category have captured the total potential in a geographical area, based on the population of that area and the average consumption per user nationally. The brand development index is usually calculated for separate metropolitan areas and is used to determine high-potential (underdeveloped) areas for new product entries or for primary demand promotions.

Brand Equity The value of a brand. From a consumer perspective, brand equity is based on consumer attitudes about positive brand attributes and favourable conse-quences of brand use.

Brand Extension The practice of marketing new products under well known brand names in an effort to capitalize on the positive image the parent brand has in the consumer's mind. See also *line extension.*

Brand Extension Strategy A marketing strategy in which a firm uses one of its established brand names on a modified product; *i.e.,* a new line or on an entirely new product. It is, essentially, a coattails strategy in which new products entering the marketplace are supported by the existing, well-recognised brand name.

Brand Familiarity The customer's ability to recognise and accept a particular brand of products. Brand familiarity is often divided into five levels: (1) brand rejection; (2) brand nonrecognition; (3) brand recognition; (4) brand preference; and (5) brand insistence.

Brand Generic This is the second half of a product's identifying title. Brand is the first half, and identifies one seller's version, while the generic is the second half and identifies the general class of item. [Example: Jello (brand) gelatin dessert (generic)]. This is not to be confused with generic brand (such as on some low-price items in supermarkets), for which there is no individual brand.

Brand Indifference A purchasing pattern characterised by a low degree of brand loyalty.

Brand Image That perception of a product formed in the mind of the consumer which is the result of the symbols and meanings associated with a particular brand. Advertising is often employed to create a brand image; *e.g.*, automobile advertising on television commonly sells a lifestyle rather than a mode of transportation.

Brand Insistence An extreme form of brand loyalty in which the customer will search extensively for the desired product or brand and accept no substitute. Consumers who are brand insistent are known as "hard core loyals." Consumers who share their loyalty between two or three brands are said to be "soft core loyals," and those who shift from favouring one brand to another are called "shifting loyals." The least brand insistent consumers, those with no loyalty to any brand, are known as "brand switchers." See also *brand loyalty* and *brand switcher*.

Brand Loyalty The consistent preference, on the part of the consumer, for one brand over another or for one set of brands over others competing in the same category.

Brand Mark That part of a brand consisting of the signs, colours, symbols, and designs; *i.e.*, those elements which are not words and are closely identified with the product. Brand marks; *e.g.*, the red tab on the back pocket of Levi Strauss jeans, may also be a part of the firm's trademark. See also *brand, brand name* and *trade-mark.*

Brand Marketing A strategy in which of a firm's products is marketed independently, generally under the direction of a brand manager. See also *product line marketing.*

Brand Name That part of a brand consisting of the actual letters or words; *i.e.*, that part which can actually be vocalised, which comprises the name of the product or service as distinct from other identifying signs, symbols and designs incorporated into the overall design. See also *brand, brand mark* and *trademark.*

Brand Nonrecognition Customers' inability to recognise a brand, though they may recognise the product. This generally occurs because the brand name is not part of the marketing strategy geared to the ultimate consumer, even when it is used by middlemen. Products with brand non-recognition problems include novelties, school supplies and other inexpensive goods commonly found in discount stores.

Brand Personality A term attributed to the advertising agency Young and Rubicam. A brand's personality is seen to depend more upon what people think about it than upon what it is or what it does. A term distinct from brand image. Sometimes known as *brand character.*

Brand Position A product's niche in the marketplace. The term "position" refers to the product's relationship to competing brands and is generally measured in terms of how the consumer perceives the various attributes of the brand; i.e., brand position depends on consumer attitudes.

Brand Preference In the process of brand acceptance, a middle stage in which the consumer will choose a particular brand over its competitors because of previous favourable experience with the product. However, should the product prove to be unavailable, the consumer is willing to accept a substitute.

Brand Proliferation The rapid and sometimes excessive growth of similar products within a particular line. Brand proliferation often results from a marketing strategy on the part from marketing strategy on the part of large producers who are attempting to dominate shelf space in stores (breakfast foods, detergents, etc.) or to occupy a series of price levels in the marketplace (appliances, automobiles, etc.).

Brand Recognition A stage in brand acceptance in which consumers remember having heard about or seen a product, even if they have not yet tried it. Such recognition is a company's first objective for a newly introduced product. The effectiveness of advertising and other publicity programmes geared to familiarising the consuming public with such a new product or brand may be tested by either a recognition survey or a recognition test.

Brand Rejection Customers' refusal to buy a particular brand of goods because of its poor image or because of previous bad experiences with the brand. Remedies for brand rejection are: (1) change the brand's current image; (2) change the product; (3) change the target segment.

Brand Share The share of the market that one brand commands expressed as part of the total market.

Brand Strategy The plan employed to create, introduce and promote a particular brand. Strategies involved include picking a name, selecting an image to project, positioning the product in the marketplace, etc.

Brand Switcher A consumer who shows no loyalty to any brand and who looks instead for the brand that is readily available, is on sale or is novel. Consumers often maintain brand loyalty for certain items while displaying a willing-ness to accept substitutes for others. Brand switchers motivated by low price and premiums are said to be "deal prone." This is particularly true in the areas of staple products, such as tuna or toilet tissue, where there is little distinguishable difference between brands and consumers will often select the brand on sale that particular day. Brand switchers motivated by the desire to try something different are said to be "variety prone." This trait shows up in the snack food industry, for example, where consumers may opt for a new cookie or other taste treat just for the sake of change. See also *brand loyalty* and *brand insistence*.

Brand Switching A purchasing pattern characterised by a change from one brand to another.

Brand-Switching Matrix A two-way-table that indicates which brand's sample of people purchased in one period and which brands they purchased in a subsequent period, thus highlighting the switches occurring among and between brands as well as the number of persons who purchased the same brand in both periods.

Brandaid A decision support system for determining the marketing mix for a particular brand. The model has submodels dealing with advertising spending level, price and salesperson effort (*i.e.,* dollars per customer per year). Its parameters can be calibrated by combining historical data (*e.g.*, on sales, market, share, advertising spending, etc.) with structured subjective judgements.

Branded Merchandise Goods that are identified by brands. This contrasts with generic brands, which are identified only by commodity type.

Branding, Line Family Using a family brand to cover only some of a firm's products. It contrasts with those cases where the term *family brand* is used only to designate the firm's entire product line.

Brandstanding In advertising and promotion, the tying together of a brand with an event, idea or issue. The tactic employed generally involves the linking of a brand name (without regard to its particular attributes) to some highly publicised event or other activity; *e.g.*, marathon runners frequently wear numbers which also carry the name of the race's sponsor

Breach of Warranty The failure of a manufacturer to honour the warranty issued with a product; i.e., refusal to back up claims concerning proper performance.

Break-bulk One of the functions of a retailer inwhichhe sells goods in smaller quantties than he bought.

Break-down Approach A method used to allocate a firm's advertising budget. In the break-down approach, the firm begins with a predetermined total budget, which is then allocated by the person or department incharge of promotions to particular lines of merchandise offered by the firm. See also *build-up approach*.

Break-even Analysis A mathematical analysis in which the fixed and variable costs of production are compared to projected revenue in an effort to reveal the break-even point; *i.e.*, that point at which expenses and revenues are blalanced.

Break-even Chart A graphic representation of fixed and variable costs juxtaposed to total revenue in suh a manner that the firm's break-even pointis revealed.

Break-even Point The point at which an enterprise has earned enough money to defray all the fixed and variable costs of operation. Break-even points may be calculated for individual products at specific price points or for an entire business.

Breakthrough Opportunity A marketing situation which enables an innovative firm to establish a new marketing strategy, develop and market a new product or create a new marketing mix. Therefore, remain profitable for an extended period of time. The breakthrough opportunity gives the firm, in effect, a temporary monopoly and an edge over competitors. It also helps the firm to capture a large portion of the market share, which may serve to discourage imitators from entering the market. The advantage will remain until competitors decide to meet the innovator in head-on competition. The longer other firms can be discouraged from entering the market, the longer the breakthrough opportunity will remain profitable.

Bretton Woods Agreement An agreed statement of aims for postwar monetary policy which resulted from an international monetary and financial conference held at Bretton Woods, New Hampshire, in July 1944. Its aims were: (1) to make all currencies freely convertible and thereby encourage multilateral trade; (2) to keep exchange rates stable; (3) to provide some means of assisting a country with temporary difficulties with its balance of payments; and (4) to encourage economic growth and development.

Broadcast Quality The media industries' standard for material that can be aired. Technical format and content are both aspects of broadcast quality. For example, 3/4-inch tape is broadcast quality, VHS tape is not. Publicity submissions that are not broadcast quality generally will not be used.

Broadcast Television A method of distributing television signals by means of stations that broadcast signals over channels assigned to specific geographic areas.

Broken Case Lot Selling Breaking of cases to sell smaller quantities, done by many wholesalers to accommodate retailers who cannot afford to buy in full shipping case lots.

Broken Lot An amount less than some understood standard unit of sale.

Broker A non-merchant middleman or marketing intermediay who brings buyers and sellers of a product togethrr. Generally a broker does not take title to merchandise nor does he have physical possesion of the goods. Mot commonly operates in the grocery business. See also *commission buying office and commission house*.

Brokerage Allowance A discount paid to buyers, particularly large organisations such as grocery chains, for performing the broker functions. These organisations request the broker's commission in the form of a a price reduction. The practice is technically a violation of the Robinson-Patman Act.

Brown Goods Merchandise in the consumer electronic audiovisual field, such as televisions, radios stereo sets, etc. The name came from the brown (furniture colour) cases in which such merchandise is frequently manufactured. At one time the term also included all furniture.

Bubble Plane A store layout plan that shows the rough placement and adjacency of key elements of a proposed store.

Budget A forecasting tool that structures a firm's short-range future plans on the basis of estimated revenues and expenditures expressed in numerical terms. Budgets are often established for a fiscal year. There are several different types of budgets or sub-budgets. A cast budget is a forecast of expected cash receipts and disbursements for a specified period of time designed to preclude possible cash-flow problems. The *cash budget* indicates the firm's cash requirements and its possible need to borrow additional funds by projecting buying and selling patterns for several successive future time periods. A *production budget* is a forecast of the number units a firm must produce in order to fill expected sales and maintain inventory for a given budget period. The quantitative data used to determine the production budget is derived by adding projected sales to the number of units expected to remain in inventory at the end of the budget period and subtracting the number of units on hand at the beginning of the budget period. A *cost-of-goods-sold budget* is used to determine the price paid for any merchandise required to obtain the sales of the period. It is based on estimates of the cost of materials used in the manufacture of the goods. A *sales budget* sets forth in detail all of a firm's anticipated sales for a given period and makes possible the allocation of the money and materials which will be needed if the firm is to achieve its sales objectives. Commonly, each product offered will require its own sales budget. The sales budget is based on studies of past sales and estimates of future business conditions. See also *sales expense budget.*

Buffer Inventory See *reserve stock*

Buffer Stock See *reserve stock*

Build-up Approach A method used to allocate a firm's advertising budget. In the build-up approach, the firm begins by ascertaining the advertising needs of each line of goods offered by the firm and determined by the person incharge of each line. Any necessary adjustments are made by the individual or group in charge of promotions and the total is added together to determine the total budget. The firm does not begin with a predetermined total budget as is the case with the break-down approach. A sophisticated form of the build-up approach may be seen in the objective-task method. See also *break-down approach.*

Building Method See *objective-task method*

Bulk Checking The process of checking arriving merchandise by comparing the package markings against the invoice or packing list without actually opening the packaging to verify contents.

Bulk Delivery See *bulk merchandise delivery*

Bulk Freight Generally refers to unpacked merchndise such as gran or coal.

Bulk Goods (1) Goods such as coal, grain, or gravel which arc sold and delivered in loose or unpackaged form. (2) Any large shipment of one item.

Bulk Marking The practice of placing the price only on the original shipping containers or at least bulk packages; individual units are not market until the merchandise is transferred from reserve to forward stock. It is also referred to as deferred marking.

Bundle of Benefits Concept A theory that customers purchase not only the goods offered by a firm, but also the advantages and capabilities those goods are expected to provide. The real value of thc mcrchandisc, therefore, resides in what the goods can do for the consumer, and not in the goods themselves. For example, the purchase of a home computer would be meaningless to the average consumer unless he perceives some real time and labour saving advantages to be gained in the computer's use. If the consumer needs equipment that can help with his income tax, communicate with his bank and pay his bills, allow him to write reports and store records, then he will purchase the home computer and expect it to provide him with those benefits. The same argument may be made for the industrial customer.

Bundle of Services Concept A theory in support of leasing rather than purchasing industrial equipment. The theory takes into account the comparative costs of leasing and buying, including the service and maintenance costs inherent in purchased equipment. According to the bundle of services concept, leased equipment is morc cost cffective.

Bundling Offering several complementary products together or offering additional services in a single "package deal." The pricc of the bundle is typically lower than the sum of the prices of the individual products or services included in it. Groups of services or products may be bundled in different combinations appealing differently to different segments in order to price discriminate among these segments and to avoid cherry picking.

Bureaucratic Organisation This term is associated with government, where official decision making is circumscribed by laws, rules and regulations which often result in inflexibility, "red tape" and slowness to act. The term is sometimes applied to the hierarchical business structure, which is thought to lead to slow decision making and slow response to change. It should be noted however, that business—unlike government—operates in a competitive environment that does not reward slow decision making if it results in poor sales or customer service. Comment: To combat any tendency towards bureaucracy, particularly in large corporations, companies have speeded up decision making by measures such as decentralised and flatter organisation structures along with computerised information and communication systems that alert management quickly to problems requiring resolution.

Bushelman A formerly common term referring to a repairer of garments, especially in the alteration room for men's clothing.

Business Analysis In new product development, efforts made to estimate the profitability of new products before large amounts of money have been spent on their development.

Business Associated Stores Stores associated with one another because of physical proximity

Business Cycle The fluctuations in business conditions which occur with some regularity over a period of time. The fluctuations are generally identified as prosperity, recession, depression and recovery. During the prosperity stage, income and employment are high. During a recession, income, employment and production begin to decline. If left uncorrected, the recession may become a depression, a period when business activities, employment and incomes decline rapidly. The recovery that generally follows a depression once again shows an increase in production and employment.

Business Domain That sector of a market which a firm targets as its business environment. It may be defined in terms of a line of products, a particular group of customers or some other combination of market factors.

Business/Professional Advertising Association (B/PAA) An association of business communications professionals in the fields of advertising, marketing, and marketing communications. Operates an employment service, conducts seminars, and sponsors annual Pro-Comm Awards

Business Portfolio Matrix See *Boston Consulting Group Matrix*

Buyback In international trade, and aggreement in which the seller of raw materials or producer goods agrees to accept the finished product manufacured from these goods as full or partial payment.

Buyclasses The three types of industrial buying: (1) the straight rebuy, (2) the modified rebuy, and (3) new task buying.

Buyer In retailing and wholesaling, an executive responsible for the selection and purchase of merchandise and its ultimate resale at a profit. The term is sometimes applied to industrial or institutional purchasing agents who buy the goods and services required for the operation of the firms or institutions.

Buyer Behaviour See *consumer behaviour*

Buyers' Costs The costs that buyers incur when acquiring and using products and services. Such costs include the price of the item being acquired, cost of information search, shipping costs, transportation costs, installation costs and postpurchase costs that may affect buyers' perceptions of value of the item being acquired.

Buyers Market An economic situation in which supplies of merchandise exceed demand. Such conditions favour the retail buyer rather than the manufacturer.

Buyflow The communication network between all individuals involved in a buying decision and the actions that take place during the course of making the purchase decision.

Buygrid Framework It consists of two dimensions: buyclasses and buyphases. The *buyclasses* are new task purchase, modified rebuy, and straight rebuy. The *buy phases* are need recognition, need definition, need description, seller identification, proposal solicitation, proposal evaluation and selection ordering procedures and performance review

Buying In retailing, the purchase of goods at teh wholesale level for resale at tehretail level.

Buying Allowance A reduction in price on specific goods offered by a producer or manufacturer to a purchaser as an incentive to buy.

Buying by Committee See *committee buying*

Buying Calendar A retail buyer's plan of merchandising activities for a period (often six months) which includes special prootions and other seasonal events.

Buying Centre In industrial marketing the buying centre is made up of those persons who are responsible for purchase decision-making in an organization. They may be the actual users of the products and services, purchasing officers, persons with influence over buying decisions (salespersons, executives *etc.),* gatekeepers, etc.

Buying Committee In large retail organisations, especially those which handle large numbers of staple products, the buying committee assists individual buyers in making decisions regarding specific merchandise.

Buying Criteria The factors considered by buyers in their evaluation of alternative suppliers, such as dependability, product quality, cost, vendor production capacity, after-sale service, vendor reliability and integrity, reciprocity and emotional factors. They can be categorised as product-related, *e.g.,* technical specifications; company-related, *e.g.*, reputation and salesperson-related, e.g., expertise and trustworthiness.

Buying Decisions The different buying situations a buyer would face in the course of purchasing a product or service to satisfy a need. Three buying decisions can be distinguished: (1) *product decision*, deciding on which product(s) will be purchased with available resources: (2) *brand decision*, deciding on which brands will be purchased among competing brand(s) of the same product; and (3) *supplier decision*, deciding on which supplier(s) will be patronized among competing suppliers.

Buying Error The failure to purchase appropriate goods for the store's customers. When the inappropriate goods do not move, a markdown is generally required to alleviate the situation.

Buying Group A group of non-competing stores organised for the purpose of buying merchandise.

Buying Hours Specific store hours during which buyers will see salesmen.

Buying Influence The buying centre members or their sources of information who have influence upon the other buying centre members such that these other individuals can change in the their behaviour and/or attitudes in the process of making a specific buying decision.

Buying Motives The forces that have been activated into a state of tension causing the buyer to seek satisfaction of a specific need. Organisational buyers are influenced by both rational appeals (*e.g.*, economic factors such as cost, quality and service) and emotional appeals (*e.g,* status, security and fear).

Buying Office The buying office is made up of buyers in national or international market centers who daily shop the market in order to provide their clients or member stores with information and to select and buy merchandise for them. Buying offices are either independent (salaried office or commission buying office) or store-owned (privae office, cooperaive office, and corporate office).

Buying Plan A breakdown of the dollar open-to-buy figure of a department or merchandise classification to indicate the number or value of units to purchase in different classifications and subclassifications.

Buying Policy Index A leading indicator of business activity, published monthly by National Bureau of Economic Research, based on the proportion of purchasing agents reporting their buying commitments for the months ahead.

Buying Power (1) In retailing, the capacity to buy large amounts of merchandise, thereby commanding a most favorable price from vendors. (2) The potential income consumers control in the marketplace.

Buying Power Index A measurement developed by *Sales & Marketing Management*, which combines three elements (population, effective buying income and retail sales) into one index which expresses a market's capacity to buy. The index is calculated as a percentage of the total U.S./Canada market potential.

Buying Roles Any behaviour pattern on the part of the customer acted out in the process of purchasing a specific kind of merchandise.

Buying Style The way a customer buys a given product or service. Buying styles range from deliberate buying to impulsive buying.

Buying Trip The retail buyer's planned visit to the market for the purpose of selectign and buyingmerchandise.

C

Cable Television Ordering System Asystem which allows cable television viewers to select and order merchandise viewed at home on their television sets.

Cadre Cadres receive special treatment from their managers because they are perceived to be particularly competent motivated and trustworthy. A salesperson who receives a relatively large amount of latitude, support and attention from his or her sales manager. In return for the special treatment, cadres are expected to perform assignments that are outside the formal job description.

Cafeteria (1) A self-service restaurant in which moderately priced food is displayed on counters. (2) A comparable restaurant for employees of a store or other business where food is served at approximate cost.

Call credit A sum deducted from a customer's account when merchandise is picked up by the store's delivery system and returned to the store.

Call Frequency The number of sales call per time period made on a particular customer. Comment: The call frequencies assigned to customers are used by salespeople to plan their own route and sale call schedules.

Call Report A sales person's formal presentation to a supervisor of data regarding calls made to prospects, customers, or in a specific market during a given period of time.

Call System A system of equalizing sales opportunities among salespeople—*e.g.*, some stores rotate salespeople, giving each an equal opportunity to meet arriving customers.

Call Tag A form notifying a delivery driver to pickup an article or parcel at a customer's address and return it to the store.

Campaign Plan A direct mail promotion which extends over a period of time and which is designed to arouse and build interest in an upcoming event or new product. The final mailing is the actual announcement of the event or product. Also known as a *teaser campaign.*

Cancellation (1) A retracton of an order for merchandise sentfrom the buyer to the vendor. (2) Surplus merchandise sold by retailers to discount houses, often in broken lots

Canned Sales Presentation A standardized sales presentation that includes all the key selling points arranged in the order designed to elicit the best response from the customer.

Canned Sales Talk A prepared sales talk repeated from memory.

Cannibalisation A condition in which a new product is introduced into the marketplace and sells at the expense of another product in the company's line; *i.e.,* it eats into the profitability of the other product. The opposite of enhancement.

Canvassing Door-to-door or telephone sales technique that involves the solicitation of orders for merchandise which will be delivered at some time in the future.

Capacity Requirements Planning (CRP) The evaluation of planned production to determine if it can be accomplished within the capacity limitations of manufacturing facilities. A capacity load projection is completed for each item in the master production schedule. The calculated load requirement is compared to available capacity, thus determining underutilisation or overutilisation of facilities.

Capital 1. The produced wealth that assists directly in further production and that furnishes satisfaction or gratification to the user only indirectly or incidentally, if at all. 2. The owner's investment tin a business. 3. All economic goods in existence at a given period of time used by society for production.

Capital Consumption Allowance The sum of depreciation on major capital goods plus capital goods destroyed or damaged plus depreciation on minor capital goods.

Capital Equipment See *capital goods*

Capital Goods Those materials, such as plants, installatons, and equipment, used to produce other products. Also called capital-investment goods.

Capital Intensive A product or an industry in which plant and equipment requirements are large relative to labour.

Capital Intensive Industry An industry which invests heavily in equipment machinery and automated devices while using relatively little labour. Expenditures for meeting the requirements of plant and equipment are therefore relatively high. Also referred to as a cost intensive industry. See also *labour intensive industry*, its opposite.

Capital Investment Goods Those materials, such as plants, installations, and equipment, used to produce other products. Also called capital-investment goods.

Capital Items See *capital goods*

Capital Turnover A financial ratio used to measure the number of times the cost of the average investory investment is converted into sales during a given period.

$$\text{Capital turnover} = \frac{\text{Sales at retail during a specified period}}{\text{Average inventory value at cost}}$$

Captive Market Customers, commonly at the retail level, who have little choice about where they shop. For example, the customers of retail or service establishments in hotels or airports where alternative or competitive businesses are relatively inaccessible, constitute a captive market.

Captive Product Pricing A pricing strategy used by makers of products which require supplies, accessories or ancillary equipment for operation. The principal product is moderately priced while the supplies and accessories are given substantial markups.

Carbon-Copy Theory In personal selling, a theory that new salespersons are best trained by memorising the techniques of a master salesperson.

Career Plateau A situation in which the likelihood of a salesperson's receiving increased responsibility (*e.g.*, a promotion, a bigger territory) is low. Career plateauing can lead to substantial opportunity costs for sales personnel on the company. Factors contributing to a career plateau include both personal (*e.g.*, low motivation, feelings of job burnout) and organisational (*e.g.*, in-adequate sales training, little company growth) characteristics.

Carload Freight Rate A reduced rail shipping rate allowed to large freight shipments which make up a full carload.

Carousel The materials handling equipment that delivers the desired item to the order picker. Typically a carousel consists of a series of bins mounted on an oval track. The entire carousel rotates bringing the bin to the operator.

Carriage Trade An old expression that refers to a wealthy class of patrons accorded special services.

Carrier In transportation, a car, truck vessel, plane, helicopter or train.

Carrying Charge The sum paid for credit service on certain charge accounts. It is an interest usually charged on the unpaid balance.

Carrying Cost See *inventory carrying costs*

Carry Over Effect Any effect that present marketing expenditures, such as advertising expenditures or new package design, may have on future sales. When a time period has elapsed between the expenditure and the visible results of that expenditure, it is known as a *delayed response effect*.

Carry Over Models Models in which the effect of a marketing mix variable is assumed to last beyond a single time period. A transformation often applied in modeling the effect of lagged marketing expenditures (*e.g.*, advertising expenditures in previous periods) on the current period's sales in the Koyck transformation. When it is assumed that the effect of the marketing expenditure decays geometrically over time (*i.e.*, loses a constant proportion of its remaining impact in each subsequent period), then the Koyck transformation allows the analyst to estimate all of those lagged marketing expenditure effects using a single one-period-lagged-sales term to predict current sales. The transformation thus greatly simplifies the task of estimating lagged effects in sales response models. The validity of the assumptions required for the transformation to be appropriate has, however, been challenged.

Cartage The fee paid to a carrier for transporting cargo from a pickup point to destination.

Case Method of Teaching Teaching based on an actual problem faced by a business. Students are required to gather additional information and to form an opinion concerning the action that should be taken.

Cash-and-Carry Wholesaler A limited service wholesaler who carries merchandise in inventory, which he sells on a customer-pick-up, cash only basis. Commonly found in the grocery business, the cash-and-carry wholesaler offers lower prices than his full-service counterpart.

Cash Before Delivery A term of sale requiring payment to the seller before goods are transferred to the purchaser. No credit is extended and no risk is assumed by the seller.

Cash Cow In large business enterprises, cash cows are units which enjoy high earnings but often have low growth potential. Because they generate large amounts of cash, these units are often "milked" to support other divisions of the enterprise, thus the term cash cow.

Cash Discount A reduction from invoice price granted to a buyer of goods for prompt payment of his bill. For example, if the terms of the bill are 2/10, net 30, the buyer may deduct 2% from the billed amount if paid within 10 days, otherwise the full amount is due in 30 days. Cash discount does not imply that full cash payment must be made at time of purchase or delivery. See also *dating*.

Cash Flow The movement of money both into the business, as receipts or revenues and out of the business, as disbursements, for a given period of time.

Cash Flow Analysis An examination of the timing of cash receipts and disbursements to identify periods of time in which working capital may be either inadequate to meet the needs of the business or excessive. A cash flow analysis expresses future income and expenditures in a dollar amount and predicts future cash flow based on an anticipated sales volume. It may be prepared on a weekly or monthly basis for semi-annual or annual projections. The steps in preparing a cash flow analysis include: (1) establishing the period; (2) estimating sales; (3) estimating the anticipated future cash inflows from the estimated sales level; (4) analyzing the expected cash outflow; (5) comparing the estimated inflow with the estimated outflow to determine the net cash gain or loss for the period; and (6) providing an estimated cash balance. The primary use of a cash flow analysis is to help plan the firm's needs for short-term capital.

Cash Flow Statement An itemised list of cash receipts and disbursements over a particular period of time.

Cash in Advance (CIA) A term of sale requiring payment to the seller before goods are transferred to the purchaser. No credit is extended and no risk is assumed by the seller. Also called *cash before delivery.*

Cash on Delivery (C.O.D.) A term of sale requiring payment for goods in cash upon their receipt by the purchaser.

Cash Register Bank An assortment of change for the use of the salesperson or transaction station operator. It is prepared at the end of the day by the person operating a cash register or prepared by a cashier for the cash register operator.

Cash Sale A transaction in which the customer pays money for merchandise at the time of purchase.

Cash Terms An agreement to pay cash for purchased goods, usually within a specified period of time.

Cash with Order A term of sale requiring that a payment sufficient to cover the cost of the merchandise and delivery accompany the customer's order.

Casual Exporting Activities of firms which engage in some export business but who do not actively seek it. Also known as accidental exporting.

Catalog A book or pamphlet listing merchandise for sale, usuallywith descriptive comments and illustrations.

Catalog House A merchant whose business is based primarily on orders deriving from catalogs and mail order solicitation for orders from retailers. Catalog houses now supply a very small percentage of the merchandise sold by stores. Also known as mail order wholesalers.

Catalog Retailing A form of selling in which the retailer provides the consumer with a merchandise catalog and the consumer submits his order by mail, telphone, or in person in a facility maintained by the store for that purpose.

Catalog Showroom A warehouse showroom where catalog selling and in-store retailing are brought together. Merchandise is presented in catalogs which the customer consults before giving his order to a clerk; who has the merchandise brought in from the warehouse. Catalog showroom merchants concentrate on nationally advertised name brand products; which they offer at prices below regular retail. Also called a *catalog store.*

Catalog Store See *catalog showroom*

Catchment Area The geographic region in which the majority of a firm's customers may be found.

Categorisation A cognitive process by which objects, events, and persons are grouped together and responded to in terms of their class membership rather than their uniqueness.

Category Based Processing A cognitive process in which an individual attempts to categorise new stimuli. If a stimulus can be considered as an example of an existing category, it is evaluated by the affect associated with the category, rather than by careful consideration of its attributes (as in piecemeal processing). The category schema is the basis for evaluation.

Category Killer A type of destination store that is usually large and that concentrates on one category, thus making it possible to carry both a broad assortment and deep selection of merchandise, coupled with low price and moderate service.

Category Manager This manager reports to the marketing manager and is responsible for the marketing of the several brands falling under a generic product category such as coffee, dessert and oral hygiene. This manager (companies sometimes use other titles, for example, unit business manager) is responsible for maximising the total profit from the mix of brands in the category. This may be done by allocating funds and marketing effort according to the profit potential of each brand in the mix; also deleting weak brands and adding new brands with higher profit potential. The category manager is chosen for business as well as marketing skills and works closely (sometimes as a member of a team) with other functional managers such as production, finance and research and development to achieve maximum profitability for the product category.

Cause Related Marketing Marketing efforts (*e.g.*, corporate sponsorship of the Olympic Games) in which a particular brand or product is linked to a particular cause or special event. The primary objective of cause related marketing is the generation of revenue, although such activity may result in increased goodwill on the part of the public. Not to be cauuse with cause marketing.

Cease and Desist Order An order, often emanating from a court or administrative agency, which prohibits the continuance of a particular activity, *e.g.*, the Federal Trade Commission may order a company to cease and desist from particular marketing practice which has been judged deceptive.

Celebrity Marketing A form of person marketing in which the promotion of entertainers, sports figures, etc. is undertaken by managers, publicity directors or agencies such as the William Morris Agency. In celebrity marketing, the goals of the marketing campaign are to create, maintain or alter attitudes toward a particular celebrity or group of celebrities through media appearances, press coverage and other publicity. See also *person marketing* and *political candidate marketing*.

Celebrity Testimonial A type of promotion in which big-name personalities are used to praise or recommend a particular product, service, idea or institution. For example, retired professional athletes are often used in beer commercials. Similarly, the same professional athletes may be used to solicit contributions to a charity or to promote prosocial behaviour such as not driving while intoxicated.

Census Block Usually a well-defined rectangular area bounded by streets or roads. However, it may be irregular in shape and may be bounded by physical features such as railroads or streams. Census blocks do not cross boundaries of countries, tracts, or block numbering areas.

Central Buying The concentration of th eauthority and responsibility for merchandise selection and purchasefor a chain of stores or the branch stores of a department store in the hands of the headquarters staff rather than in the individual units. The central buying function is generally located in the flagship store or the central market.

Central Market A geographical area containing a large concentration of suppliers. The central market may be a merchandise mart or simply a cluster of suppliers in the same section of a city, such as the garment centre in New York. Central markets provide convenient places where buyers and sellers can meet to exchange goods and services.

Central Office Edit The thorough and exacting scrutiny and correction of completed data\collection forms, including a decision about what to do with the data.

Central Place Theory 1. (retailing definition) A model that ranks communities according to the assortment of goods available in each. At the bottom of the hierarchy are communities that represent the smallest central places (centres of commerce). They provide the basic necessities of life. Further up the hierarchy are the larger central places, which carry all goods and services found in lower-order central places plus more specialised ones that are not necessary. (See also *concentric zone theory, dialectic process, gravity model, natural selection theory, retail accordion theory, retail life cycle,* and *wheel of retailing theory*). 2. (geography definition) A normative theory that explains the size, number and spacing of distribution centres to serve a dispersed population.

Centralised Adjustment System A separate office or department, staffed by trained personnel, in which all customer complaints, adjustments, or refunds are handled rather than in the selling department.

Centralised Management The practice of referring matters for decision to higher levels of management particularly to corporate management.

Centralised Organisation The concentration of the decision-making power and activities in teh headquarters or flagship store.

Centralised Sales Organisation A sales force, reporting to corporate or group management, that sells the products of two or more divisions. This may be appropriate when the products of the divisions are distributed through the same channels.

Centre of Influence Method A prospecting method used by salespeople in which the salesperson cultivates well-known, influential people who are willing to provide sales leads.

Cents-off Deal A form of price promotion in which particular consumer products are marked down and prominently labeled to indicate the number of cents reduction, the implication being that the reduction is from the regular retail price. A common practice in the grocery business.

Cents-off Offer A consumer sales promotion technique offering a certificate good for a discount off the posted purchase price of a particular product.

Certification Mark A word or symbol used to designate a product or service as being the holder of some particular certification as to quality, safety, etc. The mark of the Under-writers Laboratory is a common certification mark indicating that a product meets certain safety standards.

Chain Discount See *series discount*

Chain Prospecting A method used by salespersons to gather new leads by obtaining additional names from current prospects. When the current prospect is a satisfied customer, the leads are called referral leads. Also called the *endless chain method.*

Chain Store A unit of a chain store system.

Chain Store System A group of stores, usually a dozen or more, commonly owned and centrally merchandised and managed. In the U.S., the largest chains are grocery and automobile service stations. The term has also come to be applied to large mass merchandising organisations (J.C. Penney, Sears), franchise chains (Burger King, McDonald's) and specialty chains (Lerner Shops, etc.). See also *voluntary chain.*

Channel Captain The organisation (usually a manufacturer or wholesaler, but sometimes a retailer) which dominates and controls a channel of distribution. The ability to assume this role is almost always based on economic power. The channel captain assumes leadership within the channel and often sets distribution policy.

Channel Conflict In marketing, channel conflict is dissonance between two or more members at different levels of the channel (thus, vertical conflict). It is commonly found when one member of the channel, *e.g.*, a dominant manufacturer, attempts to control the entire distribution system. Horizontal channel conflict is found when there is dissonance (not to be confused with normal competition) between two or more members of a channel who are operating at the same level. For example, one retailer may feel that another is gaining unfair advantage by intimidating a supplier on which both depend. See also *intertype channel conflict.*

Channel Control The actual impact that a channel member achieves on an associated channel member's beliefs, attitudes and behaviour.

Channel Cooperation The positive interaction between all members of a channel of distribution, resulting in increased sales and profits for all participants. In general, it is up to the channel captain to win the voluntary cooperation of other channel members. The channel captain may accomplish this by providing advertising materials, training a middleman's sales force, giving financial advice to a channel member, etc. In retailing, retail channel captains assist manufacturers by providing information on consumer preferences and buying patterns. If the channel captain is unsuccessful in fostering voluntary cooperation, it may attempt to coerce its channel members into cooperation by such methods as exclusive dealing, tying agreements, full-line forcing, resale restrictions, reciprocity, price maintenance, price discrimination, and refusal to deal. However, many of these methods are, if no illegal, closely monitored and limited by government regulations. See also *channel of distribution.*

Channel Effectiveness A channel performance dimension based on how well the channel satisfies customer needs and wants, such as for lot size, delivery time, location convenience and assortment breadth.

Channel Efficiency A channel performance dimension focusing on how well the firm minimises costs associated with performing necessary channel functions.

Channel Fit In product marketing, channel fit refers to the degree to which a new product fits into existing channels of distribution. A product is said to have good channel fit when it is simply added to an existing line and does not require the opening up of another channel; *e.g.*, a product which can be sold through the same wholesalers and retailers who handle the company's other products.

Channel Flows The various members of a marketing channel (manufacturers/producers, distributors, retailers, customers, etc.) may be connected by one or more forms of movement called flows. These include: (1) physical flow—the actual movement of products or the delivery of services toward the customer; (2) title or ownership flow—the transfer of title to goods from one channel member to another; (3) financial or payment flow—the granting of credit downward in the channel and the movement of payments upward; (4) communication or information flow—includes such activities as the transfer of product information downward, personal selling efforts and various promotional and advertising campaigns.

Channel Functions The job tasks or activities that need to be performed in the channel.

Channel Interdependency A relationship among members of a channel of distribution in which the activities of one member may, to a considerable degree, influence the activities of others.

Channel Length The various levels of wholesaling middlemen and retailers etc. taken as a whole. Consumer goods often go through a four-link channel (and sometimes five) employing both the wholesale and retail middlemen on their way from producer to consumer. Industrial goods generally go through fewer channels, as they are often sold directly by the producer to the industrial customer. The length of the channel is affected by the product market characteristics, company characteristics and the economic environment. A financially strong company in a healthy economic environment, favours short channels when producing high priced goods aimed at a small number of customers. This channel length is particularly favourable because there are few legal restrictions impeding the marketing of goods. A financially weak company, in an unhealthy economic environment, favours long channels when producing low-priced goods targeted for mass consumption. This channel length, however, has many legal restrictions.

Channel Member Commitment The degree to which a channel relationship is stable, loyal has been built and each channel member is willing to make sacrifices to maintain the exchange.

Channel Member Dependence A channel member's need to maintain a particular channel relationship in order to achieve desired goals.

Channel Member Satisfaction A channel member's affective state reflecting its overall approval or disapproval of a channel relationship with another firm.

Channel Number The number of different marketing channels employed by a marketer. The number of different channels varies if the company is selling to entirely different market or to different market segments. For example, a cosmetic manufacturer such as Revlon sells its high-priced line directly to department stores, but its low-priced products are sold through middlemen to drug stores. The number of channels also depends on geographic regions and the sizes of buyers.

Channel of Distribution A channel of distribution is the route along which goods and services travel from producer/manufacturer through marketing inter-mediaries such as wholesalers, distributors and retailers to the final user. A channel may thus be likened to a pipeline or pathway. The firms which participate in this exchange process may themselves be regarded as the distribution channel; *i.e.,* the chain of institutions acting in concert and providing for the flow of goods and services. This flow may involve the physical movement of the product or simply the transfer of title to it.

Channel Performance An outcome measure of the channel of distribution. The performance of a distribution channel can be assessed by considering a number of performance dimensions, including channel effectiveness, channel efficiency, channel productivity and channel profitability.

Channel Power The capacity to make other members of a channel of distribution confirm to one's wishes. The member who exerts this power is called the *channel captain or channel leader.*

Channel Productivity A channel performance dimension based on the degree to which the channels' total investment in the various inputs necessary to achieve a given distribution objective can be optimised in terms of outputs.

Channel Profitability A channel performance dimension based on the financial performance of channel members in terms of ROI, liquidity, leverage, growth in sales and profits, etc.

Channel Specialisation The channel members' choice of unique positions in the channel based on their capacities, interests, goals, expectations, values and frames of references. Hence, each performs those tasks (participates in those channel flows) which it can perform at a comparative advantage.

Channel Vision A firm's view of the allocation of marketing functions among the members of a channel of distribution and its recognition of places in the channel where there are opportunities for improvement.

Channel Width The number of different outlets or individual firms employed at each level of the channel of distribution. Channel width may be intensive, selling through almost any available wholesale or retail outlet or exclusive, selling through only one wholesaler or retailer in a given area. Prestige items, such as automobiles, appliances, etc. use exclusive distribution or selective distribution—the use of more than one but fewer than all the firms that might carry a product.

Checklist A memory-jogger list of items, used to remind an analyst to think of all relevant aspects. It finds frequent use as a tool of creativity in concept generation and as a factor-consideration list in concept screening.

Cherry Picking A buyer selection of only a few items from one vendor's line and others from another line, failing to purchase a complete line or classification of merchandise from one resource. It also sometimes describes a customer's tendency to buy only items on sale.

Chief Marketing Officer (CMO) In large business organizations, a management level executive responsible for promoting the marketing perspective within the firm and for developing the firm's strategic marketing plan.

Chinese Marketing A form of faulty reasoning (based largely on wishful thinking) in which a market is viewed as containing an unrealistically large number of potential customers. The underlying assumption that the bigger the target market the better. The term comes from a book published in the 1930s by Carl Crow entitled *Four Hundred Million Customers* in which the author claimed that the Great Depression could be ended if the U.S. could simply sell some product to each of the then 400 million Chinese.

Choice Choice involves evaluating alternative actions or behaviours and forming a behavioural intention or plan to engage in the selected behaviour. Choice is the outcome of purchase decision making.

Choice Alternatives The different behaviours considered by consumers in decision making; they are usually the products or brands considered for purchase.

Choice Criteria Those critical attributes employed by a purchaser when evaluating merchandise offered for sale. Among criteria commonly used are convenience of retail outlet, price, quality, etc.

Choice Rule A method by which an individual is hypothesised to make choices or decisions. A choice ruler specifies the manner in which the individual evaluates each alternative under consideration.

C.I.F. (Cost, Insurance and Freight) A shipping term meaning that the seller of goods pays the cost of transporting the goods to their shipping point (dock, railroad platform, etc.), pays the charges incurred in loading the goods on the conveyance employed and finally, pays all insurance and transportation costs to the goods' destination. The buyer pays landing costs and all charges incurred in unloading as well as any duties or taxes levied by the importing country.

Circular Routing A method for scheduling sales calls that involves circular patterns.

Circulation In the print media, circulation refers to the number of copies of a single issue of a magazine or newspaper which are offered for sale or distributed free. Because circulation implies that someone has looked at the publication, the figure for circulation will always be lower than the actual number printed, as a certain percentage of each issue never reaches a reader.

Class Rate The standard rate established by government regulation, for shipping various commodities. These rates were originally established to guarantee fair prices to all users of both common and contract carriers and to avoid the abuses of railroad shipping prevalent in the 19th century. Class rates are established for shipping certain categories of goods between two geographical points, with distance and weight determining the rate. In general, the greater the distance and the greater the weight, the lower the rate. Conversely, the shorter the distance and the less the weight, the higher the rate. Both commodity rates and exception rates may be used as substitutes for the class rate where appropriate and where allowable by law. See also *commodity rate* and *exception rate.*

Classic Merchandise The merchandise that is not influenced by style changes, for which a demand virtually always exists.

Classical Conditioning 1. (consumer behaviour definition) A process through which a previously neutral stimulus, by being paired with an unconditioned stimulus, comes to elicit a response very similar to the response originally elicited by the unconditioned stimulus. 2. (consumer behaviour definition) A traditional learning approach often credited to the work of Ivan Pavlov. It is the belief that when a stimulus that elicits a response is paired with another stimulus, the second stimulus will elicit behaviour similar to the original response.

Classical Functionalism A strategy in which marketing functions (classically there are eight: buying, selling, transporting, storing, standardising and grading, financing, risk bearing, and collecting and disseminating market-ing information) are viewed as discrete tasks; *i.e.,* they are not integrated into a comprehensive marketing programme.

Classical Probability A probability determined by the relative frequency with which an event occurs when an experiment is repeated under controlled conditions.

Classification A grouping of merchandise into a homogeneous category usually smaller than a department. It is particularly useful for control purposes.

Classification Control A form of dollar inventory control in which the dollar value of each classification of goods is smaller than the total stock of the department—*e.g.*, the sporting goods department may be divided into several classifications or dissections, such as golf, fishing, active sport, etc.

Classification Merchandising In retailing, classification merchandising is the practice of planning the breadth of an assortment on the basis of related types or classifications of merchandise. Data reporting is then controlled by these classifications. The theory behind this practice is that small, homogeneous classes of merchandise are preferable for purposes of control.

Classified Advertising In newspapers and magazines, classified advertising refers to those ads placed in special columns arranged by type of product or service. The format and typefaces used in these columns are generally fairly uniform. See also display advertising.

Clearance Sale A special offering of goods at lowered prices to clear the store or department of sow-moving, shop-worn, and other unsold seasonal items. Generallyoccurs at the end of a season to make room for new merchandise.

Clearing House The central processing location where coupons or other sales promotion offers are collected, analysed and sorted for payment or fulfilment.

Client Public Those persons who are the direct recipients of the services and products provided by non-profit organisations.

Close The culmination of a sales presentation in which a salesperson attempts to get a customer to commit to buying a product or service.

Close-out An offer at a reduced price to clear slow-moving or incomplete stock. It is also an incomplete assortment, the remainder of a line of merchandise that is to be discontinued, offered at a low price to ensure immediate sale.

Close Rate The number of actual sales made by a salesperson divided by the number of calls made to potential customers. This is one factor used in the evaluation of salespersons, since it indicates the proportion of successful sales or closings. See also *closing*.

Closed-door Discount House A retailer selling goods to consumers who, by virtue of place of employment, membership in a union or other affiliation, are regarded as "members." Closed-door discount houses charge prices as much as 40% below those found in department stores and depend on high volume and low overhead to make a profit. They carry nationally branded, high quality merchandise for which there is strong consumer demand. Also known as a *membership club* or *wholesale club*.

Closed Stock Items sold only in sets, with no assurance to the customer that the same pattern and quality can be bought at any later time. Thus there is no provision for replacing broken pieces.

Closing The step in the sales process when the salesperson must ask the customer to conclude the purchase. Closing techniques include asking for the order, recapitulating the points of the agreement, offering to help write up the order or indicating what the buyer will lose if the order is not placed immediately. Alternatively, the salesperson may offer some incentive to the buyer, such as a special price or an extra quantity of the goods in question at no extra charge.

Club Plan Selling An arrangement in which a consumer is awarded prizes or granted discount buying privileges by getting new customers to join the club. The club is the group of customers served by the selling organisation and one joins by making purchases.

Cluster Analysis A body of statistical techniques concerned with developing natural groupings of objects based on the relationships of the p variables describing the objects.

Cluster Sample A probability sample distinguished by a two-step procedure in which (1) the parent population is divided into mutually exclusive and exhaustive subsets and (2) a random sample of subsets is selected. If the investigator then uses all of the population elements in the selected subsets for the sample, the procedure is one-stage cluster sampling; if a sample of elements is selected probabilistically from the subsets, the procedure is two-stage cluster sampling.

Clustering Techniques In the analysis of marketing research data, clustering techniques are methods used to find usable patterns within sets of data. Patterns may be established for such factors as demographic data, customer attitudes, psychographic data and purchasing behaviour. Using a computer, researchers attempt to search the data for homogeneous groups of people and then proceed to analyse the data in search of new or improved marketing strategies.

Clutter In advertising, clutter (the crowding together of advertising messages in the print and electronic media) results in a loss of advertising effectiveness. Advertisers may avoid clutter by buying more time or reserving more space in the media used. They may also pay a premium for positioning their advertisements in such a way as to avoid clutter. For example, in magazine advertising, the inside front cover is considered a less cluttered position for an ad. Advertisers may also select those media that minimise clutter, refuse to accept piggyback ads or otherwise regulate the amount of advertising and hence, the amount of clutter.

Clutter Advertising The extent to which multiple messages compete for the consumers' (limited) attention. It often is used to indicate multiple competing messages in one medium (such as television) or place.

Coding In market research data analysis, the translation of gathered information into a form (usually numerical) which can be more readily analysed.

Coefficient of Income Sensitivity A comparison between a product's percentage variation in sales over a number of years and a 1% change in personal disposable income. Used to forecast the effect of a 1% change in a available discretionary funds on a product's sales.

Coercive Influence Strategy A means of communication that puts direct pressure on the target to perform a specific behaviour or set of behaviours with adverse consequences of noncompliance stressed or implied and mediated by the source.

Cognition The sum total of an individual's beliefs, attitudes, perceptions, needs, goals and learned reactions about some aspect of the individuals' world. A cognition is the pattern of meaning of a thing. The mental processes of interpretation and decision making, including the beliefs and meanings they create.

Cognitive Component In attitude research, particularly in the tripartite view or structural approach, the cognitive component is the knowledge and beliefs a consumer has about a product or service, including evaluative beliefs. It is the intellectual component of attitude. See also *attitude* and *conative component*.

Cognitive Consonance The opposite of cognitive Consonance The opposite of cognitive dissonance, cognitive consonance is the feeling of satisfaction experienced by a customer at the point of or immediately following, a decision to purchase. The customer has a feeling of well-being and the sense that the correct decision has been made.

Cognitive Dissonance Doubt and anxiety suffered by a customer at the point of or immediately following, a decision to purchase. This dissonance is the result of a conflict between two or more of the purchaser's cognitions (beliefs or perceptions) regarding the purchased product.

Cognitive Processes Those mental activities which involve thought and reasoning, as, for example, learning and judging.

Cognitive Response The thoughts a consumer has to a persuasive message such as *support arguments* or *counter arguments*.

Cohorts In the study of demographics, cohorts are the members of each of the various age groups that make up the total population.

Cold Canvassing Door-to-door or telephone solicitation of orders for merchandise without the benefit of leads or prior appointments.

Cold Storage Warehouse A form of public warehouse designed for the storage of perishables requiring refrigeration. For example, butter, furs and meat products are generally stored in cold storage warehouses. See also *public warehouse*.

Collaborative Agreements A cooperation strategy between companies to jointly pursue a common goal. It is also referred to as *strategic alliances* or *global strategic partnerships.*

Collect on Delivery (C.O.D.) The buyer must make payment for the purchase at time of delivery of goods. It is considered a poor substitute of cash before delivery for cash in advance because if the purchaser refuses, the seller incurs return freight charges and any deterioration of the product in the process. See also *cash on delivery.*

Collect Rate Shipment A freight bill is a carrier's method of charging for transportation services. If it is collect, the buyer is responsible and must pay transport costs upon arrival of the shipment.

Colour Separation A negative of one of the four colours (black, blue, red and yellow) used in the four-colour printing process to reproduce colour photographs and other colour elements.

Combination Compensation Plan 1. (sales definition) A compensation plan for salespeople that combines a base salary with commissions and/or a bonus. (2) (sales definition) A sales force compensation plan that offers a base salary plus some proportion of incentive pay consisting of commissions, bonuses or both. When salary plus commissions is used, the commissions are typically tied to sales volume or profitability, just as with a straight commission plan. The only difference is that the commissions are smaller in a combination plan than when the salesperson is compensated solely by commission.

Combination House A middleman organisation which serves the wholesale, retail and institutional markets.

Combination Offer A form of consumer fraud involving the sale of a product at a low price tied to the purchase of a continuing service. The sale of food freezers tied to the purchase of frozen foods is a notorious example as the food is frequently of inferior quality.

Combined Target Market Approach A method of market segmentation in which two or more distinct market segments are combined into one larger target market. A single marketing strategy is then used to appeal to the larger group. Combiners, *i.e.,* firms adopting this method, do so in an attempt to increase the size of their target markets, to gain certain economies of scale, to minimise their risks, or two allocate limited resources economically. They try to extend or modify their basic offering to appeal to these combined customers and rely heavily on promotion to convince each sub-segment that the product will satisfy its needs. See also *market segmentation*.

Commercial (1) Relating to trade, commerce, stores, office buildings, as well as other business activities and properties. (2) A paid advertisement appearing in the broadcast media of radio and television.

Commercial Auction An agent business unit that effects the sale of goods through an auctioneer, who, under specified rules, solicits bids or offers from buyers and has the power to accept the highest bids of responsible bidders and thereby, consummates the sale.

Commercial Bribery The illegal attempt to influence business decision-making by offering gifts or favours to the person charged with making the decision.

Commercial Marketing The application of marketing strategies. concepts and techniques to profit making endeavors as distinct from their use in the nonprofit sector.

Commercialisation The final stage in new product development in which a manufacturer is committed to the production of a new product.

Commissary Store (1) A store operated by the military (and commonly staffed by civilian employees) for the benefit of military personnel and their dependents. (2) A store operated by a large employer for the benefit of its employees. Commissary stores generally sell food products and other supplies at prices substantially below those on the open market. Also known as company stores.

Commission A method of compensation in which payments are directly tied to the sales and/or profits achieved by the salesperson. Typically, the salesperson receives a percentage of sales as salary. This is the commission. Various combinations of salary and commissions may be used. In the "salary-plus-commission" method of compensation, the employee receives a straight salary plus a percentage of total sales during a specified period. "Straight commission" denotes a fixed or sliding percentage rate related to the salesperson's sales or profit volume with no straight salary. This method is prominent in the insurance and the securities investment industries. See also *straight commission.*

Commission Buyer of Farm Products A wholesale establish-ment primarily engaged in buying farm products on a commission basis from farmers for others.

Commission Buying Office An office that receives its remuneration in the form of commissions on orders placed from manufacturers rather than from retailers.

Commission House An agent who usually exercises physical control over and negotiates the sale of the goods the agent handles. The agent generally enjoys broader powers as to prices, methods and terms of the sale than does the broker, although the agent must obey instructions issued by the principal. The agent often arranges delivery, extends necessary credit, collects, deducts fees and remits the balance to the principal.

Commission Merchant An agent middleman who, although he often has physical control over the goods he sells, does not take title to them. Commission merchants most commonly represent the sellers of such agricultural products as grain, livestock, and produce, which are usually accepted on consignment. They have the authority to negotiate prices and terms of sale on behalf of their principal and may arrange delivery, extend credit, make collections etc. In this respect the commission merchant has more freedom than the broker.

Commission Method of Compensation The traditional compensation method whereby advertising agencies have been paid on the basis of a percentage of the cost of media time and/or space they purchased for a client. The usual commission has been 15 percent of the total cost of the media space and time purchased. Recently, clients have been moving towards the negotiation of specific fees for the services rendered by advertising agencies.

Commission with Draw A method of compensation for salespeople in which payments are based on a percentage of sales but in which regular payments are made from an account set aside for that purpose (the draw).

Commissioner A specialised type of buying agency that brings the buyer in contact with proper vendors in foreign markets and an interpreter. Also, the commissioner facilitates the procedures of foreign exchange and shipping.

Committee Buying Purchasing activities collectively performed by a group of buyers on behalf of a multi-unit operation. See also *buying committee*.

Commodity Although the term is imprecise, commodities are generally agricultural or mineral products, *e.g.*, wheat, cattle, eggs, cotton, orange juice, silver, hides, coffee, lumber, etc. Occasionally the term may be applied to manufactured goods, but never to services.

Commodity Approach to Marketing An approach to the study of marketing in which the movement of goods from producer to consumer is viewed as a key to understanding the marketing process.

Commodity Exchange A non-profit organisation which provides members with a place in which commodities are traded, either among themselves or for others, on a commission basis. The exchange does not engage in buying or selling, but does make and enforce rules and may adjust disputes among member-traders.

Commodity Products Those products of basic industry which, although they may carry brand names, are not clearly distinguishable from one another in the public eye, *e.g.*, tires, bearings, steel, electronic components, etc.

Commodity Rate An allowable deviation from the class rate charged by shippers to their customers. The reduced commodity rate may be awarded to the customer for regular use or for the size of the quantity shipped. However, the commodity rate is still subject to government regulation. See also *class rate* and *exception rate*.

Common Area (of Shopping Centre) The area within a shopping centre that is not for rental by tenants but is available for common use by all tenants, their customers and invitees.

Common Carrier A transportation firm (rail, truck, barge, etc.) engaged in shipping merchandise. Common carriers operate on regular schedules over established routes, charge published standard rates and are available to all shippers. All are subject to one or more forms of government regulation. See also *contract carrier* and *private carrier*.

Common Costs The common or general costs that support a number of activities or profit segments. These costs cannot be traced to a product or segment.

Common Law This term refers to that part of the law that grew up without benefit of legislation and resulted from court decisions; these rulings then became the precedent for subsequent litigation. According to legal theory, the colonists brought the common law of England with them to America.

Common Market An association of countries who have reduced or eliminated the trade barriers which existed between them and are parties that share a common external tariff agreement. In addition, common markets generally provide for the free flow of labour and capital from country to country. See also *European Economic Community.*

Communication A method of data collection involving questioning of respondents to secure the desired information using a data collection instrument called a questionnaire.

Communication Adaptation A strategy employed in international trade in which a company exports the same products that it manufactures for the domestic market but changes the advertising and other promotional messages which accompany them in the foreign market.

Communication Process A process consisting of five components: (1) a source (or sender), (2) an encoding process in which the message is put into a transmittable form, (3) a decoding process at which time the message is translated into a comprehensible form, and (5) the reception of the message at its destination.

Communications Act (1934) See *Federal Communications Commission*

Community Relations A firm's interactions with the locality in which it operates, with emphasis on disseminating company information to foster trust in the company's activities.

Community Shopping Centre A medium-sized shopping centre generally anchored by a variety and/or junior department store and complemented by as many as 50 smaller retail stores and related businesses. Most community shopping centres have a gross leasable area of between 1,00,000 and 3,00,000 square feet and require a surrounding population of at least 50,000 to operate profitably. The radius of attraction extends to approximately 10-15 minutes of drive time.

Company Demand See *sales potential*

Company Marketing Environment See *marketing environment*

Company Marketing Opportunity A niche in a market perceived by a company as having sales potential.

Company Store See *commissary store*

Comparative Advantage A theory of international marketing in which a country is said to have a comparative advantage when it can produce certain goods (or, for that matter, all goods) more cheaply than another country. In terms of actual trade, however, it is to each individual country's advantage to specialise in the production of those goods which it produces most advantageously; *i.e.,* in which it has a relative advantage and not in the production of all goods.

Comparative Advertising A form of competitive advertising in which specific brands are named and compared in terms of their specific characteristics and attributes. The objective is to demonstrate the superiority of the advertised product. Also known as *comparison advertising.*

Comparative Marketing In international marketing, the study of the differences and similarities between various national systems regarding supply and demand as well as distribution.

Comparative Prices Statements in advertisements or signs comparing specific prices with previous prices, other prices or prices goods are estimated to be worth.

Comparative Rating Scale A scale requiring subjects to make their ratings as a series of relative judgements or comparisons rather than as independent assessments.

Comparison Advertising See *comparative advertising*

Comparison Shopping A retail trade practice in which one retailer obtains information about his competitor's activities by sending a comparison shopper to the store. Comparison shopping may be carried on by an outside agency organised for the purpose or by the store's own comparison department.

Compensation Deal In international marketing, a form of counter trade in which payments are partly in the form of currency and partly in the form of goods.

Compensatory Import Charges Taxer that correspond to various international taxes, such as value-added taxes and sales taxes.

Compensatory Rule In evaluating alternatives, the compensatory rule suggests that a consumer will select the alternative with the highest overall evaluation on a set of choice criteria. Criteria evaluations are done separately and combined arithmetically such that positive evaluations can offset or balance (compensate for) negative evaluations. This term is also called compensatory integration procedure, compensatory model and compensatory process.

Competition Although competition may take a number of forms, in its marketing context it is a form of business activity in which two or more parties are engaged in a rivalry for customer acceptance. See also *price competition, monopolistic competition, oligopolistic competition, perfect competition*, and *pure monopoly*.

Competitive Advantage A position of superiority one firm may establish over its competitors in the marketplace. The four *Ps* of marketing are all possible avenues to a firm's finding itself in a favourable marketing situation. See also *four Ps of marketing*.

Competitive Advertising Advertising which features specific brands rather than broad product categories and which is intended to motivate the consumer to buy the particular product. Also called *selective advertising*.

Competitive Analysis The analysis of factors designed to answer the question, "how well is a firm doing compared to its competitors?" The analysis goes well beyond sales and profit figures in assessing the firm's ratings on such factors as price, product, technical capabilities, quality, costumer service, delivery and other important factors compared to each of the major competitors.

Competitive Bidding The practice of competition in which firms submit offers or bids that detail the services and product specifications to be offered at a stated price.

Competitive Brands The brands that are considered as alternatives by buyers in a particular market segment; sometimes called the evoked set. Occasionally, it is used to mean a (smaller) set of products which a particular seller wishes to be competing with; more rarely, it means the full set of competitors in fact competing in a given market.

Competitive Environment To any company in the marketplace, the competitive environment is the sum total of other firms marketing products similar to or substitutable for the company's own. For example, to a marketer of sugar, the competitive environment would include all other companies marketing sugar as well as those marketing artificial sweeteners.

Competitive Frame The list of specific brands with which a given brand competes most directly for customers.

Competitive Intelligence The systematic gathering of data and information about all aspects of competitors' marketing and business activities for the purposes of formulating plans and strategies and making decisions.

Competitive Monopoly See *differentiated oligopoly*

Competitive Parity Approach to Promotional Budgeting See *competitive-parity method*

Competitive Parity Budgeting An advertising budget method whereby an advertiser chooses to use a level of spending on advertising that is similar to the advertising spending level being used by major competitors.

Competitive-Parity Method An approach to promotional budgeting in which a firm's expenditures are set in proportion to what it believes the competition is spending. The competitive-parity method is widely regarded as a defensive strategy.

Competitive Position The position of one business relative to others in the same industry. There are a multitude of factors contributing to (and which can be used to measure) competition. The major categories are: (1) *market position*—relative share of market, rate of change of share, variability of share across segments, perceived differentiation of quality/service/price, breadth of product, and company images; (2) *economic and technological position*—relative cost position, capacity utilisation, technological position, and patented technology, product or process; and (3) *capabilities*—management strength and depth, marketing strength, distribution system, labour relation, relation-ships with regulators.

Competitive Sell See *comparative advertising*

Competitive Stage See *maturity stage*

Competitive Strategy A plan that attempts to define a position for the business that utilizes the competitive advantages that the business has over its competitors.

Complement of Markup Percentage One hundred percent less markup percentage on retail.

Complementary Goods See *complementary product*

Complementary Product A product which is accessory to or which in some way supplements another product as, for example, software supplements a computer.

Complete Segmentation A form of market segmentation in which each potential customer is treated as an individual rather than as part of an aggregation because each is seen as identifiably distinct from all others. See also *custom marketing*.

Completed Fertility The average number of births for all women in a society.

Completely Randomised Design An experimental design in which the experimental treatments are assigned to the test units completely at random.

Compliment Approach A sales approach in which the salesperson begins the sales call be complimenting the prospect.

Component Parts The industrial products (or subassemblies) that either are ready for direct assembly into the finished product or require only a minor amount of further processing. Examples are switches, transistors, motors, gears, nuts, bolts and screws.

Compound Duties The duties that provide for specific, plus ad valorem duties to be levied on the same articles.

Comprehension The cognitive processes involved in interpreting, understanding and making sense of concepts, events, objects and persons in the environment.

Comprehensive Layout A detailed mock-up of a print ad presented to clients in order to gain their approval for the advertising approach before significant production costs are incurred for obtaining artwork and typesetting.

Computerised Buying The use of computers in managing the purchasing process. Such tasks as calculating current inventory figures, computing economic order quantities, preparing purchase orders, developing requests for vendor quotations, expediting orders and generating printouts of dollars spent on vendors and products can be part of the system. Some systems may have decision support models to assist in analysis of purchase alternatives.

Conative Component In attitude research, particularly in the tripartite view or structural approach, the conative component is the readiness of an individual to purchase a particular product or service or take some other action. It is the active component of attitude. For example, the customer may be very, somewhat or not at all likely to buy a Honda Civic, take a vacation in the Middle East or participate in anti-nuclear power plant demonstrations. See also attitude and cognitive component.

Concentrated Marketing A marketing strategy in which a firm's resources are devoted to capturing a large share of a narrow market segment.

Concentration The process of bringing goods from various places together in one place. It includes the sorting processes of accumulation and assorting.

Concentration Ratio (1) (environments definition) A statistical measure, such as the percentage of a total industry's sales accounted for by the largest three firms in the industry, representing the degree of concentration of a market. (2) (strategic marketing definition) The proportion of industry shipments accounted for by the four largest firms in the industry, expressed as a percentage. This measure describes the structure of competition and yields insights into the intensity of rivalry in an industry.

Concentration Strategy In this strategy, a company chooses to pursue a large share of one or more submarkets rather than chasing a small share of a large market. The strategy can be somewhat risky if the demand in the submarket falls away or if one or more competitors enter the submarket.

Concentric Zone Theory A theory of urban land-use patterns, developed by William Burgess, that states that a city will assume the form of five concentric urban zones: the central business district, the zone in transition, the zone of working persons' homes, the zone of better residences and the commuters' zone. Growth is accomplished by the expansion of each zone into the next zone.

Concept A briefly stated idea or theme for possible use as the organizing idea for an advertisement or advertising campaign.

Concept Evaluation Stage A stage of the new product development cycle in which ideas for new products are evaluated. Initially, the product idea may be evaluated on the basis of words, pictures or models. The purpose of the concept evaluation stage is to determine whether an idea is worth further investment. The concept evaluation stage follows the idea generation stage.

Concept Statement A verbal and/or pictorial statement of a concept (for a product or for advertising) that is prepared for presentation to potential buyers or users to get their reaction prior to its being implemented. Product concepts are followed by prototypes, advertising concepts by one of several forms of semifinished production.

Concept Statement, Commercialised A term used in distinguishing two types of product concept statements. A commercialised product concept statement is prepared in an advertising format, as a persuasive statement. A noncommercialised product concept statement is prepared in neutral, non persuasive format.

Concept Test A qualitative or quantitative examination of consumer reactions to a proposed advertising idea.

Concept Testing An early stage in the product development process, concept testing attempts to determine consumer reaction to new product concepts before large amounts of money are committed to their production. Typically, potential customers are shown pictures of proposed products and are asked to react to them.

Concept Testing and Development The process in which a concept statement is presented to potential buyers or users, for their reactions. These reactions permit the developer to estimate the sales value of the concept (whether product or advertising) and to make changes in it so as to enhance its sales value.

Conclusive Research Research studies, often based on such methods as surveys, observation, simulation and experimentation, which generate large quantities of reliable data. Firms often employ conclusive research in an effort to solve specific problems and employ its results as a basis for decision making.

Conditional Sales Contract A retail installment contract which requires the buyer to pay monthly payments to a retailer or other creditor. The retailer retains title of ownership until all payments have been made, so that merchandise may be repossessed whenever the buyer fails to meet the terms of the contract. If the repossessed item is resold, the resale price is credited to the customer's balance, but the customer remains liable for the remainder of the balance due.

Confidence Interval In random sampling, a confidence interval is the range on either side of an estimate which is most likely to contain the actual value with some stated percentage of certainty. The size of the sample determines the percentage of certainty. For example, if a sample of 100 were taken in a random sample concerning a new brand of mouthwash and it was found that 10 per cent of the sample preferred the new mouthwash over existing brands, then it may be stated (with 95% certainty) that between 4 and 16 per cent of the population actually prefers the new mouthwash.

Confined Merchandise In retailing, merchandise sold by a producer or distributor to a limited number of stores so that, in effect, each retailer has exclusive resale rights in his trading areas.

Confirmation In consumer satisfaction theory, confirmation refers to a situation in which a product performs exactly as it was expected to, *i.e.*, repurchase expectations are confirmed.

Confirmation (or Order) From a retailer's standpoint, the official order of a store for goods made out on the retailer's order form and countersigned by the buyer and merchandise manager. It is distinguished from the memoranda that buyers often make out on vendors' order blanks that are not official orders and are not binding on the store. From the vendor's standpoint, it is the acknowledgement of a buyer's order by the vendor. It is the buyer's legal acceptance of the offer made by the buyer generally in writing.

Confiscation (1) In international marketing, the seizure of foreign owned property by a government without provision for reimbursement of the owners. (2) The seizure of private property by a government, often as a penalty.

Conglomerate Merger A merger of two or more corporations in unrelated industries, such as a cosmetics manufacturer and a children's clothing manufacturer. The two firms need not be on the same level of the channel of distribution. For example, an apparel manufactures may merge with a retail store or a car rental agency may merge with a food manufacturer. The companies involved undertake the merger in order to provide a diversity of operations for each other and to protect their profits from economic fluctuations.

Congruent Innovation The development of products which, because they are so slightly changed, are virtually identical to their antecedents. They frequently differ only in terms of higher or lower quality or in that they incorporate a relatively insignificant new feature. Congruent innovation almost never disrupts existing consumptive patterns.

Conjoint Analysis A statistical technique in which respondents' utilities or valuations of attributes are inferred from the preferences they express for various combinations of these attributes.

Conjoint Measurement A measurement tool used in product planning in which product attributes are analysed in an effort to determine which are most attractive to potential customers. Also known as *benefit structure analysis* and *trade-off analysis*.

Conjunctive Rule A decision-making rule of thumb or heuristic in which the consumer is assumed to set up minimum cutoffs for each of several attributes or dimensions of a product or thing. If the brand or item does not meet all of the minimum criteria, it is rejected. The evaluation rule leads to an acceptable or nonacceptable decision. For example, a conjunctive rule may be that a slice of bread must have at least 3 grams of protein, minimum percentages of specific vitamins, less than 100 mg sodium and less than 75 calories per slice to be acceptable. A brand must meet all of these minimum attributes or it is unacceptable. A shortfall in one attribute is not offset by excessive endowment in another attribute.

Conscious Parallelism Identical or similar actions taken by two or more firms in the market, especially regarding price changes, which may be seen as collusion. See also *price leader*.

Consensus A judgemental technique for forecasting business results, which is based on the combined opinions of groups of individuals.

Consent Order An order issued after a defendant agrees to discontinue a complained-of practice without admitting any violation of the law.

Consideration (1) (sales definition) A sales manager leadership style wherein sales managers are supportive, friendly and considerate of their sales personnel; they consult with them and represent their interests; and they recognise their contributions. In essence, a sales manager using this kind of leadership style exhibits relationship-oriented behaviour. (2) (retailing definition) Something of value received or given at the request of the promiser in reliance on and in return for the promiser's promise. It may be a payment of money or merely an exchange of promises, as when a buyer orders goods and the vendor confirms the order. The buyer promises to buy and take the goods and the vendor promises to sell and ship them.

Consideration Set The group of alternatives that a consumer evaluates in making a decision.

Consignee A person or firm to whom shipments are made.

Consignment Merchandise shipped by a producer to a distributor or retailer with the understanding that the producer retains title to the goods until they are sold. Consignment sales offer the producer the opportunity to control its terms of resale and help overcome dealer resistance to the product.

Consignment Sale In this sale, title remains with the vendor until the goods are resold by the retailer; however, any unsold portion of the goods may be returned to the vendor without payment.

Consistency of Product Mix A firm's product mix has three attributes: width, depth and consistency. A firm's lines are said to be consistent when they share certain common characteristics such as similar end use, shared distribution channels, common production facilities, etc.

Consistency Theory A theory that purports that attitudes, values, and behaviour tend to be consistent in the cognitive structures of the individual.

Consolidated Delivery Service A private business organised to deliver products for retailers. A fee is charged for every package delivered.

Consolidated Metropolitan Statistical Area (CMSA) Large metropolitan complexes within which individual components, designated as PMSAs, have been defined. These components exhibit a high degree of integration as do, for example, Dade and Broward counties in Florida, which form a PMSA. See also *Metropolitan Statistical Area (MSA)* and *Primary Metropolitan Statistical Area (PMSA)*.

Consolidation (1) (physical distribution definition) The small shipments combined or consolidated into large shipments to reduce transportation expenditures. Larger volume shipments typically qualify for quantity discounts. Generally the larger the shipment the lower the freight rate per hundred weight. (2) (environments definition) The joining of two or more independent business firms into a new firm. Unlike a merger, the acquired company does not maintain its identity.

Consolidator A person or firm providing the service of combining small shipments into larger shipments to reduce transportation expenditures.

Consortia In international marketing, a partnership arrangement similar to the joint venture with the exception that it typically involves a large number of participants and functions in a market in which it was not previously involved. Consortia help to bring together financing and spread risk among more participants.

Conspiracy An agreement between competitors, made prior to contacting customers, concerning their relationships with the customers.

Constant Dollar Value The adjustment of dollar values by purchasing power to eliminate or allow for the effects of price changes on data in dollars reported overtime. This is sometimes referred to as real dollars.

Constant Dollars A dollar amount modified so that the effects of inflation have been removed. A base year is selected and all subsequent calculations and comparisons are relative to the dollar value in that year. All the resultant dollar values are then constant and comparable. Used in time series analysis, other statistical series, and economics.

Constant Sum Method A type of comparative rating scale in which an individual is instructed to divide some given sum among two or more attributes on the basis of some criterion (*e.g.,* their importance to him or her).

Constitutive Definition A definition in which a given construct is defined in terms of other constructs in the set, sometimes in the form of an equation that expresses the relationship among them.

Constrained Decision Making Limitations imposed upon the decision-making discretion of a business, especially as a result of franchise agreements.

Construct Validation An approach to validating a measure by determining what construct, concept or trait the instrument is in fact measuring.

Consultative Selling A customised sales presentation approach in which the salesperson is viewed as an expert and serves as a consultant to the customer. The salesperson identifies the prospects's needs and recommends the best solution even if the best solution does not require the salesperson's products or services.

Consumable Supplies The products that are used up or consumed in the operation of a business. Examples are cleaning compounds, business forms, soaps and small tools.

Consumer Traditionally, the ultimate user or consumer of goods, ideas and services. However, the term also is used to imply the buyer or decision maker as well as the ultimate consumer. A mother buying cereal for consumption by a small child is often called the consumer although she may not be the ultimate user.

Consumer Advertising Advertising directed to the ultimate consumer, *i.e.,* the general public.

Consumer Advocate One who speaks for or represents the interests of the consuming public, particularly with respect to social, economic and ecological matters.

Consumer Analysis See *consumer research*

Consumer Behaviour The actions of consumers in the marketplace and the underlying motives for those actions. Marketers expect that by understanding what causes consumers to buy particular goods and services they will be able to determine which products are needed in the marketplace, which are obsolete and how best to present those goods to the consumer.

Consumer Behaviour Odyssey A team of researchers that traveled across the country in the summer of 1986 interviewing, filming and recording the behaviour of consumers engaging in various consumption activities.

Consumer Bill of Rights (1962) Principles stated by President Kennedy in 1962, which outlined the rights consumers should expect from the marketplace and thereby provided the framework for much subsequent consumer legislation. As stated by Kennedy, the consumer is entitled to be safe from injury, to be correctly informed about products, to have a proper forum in which to be heard when problems and complaints arise, to have a choice in the selection of goods and/or services, and to have a voice in the decision-making process through which goods and/or services become available in the marketplace.

Consumer Choice Model A model attempting to represent how consumers use and combine information about alternatives in order to make a choice among them.

Consumer Cooperative A retail operation owned by its customers and usually incorporated on the basis of one vote for each customer-member. Merchandise is commonly sold at the prevailing market price and profits are divided among the customer-members in proportion to their patronage of the store.

Consumer Credit The ability of individual consumers to obtain money, goods or revenues on the strength of their promise to pay at some specified time in the future, generally in installments. Such purchases are thus referred to as being on "time."

Consumer Credit Protection Act (1968) A federal statute, passed in 1969 and amended in 1970, which requires finance companies, banks, retailers and other grantors of consumer credit to reveal to the consumer the true cost of credit, both in terms of annual percentage rates and dollar amounts. The legislation was designed to allow consumers to compare competing sources of credit. The 1970 amendment protects the holder of credit cards from liability if the cards are fraudulently used. Commonly referred to as the Truth-in-Lending Act.

Consumer Decision Making Unit The decision maker in the family, organisation or group. The decision making unit need not necessarily be a single individual, but may be a committee or informal set of individuals that makes the final choices. Often the decision reflects not only the attributes of the products being considered, but also the influence patterns found in formal groups and informal groups.

Consumer Demand The level of desire for goods coupled with the ability to purchase these same goods. Most frequently applied to the ultimate consumer, but may include industrial, governmental and institutional customers as well. See also *demand.*

Consumer Demographics Vital statistics of the consuming population including size, age, sex, birth and death rates, location, income, race, education, etc.

Consumer Diary A booklet in which each member of a representative sample of consumers records what he or she is actually viewing on television and/or listening to on radio for one week. The consumers are also asked to provide information about their age, sex, occupation, etc. Use of the consumer diary is intended to give advertisers insight into the make-up of the broadcast media audience.

Consumer Education The formalized teaching efforts to provide consumers with skills and knowledge to allocate their resources wisely in the market-place.

Consumer Expenditure Survey A survey of a representative sample of the U.S. population conducted by the U.S. Bureau of the Census for the Bureau of Labour Statistics to provide a continuous flow of data on the buying habits of American consumers. The survey consists of two components: an interview panel survey of five interviews every three months and a diary or record keeping survey of households for two consecutive one-week periods.

Consumer Finance Company A lending agency licensed under state laws to engage in the business of lending money to consumers. It is also referred to as a personal finance company.

Consumer Goods Goods produced for the ultimate consumer and nearly always sold at the retail level. These products are for personal, nonbusiness use and may fall into one of three categories: (1) convenience items (milk, cigarettes, magazines etc.), (2) shopping items (apparel, automobiles etc.), (3) specially items (gourmet foods, etc.)

Consumer Goods Pricing Act (1975) Federal legislation that halted all interstate usage of resale price maintenance agreements. This law ended many of the so-called "fair trade" agreements among producers and distributors involved in interstate commerce.

Consumer Information The policies aimed at providing consumers with marketplace information and fostering effective utilisation leading to improved consumer choice.

Consumer Information Processing (CIP) The mental processes by which consumers interpret information from the environment to make it meaningful and integrate that information to make decisions.

Consumer Laws Legislation enacted on the local, state or national level to protect consumers from unscrupulous business practices. On the federal level in the United States, these laws include the Kefauver-Harris Drug Amendments to the Food and Drug Act (1962), the Wholesome Meat Act (1967), the National Traffic and Motor Vehicle Safety Act (1966), the Child Protection and Toy Safety Act (1969), the Federal Hazardous Substances Labeling Act (1960), the Fair Labeling and Packaging Act (1966), the Consumer Protection Credit Act (1968), the Consumer Product Safety Act (1972), and Equal Credit Opportunity Act (1976) among many others.

Consumer Market The consumer market consists of persons who purchase goods and services for their own use or for the use of persons in their household; *i.e.,* they do not resell the purchased product nor do they use it in some other business enterprise.

Consumer Motivation The driving force in an individual that impels him to act in the marketplace. It may be positive or negative depending on how he perceives his needs and goals. See also *motive*.

Consumer Movement A mix of people, ideas and organizations representing previously unrepresented groups or concerns and having change or reform as common ends.

Consumer Panel In marketing research, a group of individuals brought together for the purpose of determining consumer preferences with regard to products or ideas. The panel members are interviewed collectively and their expressed opinions are tabulated for use in new product development, etc.

Consumer-perceived Risk A consumer's perception of the possible effects, mostly negative, of an incorrect purchase decision. Includes functional risk, physical risk, financial risk, social risk and psychological risk.

Consumer Price Index (CPI) A measure of the changes in the retail prices of a representative "market basket" of goods and services purchased for day-to-day living by urban consumers. 1967 is the index base year, with current prices expressed in relation to that year. The items making up the "market basket" are of constant quality and quantity. The CPI, which is issued monthly by the U.S. Bureau of Labour Statistics, is limited to measuring the effect of selected price changes on the cost of living and is not a true cost of living index, which would measure such variables as the total amount families spend to live, how price fluctuations effect the standard of living or the relative difference in the cost of living between geographic areas. The consumer price index or inaccurately, the cost of living index.

Consumer Product A product produced for and purchased by, households for their use.

Consumer/Product Relationship The relationship between consumers and a product or brand. It is how consumers perceive the product as relating to their goals and values. The consumer/ product relationship is important to consider in developing marketing strategies.

Consumer Product Safety Act (1972) Federal legislation which established the Consumer Product Safety Commission (CPSC). The act stipulates that manufacturers must notify the Commission within 24 hours of discovering that they have produced and sold product which represents a substantial hazard to consumers. A recall procedure must be instituted by the manufacturer to correct the defect. The Act grants the Commission jurisdiction over most consumer products, the exceptions being those already regulated by another agency such as the Food and Drug Administration. The Commission is authorised to protect consumers by setting standards for product safety, testing products, investigating consumer complaints about defective products, banning dangerous products, and monitoring injuries received from those products. In recent years, such products as cribs for infants have been recalled by the Commission for presenting hazardous defects. See also *Consumer Product Safety Act (1972).*

Consumer Product Safety Commission Improvements Act (1976)

An amendment to the Consumer Product Safety Act (1972) intended to improve the effectiveness of the Commission by providing standards, enforceability, litigation procedures, and funding. See also *Consumer Product Safety Act (1972).*

Consumer Protection The body of federal, state and local government legislation designed to assure safety, purity, quality efficacy, purity, quality and efficacy of many products, services and the reliability of statements in advertising about them.

Consumer Relations The communications efforts used to support the sale of a product or service. This generally includes product publicity, company image advertising, interaction with consumer groups and customer inquiry response systems.

Consumer Research The study of the ultimate consumer to determine the factors that influence purchase decisions involving time, money and effort in the consumption of goods and services. Consumer behaviour includes the related studies of demography, sociology, anthropology, and psychology. Marketers look to consumer research to help them identify their target markets and determine how to market their goods and/or services to those target markets most efficiently.

Consumer Sales Promotion Externally directed incentives offered to the ultimate consumer. These usually consist of offers such as coupons, premiums, rebates, etc., designed to gain one or more of the following; product trial; repeat usage of product; more frequent or multiple product purchases; introduce a new/ improved product; introduce new packaging or different size packages; neutralise competitive advertising or sales promotions; capitalise on seasonal, geographic or special events; encourage consumers to trade up to a larger size more profitable line or another product in the line.

Consumer Satisfaction 1. (consumer behaviour definition) The degree to which a consumer's expectations are fulfilled or surpassed by a product. 2. (consumer behaviour definition) The post-purchase evaluation of a consumer action by the ultimate consumer or the decision maker. The beliefs, attitudes and future purchase patterns; word-of-mouth communication; and legal and informal complaints have been related to the post-purchase satisfaction/dissatisfaction process.

Consumer Sentiment Index The Index of Consumer Sentiment (ICS) was developed at the University of Michigan Survey Research Center to measure the confidence or optimism (pessimism) of consumers in their future well-being and coming economic conditions. The index measures short-and long-term expectations of business conditions and the individual's perceived economic well-being. Evidence indicates that the ICS is a leading indicator of economic activity as consumer confidence seems to precede major spending decisions.

Consumer Socialisation The process by which consumers' form attitudes and opinions within the context of the society around them and develop the skills necessary to become develop the skills necessary to become consumers within that society. The process is an on-going one, beginning in childhood and continuing throughout life.

Consumer Sovereignty A concept in marketing in which the consumer is seen as the final arbiter in the marketplace, having the power to decide which products will be successful and which will fail.

Consumer Stimulants Various promotions and incentives employed to attract the consumer and to stimulate demand. Consumer stimulants may take the form of free samples delivered to the home, cents-off deals and premiums offered at retail, contests and sweepstakes and other promotional activities.

Consumer Surplus The difference, as perceived by a consumer, between the value of a purchase and the price he pays for it. A consumer surplus exists if the consumer feels he is getting more than his money's worth and if he would even be willing to pay a somewhat higher price for the same goods.

Consumerism A social movement stemming from the efforts of consumers to promote and protect their own interests in the marketplace. Sometimes organised, sometimes not, these efforts centre upon concern for the consumer's rights to safety, information, fair pricing, truthful advertising and quality control.

Consumers' Goods Goods that directly satisfy human wants in consumption and that assist in further production only indirectly or incidentally, if at all.

Consumers' Surplus The difference between the maximum price that consumers are willing to pay and the lower amount they actually pay.

Consumption The direct and final use of goods or services in satisfying the wants of free human beings.

Consumption Function A schedule of the amounts of their disposable income that individuals tend to devote to consumption at various levels of income.

Consumption Patterns The patterns in which consumers use or do not use, a product. Consumption patterns are commonly employed as a basis for market segmentation.

Container-on-Flat Car (COFC) A shipment of goods in a container on a rail flatcar. Shipments moving as COFC receive special rates.

Container Premium Packaging for goods which is reusable for another purpose, thus serving as an added inducement for the consumer to purchase the goods. For example, coffee sold in reusable cannisters or wine sold in bottles which can later be used as carafes.

Containerisation The consolidation of a number of smaller packages or boxes into a large standardised container which can be sealed at its point of origin and shipped unopened to its destination. Constainersed freight is subject to less damage and pilferage than loose cargo and is cheaper to handle.

Containerising The practice in transportation of consolidating a number of packages into one container that is sealed at the point of origin and remains sealed until it reaches the point of destination.

Content Analysis The analysis of articles and news stories in various media used as a method of identifying positive and negative mentions about an organisation, product, service or issue. It is a method used to measure impact of publicity and other promotional and pubic relations efforts.

Content Label A tag or label affixed in confirmance with the requirements of the Federal wool, fur or textile fiber products acts intended to protect the consumer against the misbranding, mislabeling and false advertising of furs and other textile products.

Content Validity An approach to validating a measure by determining the adequacy with which the domain of the characteristic is captured by the measure; it is sometimes called face validity.

Contest A sales promotion device in which the participant competes for prizes by submitting an entry which requires a degree of skill or judgement to prepare, *e.g.,* a statement or jingle. Unlike games and sweepstakes, the element of pure chance is eliminated in contests. See also *game* and *sweepstake.*

Contingency Contract An agreement to deliver goods or services at a price to be determined either by the actual costs incurred while performing the service or producing the product or by the measured value realized after the service has been performed or the product has been used.

Contingency Planning Development of plans to provide an alternative to the main plan in the event of threats or opportunities that were thought to have a low probability or occurring at the time of the preparation of the main plan. The contingency plan deals not with unforeseen events, but with events that were foreseen but considered unlikely to occur.

Contingency Pricing A payment plan in which a service organisation does not receive payment for services performed until the customer's satisfaction can be assured.

Contingent Reward Leadership A leadership style wherein sales managers maintain close supervision with their salespeople. In essence, using this leadership style entails identifying and clarifying job tasks for the salespeople, defining the objectives, recommending how to execute job assignments and indicating how successful performance will lead to attainment of desired job rewards.

Continuity In advertising, the flow of advertising messages over a period of time. In some respects continuity is like a schedule or plan in that it provides some control over the spacing and frequency of ads.

Continuity Plan Any type of consumer sales promotion technique that encourages customers to purchase products on a continuing basis or over time. The plan often is based on some sort of saving or accumulation scheme such as trading stamps, points, coupons or the like.

Continuity Series In direct marketing, a multi-part product such as a *set of books*, which is shipped one part at a time to the customer.

Continuous Demand The need and/or desire for goods or services which remains stable for a prolonged time period. See also *demand.*

Continuous Innovation A continuing process by which new products are developed and introduced into the marketplace. Rather than representing some new departure, these new products commonly were already in production and have been slightly altered or improved.

Continuous Media Pattern A timing pattern used in a media plan whereby the advertising messages are scheduled continuously throughout the time period covered by the media plan.

Contraband Merchandise which is forbidden by law to be imported or exported, be which is sometimes smuggled into a country and unlawfully sold.

Contraceptive Social Marketing (CSM) The application of commercial marketing technology to the promotion of contraceptive products (condoms, birth control pills etc.) as part of public or private nonprofit family planning programmes.

Contract An agreement between two or more parties which is generally set forth in writing and is enforceable by law. The legality of any contract depends on the following factors: (1) a lawful promise; (2) competent parties; (3) an offer and its acceptance; (4) agreement. The contract must be in writing if it involves a certain amount of money (as determined by the state) or if it extends for more than one year.

Contract Carrier A transportation company which ships goods for one or more clients on the basis of a legal or business agreement. Unlike the common carrier, the contract carrier does not maintain regularly scheduled routes. See also *common carrier* and *private carrier*.

Contract Department A unit in a department store set up to sell in quantity to institutions such supplies as food, bedding, floor coverings; a department that arranges for the sale of goods in quantity to large buyers at special prices.

Contract Farming A contractual arrangement between farmers and middlemen or manufacturers in which the farmer receives supplies and/or working capital and the manufacturers or middlemen agree to purchase the farmer's crop, sometimes at a guaranteed price.

Contract Manufacturing (1) In international marketing, a form of joint venture in which a foreign company contracts with local manufacturers in the host country to produce a product. See also *joint venture.* (2) A business arrangement in which one manufacturer produces goods for another manufacturer, a practice common in the apparel industry.

Contract Typing This exists when a person agrees to sell one product, the "typing product," only on the condition that the vendee also purchase another product, the "tied product." It is also called a tie-in arrangement and is generally illegal under the Sherman Antitrust Act or Clayton Act.

Contract Warehouse A storage facility which combines public and private warehousing services. It is like a public warehouse in that it serves a variety of customers. It differs from a public warehouse, however, in that the arrangements are long term rather than on a month by month basis. The contracts may also include special warehouse services such as packaging or assembly. It provides the stability of a private warehouse, therefore, through long term leases and special services. Independently owned and operated. See also *public warehouse and private warehouse.*

Contractual Vertical Marketing System A system in which independent channel members at two or more levels have entered into formal agreements to coordinate their marketing efforts in an attempt to take advantage of the economics of scale. Contractual vertical marketing systems are generally of three types: (1) voluntary chains, (2) retail cooperatives, and (3) Franchise operations. See also *corporate vertical marketing*

Contractual VMS See *contractual vertical marketing system and administered vertical marketing system.*

Contracyclical Pricing A pricing strategy which runs counter to the usual economic cycle in that during periods of prosperity the firm increases production and reduces prices (because of the high level of demand) and during an economic downturn, reduces production and increases prices(because of reduced demand).

Contribution In marketing cost analysis and break-even analysis, contribution generally means the sum of money generated by sales after variable costs have been subtracted. The term may also be applied to the amount of money a unit in a firm contributes toward discharging the firm's overall fixed costs.

Contribution-Margin Approach to Cost Analysis In marketing cost analysis, an accounting system in which only direct expenses are charged to each marketing unit within firm. The term contribution refers to the amount of money contributed by the unit which is to be applied to the firm's total fixed expenses. Margin refers to that amount of money which is the unit's profit margin, *i.e.,* gross sales less variable costs. The system is particularly useful when a number of alternatives under consideration are used, while other costs are ignored. The system focuses on variable costs which can be allocated more readily than some fixed costs, especially those fixed costs which do not change over short periods of time and which can, therefore, be ommitted from the analysis. See also full-cost approach to cost analysis and marketing cost analysis.

Contribution Pricing A pricing strategy in which under special conditions (*e.g.,* the promise of a very large order), a firm sets the price of its product lower than that which would cover the full cost of production. Contribution pricing covers the variable costs associated with the production of the specific product and makes a contribution toward meeting the firm's overall fixed costs even though prices at this level may not contribute to the affirms' overall profits.

Control In marketing, that aspect of management concerned with monitoring the firm's performance in the marketplace with particular attention given to determining whether or not the basic objectives of the firm are being achieved.

Control Audit An examination and evaluation of the results of a marketing plan. A control audit is designed to help identify and correct any deviations form the plan and to monitor the plan's progress. See also *marketing plan, control, and marketing audit.*

Control Group A group of subjects in an experiment who are not exposed to any of the experimental treatments or alternatives whose effects are to be measured; the control group is used to assess what part of the total observed effect was due to things other than the experimental variable(s).

Controllable Cost The cost that varies in volume, efficiency, choice of alternatives and management determination. It is also any cost an organisational unit has authority to incur and/ or ability to change.

Controllable Factors In marketing, those factors over which the firm has significant control, *e.g.,* choice of product, choice of customer, how the product is to be distributed, selling price, overall marketing objectives, etc. Also referred to as controllable variables.

Controlled Brand A brand of merchandise owned by its manufacturer whose distribution is restricted to a limited number of distributors, generally selected because they are (1) not large enough to support a private brand of their own and (2) are not in direct competition with one another.

Controlled Circulation The distribution of a newspaper or magazine, usually free, to selected individuals who are members of an audience of special interest to advertisers.

Controlled Test Market A market in which an entire marketing test program is conducted by an outside service.

Convenience Goods Those items usually purchased by the customer is small quantities, at frequent intervals, and with a minimum of comparison shopping. They are usually staples (bread, milk, etc.) or goods needed in an emergency (first aid supplies, small hardware, etc.) or impulse items (candy, magazines, etc.) Because convenience of access is of primary importance to the customer, he is often willing to accept a number of brands as acceptable substitutes for one another.

Convenience Sample A method of non-probability sampling in which the researcher interviews those members of the population most readily available. For example, "man-in-the-street" interviews are a form of convenience sample. See also *non-probability sampling.*

Convenience Store A grocery store, generally small, which carries a limited line of high-demand daily necessities, is open for extended hours and charges prices higher than a supermarket. Appeals to the customer seeking to avoid the time and effort involved in shopping at a larger store or who is shopping at off hours. Convenience stores are generally placed at highly accessible locations.

Conventional Channel A channel of distribution which is loosely organized (as compared to a vertical marketing system) and in which the members are largely autonomous. Most consumer goods follow a conventional channel from manufacturer to wholesaler to retailer to ultimate consumer.

Convergent Validity The confirmation of the existence of a construct determined by the correlations exhibited by independent measures of the construct.

Converter In the textile and paper trades, a wholesaling firm engaged in manufacturing activities to a significant degree. Also, a firm or merchant who purchases grey cotton cloth (woven but not finished) and has it bleached, dyed, printed or mercerised before sale.

Conveyor A materials handling device widely used in shipping and receiving operations. Conveyors are classified as power or gravity with roller or belt movement.

Cooling-Off Laws Local laws which allow customers a period of time (usually three days) in which to reconsider a purchase and if they so choose, to cancel the commitment. These laws have been passed to protect consumers from deceptive or high-pressure practices employed by telephone and door-to-door salespeople.

Cooperative A term applied to a wide range of organisations, which may include apartment houses, credit unions, mutual insurance companies, electric power distributors and a number of marketing enterprises which are jointly owned by their members and which were established to take advantage of the economic power inherent in large size. In marketing, cooperatives include such organisations as consumer cooperatives (usually retail outlets owned by shareholding customers), marketing cooperatives (associations of the producers of certain commodities; *e.g.,* citrus fruit) or supply cooperatives (which sell goods to members at less than open-market prices). Members of cooperatives, who usually own shares in the organisation, may be individuals or companies. Co-operatives are distinguished from profit-making ventures in that they render economic services to their members or shareholders on a nonprofit basis. In addition, they tend to eliminate at least one merchant middleman in the distribution channel by making purchases a step closer to the producer/manufacturer level.

Cooperative Advertising A strategy in which advertising costs are shared by seller and reseller (commonly manufacturer and retailer). Ads are run at the local level by the retailer and part of the cost is reimbursed by the manufacturer upon receipt of verification that the ads were actually run. This arrangement, because it involves more than one level of the market, is called *vertical cooperative advertising.* When the cooperative effort is at one level of the market (as with two or more retailers sharing advertising costs) it is called *horizontal cooperative advertising.* Also known as *vertical advertising, dealer-cooperative advertising.* Also known as *vertical advertising, dealer-cooperative advertising,* and *manufacturer's cooperative advertising.*

Cooperative Buying Any and all consolidations of orders by a number of stores or store buyers in separate stores. It is also called affiliated buying.

Cooperative Chain A group of retailers who on their own initiative have banded together for the purpose of buying, merchandising or promoting. It is also called a *cooperative group.*

Cooperative Exporting The cooperation of domestic firms for the purpose of international exports. Firms that compete domestically may collaborate internationally.

Cooperative Group A contractual marketing system is which retailers combine to form a wholesale warehouse operation. Its services to retailer members are primarily large-scale buying and warehousing operations.

Cooperative International Marketing Organisation A cooperative group composed of several domestic manufacturers who have come together to market their goods abroad. The cooperative organisation is partly under the administrative control of its member firms. This type of international marketing middleman is used frequently by producers of primary products such as fruits, nuts, grains, etc. See also *indirect export*.

Cooperative Marketing The process by which independent producers, wholesalers, retailers, consumers or combi-nations of them act collectively in buying or selling or both.

Cooperative Wholesaler A wholesale business owned by retail merchants. Typically, the wholesale establishment buys in its own name. Examples exist in the food, drug and hardware lines.

Coordinated Advertising Campaign See advertising campaign and product line marketing.

Copy In advertising, copy refers to the words (either written or spoken) which express the message in an advertising piece or commercial.

Copy Platform A statement prepared by the advertiser (often in association with an advertising agency) setting for the advertising strategy, a summary of the rationale for the strategy and related background information.

Copy Research The testing of audience reactions to advertising messages while the advertising is being developed (called *pre-testing*) or after the advertising has been produced in final form (called *post-testing*).

Copy Strategy Statement A description of the objectives, content, support and tone of the advertising a firm desires for its product. The statement may be directed to either an inhouse advertising department or to an advertising agency. In the copy strategy statement, the advertiser also sets out the style, tone, words and format selected for the message. Since this is done prior to the preparation of the advertising campaign, it serves to give direction to the advertising specialists and inform them as to their client's preferences. See also *advertising message*.

Copy Thrust In advertising and promotion, copy thrust refers to the message to be communicated by the written copy and the accompanying illustrations. It flows directly from the objectives of the promotion, whether it is intended to inform the customer of a sale, or to persuade the customer that the product is worthwhile, etc. See also *advertising objectives*.

Copyfitting The process of calculating how much space a given amount of text will require on a printed page and re-writing the copy, if necessary, to fit into the available space.

Copyright A grant of property rights to a writer or artist which protects his work from unauthorised sale, reproduction, display, performance, etc. In the U.S., copyright protection is granted under the terms of the Federal Copyright Act. Works created on or after January 1, 1978 are protected for the lifetime of its creator plus 50 years.

Copywriter A person with good verbal abilities who is talented in creating advertising ideas and skilled at writing advertising copy.

Core Product The central benefit or purpose for which a consumer buys a product. The core product varies from purchaser to purchaser. The core product or core benefit may come either from the physical good or service performance or from the augmented dimensions of the product.

Corporate Buy Agreement A contractual buy-sell agreement in which the volume needs of multiple sites are aggregated. Usually, the buyer negotiates a favourable price and commits to a minimum annual purchase volume.

Corporate Culture The patterns and norms that govern the behaviour of a corporation and its employees; particularly, the shared values, beliefs and customs.

Corporate Image The perception of a company formed in the mind of the customer. Corporate image is the revealed personality of the organisation.

Corporate Licensing The use of a firm's name to enhance the saleability of a product. For example, the way in which Murjani International employs the Coca-Cola logo on its clothing.

Corporate Marketing System A marketing channel that achieves vertical co-ordination through the joint ownership and operation of two or more channel members on different levels of distribution.

Corporate Purpose The raison d'etre of a firm that describes the scope of the firm and its dominant emphasis and values. The purpose (or mission) of an organisation is a function of five elements: (1) the history of the organisation; (2) the current preferences of the management and/or owners; (3) environmental considerations; (4) the resources of the organisation; and (5) the distinctive competences of the organisation.

Corporate Relations The use of communication and public relations techniques to build favourable attitudes toward a particular company with competitors, consumers, the financial community, stockholders and other publics.

Corporate Strategy The overall plan that integrates the strategies of all the businesses within the corporation. It usually describes the overall mission, the financial and human resource strategies and policies that affect all businesses within the corporation, the organisation structure, the management of the interdependencies among businesses, and major initiatives to change the scope of the firm such as acquisitions and divestments.

Corporate Vertical Marketing System A system in which a large corporation controls two or more levels of a marketing channel. For example, a manufacturer may own the distribution facilities for his product as well as the retail outlets through which it is sold. See also *administered vertical marketing system* and *contractual vertical marketing system*.

Corrective Advertising An advertising message designed to disclaim previous statements. Corrective advertising is sometimes ordered by the Federal Trade Commission (FTC) when an advertisement is deemed to be unfair and/or deceptive. For example, when it was found that Listerine mouthwash did not actually kill germs, the FTC ordered corrective advertising explaining that Listerine does not kill germs, but does fight bad breath. See also *affirmative disclosure*.

Correlation Analysis In market factor analysis, a procedure which makes it possible to translate the behaviour of variables in the marketing environment into estimates of future sales. Correlation analysis involves the sophisticated manipulation of market factor statistics in an effort to project potential sales for a product or service.

Cost (1) The amount spent on producing or manufacturing a commodity. Cost usually refers to money, but may be used in a broader context to include time and effort, etc. (2) The price a vendor charges a retailer for goods. (3) In retailing, any money expended to bring merchandise into a store, including the wholesale price of the merchandise, freight charges, etc. See also *price* and *value*.

Cost Allowance A reduction in invoice price made by a manufacturer or supplier to compensate the buyer for an incorrect shipment, goods damaged in transit, delay in delivery etc.

Cost Analysis A sales management evaluation and control method for monitoring sales force performance. A cost analysis involves monitoring the costs of various selling functions across individual salespeople, districts, products and customer types. When put together with the data from a sales analysis, this procedure allows a firm to judge the profitability of various products, customer types, and territories.

Cost and Freight A shipping term meaning that the seller of goods pays the cost of transporting the goods to their shipping point (dock, railroad platform, etc.), the loading charges and the cost of transporting the goods to their destination. Responsibility for the cost of insurance is transferred to the buyer at the time the goods are loaded abroad the vessel or vehicle.

Cost Benefit Analysis A technique used for sorting out alternatives in order to find that one which will produce the smallest cost-benefit ratio; *i.e.,* the alternative which will provide the greatest benefit (not necessarily expressed in terms of profit) for the lowest expense. Cost-benefit analysis is frequently used in planning government expenditures. Also called *crossover analysis, cost-utility analysis* and *cost-effectiveness analysis*.

Cost Centre A division, department, or subdivision thereof; a group of machines, people or both; a single machine, operator or another unit of activity into which a business is divided for cost assignment and allocation.

Cost Code The system of symbols used to indicate the cost of merchandise on price tickets while concealing that information from the customer. For example, lettrs from an easily remembered word or expression with ten nonrepeatignletters corresponding to numerals may be used.

Cost Department A manufacturing or processing department within a retail store that is operated on the cost method of accounting. Also, one of the independent departments selling merchandise or service (principally service) but carrying no inventories at retail value— *e.g.,* restaurant, barber shop, fur storage and beauty parlour.

Cost-Insurance Freight (C.I.F.) Under this contract the risk of loss or damage to goods is transferred to the buyer once the goods have passed the ship's rail. But the seller has to pay the expense of transportation for the goods upto the port of destination, including the expense of insurance.

Cost Intensive Industry See *capital intensive industry*

Cost Inventory The actual cost or market value, whichever is lower, of the inventory on hand at any time. The term seldom refers to the original price paid for the merchandise, but rather the present depreciated worth. If the original price is to be designated, the term generally used is billed cost of inventory.

Cost Method of Inventory Determination of the cost of inventory on hand by marking the actual cost on each price ticket in code and computing inventory value using these unit cost prices.

Cost Multiplier The complement of the markup percent. This figure indicates the average relationship of cost to retail value of goods handled in the accounting period. It is also referred to as the cost complement or cost percent.

Cost of Goods Purchased The net price paid to the vendor for merchandise, plus the price paid for transportation and delivery. In calculating the net cost of delivered purchases, cash discounts are subtracted from the above amount. In calculating the net cost of purchases, cash discounts are subtracted from the original invoice price, without consideration of transportation and delivery fees.

Cost of Goods Sold The price paid for any merchandise required to obtain the sales of the accounting period. It generally includes all charges (invoice costs) for goods on hand, goods on order, freight-in charges and workroom and alteration costs. The cost of goods sold may be calculated either before or after cash discounts have been deducted (or alteration and workroom costs added). The cost of goods sold may be determined by subtracting the closing inventory at cost from the operating inventory plus purchases at cost.

Opening inventory (at cost) +
new purchases for period (at cost) –
closing inventory (at cost) =
cost of goods sold

Cost of Industrial Sales Call The cost includes the salaries, commissions, bonuses, travel expenses, and entertainment expenses that a company encounters each time a salesperson makes a face-to-face presentation to one or more persons.

Cost of Living The money required to maintain a particular standard of living expressed in terms of the purchase of specified goods and services.

Cost-of-Living Allowance (COLA) An adjustment to wages and earnings, particularly during periods of rapid increases in prices, to keep them in line with the cost of living.

Cost-Oriented Audit An examination and evaluation of the results of a marketing plan from the point of view of costs and cost-effectiveness.

Cost Oriented Strategy An approach to improving performance by reducing the costs per unit. The cost advantage can be used to improve profit margins or increase market share by cutting prices.

Cost Per Thousand (CPM) In advertising, the expense involved in reaching one thousand potential customers with a specific advertisement or advertising campaign.

Cost-Plus A method of determining the selling price of goods or services whereby cost is increased by an agreed-upon increment.

Cost Plus Pricing A method for determining selling prize based on the cost of manufacturer (to the producer) or cost of acquisition (to the distributor or retailer) in which a standard markup is added to the cost figure. Current demand and the competitive situation in the marketplace are not factored into this cost-based pricing strategy.

Cost Tradeoff The planned increase in one marketing cost (such as transportation) to bring about a decrease in other costs (such as storage). For example, in the attempt to minimize the overall marketing costs, the marketer may find that a more expensive form of shipping (such as air freight) compensates for the fact that the goods will not have to be stored for extended periods of time.

Counter Advertising Advertising whose aim is to counter, or controvert, the affect of other advertising. For example, anti-smoking advertising.

Counter Marketing Efforts aimed at eliminating entirely the demand for a product, service or idea Counter marketing is generally carried out by parties who find the product in question undesirable or unwholesome. The efforts of the federal government and the American Cancer Society to discourage cigarette smoking are an example of counter-marketing. Also known as *unselling*.

Counter Purchase In international marketing, a form of counter trade in which the trading parties negotiate two contracts. Under the terms of the first contract the seller receives cash from the buyer. Under the terms of the second contract the seller agrees to buy goods from the original seller at a monetary value equal to that in the first contract; *i.e.,* the original seller, in return for cash payment agrees to become a buyer at some future time (generally within 6 to 12 months).

Counter Segmentation A strategy in which the number of market segments targeted by a company are reduced, generally through the elimination of products which have been serving narrow segments of the population.

Counter Trade International business in which some payments are made in the form of goods rather than currency. Countertrade includes four types of transaction: barter, compensation deals, counterpurchase and buyback.

Countervailing Duty A tariff levied on goods entering a country which have been granted an export subsidy or bounty by the government of the exporting country. The countervailing duty is meant to offset the advantage the exporter thus gains in the import market over domestic producers.

Countervailing Power 1. (economic definition) The power exercised by large organisations with diverse and conflicting interests in the marketplace. 2. (environments definition) The ability of individuals, companies, or groups to offset the power of large enterprises or large purchasers.

Country of Origin Effect The effect that the country of origin of the product has on the buyer's quality perceptions of the product.

Coupon A printed certificate employed by producers, distributors, or retailers as a sales promotion device. The coupon is redeemable by the customer for specified goods or services at a reduced price. Coupons are used to introduce new products, to promote multiple purchases, to encourage the purchase of larger sizes or the trial purchase of smaller sizes, to quickly increase the sales volume of a particular line, to introduce new product features, etc.

Coupon Fraud A planned misredemption of coupon offers designed to illegally obtain the value of a coupon without adhering to the published rules for redemption.

Coupon Redemption The use of a seller's value certificate at the time of purchase to obtain either a lower price or greater value than normal. Also, this term is used to describe the act of accepting a seller's certificate by a retailer or other intermediary.

Couponing A promotional strategy in which coupons are employed to achieve two objectives: (1) in the short term, to increase the sales volume of a particular product over a specific period of time, and (2) in the long run, to increase the market share of the promoted product.

Courtesy Days The days on which stores extend to credit customers the privilege of making purchases at sale prices in advance of public advertising of the sale.

Coverage The extent to which a medium reaches an audience. In the electronic media coverage includes the number of homes reached by the station's signal. In the print media coverage refers to the ratio of circulation to the total number of individuals, families or organisations in a geographic area. Sometimes called *penetration*.

Creative Boutique A limited-service advertising agency that focuses its work on the development of highly effective (creative) advertising messages for its clients.

Creative Selling A sales approach which involves a thorough knowledge of both the product and the ascertained needs of the customer. The product (or service) is demonstrated, explained and persuasively presented to the customer in such a way as to demonstrate how the product (or service) will satisfy the customer's needs. Considered a high level sales technique, the opposite of routine order-taking.

Credit In its marketing sense, credit is the capacity of an individual or organisation to buy and sell under a variety of arrangements other than cash-and-carry. An essential component in the concept of credit is faith or trust, *i.e.,* the notion that the persons who promises to pay in given period of time will, in a fact, do so.

Credit Bureau An agency that acts as a clearinghouse by collecting and maintaining credit information about individuals or firms and by providing it to members or subscribers.

Credit Limit The maximum quantity of credit that may be allowed to be outstanding on an individual customer account.

Credit Union A cooperative financial institution charactered by a state or by the federal government which serves the members of a homogeneous group (the employees of a firm, the members of a union, etc.). Credit unions resemble savings and loan institutions in the services they provide to their members.

Crisis Management An attempt by an organization to reduce, minimise or control the impact of a calamitous event through various communication techniques.

Critical Path Method (CPM) An analytical process which breaks large projects down into component parts and analyses the time needed to complete each part. The sequence of individual operations leading to the completion of the whole project is called the critical path. The critical Path method provides the manager with an estimate of the least possible amount of time required for completion of the total project, thus enabling him to estimate the time required for production.

Cross Branding A form of brand promotion calculated to enhance an existing product by drawing on the brand strength of one or more of its ingredients or constituents. For example, advertising for a food product may include reference to a well-known and respected ingredient in an effort to trade on the ingredient's brand equity

Cross Classification Matrix A device, usually in the form of a grid, employed to isolate specific subdivisions in a market for purposes of segmentation.

Cross Elasticity A concept which relates the change in price of one product to a change in demand for another product. Cross elasticity may be positive, the increase in price for Product A may generate increased demand for Product B (which may now be a cheaper alternative) or it may be negative—reducing demand for Product B (because demand for Product B is dependent on sales of Product A). Also known as *price cross elasticity*.

Cross Elasticity of Demand A measure of the extent to which a change in the price of one product affects the sale of another—*e.g.*, a small percentage change in the price of Product A may result in a large change in the sales of Product B.

Cross Impact Analysis A forecasting technique often used in futures research that logically studies the effects of the interaction of specified events with each other. The wide variety of impacts that can occur are analysed and assessed to determine the overall effect. It has been used to assess market and product opportunities.

Cross Over Analysis See *cost benefit analysis*

Cross Ruff A consumer sales promotion technique in which a noncompetitive product is used as the vehicle to distribute a coupon, sample or other sales promotion offer for another product.

Cross Sectional Study An investigation involving a sample of elements selected from the population of interest that are measured at a single point in time.

Cross Selling 1. (retailing definition) The process of selling between and among departments to facilitate larger transactions and to make it more convenient for the customer to do related item shopping. 2. (sales promotion definition) A consumer sales promotion technique in which the manufacturer attempts to sell the consumer products related to a product the consumer already uses or which the marketer has available.

Cross Tabulation A count of the number of cases that fall into each of several categories when the categories are based on two or more variables considered simultaneously.

Crude Birth Rate The number of live births per year per thousand population.

Cue In psychology and hence in consumer research, a cue is a minor stimulus which guides behaviour, often without the conscious awareness of the individual consumer. A cue helps determine when, where and how the consumer responds to products and services in his/her environment. The advertisements seen or heard by the consumer, the exposure of the consumer to the good or service and the attitudes of other people toward the good or service are all cues that influence the consumer's decision to buy.

Cultural Ecology The study of the process by which a society adapts to its environment by social transformations and evolutionary changes.

Cultural Environment The aggregate of patterns and norms that regulate a society's behaviour including the value, beliefs and customs that are shared and transmitted by the society.

Cultural Lag The differences in the rates of change in various parts of the same culture, such as the relatively slow rate of acceptance of products or ideas by some market segments compared to others. It is also used to indicate the failure of a society to keep up with technological and environmental changes in its economic, social, legal and political policies.

Culture From a marketing standpoint, culture most directly relates to the way people behave in the marketplace. Culture is as anthropologist A.L. Kroller has stated, "a set of patterns, of and for behaviour, prevalent among a group..." which includes the group's laws, customs, norms and institutions.

Cumulative Markon The total of mark on on the beginning inventory in any accounting period plus the aggregate purchase Markon during the period, including additional markups, before any markdowns. It is the difference between the total cost and the total original retail value of all goods handled to date, commonly expressed as a percentage of cumulative original retail.

Cumulative Markup The average percentage markup for the period. It is the total retail price minus cost divided by retail price.

Cumulative Quantity Discount A discount based on all purchases made during a specified period from a producer, manufacturer, or wholesaler. The objective is to encourage repeat orders on the part of buyers. Also called a deferred or patronage discount.

Curiosity Approach A technique used by a salesperson in the first few minutes of contact with a prospect. The salesperson presents the prospect with an unexpected question or gadget to arouse the prospect's immediate interest and curiosity. See also *approach*.

Currency Revaluation An increase in the value of one currency *vis-a-vis* other currencies. Revaluation takes place when currency values adjust in the foreign exchange markets in response to supply and demand pressures.

Current Ration The sum of a firm's current assets divided by the sum of its current liabilities. A measures of the firm's ability to meet its financial obligations.

$$\text{Current ration} = \frac{\text{Current assets}}{\text{Current liabilities}}$$

Current Population Survey (CPS) A monthly nationwide survey of a scientifically selected sample of about 71,000 housing units in 729 areas, covering about 1,200 countries and cities in every state and the District of Columbia. The U.S. Bureau of the Census issues a series of publications on the results under the title *Current Population Reports*.

Custom House Broker An individual or firm specializing in the expeditious clearance of imported goods through U.S. Customs. Custom house brokers are licensed by the Treasury Department and are employed by importers who do not have representation at the port of entry of their goods. Sometimes known as *customs brokers* and (because they may assume additional duties) foreign freight forwarders.

Customary Price A price which, because it has not changed in a long time, has become traditional or customary. Inflation has made customary prices virtually impossible to maintain, but in the past such items as postcards, soft drinks and candy bars had such stable prices that the consuming public came to expect them to remain constant. Sometimes referred to as a custom price.

Customer Any person who buys merchandise from a store or other marketer. The customer of a retail establishment is the ultimate consumer. The store itself, however, is the customer of all the vendors with whom it does business.

Customer Demand The amout and dollar value of merchandise purchased by customers in a specified period of time.

Customer Profile The demographic and psychographic characteristics of the people who comprise the target market and the purchasing patterns they display. Generally presented as a perentage figure which may be compared to the population as a whole.

Customer Service Standards In the distribution of goods, the quality of the service that a firm's customers can expect to receive. These standards include the receipt of the goods in undamaged condition, speedy and reliable delivery availability of items ordered and accuracy in order filling. In general, most companies try to meet or exceed the standards set by their competitors, since service is another way in which similar firms may compete.

Customer Services (1) Any and all activities performed by a retailer for its customers' convenience and not directly related to the sale of a specific product within the store. For example, gift wrap, credit and delivery. See also *accommodaton services* and *store services* as well as individual services. (2) Activities provided by a vendor for a client to factilitate the buying process and to establish a good relationship.

Customer Switching Cost The costs that tend to tie buyers to one supplier. These costs tend to be high when the product is durable or specialised, when the customer has invested a lot of time and energy in learning how to use the product or when the customer has made special-purpose investments that are useless elsewhere.

Customisation Tailoring the product to the special and unique needs of the customer. Each buyer is potentially a unique segment

Customised Sales Presentation A sales presentation developed from a detailed analysis or survey of the specific prospects needs.

Customs Union An association of countries which have agreed to reduce or eliminate the trade barriers existing between them and who have, in addition, agreed to levy a tariff on goods imported from countries outside the union.

Cutthroat Competition The temporary reduction of prices, often to unreasonable levels, such as below costs, for the purpose of eliminating competitors so as to be able to control a product's or service's price.

Cycle Billing A procedure by which customers receive monthly invoices on a rotating alphabetical basis throughout the month rather than all at the first of the month.

Cyclical Demand Demand for products and services which is responsive to changes in the country's economic cycles.

D

Daily Seller Report Lists merchandise which is selling in largest quantities on a day by day basis.

Data Information of a concrete nature such as statistics or measurements used as a basis for reasoning and decision making.

Data Bank An information system, generally a computer, in which a variety of factual data is organised and stored and made available for quick retrieval.

Data Reduction That step in marketing research in which collected data is summarised so that it may be analysed.

Database See *Data Bank*

Database Marketing A system in which marketing activities are based on data (often stored in a computer) gathered through marketing research projects and kept available for further use.

Date of Invoice (DOI) A form of dating denoting that the discount period begins with the date of the invoice. The cash discount period runs a speified number of days from the date of the invoice.

Dating On invoices, dating refers to the time period during which discounts may be taken by a reseller customer (typically a retailer) as well as to the date on which the total dollar amount on the invoice becomes due. See also *cash discount*.

Dating Period See *dating*

Day-After-Recall (DAR) A method of testing the performance of an ad or a commercial whereby members of the audience are surveyed one day after their exposure to an ad or commercial in an advertising vehicle to discover how many of the audience members remember encounter-ing that specific ad or commercial in the advertising vehicle.

Dead Area In a store, space where displays normally cannot be set up due to physical obstructions such as corners, stairs, etc., and which adversely affect the retailing function

Dead Stock Merchandise which has remained unsold for an extended period of time.

Deal Usually at retail a temporary special offering of merchandise, either in the form of a price reduction (cents-off deal etc.) or as multiple units at a special price.

Deal Merchandise A product that a seller may offer at a reduced price or that may have been specially bundled, processed or manufactured for a limited period of time.

Deal Prone A description of the behaviour of that group of consumers who make product purchase decisions on the basis of whether or not a particular product is being sold under some sort of deal condition.

Dealer An individual or firm which sells merchandise without altering it. The term is most frequently applied to retailers, *e.g.*, automobile dealer, but is sometimes used synonymously with wholesaler or distributor.

Dealer Brand See *private brand*

Dealer-Cooperative Advertising See *cooperative advertising*

Dealer Display In retail stores, promotional posters, placards, signs, etc. provided by manufacturers or distributors which are often displayed at point-of-sale. Actual merchandise is sometimes incorporated into the display.

Dealer Helps Nonpersonal services provided the retailer by the manufacturer or wholesaler such as readying merchandise for resale through packaging, labeling, price ticketing, etc.

Dealer-Listing Ads See *manufacturers' dealer-listing ads*

Dealer Loader (1) A gift from a manufacturer to a middleman to encourage him to order. (2) A retail point-of-purchase fixture provided by a manufacturer or supplier and generally placed near the register or checkout counter to display merchandise. Sometimes called a display loader.

Dealer-Service Salesperson See *manufacturer's salesperson*

Decennial Census The complete count of the population every ten years by the U.S. Bureau of the Census, as is provided by the U.S. Constitution. This enumeration and compilation of information about the characteristics of the U.S. population is a rich source of information for marketing.

Decentralised Adjustment System A system in which customers take their complaints directly to the selling department involved. Salespeople may make most of the adjustments, although the final approval of the department head or selling supervisor is often a requirement.

Decentralised Management The practice of delegating decision-making authority to lower levels of management and in some cases, to non-managers authorised to make decisions, such as salespeople. Comment: It is particularly important in marketing that decisions are made by managers or others close to the company's markets.

Decentralised Organisation In an organisational structure, a decentralised organisation is one in which authority and responsibility have been distributed to the greatest possible number of members, departments or employees at the lowest possible level of the organisational hierarchy. For example, in multinational marketing, a decentralised organisation implies that many of the marketing and other decision making processes reside in the individual local firms and subsidiaries in the host countries, rather than with the parent in the home country.

Decentralised Sales Organisation In this organisation, each division has its own sales force. This is appropriate when company divisions sell different products to different markets through different channels and when the divisions are large enough to afford their own sales forces.

Deception An unethical sales practice involving withholding information or telling "white lies."

Deceptive Advertising The adverising intended to mislead consumers by falsely making claims, by failure to make full disclosure or by both.

Deceptive Packaging The packaging of products offered for sale in a manner calculated to deceive the purchaser, *e.g.*, large boxes only partially filled with merchandise.

Deceptive Practice Business practices calculated to deceive the consumer. Most deceptive practices fall into one of two categories: (1) deceptive advertising and promotion and/or (2) fraudulent and confusing selling practices.

Deceptive Pricing Pricing tactics which are calculated to deceive or confuse the purchaser. Included are all misrepresentations of credit terms as well as the use of fraudulent reference prices and other deceptive markdown practices.

Deceptive Promotion A promotional practice calculated to deceive or mislead the consumer. The misrepresentation of price or performance is common in deceptive promotions.

Decision Calculus Models The quantitative models of a process that are calibrated by examining subjective judgement about outcomes of the process (*e.g.*, market share or sales of a firm) under a variety of hypothetical scenarios (*e.g.*, advertising spending level, promotion expenditures). Once the model linking process out-comes to marketing decisions variables has been calibrated, it is possible to derive an optimal marketing recommendation (Little 1970; Chakravarthi, Mitchell and Staelin 1981; Little and Lodish 1981). Examples for advertising decisions include ADBUDG, ADMOD, and MEDIAC. Examples for overall brand/product decisions are BRANDAID and STRATPORT. Examples for salesforce decisions include CALLPLAN and DETAILER.

Decision Making, Consumer 1. (consumer behaviour definition) The process of selecting from several choices, products, brands or ideas. The decision process may involve complex cognitive or mental activity, a simple learned response or an uninvolved and uninformed choice that may even appear to be stochastic or probabilistic, *i.e.*, occurring by chance. 2. (consumer behaviour definition) The process by which consumers collect information about choice alternatives and evaluates those alternatives in order to make choices among them.

Decision-Making Unit (DMU) In purchasing, that person or person responsible for deciding what is to be purchased for the firm.

Decision Process See *adoption process*

Decision Support System (DSS) A type of management support system based on interactive computerised information retrieval. Managers access a central computer's processing unit through a terminal or personal computer, input their data and have the data processed for immediate results. See also *marketing information system (MIS)*.

Decision Tree In marketing planning, a method of graphically depicting a series of alternative courses of action in the shape of a tree with each branch of the tree representing a possible decision along with its projected outcome. Decision trees aid managers in visually understanding an array of alternatives.

Decision Variables, Marketing These correspond to the major marketing functions that influence revenue and profit. They are summarised in the wellknown four P's: product, price, promotion and place (distribution). Other marketing decision variables may include service policies, credit and so forth.

Decline Stage The next to last stage in the life cycle of a product (it precedes abandonment) when sales are in decline and profits more difficult to achieve. See also *product life cycle (PLC)* and *retail life cycle*.

Decoder See *decoding*

Decoding The translation of a message from the form in which it was transmitted into a form in which it was transmitted into a form comprehensible to the recipient.

Defender A model representing customers' brand choice decisions as a function of brand attributes. Key features include the incorporation of heterogeneous customer preferences and the representation of attribute levels in a "per dollar" multiattribute space. Based on the model, several qualitative, normative implications hold regarding the optimal competitive response by "defending" brands against a new market entrant.

Defensive Pricing A strategy in which a company prices its products so as to protect (or defend) established products or market share, *e.g.*, a new product may introduced at a price higher than another of the firm's products so as not to cannibalise it.

Deferred Billing A billing method that enables customers to buy merchandise and not pay for it for several months, with no interest charge.

Delivered Price A price quotation at wholesale or retail level which includes the cost of delivery. This price strategy is also known as *freight allowed pricing.*

Delivered Pricing A form of geographical pricing in which the price quoted by the manufacturer includes both the list price and the transportation costs. In such cases, the prices are quoted as F.O.B. destination, meaning the manufacturer bears the responsibility of selecting and paying for the method of transporting the product.

Delivery Duty Paid Under this contract the seller undertakes to deliver the goods to the buyer at the place he or she names in the country of import with all costs, including duties, paid. The seller is responsible under this contract for getting the import license if one is required.

Delivery Period The normal time between the placing of an order and the receipt of stock.

Delivery Reliability The degree to which a seller delivers a product according to the schedule promised at the time of sale.

Demand The concept demand has two components. On the one hand, purchasers must have a need or desire for the product or service offered for sale and on the other hand, must be willing and able to pay the price asked by the seller. This condition (in which the buyer can actually fulfill his needs) is known as *effective demand.*

Demand Analysis In a broad context, demand analysis involves an examination of the factors which govern the sale and use of a product or service, *e.g.*, such factors as economic conditions, price, scarcity and buying habits. In a more narrow context, demand analysis is concerned with explaining changes in the demand curve and the relationship between price levels and demand in the market-place.

Demand-Backward Pricing A method of setting prices which starts with what is considered an acceptable final (retail) price and works backward to what a producer can actually charge. The producer determines how much may be spent on producing the item by starting with this acceptable final price and subtracting both the margins which channel members typically expect and the average or planned marketing expenses. Demand-backward pricing, to be effective, requires demand estimates, since the quantity demanded will affect production costs. The producer must also determine whether quality will play a significant role in demand or if improved quality may be sacrificed to reduce costs of production. Also known as demand-minus pricing.

Demand Creation The user of price reductions and/or other incentives, such as premiums rebates, etc., to create or increase immediate sales response for the product or service among consumers or resellers.

Demand Density A measure of the extent to which potential demand for the retailer's goods and services is concentrated in certain census tracts, ZIP codes or other geographic parts of the community.

Demand/Destination Areas The departments in stores in which demand for their products or services are created before customers get to their destination.

Demand Expansibility Demand for a product or service which can be increased through the use of advertising alone. No change in price or any other variable is necessary to affect the change.

Demand Factors The elements that determine the consumers' willingness and ability to pay for products.

Demand Industrial The demand includes the goods and services that are required by all individuals and organisations that are engaged in the production of other goods and services.

Demand-Oriented Pricing A strategy used in setting retail prices based on the level of demand for the product on the part of the customers. Merchandise for which there is strong demand will carry a higher price than merchandise for which there is relatively weak demand.

Demand-pulled Innovation Innovation that is caused or at least stimulated by the needs, wants or desires of customers. This contrasts with supply-pushed innovation. Other terms for these two ideas are market-or customer-driven innovation and technology-driven innovation.

Demarketing A marketing strategy calculated to reduce rather than increase demand for a product or service. Demarketing efforts are usually confined to periods of product shortage, *e.g.*, American oil companies discouraged gasoline consumption during the Arab oil boycott. Sometimes called *creative Remarketing.*

Demographic Environment The human population characteristics that surround a firm or nation and that greatly affect markets. The demographic environment includes such factors as age distributions births, deaths, immigration, marital status, sex, education, religious affiliations, and geographic dispersion—chracteritics that are often used for segmentation purposes.

Demographic Segmentation A method of market segmentation based on geographic location (such as world or national region, population dencity, city size, etc.) or shared socio-economic characteristics (such as age, sex, religion, education, income etc.). See also *geographic segmentation, socio-economic segmentation, and market segmentation.*

Demographics The vital statistics of a population including the size of the group and the age, sex, birth and death rates, location, income, occupation, race, education, etc. of its members. See also *market segmentation.*

Demography The study of populations of human beings, including vital and social statistics.

Demonstration (1) In the sales process, a demonstration is the involvement of the potential customer in the presentation by the salesperson. The salesperson allows the customer to use, test or experiment with the product. See also *dramatic approach*. (2) In retail selling, a demonstration is a form of in-store sales promotion in which one or more individuals explain to customers how a product is used and show how the product may be useful in the customer's own life. At times the demonstrator may be employed by a manufacturer rather than the store.

Demonstration Advertising A form of advertising in which the attributes of a product are actually demonstrated and which frequently emphasises the competitive strengths of the product.

Demonstrations, as Retailer Sales Promotion An exhibition of a product in use or in its ultimate form as an inducement to prospective purchasers. Examples are preparation and dispensing of food products in supermarkets, sampling of beverages in liquor stores or demonstration of cooking equipment in department stories—all intended to call additional attention to the product or service.

Demurrage A carrier charge incurred when freight cars are retained beyond the specified time allowed for loading or unloading. Railroads charge demurrage for delays in excess of 48 hours in returning a car to service.

Department Manager In retailing, the department manager is the individual responsible for running a particular selling area in a store. In some stores, the department manager may be involved in both the buying and selling of merchandise. In other more centralised organisations, however, the department manager is primarily involved in the presentation of merchandise, supervision of personnel and customer service.

Department Store A large-scale retailing institution which sells a wide variety of goods including hard lines and which with some exceptions, provides its customers with extensive services. The department store takes its name from the units (departments) in which related kinds of merchandise are grouped for purposes of promotion, service and control. Although the traditional department store with its downtown flagship and its emphasis on fashion and service (exemplified by such stores as Macy's, Marshall Field and the May Co.) is the most clearly recognised form of department store, there are other retail organisations which fall into this category. Included all departmentalised specialty stores with their narrower assortment of goods concentrated at the high end in terms of price and fashion (for example Lord and Taylor, Neiman-Marcus) and chain department stores, which include the great mass merchandisers with their common format (Sears, J.C. Penney) and which have taken on many of the aspects of the traditional department store even though the profit base is the entire store rather than the individual department. The discount department stores (K-Mart, Wal-Mart) characterised by low margins and self-service, sell merchandise in such great varieties that they also may be regarded as department stores. Store ownership groups round out the category (for example, Federated Department Stores, Allied Stores). These organisations, generally unknown to the public, pull together a number of department stores and their branches into a single centrally managed (but individually merchandised) retailing group. See also *chain store system, promotional department store, junior department store, specialty store, department store ownership group, discount store.*

Department Store Ownership Group A retailing organisation in which the member stores (usually once independent department stores) are centrally owned and controlled in terms of broad policy-making, but which are operated and merchandised autonomously. The individual stores and their branches operate under their original names and the general public is seldom aware of their affiliation with the group. Also known as a department store chain.

Departmentalised Specialty Store A term used to designate a concern organised in the same way ass a department store but handling a narrower range of merchandise.

Departmentalising The process of classifying merchandise into somewhat homogeneous groups known as departments.

Depreciation The reduction in value of property due to wear and tear or the passage of time. Depreciation may be clearly observable as in the rusting away of machinery or it may be less easily detectable as in the eroded value of fashion goods held too long in inventory.

Depression A phase of the business cycle characterised by a rapid decline in grass national product and employment.

Depth Interview A technique used in motivation research which uses an informal open discussion to uncover unconscious motives and to delve beneath the superficial answers of the participants. See also *motivation research*.

Deregulation The systematic discontinuance of laws and regulations which once controlled business activities but have subsequently been deemed undesirable. For example, the deregulation of the airline industry allowed airlines to compete on the basis of rates and charges, whereas they had previously been forced to compete on the basis of peripheral services to customers. Similarly, the Motor Carrier Act (1980) deregulated the trucking industry, so that private carriers were permitted to solicit back haul merchandise for the first time in nearly fifty years.

Derived Demand Market demand for a product which can be traced to the demand for another product. Most derived demand is, finally traceable to consumer demand.

Description Buying. In industrial buying, the practice of purchasing a product on the basis of a written or verbal description of the product without first inspecting it. Description buying is facilitated by guarantees of quality in the form of grading, branding and buying by specification. For example, accepted government standards of grading produce allow these goods to sold without further inspection or sampling by wholesalers or retailers.

Descriptive Billing A type of charge statement prepared for the customer in which a printout of the period's (usually a month) purchases appear on one statement with a description of the item purchased, the date and the price but the original sales check is not included in the statement; only the description is.

Descriptive Labelling The use of descriptive information (e.g., size, ingredients or use) on labels. This contrasts with grade labeling, in which code letters or numbers are used to describe the relative quality of goods.

Descriptive Research Market research calculated to yield information about a particular problem, *e.g.,* how consumers behave under specific marketplace conditions or how one can identify the users of a given product.

Designated Market Area (DMA) The geographic area surrounding a city in which the broadcasting stations based in that city account for a greater share of the listening or viewing households than do broadcasting stations based in other nearby cities. It also is the specific geographic area to which a country in the United States is exclusively assigned on the basis of the television viewing habits of the people residing in the country.

Destination Merchandise A type of merchandise that motivates or triggers a trip to a specific store.

Destination Store A store to which a consumer generally makes a special trip with the intent of shopping.

Detail Salesperson The missionary salesperson employed by a pharmaceutical company to call on physicians and attempt to get them to prescribe their firm's products.

Detailer A decision calculus model providing a decision support system for allocating a salesforce's selling effort across the items in a firm's product line. The model's parameters are calibrated using subjective responses to a series of questions concerning projected sales under various levels of detailing effort and over various time periods.

Detailing The personal sampling and other promotional work among doctors, dentists and other professional persons done for pharmaceutical concerns, in order to secure goodwill and possible distribution or prescription of the product.

Detention A carrier charge incurred when trailers of motor carriers are retained beyond the specified loading or unloading time. The permitted time is specified in the tariff and normally is limited to a few hours.

Determining Dimensions The needs and preferences of the customer which affect the purchase of a specific product type or specific brand in the marketplace. Such factors as a product's value as a status symbol, colour of the product, demographic characteristics of the customer, behavioural needs, attitudes, the degree of a customer's urgency for satisfaction of his/her needs and brand name are examples of determining dimensions. See also *qualifying dimensions.*

Devaluation A reduction in the value of a nation's currency, undertaken by the government of that nation, in relation to other currencies or to gold. A devaluation may be undertaken to bring a nation's currency more into line with other currencies in an effort to facilitate international trade by making exported goods more affordable to foreign consumers. See also *revaluation*.

Developing Country A country with semideveloped markets whose 1987 GNP per capita ranged from $1,001 to $2,500. The characteristics of this category of country are: (1) more than 33 percent of the population is engaged in agriculture and less than 30 percent of the population is urban; (2) at least 50 percent of the population is literate; and (3) there are often highly developed industrial sectors and consumer markets are also of significant size on a per capita basis.

Development Time The time it takes to develop a new product, usually expressed in months. Development time is a function of several factors, such as product complexity, newness, clarity of customer requirements, effectiveness of new product development process, prototyping quality, highly effective development leadership, priority and prior experience.

DEX/UCS The standard for electronic exchange that utilises a uniform communications system to allow suppliers who ship direct store delivery to communicate invoice data to retailers at their receiving facilities.

Dialectic Process An evolutionary theory based on the premise that retail institutions evolve. The theory suggests that new retail formats emerge by adopting characteristics from other forms of retailers in much the same way that a child is the product of the pooled genes of two very different parents.

Dialog System The part of a decision support system that permits users to explore the database by employing the system models to produce reports that satisfy their particular information needs. It is also called a language system.

Dichotomous Question A fixed-alternative question in which respondents are asked to indicate which of two alternative responses most closely corresponds to their position on a subject.

Differential Advantage The advantage one firm holds over its competitors because o f its wide range of experience, greater resources, higher level of competence, superior reputation, familiarity to the consuming public, etc.

Differential Pricing A form of demand-oriented pricing commonly applied to markets which can be divided into segments—some in which demand for the product or service is elastic and some in which demand is inelastic. Marketers attempt to sell at a high price in market segments having inelastic demand and at a lower price in segments having elastic demand.

Differentiated Oligopoly An oligopoly that produces and markets products that consumers consider close, but less than perfect, substitutes—e.g., automobiles.

Differentiated Marketing A marketing strategy in which a manufacturer produces a number of related products, each with a narrow segment of the total market as its target. The manufacturer attempts to build sales by addressing various segments of the market individually rather than by marketing a single product for all customers. See also *undifferentiated marketing* and *market segmentation*.

Differentiation In organisational structure, differentiation is the structuring of jobs in such a way as to allow for specialisation of functions and provide greater efficiency within the organisation. The larger the organisation, the greater the opportunity for differentiation. In large companies, the marketing task may be differen-tiated into such specialised units as commercial research, advertising and promotion, application development, sales and customer service.

Diffusion Model A model representing the contagion or spread of something through a population. Diffusion models in marketing often are applied to the adoption of a new product or the exposure of potential customers to some information about a product (*e.g.,* an advertising message). Numerous specific mathematical formulations have been applied to diffusion processes and these are reviewed by Lilien and Kotler (1983 Chapter 19) and Mahajan and Wind (1986). The most widely cited of these models was introduced to marketing by Bass (1969). The most widely cited of these models was introduced to marketing by Bass (1969). It incorporates explicitly an innovation effect and an invitation effect. When both effects are present, the time path of adoption follows an S-shaped curve.

Diffusion of Innovation The process by which the use of an i innovation is spread within a market group, over time and over various categories of adopters.

Diffusion Process The process by which a product is adopted in successive stages by members of a target market. Consumers are generally classified as innovators (thee first group of customers to buy a product), early adopters, members of the early and late majorities, laggards, and finally, non-adopters (those who do not buy the new product). This classification is implemented in an effort to describe the behaviour of consumers as a product is diffused through the marketplace. See also *adoption process*.

Diminishing Marginal Utility A situation in which the marginal utility, *i.e.,* the extra utility added by consumption of a last unit, tends to decrease.

Diminishing Return A situation in which after a point the extra output resulting from an increase in some input(s) relative to other fixed inputs tends to become less and less.

Diminishing Utility A situation in which consumption of successive new units of a good causes total utility to grow at an increasingly from an rate, *i.e.,* psychological factors cause a consumer to have a lesser appreciation to the later units.

Direct Advertising A mass or quantity promotion, not in an advertising medium but issued from the advertiser by mail or personal distribution to individual customers or prospects. Also, it is the advertising literature appearing in folders, leaflets, throw-aways, letters and delivered to prospective customers by mail, salespeople, dealers or tucked into mailboxes.

Direct Channel A channel whereby goods and services are sold directly from producer to final user without involvement of other independent middlemen.

Direct Competitor A firm competing head-to-head with another firm, generally offering potential customers similar or identical products or services.

Direct Cost Costs involved in doing business which can be directly ascribed to a particular product or to an organisational unit. Commonly, materials and supplies, wages and overhead are regarded as direct costs which vary with the volume of production. See also *overhead, fixed cost, variable cost* and *indirect cost.*

Direct Cost Method of Inventory A system under which the cost value of each item sold is recorded along with the selling price so an accurate costing of sales may be obtained.

Direct Denial A method for answering prospect objects by making strong statements indicating that the prospect has made an error.

Direct Derivation In market factor analysis, a procedure which makes it possible to translate the behaviour of variables in the marketing environment into estimates of future sales. Direct derivation involves the relatively non-technical examination of statistics in an effort to project the market potential for a product or service.

Direct Export A method of exporting goods in which the domestic firm handles its own exporting, independent of any international marketing middlemen. Direct export may be achieved through the use of a domestic-based export department or division within the firm, an overseas sales branch or subsidiary, travelling export sales representatives or through foreign-based distri-butors or agents.

Direct Exporting The type of exporting in which firms enter foreign markets directly and do their own export marketing. The firm itself undertakes the complete export marketing task, which is extensive. Direct exporting includes choosing appropriate foreign markets, selecting agents or distributors to represent the firm in those markets, motivating and controlling those distributors choosing the product line for the target markets, setting prices and determining promotional strategies for those markets, handling international shipping, finance and preparing export documentation.

Direct Fixed Costs Costs that are incurred by and solely for a particular product or segment but which do not vary with an activity level.

Direct Investment A company's investment in foreign-based manufacturing facilities, rather than entering into competition with local foreign manufacturers. This form of direct export provides the company with cost economies such as cheaper labour and/or raw materials, government investment incentives and freight savings. Direct investment also leads to a better image of the investing company in the host country, closer ties to the government of the host country, better relationships with suppliers, distributors and better control over its investment than may be possible with other forms of direct export. See also *direct export.*

Direct Mail The use of the postal service to arouse the interest of consumers in a product or service being offered for sale. In a sense, direct mail efforts may be regarded as a form of advertising (in contrast to mail order retailing, which is a method of doing business). Direct mail may be employed to prospect for new customers or to maintain contact with existing ones. Sales letters, postcards, circulars and catalogs are frequently used in direct mail activities.

Direct Mail Advertising The use of the mail delivered by the U.S. Postal Service or other delivery services as an advertising media vehicle.

Direct Marketing Marketing via direct mail, telephone retailing, mail order retailing, catalog retailing, mail order ads and inserts (preprints) in magazines, door-to-door retailing, and such electronic media as two-way cable television. Direct marketing efforts are calculated to elicit a direct response on the part of potential customers. See also *direct selling.*

Direct Marketing Association (DMA) An association of firms using and producing direct mail and direct response advertising. The association studies attitudes toward direct marketing, sponsors institutes and workshops and serves as an industry liaison with the government in Washington, D.C. DMA provides a "Mail Preference Service" for consumers wishing to increase or decrease the amount of advertising mail they receive and a "Mail Order Action Line" to help resolve consumer complaints about mail order purchases. DMA publishes *Direct Line* (monthly), *Direct Marketing Journal* (bimonthly), Special Reports (quarterly), an annual Membership Roster, and the *Direct Mail/Marketing Manual*. The association is based in New York City.

Direct Marketing Association Catalog Council (DMACC) A professional association of catalog houses, printers, list brokers and related firms and individuals. The DMACC serves important legislative and educational functions for its membership and represents the industry in Congress. DMACC headquarters are located in New York City.

Direct Marketing Educational Foundation (DMEF) An association of individuals, businesses and organisations working to promote college-level education in direct marketing. The association sponsors seminars and institutes for both students and faculty. It also sponsors summer student internship programmes, regional institutes for faculty and visiting executive progrrammes. DMEF publishes educational materials, course oulines and career pamphlets.

Direct Marketing Minorities Opportunities (DMMO) A New York based association dedicated to educating and training minority employees for careers in direct marketing. The association places minority candidates in direct marketing firms. It also offers referrals, support groups and continuing education programs. DMMO publishes a quarterly newsletter entitled Direct Marketing Minority Opportunities.

Direct Product Profitability (DPP) The managerial accounting practice of allocating costs to specific products. It is a method of evaluating distribution alternatives such as direct store delivery. It is also used to allocate shelf space in retail stores based on profitability. The profit on sale of a product after deducting the cost of the goods and only the expenses directly related to that particular product or product line.

Direct Request Method A method for obtaining commitment from a customer by simply asking for the purchase order.

Direct Response Advertising An approach to the advertising message that includes a method of response such as an address or telephone number whereby members of the audience can respond directly to the advertiser in order to purchase a product or service offered in the advertising message. Direct response advertising can be conveyed to members of a target market by a wide variety of advertising media, including television, radio, magazines, mail delivery, etc.

Direct Response Marketing See *direct marketing*

Direct Response Retailing See *mail order retailing*

Direct Sales Force A sales force consisting of salespeople employed by the company for whom they sell products or services.

Direct-Sales Results Test A test designed to measure the effectiveness of advertising or other promotional activities by calculating the increase in revenue achieved by each dollar of promotion expenditure.

Direct Sell A type of advertising message which focuses on a single unique product benefit and hammers it home to the target audience through constant repetition. This approach is often used in conjunction with product demonstrations such as the superior absorbency of certain paper towels, the extra-strength relief of a pain reliever, and the inability of coffee drinkers to distinguish between fresh-brewed coffee and certain instants. Not to be confused with direct selling. See also image sell, which is its opposite.

Direct Selling A relatively imprecise term having two principal meanings: (1) At the industrial level, direct selling is generally taken to mean selling from producer/manufacturer to final user without recourse to middlemen—neither wholesalers nor retailers. This arrangement is also known as a zero-level channel or a direct-to-user channel. (2) At the retail level direct selling commonly refers to such activities as telephone sales, door-to-door selling or in-home parties. See also *direct marketing*.

Direct Selling Establishment An establishment primarily engaged in the retail sale of merchandise by telephone or house-to-house canvass or in the workplace.

Direct Selling Organisation A non store retailing establishment that solicits orders and distributes its products direct to consumers.

Direct Store Delivery (DSD) 1. (physical distribution definition) A system whereby goods are delivered to the buyer's store instead of going through a warehouse or distribution center. This can result in less handling and faster deliveries, but does not necessarily result in lower costs. 2. (retailing definition) Delivery by a vendor directly to a retail store of a customer, as opposed to delivery to a distribution center operated by the customer.

Direct-to-User Channel See *direct selling*

Direct Variable Costs Costs that vary directly with an activity level.

Directional and Departmental Signage A signage system that helps guide the shopper through the shopping trip and locate specific departments of interest.

Dirichlet Multinomial Model A probability mixture model commonly used to represent patterns of brand choice behaviour. Over repeated occasions on which purchases are made from the product category, the set of brands chosen are assumed to follow the multinomial distribution for any given individual. The model also assumes that individuals differ from each other in their set of brand choice probabilities. These probabilities are taken to have a Dirichlet distribution across individuals. The Dirichlet is a parsimonious distribution for the set of brand choice probabilities: for *n* brands there are *n* Dirichlet distribution parameters; *n-1* of which indicate the average share of choices for each brand and the *n*th indicating the amount of heterogeneity in preference across individuals. The model thus can be used to predict brand choice patterns exhibited over time by a set of individuals.

Disaggregated Market A market in which the customers are all so distinct from one another that no aggregates may be formed. Such markets are said to be completely segmented.

Disconfirmation In consumer satisfaction theory, disconfirmation refers to a situation in which a product performs differently than expected prior to purchase. Positive disconfirmation occurs when the product performs better than expected; negative disconfirmation occurs when the product performs worse than expected.

Discontinuous Innovation The development of products which are so new and innovative that they have no clearly discernible antecedents. An entirely new market must be developed for these products.

Discount A reduction from list or marked price similar to an allowance granted by a seller to a buyer. Discounts are most commonly granted to induce the buyer to pay for his purchases quickly (cash discount), to buy substantial amounts of merchandise (quantity discount), to perform certain middleman functions in the distribution channel (trade discount) or to place orders during the time of year when business is slow (seasonal discount). See also *trade discount*.

Discount Department Store See *promotional department store*

Discount House A retailing business unit, featuring consumer durable items, competing on a basis of price appeal and operating on a relatively low markup and with a minimum of customer service.

Discount Retailer See *discount store*

Discount Store A retail establishment which operates on very low margins in order to offer merchandise at prices well below the recognized market level. The discount store emphasises self-services. Typically volume oriented, it is distinguished primarily by its emphasis on price and value. The magazine Discount Merchandiser restricts the term discount store to retail outlets of at least 10,000 square feet doing an annual volume of $1 million. See also *promotional department store*.

Discrepancy of Assortment The difference between the lines made by the producer and the assortment wanted by the consumer. Whole-salers and retailers compensate for this discrepancy by putting together an appropriate product mix for their customers. *See* also *assorting*.

Discrepancy of Quantity The difference between the number of goods it is economical for a producer to make and the quantity normally wanted by the consumer. Whole-salers and retailers in the channel of distribution compensate for this discrepancy by regrouping the goods into increasingly smaller quantities through allocation. See also *allocation*.

Discrete-Lot-Sizing An inventory management technique to help determine order quantities. The procurement objective is to obtain a quantity of components that equals the net requirement needed at a specific time. Purchase quantities will vary from order to order because of fluctuations in component requirements.

Discretionary Buying Power The money in the hands of consumers after the payment of taxes and the purchase of necessities; popularly called hot money or loose money.

Discretionary Expenditures See *discretionary income*

Discretionary Income That portion of a person's earnings which remains after taxes have been paid, contracted payments made and the necessities of life purchased. The individual has a certain amount of discretion as to how the balance shall be spent. Such expenditures are called discretionary expenditures.

Discretionary Personal Income See *discretionary income*

Discriminant Analysis A statistical technique employed to model the relationship between a dichotomous or multichotomous criterion variable and a set of *p* continuous predictor variables.

Discriminant Consequences The consequences that differ across a set of alternatives that may be used as choice criteria.

Discriminant Validity A criterion imposed on a measure of a construct requiring that it not correlate too highly with measures from which it is supposed to differ.

Discriminative Stimulus A stimulus that by its mere presence or absence changes the probability of a behaviour. For example, a 50 percent off sign in a store window could be a discriminitive stimulus.

Discriminatory Pricing The sale of goods or services at different prices to different customers. Pricing is discriminatory when it is calculated to give one party an unfair advantage over another. Discriminatory pricing is illegal under the provisions of the Robinson-Patman Act when it reduces competition in interstate commerce.

Diseconomies of Scale Cost increases and other operating disadvantages arising out of large scale operations. For example, a business may grow so large (as in the case of General Motors) that size in itself attracts the notice of government regulators.

Disjunctive Rule As compared with the conjunctive rule or lexicographic rule, the disjunctive heuristic (or rule of thumb) assumes that the consumer develops acceptable standards for each dimension (which may be higher than the minimum cutoff levels for the conjunctive heuristic). According to Bettman, if a product, brand or alternative passes that standard for any attribute, it is accepted. The evaluation process yields groups of acceptable and unacceptable alternatives and hence the evaluation is derived rather than direct.

Dispersion The process of breaking down a supply of goods into smaller lots. It includes the sorting processes of allocation and sorting out.

Display The impersonal, visual presentation of goods or ideas. Display is frequently employed in the retail trade in store windows and interiors to facilitate customer examination and selection of merchandise. See also *visual merchandising*.

Display Advertising In newspaper advertising, display advertisements are those which feature illustrations and other visual devices as well as words.

Display Loader See *dealer loader*

Display Merchandising See *visual merchandising*

Display Stock The stock placed on various display fixtures that customers can directly examine.

Display Type The type on a printed page, brochure, poster or other advertising material that is larger than the type used for the body copy.

Disposable Income Earnings which remain after income and other taxes and mandatory payments have been deducted. Roughly equivalent to "take home pay."

Disposable Personal Income (DPI) 1. Personal income less federal, state and local taxes. 2. A consumer's total money income less taxes paid to all government agencies; popularly shortened to *disposable income*.

Disproportionate Stratified Sampling A stratified sample in which the individual strata or subsets are sampled in relation to both their size and their variability; strata exhibiting more variability are sampled more than proportionately to their relative size, while those that are very homogeneous are sampled less than proportionately.

Dissatisfaction This occurs when prepurchase expectations are negatively disconfirmed (the product performs worse than expected).

Dissatisfier See *motive*

Dissection Control The subdividing of existing departments into relatively narrow groupings, then the establishing of dollar stock control records for each grouping.

Dissociative Group A reference group from which an individual makes an effort to disassociate himself; *e.g.*, from a particular social class or ethnic group.

Dissonance See *cognitive dissonance*

Distinctive Competences The strengths of the firm. That is, the particular characteristics of the firm that make it uniquely adopted to carry out its task(s) and to fulfil its purpose(s) in the industry within which it participates. The converse to the firm's distinctive advantages are its weaknesses, which inhibit and limit the ability of the firm to fulfil its purpose.

Distinctiveness A uniqueness that one product or one firm has over others. The distinctiveness may exist in any attribute and may only be perceived, not real.

Distinctiveness Stage See *fashion cycle*

Distress Merchandise The goods that are (or soon will be) past the point where they can be sold at anything close to normal prices. This includes perishable, unfashionable, damaged and unseasonal merchandise that still may have some market value.

Distribution In a broad sense, those activities involved in physically transferring goods from the point at which they are produced to the point of their consumption Functions in the distribution process include transportation, warehousing, wholesaling, and retailing. Distribution may best be understood as that part of the marketing process which follows production; *i.e.,* those activities taking place after there is a physical product to distribute. At the manufacturing level, distribution sometimes includes selling and advertising functions as well as order processing, customer service, and delivery. At retail, distribution refers to the movement of merchandise within the organisation; *e.g.,* from distribution center to store, from stock room to department, etc. See also *physical distribution (PD).*

Distribution Centre See *break bulk centre*

Distribution Channel See *channel of distribution*

Distribution Cost Analysis An analysis of the costs incurred, both direct and indirect, in selling a company's products. Such a study is calculated to reveal which salespeople are most productive, which products are most profitable, and other data useful in managing the marketing effort.

Distribution Intensity A measure of the exposure a product is given at wholesale or retail. The more outlets, the more intense the distribution.

Distribution Intensity Response Function See *response function*

Distribution Models In modeling the key decisions of which channel of distribution to choose, management can use any of the general models for option generation and evaluation. Specialised models have been developed, however, for specific distribution decisions such as site selection and logistics. Most of the gravitational site selection models follow Huff (1964), who developed a model in which the attraction of a site is proportional to the size of the retail center and inversely proportional to the customers' distance from the site. This model has been extended to incorporate not only size of retail site, but also image. These models are extensions of the Multiplicative Competitive Interaction model. Logistics-related optimisation models have also been developed for warehouse locations and inventory management. Most of the models are based on mathematical programming or simulations.

Distribution of Income The apportionment of money and real income of an economy among individuals.

Distribution of Planning Planning efforts calculated to facilitate the storage and transfer of products as they move from producer to consumer.

Distribution Requirements Planning (DRP) A planning technique that seeks to time-phase movement of products from manufacturing through the distribution channel. The objective is to forward allocate as little inventory as practical while satisfying customer service goals.

Distribution Standards In customer service, standards of performance with respect to response time, delivery time, accuracy in order-filling, depth of inventory etc.

Distribution Strategy The decision to market goods through a particular channel to achieve the most economic or cost-effective result. See also *channel of distribution and distribution*

Distribution Structure The sum of all the distribution channels existing in an industry.

Distribution System Responsiveness In physical distribution, the responsiveness of the system is the degree to which it can react to a change in demand; i.e., a system is judged responsive if it can increase the flow of products quickly when demand increases.

Distribution Warehouse See *break-bulk center*

Distributive Traders The establishments that are engaged principally in marketing (wholesale trade, retail trade, and service industries).

Distributor A broad, generic term often used synonymously with wholesaler and more specifically, with general merchandise wholesaler. The term carries the additional meaning of "exclusive sales representative" in some segments of manufacturing. See also *wholesaler, manufacturer's agent, general merchandise wholesaler* and *industrial distributor*.

Distributor's Brand A brand that is owned and controlled by a reseller (distributor) such as a retailer or a wholesaler, as opposed to a brand owned by the manufacturer. The term applies only to the brand itself, not to the product or to its content. It is often called a *private brand* or *private label* and (with exceptions such as Sears' brands) is usually not advertised heavily.

Distributorship A type of franchise system wherein franchisees maintain warehouse stock to supply other franchisees. The distributor takes title to the goods and provides services to other customers.

Distributor Without A Yard See *drop shipper*

District Office See *manufacturer's branch office*

Diversification Diversification in marketing may take a number of forms. A firm may introduce new products into existing markets or it may introduce existing products into new markets. In a complete departure,it may introduce new products into new markets. Some diversification is accomplished through mergers and acquisitions. The object of diversification is almost always expansion with a concurrent increase in profits.

Diversion 1. (physical distribution definition) The changing of the destination of a shipment while it is enroute and prior to arrival at the originally planned destination. 2. (sales promotion definition) The situation in which agents or retailers in one part of the country buy a product under deal conditions and then resell the product to channel members in another part of the country where the manufacturer is not offering the deal.

Diversion in Transit A practice in rail transportation in which the final destination of goods is determined after they have left the shipping point. As long as the route involves no backtracking, the shipper receives the regular carload rate from the railroad. This practice allows producers of goods, especially perishables, to move them in the general direction of their markets before a final destination is known.

Diverters 1. An unauthorised, but legal, member of a marketing channel. 2. Firms that buy unwanted merchandise from retailers and manufacturers and resell the merchan-dise to other retailers.

Divestiture The selling off of some of their businesses by large companies, usually for economic reasons but occasionally upon the insistence of the government (as was the case with A.T. & T. in the early 1980s).

Divest Strategy The sale or liquidation of businesses or product lines in order to limit losses and/or because the resources freed up can be better use in other businesses.

Divisional Organisation A form of organisation that breaks the company into two or more business units (commonly called divisions). A division is a profit center and the division manager is responsible for attaining profit goals. A division may be responsible for a share of the company's existing product lines or for a separate business. The division manager reports to a top corporate executive. A division may be organised functionally or (as it expands) with the assistance of product managers, market managers or category managers.

DMA See *Direct Marketing Association (DMA)*

DMACC See *Direct Marketing Association Catalog Council (DMACC)*

DMEF See *Direct Marketing Educational Foundation (DMEF)*

DMMO See *Direct Marketing Minorities Opportunities (DMMO)*

DMU See *decision-making unit (DMU)*

Documentary Collections (Drafts) This is a method of payment using a bill of exchange. A bill of exchange is negotiable instrument that is easily transferable from one party to another.

DOG A business unit or product which has proved unprofitable and which is viewed as having little future potential.

Dollar Control The control of sales, stocks, markdowns, and markups in terms of dollars rather than in terms of pieces or items.

Domestic-Based Export Agent An independent international marketing middleman used in indirect export. The domestic-based export agent negotiates foreign purchases for the domestic manufacturer and receives compensation in the form of a commission. Trading companies are one form of domestic-based export agents. See also *indirect export.*

Domestic-Based Export Department In direct exporting, the part of a domestic firm whose activities are directed toward selling goods abroad. This is a self-contained unit of the producer and does not involve the use of an independent international marketing middleman. The department may eventually evolve into a division or a subsidiary of the producer. See also direct export.

Domestic-Based Export Division See *domestic-based export department*

Domestic Based Export Merchant An independent international marketing middleman used in indirect export. The domestic-based export merchant buys the manufacturer's product and sells it abroad. See also *indirect export.*

Domestic-Based Export Subsidiary See *domestic-based export department*

Domestic-Only Orientation A marketing strategy which excludes all foreign business, both import and export.

Domesticated Markets The markets that once were competitive that have been restructured as a result of voluntary, long-term binding agreements. A significant proportion of all transactions in these markets are planned and administered on the basis of negotiated rules of ex-change. The benefits are reduced uncertainty, reduced transactions costs and access to economies of scale.

Domestication A process in which foreign businesses are forced to give up control of their operations by the government of the host country. The final step in the domestication process is the outright ownership of the corporation's property by nationals.

Domestics A subdivision of the piece goods classification of department store merchandise, including muslins, sheets, pillowcases, tubing, cotton, outing flannel, etc.

Donor Market A target audience asked to give money, goods, body organs or blood to an organisation or individual without expecting a tangible benefit in return. Comment: Donor marketing can be carried out by for-profit organisations. For-profit organisations (although this is rare).

Door-to-Door Retailing Retailing in which the selling is done directly to the consumers in their own homes. Products sold door-to-door are often those which the customer has not been actively seeking out (such as encyclopedias, vacuum cleaners, etc.).

Door-to-Door Selling See *door-to-door retailing*

Double-Barreled Question A question that calls for two responses and thereby creates confusion for the respondent.

Double Search Marketplace activity characterised by consumers looking for products they need and producers looking for customers—each is searching for the other.

Double Stack A system for stacking two containers vertically on a single railcar. This system doubles the carrying capacity of each railcar and significantly reduces product damage.

Downsising An act of eliminating levels, units, groups or individuals in an organisation.

Downward-Flow Theory See *fashion adoption process*

DPI See *disposable income*

Dramatic Approach A technique used by a salesperson in the first few minutes of contact with a prospect. The salesperson presents an eye-opening demonstration of how the good or service works. Often the prospect may be involved in the demonstration. See also *approach.*

Draw The money paid to salespeople against future commissions, usually in a period when commissions are low, in order to ensure that they may take home a specified minimum level of pay each month.

Drawing Account See *commission withdraw*

Drayage See *cartage*

Drive In psychology, and hence in consumer research, a drive is a strong stimulus that necessitates action. For example, an individual may have a drive to succeed in a professional career. When such a drive is directed toward a particular object that will help realise (and thus reduce) the drive, it becomes a motive. Thus, the same individual may attend college in his/her chosen field in order to achieve success. The drive to succeed has now become the individual's motive to attend college. Marketers investigate the drives that motivate customers to determine how their products may be used to help the customer realise the drive and how best to present and promote their products to the customer. Thus, in the same example, an apparel manufacturer may gear a promotion to "dressing for success" as a way of marketing clothing geared to the success-driven consumer.

Drop Shipment (1) A shipment of goods arranged by a limited-service wholesaler called a *drop shipper.* (2) In retailing, the term refers to merchandise shipped by a manufacturer to the individual branch stores of a chain or department store organisation rather than to a warehouse or distribution centre.

Drop Shipment Wholesaler See *drop shipper*

Drop Shipper A limited service wholesaler who, although he takes title to the goods he sells, never actually has them in his possession. Drop shippers commonly sell bulk products like sand and gravel, coal or building materials. They receive orders from customers and then find a suitable manufacturer or supplier who ships the goods directly to the customer. The supplier bills the drop shipper who, in turn, bills the customer. Also known as a *desk jobber* or *drop shipment wholesaler*.

Drug Listing Act Federal legislation which provided the Food and Drug Administration (FDA) with access to information on drug manufacturers so as to protect consumers.

Drugstore A retail establishment which traditionally was a place where drugs and medicines were prepared and dispensed according to a physician's written prescription. As drugstores evolved, they added proprietary drugs, health and beauty aids, medical supplies, books and magazines, cigars and cigarettes, small appliances, etc. to the mix of products they stocked.

Dry Goods See *soft goods*

DSS See *decision support system (DSS)*

Dual Adaptation A strategy employed in international marketing in which the product offered for export is different from the domestic product and which is promoted differently in the foreign market.

Dual Career Path Sales The provision of a choice made available to junior sales people in an organization to receive more pay and recognition through promotions to managerial positions or through promotions within the sales rank with compensation being similar at similar levels along each path.

Dual Marketing The practice of selling the same or similar products to both individual consumers and to industrial or institutional customers. For example, automobile manufacturers sell cars to individuals through franchised dealers (retailers) while, at the same time, selling fleets of new cars to auto rental firms. See also *dual distribution*.

Dual Target Market In non-profit marketing, nonbusiness organisations are seen as functioning in a dual-target market; *i.e.,* on the one hand they have to address the sources of their funds (donors, government agencies, organised charities etc.) and on the other hand must provide for their clients and other recipients of their services.

Dummy A preliminary layout for an ad, brochure, poster or other printed advertising material showing the position and size of the headlines, subheads, body copy and artwork.

Dump Display Merchandise is simply thrown on a table or into a box, generally to project a bargain image.

Dumping Price discrimination in international trade, i.e., the sale of like goods at different prices in two or more national markets. For example, producer might sell his products in a foreign market at a predatory price level and make up the difference through profits on sales at a higher price at home.

Dun To persistentlydemand payment of a delinquent account.

Dunnage Loose material, often lumber, packed around cargo on trucks, rail cars, ships, to protect the merchandise from damage in transit.

Durable Goods Tangible capital or consumer goods having a relatively long useful life (sometimes arbitrarily put at three years.)

Dwelling Unit Typically, many goods are purchased in common. A single home, apartment, townhouse or other unit in which a single person, family or cohesive set of unrelated individuals reside.

E

Early Adopter A consumer who is generally among the first to purchase a new produt. Not quite an innovator, but anxious to keep up with the latest trends and fashions.

Early Markdown A markdown taken early in the season or while the demand for the merchandise is still relatively active.

Earned Income The income resulting from work or services performed as contrasted with income from such sources as investments or rent.

Econometric Analysis In causal research, econometric analysis is the attempt to project sales or other activities by constructing an econometric model and simulating a future outcome. The model uses two or more regression or similar analyses to simulate future events on the basis of past relationships.

Econometrics The study of economics which utilises mathematical and statistical models to verify existing theories and to develop new theories.

Economic Approach to Pricing An overall economic strategy in which price levels are viewed as being determined by the interaction between supply and demand in the marketplace.

Economic Concept of Rent The determination of the maximum allowable rent expenditure by a retailer. Achieved by subtracting all other projected operating expenses and a planned profit figure from projected sales.

Economic Determinism A philosophy, perspective or belief that economic forces ultimately are determinants of social and political change.

Economic Forecasting The use of changes in the national and international business climate to predict the effects of those changes on specific industries. For example, changes in the Gross National Product (GNP) are said to affect changes in U.S. automobile sales. When the GNP increases (indicating prosperity), auto sales are said to rise accordingly. Commonly used predictors or indicators are the GNP, the unemployment rate, the increase (or decrease) in average weekly hours worked, the increase (or decrease) in the employment cost per man hour, gross private domestic investment, corporate profits, housing starts, interest rates, disposable personal income, consumer price indexes and retail sales etc. These indicators are compiled and published in the United States both by the government and by outside organisations such as banks, brokerage houses and universities. Economic forecasting may be used to predict impending changes in the demand for both consumer and industrial goods. See also *forecasting.*

Economic Goods The goods that are so scarce relative to human wants that human effort is required to obtain them.

Economic Indicator The data collected over time that reflect economic activity and general business conditions.

Economic Infrastructure The internal facilities of a country available for conducting business activities, especially the communication, transfortation, distribution and financial systems.

Economic Life The period of time over which the benefits of an asset are expected to be received.

Economic Man A model of human behaviour assumed by economists in analysing market behaviour. The economic person is a rational person who attempts to maximise the utility received from his/her monetary outflows and sacrifices.

Economic Man Theory A view of consumer behaviour which postulates that price is the primary motivating factor for consumer purchase decisions.

Economic Needs Those customer needs which are concerned with making the best use of limited resources (from the customer's own point of view). These needs include convenience of product use, efficiency of product operation or use, dependability of the product, reliability of service, durability, improvement of earnings, improvement of productivity of property and economy of purchase or use. Economic needs govern how and why customers select certain product features over others.

Economic Order Quantity (EOQ) The optimum size of an order, calculated to minimise carrying and procurement costs, especially the cost of frequent re-ordering, while maintaining sufficient quantities to meet the average level of demand. An EOQ model is the technique used to balance the costs of holding inventory against the costs involved in placing orders.

Economic Organisation The way in which the means of production and distribution of goods are organised, such as capitalism or socialism.

Economic Shoppers The shoppers who try to maximise the ratio of total utility and dollars of expenditure.

Economic-Lot-Sizing An inventory management technique used to determine order quantity or order period which minimises the total cost of inventory maintenance and ordering. This requires continuous demand.

Economics The study of the production, distribution and consumption of the goods and services that costitute a society's wealth

Economic System The manner in which an economy is organised to utilise scarce resources to produce goods and services and to distribute them for consumption. The economic system of any given society will reflect that society's goals and the nature of its political institu-tions. Nevertheless, all economic systems must develop some method to decide what and how much is to be produced and distributed as well as by whom, when and to whom. Planned economic systems are those in which government planners decide what and how much is to be produced and distributed by whom, when, and to whom. Socialist and communist economic systems function in this manner. In market-directed economic systems, such as capitalism, the individual decisions of producers and consumers make the decisions for the consumers make the decisions for the economy as a whole. In a pure market-directed economy also known as a *free-market economy*, consumers determine a society's production by their choices in the marketplace without government intervention.

Economical Shopper A consumer who is particularly sensitive to price, quality, and merchandise assortment and who shops for the best value available.

Economies of Scale Cost reductions and other operating advantages accruing from efficient, large scale production. Such economies are generally reflected in lower unit prices.

Economy (1) a society's system of producing, distributing, and consuming goods and services.(2) The overall financial or business condition of such a system on the local, oregional, or national levels.

Economy Pack Several products, wrapped together and sold at a lower price than if each were sold separately, to provide a saving to the consumer. The economy pack most often comes directly from the producer, but middleman organisations sometimes repackage merchandise to create an economy pack.

Economy Size A large quantity of a product, such as detergent, sold in a single large package to provide the consumer with a lower per unit price.

Ecosystem The complex of interactions of all the organisms with their environments and with each other. Technically, it is a subunit of the biosphere or a unit of a landscape. The interactions of members of a distribution channel or the interaction of a company and its products with consumer environments are examples of marketing applications.

Effective Buying Income (EBI) A measurement developed by *Sales & Marketing Management* (magazine) which is the equivalent of disposable personal income, *i.e.,* it represents wages and salaries and other income (rents etc.) less federal, state and local taxes and other deductions such as contributions toward insurance coverage, pension systems etc. EBI is a bulk measurement of market potential and is viewed as most effective when employed in making generalisations about a market's capacity to buy.

Effective Demand People with money and the inclination to buy.

Effective Frequency An Advertiser's determination of the optimum number of exposure opportunities required to effectively convey the advertising message to the desired audience or target market.

Effort Scale In consumer behaviour studies, the effort scale in an attempt to graphically represent the amount of time and effort consumers are prepared to expend in shopping for a particular product.

Ego Defenses The tools the ego has available to defend the individual from psychological stresses such as the forces of the id (libido) and the superego. Ego defenses are psychological constructs such as identification, rationali-sation, reaction formation, repression, sublimation, etc.

80-20 Principle A rule of thumb in retailing which states that 80 per cent of sales are generated by 20 per cent of the merchandise.

Elaboration Likelihood Model (ELM) A model of attitude formation and change that proposes that the process by which attitudes change depends upon the message recipient's level of motivation. According to Petty and Cacioppo, the authors of the ELM, when motivation is high, the message recipient will pay attention a and respond to the quality of message arguments. When motivation is low, the message recipient will be more responsive to peripheral elements of the message (*e.g.*, music, spokesperson attractiveness, etc.).

Elastic Demand 1. A situation in which a cut in price-increases the quantity taken in the market enough that total revenue is increased. 2. A situation in which a given change in the price of an economic goods is associated with a more than proportionate change in the quantity that buyers would purchase. 3. A situation in which the percentage of quantity taken "stretches" more than the percentage drop in price.

Elastic Supply (1) A situation in which a percentage increase in price attracts a greater percentage of products offered to the market. (2) A situation in which the percentage of goods offered "stretches" more than the percentage increase in price.

Elasticity The adaptability of a market and its ability to respond to a change in price. Elasticity is calculated as the percent change in the quantity demanded divided by the percent change in price.

$$\text{Elasticity} = \frac{\%\text{ change in quantity demanded}}{\%\text{ change in price}}$$

Elasticity Coefficient (1) A measure of the responsiveness of the quantity of a product taken in the market to price changes. (2) (technical definition) E is the limit as the change in price tends to zero of a ratio composed of two ratios: the change in quantity/quantity, divided by change in price/price. E is always negative; if the absolute value of E is greater than one, demand is said to be elastic; if exactly equal to one, unitary price elasticity prevails; if less than one, demand is said to be inelastic.

Elasticity Method A system of basing a firm's advertising appropriation on supply and demand curves. The average cost of any additional expenditure is compared with the average return on increased profit, indicating the point beyond which advertising is uneconomic.

Elasticity of Demand A concept that relates quantities of goods sold to changes in price. Normally, demand for goods will vary inversely to price, other factors remaining constant. For example, if a 1% decrease in price produces an increased demand of *less* than 1%, demand is said to be inelastic. Conversely, if a 1% decrease in price produces increased demand of *more* than 1%, then demand is said to be elastic. If a 1% decrease in price produces exactly 1% in increased demand, a condition of unitary elasticity is said to exist.

Elasticity of Expectations The ratio that exists between the predicted future percent change in price and the most recent current change in price.

Elasticity of Supply An economic concept that relates the supply of goods to their market price; *i.e.,* as the price of goods advances, producers are inclined to respond by producing more, thus increasing the supply in the marketplace. If, however, supply does not respond to an increase in price it is regarded as inelastic.

Elasticon A conjoint analysis-based model for estimating self- and cross price elasticity. Subjects are asked to indicate their likelihood of buying each brand (when each brand is priced at some experimental level). A first order Markov model represents the price induced brand switching. The price demand model is fitted by generalised least-squares to the share of choice.

Electronic Banking Network See *electronic funds transfer*

Electronic Cash Register (ECR) See *point-of-sale (POS) perpetual inventory control system.*

Electronic Direct Marketing (EDM) An interactive system, such as two-way cable television, in which the concept of direct marketing is combined with the electronic media (television, radio and the telephone). EDM is calculated to elicit a direct response on the part of potential customers. See also *telemarketing and electronic retailing.*

Electronic Funds Transfer (EFT) In retailing, the use of automated electronic equipment, such as computer terminals, to move money directly from the customer's account to the retailer's account at the point-of-sale or service.

Electronic Retailing The use of electronically transmitted information to facilitate consumer shopping without the need to enter a store. Electronic retailing is a form of direct marketing in which telephone lines connected to home computers, television sets equipped with special decoders, and interactive cable television are employed to transmit information to the consumer. The potential buyer views a "menu" combining text and still graphics which includes all merchandise being offered for sale. If the consumer decides to purchase, a number is entered on a keyboard (or, in some systems, a telephone call is made to a central location and the item is ordered. Another form of electronic retailing employs transactional discs (either in the store or placed in remote locations) equipped with video-disc players or other electronic equipment on which the customer may view a merchandise "menu." Sales are commonly executed through the use of a keyboard or by an in-store clerk. Although some systems bypass the traditional retailer completely—the manufacturer sells directly to the consumer—electronic retailing is generally viewed as an adjunct to in-store shopping rather than a replacement for it.

Elimination-By-Aspects (EBA) Model A brand choice model that represents the ultimate selection decision as a series of eliminations. Each alternative available for choice is viewed as having some set of aspects (*e.g.*, product features). At each stage of the choice process an aspect is selected (with probability proportional to that aspect's importance for this consumer) and all alternatives still being considered that do not possess the selected aspect are eliminated. The process continues until only one alternative remains, and that remaining item is assumed to be the one chosen by the consumer (Tversky 1972). Although more difficult to calibrate and apply than Luce's Choice Axiom model for choices, it does avoid the independence from irrelevant alternatives property of the latter model, which is often seen as an appealing feature of the EBA model. It has led to the development of other hierarchical/sequential choice models, including the Hierarchical Elimination Model.

Embargo The most stringent form of trade restriction or quota under which specific products are barred from entering a country.

Embourgeoisement The theory, now out of vogue, that affluent workers in industry adopt middle-class standards, life styles, and purchasing patterns as the result of their higher earnings.

Emergency Goods Products purchased only when the need is very great.

Emergency Product A good (such as a portable generator) or a service (such as ambulance delivery) in which an essentially nondeliberative purchase decision is based on critical and timely need.

Emotional Buying Motive Any factor which contributes to a customer's impulse to buy certain merchandise which is rooted in the customer's self-image and personal feelings rather than in logical thought. See also *motive and rational buying motive*.

Empathy The ability to put oneself in another's place. In marketing, this allows the perceptive marketer to anticipate a customer's reaction to appeals and campaigns.

Empirical Credit System A method for determining the credit-worthiness of applicants. It is based on creditors' experience with borrowers and attributes points to traits describing the applicant (such as previous credit history, whether the applicant own or rents a dwelling, length of employment, salary, etc.).

Employee Benefit Any of the non-wage forms of employee compensation. May include paid sick leave, holidays and vacations, group medical and dental insurance, retirement programs, etc.

Employee Development A programme designed to upgrade employees through training. The programme may aim to improve the performance of employees at their present jobs or to qualify them for advancement within the organisation.

Employee Discount A certain discount from retail price offered by most general merchandise retailers to employees. It is a kind of retail reduction from the point of view or accounting. Usually stores grant a larger percentage on personal wearing apparel than on gifts purchased by the employee.

Employee Handbook A manual of facts and instructions provided to the employees of a business. May include the history and philosophy of the firm, regulations, policies, procedures, benefits, dress code, etc. Often used in the orientation of new employees.

Employee Indoctrination See *employee orientation*.

Employee Orientation A period in which all new employees are familiarised with the policies, history and operations of the business as well as the responsibilities of their particular jobs. The employees are also introduced to employee benefits and opportunities for advancement during the orientation period. An orientation booklet is provided by some firms.

The booklet may contain details about the firm's history, development, organisation, and policies as well as general information about the firm's operations and facilities. Employment policies and practices are often spelled out. Intended to give the new employees insight into the company, what is expected of them, and what they may expect in return.

Employer A person or company which hires others to work for wages, salary, or commission.

Emulation Stage See *fashion cycle*

Emulative Product A new product that imitates another product already on the market. It is somewhat different from previous products (not a pure "me-too" product), but the difference is not substantial or significant.

End of Month Dating (EOM) The cash discount and the net credit periods begin on the first day of the following month rather than on the invoice date. EOM terms are frequently stated in this manner: "2/10 net 20, EOM" Suppose an order is filled and shipped on June 16 under these terms. In such a case, the cash discount may be taken any time through July 10 and the net amount is due on July 30.

End of Month Terms In the dating of invoices, an agreement indicating that cash discounts and net credit periods begin at the end of the month the goods were shipped. Invoices dated on the 25th of the month or later are generally treated as if dated on the first day of the next month.

End-Use Application Segmentation In industrial marketing, the subdivision of a market on the basis of how the product is to be used by its purchaser.

End User A person organisation that consumes a good or service that may consist of the input of numerous firms. For example, an insurance company may be the end user for a keyboard for a personal computer, originally produced for and sold to the personal computer manufacturer.

End-Aisle Display An exhibit of a product set up at the end of the aisle in retail store to call attention to a a special offering or price.

Endless Chain Method A method of prospecting in which a salesperson asks customers to suggest other customers who might be interested in the salesperson's offerings.

Enduring Involvement The general, personal relevance of a product or activity.

Enhancement A condition in which a new product is introduced into the marketplace and which increases the sales rates of one or more other products in the company's line. The opposite of cannibalisation.

Entrapment Study A technique employed in marketing research in which the purpose of the study is not revealed to the respondent.

Entrepot A commercial center which receives and redistributes goods and which is free of import duty and/or maintains bonded warehouses. London, Amsterdam, and Rotterdam's Europort are examples of entrepots.

Entrepreneur A person who organises, launches and directs a business undertaking such as a new business, a new product, or a new production process.

Environment The complex set of physical and social stimuli in the external world of consumers.

Environmental Analysis The gathering and analysing of data about a company's or nation's external environment to identify trends and their impact upon an organisation or country. Included among the environmental forces considered are the political, cultural, social, demographic, economic, legal, international and ecological factors.

Environmental Impact Analysis The assessment of the impact of a strategy or decision on the environment, especially the ecological consequences of the strategy or decision.

Environmental Monitoring The activities aimed a keeping track of change in external factors that are likely to affect the markets and demand for a firm's products and services. Among the external factors usually considered are the economic, social, demographic, political, legal, cultural and technological forces.

Environmental Opportunity In a marketing context, a part of the business environment in which there is an unmet need for products or services which a company may exploit.

Environmentalism 1. (legislation definition) This refers to public concern over protecting, enhancing and improving the environment, which includes conserving natural resources, eliminating pollution and hazardous substances, historic preservation and preventing the extinction of plant and animal species. 2. (environments definition) That part of consumerism that concentrates on ecology issues such as air, water, and noise pollution and the depletion of natural resources. Marketing decisions and action, such as new product offerings, can impact directly on physical environments.

Equal Credit Opportunity Act (1975-1977) Federal legislation prohibiting the denial of credit to any applicant on the basis of age, sex, marital status, national origin, race, religion, receipt of payments from public assistance programmes and/or childbearing intentions. The Act went into effect in stages from 1975 to 1977. It further stipulates that creditors must provide each unsuccessful applicant with reasons for denial of credit, that married people may request separate accounts and that alimony and child care payments must be considered as income.

Equalised Workload Method A method of determining sales force size that is based on the premise that all sales personnel should have an equal amount of work. The method requires that management estimate the work required to serve the entire market. The total work calculation is typically treated as a function of the number of accounts, the frequency with which each account should be called on and the length of time that should be spent on each call. This estimate is then divided by the amount of work an individual salesperson should be able to handle to determine the total number of salespeople required.

Equilibrium Point In supply and demand, the point at which the quantity and the price of a good or service that sellers are willing to offer equals the quantity and price that buyers are willing to pay for that good or service. Graphically, the equilibrium point may be represented as the point at which the supply curve and the demand curve intersect. The price of a particular good or service so determined is known as the equilibrium price. See also *supply curve and demand curve.*

Equipment The durable goods used to support manufacturing, logistics, administrative and other business processes. The definition includes fixed equipments such as generators and drill presses, light factory equipment such as hand tools and lift trucks and office equipments such as typewriters and desks.

Equity Theory A method of explaining employee motivation which assumes that individuals must see a relationship between the amount of work they perform (input) and the rewards they obtain (outcome).

Equivalence A measure of reliability that is applied to both single instruments and measurement situations. When applied to instruments, the equivalence measure of reliability is the internal consistency or internal homogeneity of the set of items forming the scale; when applied to measurement situations, the equivalence measure of reliability focuses on whether different observers or different instruments used to measure the same individuals or objects at the same point in time yield consistent results.

Erratic Demand The need and/or desire for goods or services which is unstable and unpredictable over a protracted period.

Escalator Clause In pricing practice, a clause in an agreement which permits a producer or manufacturer to increase his prices based on a specified formula such as the cost-of-living index.

Established Trends A pattern of increased demand for specific merchandise by style, color, material content, price lines, etc. as indicated by customer preference reflected in sales or by consumer research.

Estimated Liability The projected costs to be incurred for uncertain, variable obligations such as repairs under warranty.

Ethical Shopper A customer who feels obligated to patronise small stores or local businesses to help them stay in business and is willing to sacrifice the potential price and assortment benefits available in larger stores or chains in order to do so.

Ethics This relates to moral action, conduct, motive and character. It also means professionally right or befitting, confirming to professional standards of conduct.

Ethnic Market A group of customers defined by race, country of origin, language, etc.

Ethnocentric Orientation A home country orientation or an unconscious bias or belief that the home country approach to business is superior.

Ethnocentricism The belief that one's own cultural values are or should be, the norm. Ethnocentricism is exemplified in the self-reference criteria in which one's values are taken as a reference point for all others.

Ethnography A detailed, descriptive study of a group and its behaviour, characteristics, culture, etc.

Eurocurrency A national currency deposited outside the country of denomination: for example, U.S. dollars deposited in a foreign bank.

Eurodollars U.S. dollar deposits held in banks outside the United States.

European Community An association of European countries, viz. Germany, France, Italy, Belgium, Luxembourg, the Netherlands, the United Kingdom, Ireland and Denmark, with uniform trade rules built upon the elimination of internal tariff barriers and the establishment of common external barriers. Its goal is to integrate and harmonise the economic, social and political life of members. On the economic front, the goal is the elimination of all barriers and restrictions on the movement of goods and services.

European Currency Unit (ECU) A weighted average currency unit created by weighting the current exchange rate of the twelve European Community member country currencies based on country GNP and trade. The ECU is a unit of value that fluctuates less than individual European Community currencies because it is a weighted average.

European Economic Community (EEC) The European common market resulting from the Treaty of Rome, 1957. Members include France, the United Kingdom, the Federal Republic of Germany, Italy, the Netherlands, Belgium, Luxembourg, Ireland, Denmark and Greece. Aims include the sharing of common agricultural practices, free movement of labour and capital between members and a unified transportation system. Most tariffs between members were dropped by 1970. Also known simply as the European Community (EC) or the Common Market.

Evaluative Criteria In consumer behaviour, those aspects of a product or service which a consumer considers during the process of weighting alternative courses of action.

Even-Line Pricing A method of ascribing whole number selling prices to merchandise to give the impression of high-end retailing. For example, a retailer using even-line pricing would charge $100 for an item rather than $99.95. See also *odd-line pricing*.

Event Creation The use of communication techniques such as news releases, press conferences, etc., to call attention to activities to promote a company, product or service. Also, it is the development of a special activity, showing, display or exhibit designed to demonstrate products or to connect the product to favourable products or activities.

Events Nonpersonal communications such as news conferences, grand openings, etc. designed to communicate particular messages to target audiences. See also *nonpersonal communication channels*.

Every Day Low Price (EDLP) 1. (retailing definition) A policy or strategy of retail pricing whereby presumably low prices are set initially on items and maintained, as opposed to the occasional offering of items at special or reduced sales prices. 2. (sales promotion definition) A pricing approach in which the product is offered to retailers and consumers at a consistently low cost rather than reducing price periodically through sales promotion activities.

Evoked Set In consumer behaviour, evoked set refers to the specific brands a buyer will consider when shopping a product category; *i.e.*, customers commonly do not consider every possible choice or alternative when making buying decisions. Evoked sets are relatively small compared to the total number of choices in the marketplace. See also *inert set* and *inept set*.

Ex Dock (Named Port of Importation) A term of sale indicating that the quoted price includes the cost of the goods and all costs necessary to bring the goods to the named port. Includes duty, if any.

Ex Works A shipping term indicating that the seller of goods is responsible only for making the goods sold available at this factory or works. The buyer is responsible for loading the goods on whichever vehicle he provides and for transportation to the final destination.

Exception Rate A freight rate charged by shippers to their customers. The exception rate is a deviation from the class rate allowed under special circumstances, though still subject to government regulation. It may be either higher or lower than the class rate and applies to both contract and common carriers. In general, lower exception rates may be charged to encourage competition or otherwise aid the shipping industry. Higher rates are allowed for special services, such as express or overnight delivery. See also *class rate* and *commodity rate*.

Exception Report In a marketing information system, a report to an executive of some circumstance or occurrence in the system which exceeds predetermined levels. For example, a manager may not be concerned with the level of sales as long as they do not increase or decrease by more than a preestablished percentage. If they exceed these limits he is automatically sent an exception report.

Exchange (1) In marketing, an exchange occurs when two or more parties trade products for products (swapping or barter) or products for money (buying or selling). (2) In retailing, the substitution of one item for another, usually returned merchandise. (3) A place where securities, commodities, etc. are traded.

Exchange Control A method used by some governments to regulate foreign trade. The government controls the amount of currency exchanged by requiring firms that earn foreign currency (exchange) through exporting to sell this currency to a central bank or control agency which serves as a clearing house. Similarly, importers must buy their foreign currency from the same central clearing house.

Exchange Functions The buying and selling activities in the marketing process which result in the exchange of title to goods or services. Exchange is regarded as one of the basic marketing functions.

Exchange Rate The price of one country's currency expressed in terms of another country's currency or gold. For example, a U.S. dollar is worth a certain number of British pounds sterling, Canadian dollars, French francs, Japanese yen, etc. The exchange rate is not a constant and fluctuates on a daily basis as currencies are traded in international money markets.

Exclusive Dealing A form of exclusive distribution in which the middleman or retailer, having an exclusive distributor-ship granted by a manufacturer or supplier, is prohibited from carrying competing lines.

Exclusive Distribution A form of distribution in which a product or service is offered for sale to only one distributor or retailer in a particular territory. The manufacturer or producer thus gives the exclusive right to resale to a single organisation. See also *confined merchandise*.

Exclusives Merchandise produced for one or a limited number of resellers.

Executive Any person whose function is to administer or manage the affairs of a business or other organisation. Executives are generally expected to provide leadership by directing, motivating and guiding the work of individual employees, departments and causing others to follow their lead.

Executive Panel Survey A Technique used to estimate demand for a product. The individuals surveyed are all involved in some aspect of the marketing process, such as executives with experience in marketing similar or related products.

Exempt Carrier A form of transportation (rail, highway, river, etc.) which has been granted an exemption from certain regulations by the localities in which it operates when certain specified products are being moved. For example, a barge line may be exempt from all local laws except for those governing safety when it is transporting a commodity like wheat.

Exhibit The gathering and displaying of products, people or information at a central location for viewing by a diverse audience.

Expandability of Demand The degree to which the demand schedule can be shifted through the use of marketing mix variables such as advertising and personal selling.

Ex-parte A regulatory practice of pretesting proposed regulatory rules in an effort to get reactions and comments from shippers, carriers and other interested parties.

Expectancy A salesperson's estimate of the likelihood that if he or she increases his or her effort on some job activity, a higher level of performance will occur. In essence, expectancy is the linkage between effort and salesperson performance. For example, a salesperson might estimate that there is a 50 per cent probability (expectancy) that if he or she spends 10 per cent more time calling on new accounts, his or her sales volume will rise by 15 per cent. Expectancies can influence a salesperson's level of motivation.

Expectancy-value Model This is one of the major schools of motivation emerging from the work of Kurt Lewin. According to Wilkie, the major proposition is that the strength of the tendency to act in a certain way depends on the strength of the expectancy that the act will be followed by a given consequence (or goal) and the value of that goal to the individual. It assumes that the consumer behaves purposively and evaluates, say, the purchase of a particular brand in terms of how desirable the consequences of the purchase of that brand are for him or her.

Expectation-Disconfirmation Model A model that proposes that satisfaction depends upon the consistency between expectations and performance. Dissatisfaction is proposed to result when product performance is below expectations, whereas satisfaction arises when performance equals or exceeds expected performance.

Expected Price The level at which the customer expects a product or service to be priced; *i.e.,* expected price represents what the customer thinks a product or service is worth.

Expected Profit Concept A strategy employed by firms engaged in competitive bidding. The profit which might be expected to accrue from each bid price is calculated in the knowledge that the probability of an acceptable bid decreases as projected profit increases.

Expected Value A concept used in selecting alternative courses of action. The expected value of an alternative is an average of all the conceivable consequences of that alternative with each consequence being assigned a probability percentage. When applied to the marketing of new products, the expected value concept facilitates the sorting out of the many probabilities existing in the market-place.

Expediter An expediter is one who works to speed up a shipment for delivery.

Expense Any cost incurred in the course of running one's own business, doing one's work, etc. Expenses are subtracted from the gross margin to get the net profit.

Expense Account An account maintained by salespeople that includes travel, entertainment and other expenses which they incur for business purposes and for which they are reimbursed by their employers.

Expense Centre A collection of controllable costs that are related to one particular area of work or kind of store service.

Expense Centre Accounting The grouping of expenses by their necessity in performing a particular kind of store service. For example, some expense centers are management, property and equipment, accounts payble, etc. Natural expenses are typically included as a part of the concept (*e.g.*, payroll).

Expense Item Any short-lived good or service which may be charged off as it is used, usually in the year of purchase. See also *capital goods*.

Experience Curve A graphic representation of a marketing reality; *i.e.*, that those firms having the highest share of the market will have an advantage over their smaller competitors because of their learning advantage, greater specialisation, economies of scale, etc.

Experience Curve Analysis The application of the experience curve effect, to understand (1) how the components of the total cost of a company's product are affected by cumulative experience, (2) the relationship of industry experience and average industry prices and costs, and (3) how competitive cost comparisons relate to current costs of direct competitors to their cumulative experience.

Experience Curve Effect A systematic decline in the cost per unit that is achieved as the cumulative volume (and therefore experience) increases. There are three sources of the experience curve effect: (1) *learning*—the increasing efficiency of labour that arises chiefly from practice; (2) *technological improvements*—including process innovations, resource mix changes and product standardisation; and (3) *economies of scale*—the increased efficiency due to size.

Experience Curve Pricing A strategy used in pricing manufactured goods in which the selling price is calculated on the basis of projected costs at the time of production rather than on costs prevailing during the planning stages.

Experience Survey A series of interviews with people knowledgeable about the general subject being investi-gated.

Experiment A technique for gathering primary data in which variables are manipulated in such a way that cause and effect relationships become apparent. Experi-ments provide a basis for small-scale trial runs before the firm totally commits itself to a course of action.

Experimental Demand Curve A price volume relationship estimated by simulating actual market conditions in an experiment or other form of pricing research.

Experimental Design A research investigation in which the investigator has direct control over at least one independent variable and manipulates at least one independent variable.

Experimental Gaming A method of research which utilises a simulated environment to observe behaviour.

Experimental Group A group of subjects in an experiment who are exposed to an experimental treatment or alternative whose effect is to be measured and compared.

Experimental Mortality An experimental condition in which test units are lost during the course of an experiment.

Expert Channel A personal communication channel consisting of independent experts making statements to target customers.

Expert Systems (1) (models definition) Interactive computer systems that, by applying a variety of knowledge elements (*e.g.,* facts, rules, models) within a specified domain, can solve a problem with an expertise comparable to that of an acknowledged human expert. As part of the developments in artificial intelligence, expert systems have been developed in various fields (medicine, defense, manufacturing, etc.) In recent years, a number of marketing expert systems have been developed, including ADCAD (an expert system for the design of advertising appeals and executions) (2) (marketing research definition) A computer-based artificial intelligence system that attempts to model how experts in the area process information to solve the problem at hand.

Explicit Costs Expenditures such as wages, utilities, supplies, etc., which are clearly stated and readily observable. They appear on the accounting record as costs and are charged against the operation of the business. See also implicit costs.

Exploration Stage In new product development, the initial stage during which ideas for new products are either searched out or internally generated by a firm.

Exploratory Research A research design in which the major emphasis is on gaining ideas and insights; it is particularly helpful in breaking broad, vague problem statements into smaller, more precise subproblem statements.

Exponential Smoothing In time-series analysis, exponential smoothing is the practice of making predictions on a weighted average of experiences. Experiences are weighted with regard to their occurrence in time, with the most recent experience given more weight than the others. For example, if a firm's cigarette sales for the four previous months had been 6,000, 5,000, 7,000 and 7,500 cartons, respectively, the forecast for the coming month would be above 7,500 cartons.

Export (1) To send or transport goods to another country or countries especially for the purpose of sales. (2) An export is any item sent to another country or countries.

Export Agent A manufacturers' agent who specialises in marketing goods abroad.

Export Broker An agent middleman involved in international trade, performing the functions of a broker for domestic firms exporting their goods to foreign markets. The export broker brings, buyers and sellers together and essentially provides information to each of them, connecting the needs of the buyers to the available goods of the supplier. See also *agent middleman, domestic-based export merchant* and *import broker*.

Export Commission House A commission merchant involved in international trade or selling domestic goods in a foreign market. The export commission house handles goods shipped to it by sellers, completes the sales and sends the money to each seller. The export commission house is reimbursed for its services by means of a commission paid by the seller. See also *commission merchant*.

Export-Management Company An independent international marketing middleman which manages a company's export activities in indirect exporting and is paid a set fee. See also *indirect export*.

Export Marketing The integrated marketing of goods and

services that are produced in a foreign country. Each element of the marketing mix (product, price, promotion and channels of distribution) is potentially variable.

Export Sales Representative In direct export, the export sales representative is a domestic based salesperson sent abroad at intervals to find foreign customers for the producer. See also *direct export.*

Export Selling Selling to a foreign country with the focus on the product and the emphasis on selling. The key elements of marketing mix (product, price, promotion, and channels of distribution) are all the same as in the home market. Only the place or distribution is adjusted in export selling.

Export Trading Company A firm that buys another firm's merchandise and assumes all responsibility for the marketing and distribution of the product abroad.

Exporting The sale of goods or services to customers in foreign countries.

Exposure The degree to which an advertising message is actually perceived by members o f the target audience. For an ad to be exposed it must be more than simply seen—it must be noticed to an extent that there is some measurable impact.

Expropriation The seizure of foreign owned property by a government with some provision for the reimbursement of the owners.

Extended Product Those tangible and intangible elements which accompany a product or service. Included all warranties, service contracts, supplies and such intangibles as the status and prestige associated with ownership of the product.

Extended Terms Additional time allowed the buyer of goods to pay an invoice.

Extensible Market A market which has room for expansion, either through an increase in per capita consumption or by attracting more first time customers.

Extensive Market Opportunities Opportunities in the marketplace for new growth which generally involve a company in activities not previously part of its marketing effort. For example, a company may develop an entirely new product line to appeal to its existing customers.

Extensive Problem Solving In consumer behaviour, extensive problem solving is the effort taken to understand one's needs and how to satisfy them. This is particularly applicable when a need is completely new to the individual consumer. See also *limited problem solving.*

Expressed Warranty (1) (retailing definition) A guarantee supplied by either the retailer or the manufacturer that details the terms of the warranty in simple and easily understood language so customers know what is and what is not covered by the warranty. (2) (product development definition) the spoken or written promises made by the seller of a product about what will be done if the product proves to be defective in manufacture or performance. This contrasts with promises that are only implied by common knowledge of the product or by customary practices in a trade. Expressed warranties are usually restricted to stated periods of time.

External Data Data that originate outside the organisation for which the research is being done. (See also *internal data*)

External Stimulus A cue or stimulus or prod to action that is external to the individual such as a bright light or an advertisement. An internal stimulus would be one from within the individual such as hunger pangs, the feeling of fear, or glee.

External Validity One criterion by which an experiment is evaluated; the criterion refers to the extent, to what populations and settings, to which the observed experi-mental effect can be generalised.

Extinction An agreement between lender and borrower to spread payments on an outstanding debt over a longer period of time.

Extra Dating A form of deferred dating. The purchaser is allowed a specified number of days before the ordinary dating begins. To illustrate, in the sale of blankets the terms "2/10—60 days extra" may be offered by the vendor. This means that the buyer has 60 days plus 10 days, or 70 days, from the invoice date in which to pay the bill with the discount deducted.

Extraneous Items Items such as charges for gift wrap, etc. which appear on sales checks but which must be excluded when sales are beingaudited in order to arrive at a true net sales figure.

Eyeball Control The visual examination of stock levels at periodic intervals to determine replenishment needs. Assumes that a model stock concept exists in the mind of the observer. Relies on observaion rather than record keeping.

F

Face Value The face value can be either a specific monetary amount, a percentage discount or combination offer with another product. The printed financial value of a coupon.

Facint Text Matter The positonaing of an advertisement in a periodical so that it is opposite edititorial matter.

Facilitating Agent A business firm that assists in the performance of distribution tasks other than buying, selling and transferring title (*e.g.*, bank, transportation company, warehouse).

Factor A financial institution which buys at discount the accounts receivable of other businesses. The transaction provides the business with ready cash. The factor makes a profit by collecting the outstanding debts while at the same time bearing the risks of uncollectable accounts.

Factory Outlet Originally, a manufacturer-owned retail store located at the factory site through which unwanted inventory could be unloaded. These stores now sell in season, first-quality merchandise of more than one manufacturer and are often located in factory outlet mills which complete directly with traditional retailers.

Factory Outlet Centre A shopping center that specialises in manufacturers' outlets that dispose of excess merchandise or that may serve as an alternate channel of distribution.

Factory Pack The multiple packaging of one product or of one product and another product of the same firm or one product and a sample or premium The packaging is done at the factory and arrives in the trade channel already in the promotional form.

Factory-Positioned Warehouse A facility in which goods may be stored. The factory-positioned warehouse is located near the place of manufacture and may be used to store raw materials and fabricating parts to be used in production or to store finished goods waiting to be shipped.

Factual Approach A technique used by a salesperson in the first few moments of contact with a prospect. In this approach, the salesperson turns an interesting fact connected with the product or service being sold into an enticing opening sentence. See also *approach*.

Fad A style or product that is accepted quickly by large numbers of consumers but which enjoys short-lived popularity and passes into oblivion in a relatively short time.

Fair Credit Reporting Act (1970) Federal legislation which permits any credit applicant who is rejected for credit on the basis of adverse information supplied by a credit bureau to be notified of the reasons for such a rejection. The applicant may examine the credit file and have it corrected. Adverse credit information may not be used if it is more than 7 years old and information that is only 3 months old must be verified before it is used. The Act is designed to control the practices of credit bureaus in their determination and distribution of credit ratings, protect credit applicants from the effects of erroneous information that a credit bureau may have in its files and provide applicants with the opportunity to inspect their own files so as to counter any misinformation contained therein.

Fair Debt Collection Practices Act (1978) Federal legislation prohibiting the use of abusive, deceptive and unfair debt collection practices. The legislation is essentially a list of specific practices that creditors or collection agencies may not use.

Fair Packaging and Labelling Act (1966) Federal legislation enabling the Federal Trade Commission (FTC) and the Food and Drug Administration (FDA) to take action against the use of false or misleading matter on labels, the omission of ingredients, the omission of net quantity and size of serving information on food products and the use of misleading shapes and sizes in packaging. Also known as the *Truth-in-Packaging Act.*

Family A group of at least two people in a household based on marriage, cohabitation, blood relationships, or adoption.

Family Brand A trade name or symbol whichincludes all or several of the products of one seller (e.g. Del Monte, G.E., Campbell's). Goodwill built up for one product is expected to extend to the other products.

Family Decision Making The process, interactions, and roles of family members involved in making decisions as a group.

Family Life Cycle (FLC) Those stages through which a family passes from formation to dissolution including single persons, young married couples, couples with children, couples without children at home (the so called empty nest) and finally single persons again (*i.e.,* solitary survivors).

Family Packaging The use of one design or other key packaging element to integrate the packaging of two or more individual items. The packages clearly belong to one set, but there are usually some individualisations, especially in brand name.

Farm Products Raw materials produced by farmers, such as cotton, hogs, eggs and milk. These are unprocessed goods that are handled as little as needed to move them to the next step in the production process. They become part of a physical good when they are processed in the form of textiles, frozen or canned foods, etc. This is in contrast to produce, which refers to fresh fruits and vegetables sold at retail.

FAS (Free Along Side) A term used in shipping agreements meaning that the seller of goods pays the freight charges on a shipment upto the point where the goods are placed on the dock alongside the shop (or train or truck). At that point title to the goods passes to the buyer who pays all costs associated with delays in loading or damage to goods.

Fashion Those styles (clothing, automobiles, etc.) which are currently most popular are said to be in fashion, *i.e.,* they are widely accepted by consumers at one or more levels of the market. Since styles constantly change in response to consumer demand for the new, it may be said that fashion is, in fact, change—that fashion is not something so much as it is an on-going process.

Fashion Adoption Process The mechanism by which fashions are diffused throughout a population. There are three theories of fashion adoption: (1) the downward-flow (or trickle-down) theory in which adoption and diffusion are seen as flowing from higher socio-economic classes downward to the lower classes; (2) horizontal-flow (the mass-market theory) in which fashions are believed to move from group to group in the same social class; *e.g.,* opinion leaders within the large middle class have as much influence on fashion adoption as do leading members of the upper class; (3) the upward-flow theory in which generally younger people (and sometimes young people of relatively low socio-economic levels) are seen as influencing fashions as they quickly adopt new styles which will later be diffused up the class structure. See also *diffusion process* and *fashion cycle.*

Fashion Coordination The function of analysing fashion trends in order to ensure that the merchandise offered for sale in various related apparel departments is of comparable style, quality and appeal.

Fashion Cycle A theory, similar to the product life cycle, in which styles are seen to appear and rise in popularity, flourish, peak, and finally decline and disappear The cycle may be seen as having three stages: (1) the introductory or distinctiveness stage (in which some consumers seek and are willing to pay for products different from those accepted by the majority; *i.e.,* new and innovative fashions); (2) the acceptance or emulation stage (in which a particular style catches on due to the desire of other consumers to imitate the original users; and (3) the regression or economic emulation stage (in which many consumers desire the fashion and manufacturers mass produce the product at low cost. This continues until the market passes through the growth and maturity stages and rapidly moves into sales decline). See also *product life cycle (PLC)*.

Fashion Product A subcategory of a shopping product. This subcategory contains items that are wanted by consumers for their fashion aspects.

Fast Food Outlet A food retailing institution featuring a very limited menu, pre-prepared or quickly prepared food and take-out operations.

Fast Freight Service In physical distribution, fast freight service refers to the use of special, fast trains for the shipment of perishable goods, goods in urgent demand or high value items.

Feature The use of advertising, displays or other activity, generally by a retailer, to call special attention to a product, generally for a limited period of time.

Feature Story A type of publicity material that can be used by the media at their convenience because it is not time related. A feature is often human interest-related and contains more background information than typically found in a news release. It is also known as an *evergreen* because of its relatively long life span.

Federal Communications Commission (FCC) The federal agency responsible for administering the Communications Act of 1934 and subsequent related legislation regarding the licensing of television and radio broadcasters. The Commission also exercises control over the practices of the broadcasters, in an effort to ensure they operate for the public interest, convenience and necessity. This control has frequently extended to advertising practices.

Federal Food and Drug Act (1906) Federal legislation which prohibited the manufacture, sale or transportation of adulterated or fraudulently labeled foods and drugs in interstate commerce. The Act was replaced by the Food, Drug and Cosmetic Act (1938), amended by the Food Additives Amendment (1958) and the Kefauver-Harris Drug Amendments to the Food and Drug Act (1962). Also called the *Pure Food* and *Drug Act* (1906).

Federal Hazardous Substances Labelling Act (1960) Federal legislation requiring manufacturers to place warning labels on all items containing dangerous household chemicals.

Federal Regulatory Agencies Administrative agencies that create and enforce the bulk of the laws that make up the legal environment of business. More than one hundred federal agencies exercise some degree of control over private economic activities.

Federal Trade Commission (FTC) A regulatory agency of the federal government charged with policing anti-monopoly laws. In the 1970s, the FTC emerged as a protector of consumer rights by regulating children's advertising, cigarette package labeling, the funeral industry, etc. See also *Federal Trade Commission Act (1914).*

Federal Trade Commission Act (1914) Federal legislation which established the Federal Trade Commission (FTC) and empowered it to enforce the Sherman Antitrust Act (1890), the Clayton Act (1914) and subsequent related legislation. The Act made it illegal for anyone to commit an unfair or deceptive act of commerce or to engage in deceptive business practices. Amended by the Wheeler-Lea Act (1938).

Feedback (1) In communications, the response to a decoded message transmitted back from the receiver to the sender. (2) More generally, responses fed back from consumers in the marketplace.

Fee Method of Compensation Thee compensation method whereby advertising agencies are paid by their clients on the basis of negotiated fees for the specific services rendered.

Fell-Felt-Found Method A method used by salespeople to helpfully respond to prospect objections by showing how other prospects held similar views before buying the product or service.

Fertility Rate The birth rate expressed as the number of children per woman.

Field Edit A preliminary edit, typically conducted by a field supervisor, that is designed to detect the most glaring omissions and in accuranccies in a completed data collection ınstrument.

Field Experiment A research study in a realistic situation in which one o r more independent variables are manipulated by the experimenter under as carefully controlled conditions as the situation will permit.

Field Sales Manager Lower level sales manager generally at the district or regional level. The field sales force reports to the field sales manager.

Field Salesperson A salesperson who is responsible for contacting and selling goods and services to customers in their place of business or residence.

Field Warehouser A specialised public warehouse organisation which provides cash for goods on hand. The field warehouser holds some of a manufacturer's finished goods as its own property. In exchange, it issues warehouse receipts to the manufacturer. The warehouse receipts may be used as collateral to borrow money. This is a particularly valuable service to manufacturers whose goods, are not yet sold. The manufacture's own warehouse. is used to avoid the expense of transporting the goods and the seller retains title. Control of the goods, however, passes to the field warehouser. Also known as a *custodial warehouser.*

Field Warehousing (1) (economic definition) A financing device whereby a field warehouse receipt is pledged as security for a loan. (2) (retailing definition) An arrangement by which the owner of goods leases a portion of the storage facility to a licensed warehouser who places a representative in charge, posts signs stating that a designated portion of the warehouse is in the charge of the outside organisation, and adds to or takes from stock as directed by the financial institution that has the stock as collateral.

Fighting Brand An individual brand used to meet the competition while the company's other, higher quality, better known, and more expensive brand is protected. See also *individual brand.*

Fill-Ins Goods purchased for resale to fill gaps in the inventory of regular merchandise which has been sold out.

Fill Rate An inventory's availability goal used when setting customer service objectives, *e.g.*, 99 per cent product fill rate or filling 99 out of 100 customer orders.

Financial Analyst A person who investigates, evaluates and advises clients on the value and risk of investment offerings.

Financial Institutions Marketing Association (FIMA) An association of individuals involved in marketing, public relations, sales, advertising, and/or consumer research in the banking industry. The Chicago based association publishes *Financial Marketing* (monthly) and *Marketing Alert* (bimonthly), an annual *Membership Directory*, and specialised manuals and books.

Financial Objectives The profit and return on investment sought by a company in the current year as expressed in the marketing plan.

Financial Quota A quota that focuses on financial criteria such as gross margin or contribution to overhead. Financial quotas are used to make salespeople conscious of the cost and profit implications of what they sell. Financial quotas are often stated in terms of direct selling expenses, gross margin, or net profit. They are most applicable when the firm's market penetration approaches saturation levels. In such instances, increasing sales or market share is difficult, so an emphasis on selling efficiency and cost control becomes a logical mechanism for increasing profits.

Financial Ratios The series of ratios used to measure a company's productivity, solvency, liquidity and other items on the company's balance sheet. The ratios indicate trends in these financial areas and provide a means of comparing companies within an industry. The financial ratios are grouped into two types. (1) those that summarise an aspect of the business operation for a period of time (generally one year) and 2) those that summarise an aspect of the company's financial position of a given moment in time.

Financing Function A facilitating marketing function by which funding is provided to manufacture, transport, sell, buy and store products.

Fixed Capital Durable capital that may be used repeatedly over a considerable period of time.

Fixed Cost An expenditure that remains constant regardless of changes in sales volume. Rent, property taxes, and depreciation are examples of fixed costs. Also called fixed expenses.

Fixed Cost, Average The total fixed cost divided by the numbers of units produced and marketed.

Fixed Cost Contribution per Unit The selling price per unit less the variable cost per unit.

Fixed Cost, Total The sum of costs incurred by a firm that tend to remain at the same level (fixed) no matter how many units of a product are produced and marketed.

Fixed Exchange Rate An exchange rate that is fixed by government policy and that is not free to fluctuate in response to market forces.

Fixed Stock A definite amount of a good already produced, on hand and ready for sale. It cannot be increased in the short run and can be decreased only by sale.

Flagship Store In a local department store organisation, the main or downtown store, especially when it is large or dominant in relation to other company stores.

Flash Report As soon as the day's sales figures have been read on whatever kind of register is in use, a tentative, unaudited report is released to give management the day's results for comparison with budget or perhaps last year's sales figure.

Flat Organisation This term (and the term horizontal organisation) refers to an organisation with few or no interning levels of management between the top executive and the workers. It presents a stark contrast to the classic hierarchical organisation and bureaucratic organisation with their layers of managers each of whom supervises a lower layer, leading finally to the supervision of workers. The underlying concept of the flat organisation is that trained workers with assigned goals and with the authority to achieve the goals in their own way, will—working individually or in groups—be more productive than workers who are closely supervised by managers. Comment: A truly flat organisation would be feasible only for a small business or service organisation or institution in which all employees report directly to the boss. For a large organisation wishing to delegate more authority down the line, a more descriptive term would be "flatter" organisation. Layers of management are reduced to the minimum and workers are given more authority and responsibility to achieve their assigned goals. It should be noted, however, that in the case of a business (particularly where stock is issued to the public) the hierarchy cannot be dispensed with entirely. The corporations is charged with many fiduciary and legal requirements. Consequently, top management must provide policies, direction and controls to ensure that managers and workers at all levels understand and comply with these requirements.

Flat Rate A price charged for advertising space or time that does not include discounts based on the quantity of space or time purchased by the advertiser.

Flexible Break-Even Analysis A form of business analysis used to project the performance of a product in the marketplace at various price points. Break-even analysis reveals the number of units of a product that must be sold for total revenue to equal total product cost. Flexible break-even analysis allows the market researcher to estimate the expected sales volume at a number of different prices.

Flexible Pricing A variable pricing policy which allows for bargaining between buyer and seller as well as for the adjustment of prices to confirm to peaks and slumps in the normal business cycle. Flexible prices are commonly found in the industrial market but occur at the retail level in the used car, appliance markets etc.

Flighting An advertising continuity or timing patterning which advertising messages are scheduled to run during intervals of time that are separated by periods in which no advertising messages appear for the advertised item. Any period of time during which the messages are appearing is called a flight and period of message in activity is usually called a hiatus.

Floating Exchange Rate An exchange rate that is determined by private supply and demand and that is free to respond to market forces.

Floor Audit The use of floor sales registers for all transactions, both cash and credit, so as to obtain from the register readings the total sales for each salesperson, department and type of sale.

Floor Plan Financing A form of short-term financing commonly used by retailer of big ticket items such as home appliances, boats, and automobiles. The retailer borrows money from a lending institution and uses it to pay the vendor (a manufacturer or distributor) for the goods at time of receipt. The lending institution holds title to the goods as collateral and is repaid by the retailer as the goods are sold.

Fluctuating Demand In industrial marketing, the volatile demand for industrial goods and services, particularly for new plants and equipment. This demand is generally regarded as less stable than the demand for consumer goods and services. See also *accelerator principle*.

F.O.B. (Free on Board) A term used in shipping agreements meaning that the buyer of goods pays the freight charges from the FOB point (the point of origin), *e.g.*, the factory, port-of-entry, etc. Title to the merchandise passes to the buyer at the FOB point, for example at the time the goods pass the ship's rail.

F.O.B. (Free on Board) Factory A shipping agreement in which the seller of goods places them on a carrier at the factory site at no charge to the buyer (thus "free on board"). The buyer assumes title to the goods as soon as they are on board the carrier and pays the freight from the factory to destination.

F.O.B. Destination A shipping term that indicates the seller pays the freight to the destination. Title does not pass until the merchandise reaches its destination; thus, the seller assumes all risks, loss or damage while goods are in transit, except for the liability of the carrier.

F.O.B. Factory Pricing See *F.O.B. (free on board) factory*

F.O.B. Origin Pricing A form of geographical pricing in which the seller quotes prices from the point of shipment. Free-on-board (F.O.B.) means it is the buyer's responsibility to select the mode of transporting the goods, choose the specific carrier, handle all claims and pay all shipping charges.

Focus Group 1. (consumer behaviour definition) A method of gathering qualitative data on the preferences and beliefs of consumers through group interaction and discussion usually focused on a specific topic or product. Also, it is a group of respondents brought together for this purpose. 2. (marketing research definition) A personal interview conducted among a small number of individuals simultaneously; the interview relies more on group discussion than on a series of directed questions to generate data. It is also called group indepth interview.

Focus Group Interview A form of indirect iterview used in marketing research. In a focus group interview, a small group of consumers is invited to participate in a spontaneous discussion in the hope that the discussion will reval the participants' real feelings about the products.

Follower Advantage The ability of nonpioneering market entrants to gain long-term competitive advantages due to late entry. Mechanisms that lead to follower advantage include resolution of demand and market uncertainty, shifts in technology or customer needs, the ability to free-ride on first-mover investments in buyer education and infrastructure development and learning from the pioneer's product, positioning, or marketing mistakes.

Food and Drug Administration (FDA). The federal agency responsible for monitoring the purity of foods, food additives and drugs in interstate commerce. Maintains a testing programme to insure this, and enforces penalties against misbranding, adulteration and other related offenses. Created by the federal Food and Drug Act (1906).

Food Broker A manufacturer's agent who specialises in the distribution of grocery items. Food brokers call on grocery wholesalers and large retailers on behalf of their clients and are directly involved in marketing strategy, planning and promotion of the goods they carry.

Food Court In a shopping center, a concentration of restaurants and food service facilities in a particular area apart from stores, usually with a shared eating area.

Food Marketing Institute (FMI) A Washington, D.C. based association of grocery retailers and wholesalers. The association represents the industry to both the government and to consumers. FMI conducts research, collects statistical data, and maintains a library. It publishes *Washington Report* (weekly) and *Issues Bulletin* (monthly), as well as three important annual publications, *Supermarket Industry Financial Review*, *Facts About New Supermarkets*, and *Food Marketing Industry Speaks.*

Foot-in-the-Door Technique A technique in which compliance is gained for a relatively large request by first gaining compliance to a relatively minor request; the compliance with the minor request positively affects later compliance with the larger request. For example, getting someone to make a small donation to a charity can be used to increase the probability that he/she will donate more later. The first, small request is the foot in the door.

Foote, Cone & Belding (FCB) Grid A two-dimensional grid developed by the Foote, Cone and Belding advertising agency for analysing consumers and products. The grid divides products on the basis of whether they are higher or lower in involvement and on the basis of whether they are "think" products or "feel" products.

Forced Sale A sale of products at less than market price due to the urgent need for a merchant to liquidate merchandise assets, generally, to meet the demand of creditors. It is also the sale of goods or property under order from the court: an ordered public auction sale.

Forecasting The practice of predicting future demand in the marketplace over a given period of time. Both subjective and statistical methods may be used. See also *sales forecasting*

Forecasting Models In forecasting sales, share, or other marketing objectives, a variety of models have been used, including time series models (*e.g.*, moving averages, exponential smoothing, decompositional), econometric models (*e.g.*, regression, input-output) and judgemental models (*e.g.*, Delphi technique). Most common of the econometric models are those including marketing mix variables of the firm and its competitors, thus offering diagnostic insights.

Foreign-Based Export Agent In direct export, a foreign company which sells the goods on behalf of the exporting company. The agent may have either exclusive or general rights to represent the exporter in that country. See also *direct export.*

Foreign-Based Export Distributor In direct export, a company located in the host country that buys and owns goods from the exporter. See also *foreign-based export agent* and *direct export.*

Foreign Direct Investment Investing in a country with control or influence over the direction of the investment. For balance of payments purposes, any holding of more than 20 percent of these shares of a company is considered direct as opposed to portfolio investment.

Foreign Exchange Any currency that is purchased or sold in the foreign exchange market.

Foreign Exchange Market The buyers and sellers of currencies that are traded for both spot and future delivery on a continuous basis.

Foreign Trade Zone (FTZ) A city (frequently a seaport) designated by a county which may receive foreign goods to store and further process them without the importer paying import duties unless the goods actually enter the country. Foreign trade zones facilitate international trade in that exporters can ship from the zone where large quantities of goods are stored to other countries without being involved in the country's trade restrictions—these zone is, in fact, an enclave free of these regulations. Also known as a *free trade zone* or *free port.*

Fork-Lift Truck A material handling device to move unit loads. It is capable of moving loads both horizontally and vertically. The most common power sources are propane gas and electricity.

Formative Research The market research, usually on target customers, carried out before a marketing program is begun in order to help formulate effective strategy and tactics.

Form Utility The usefulness (or consumer satisfaction) derived from the physical transformation raw materials undergo in processing or manufacture. Form utility may be regarded as the economic utility derived from the actual physical product.

Formula Pricing A pricing strategy in which final price is established through the use of a formula, *e.g.*, price may be set at three times cost without consideration of any other variables or with competitive conditions in the marketplace.

Formula Selling A selling approach in which the sales presentation is designed to move the customer through the stages in the decision-making process such as get the customer's attention, develop interest, build desire and secure action (AIDA).

Forward Buying 1. (industrial definition) The practice of buying materials in a quantity exceeding current requirements in order to receive volume discounts or to ensure availability. 2. (sales promotion definition) A situation in which retailers buy more of a product on deal than they intend to sell during the deal period. These additional products are warehoused or stored and sold later at full price or margin.

Forward Dating Refers to the payment due date on invoices for merchandise. The payment due date is moved forward by the manufacturer or supplier in an effort to make the terms of sale more attractive to the retailer. This tactic is frequently employed to encourage retailers to buy large quantities of merchandise to meet anticipated high demand *e.g.*, during the Christmas selling season.

Forward Integration A marketing system in which a producer or manufacturer owns or controls the distribution channels (upto and sometimes including, retail outlets) through which his product passes on its way to the ultimate consumer.

Forward Invention In international marketing, the development of new products for foreign markets.

Forward Market Segmentation A means of identifying segments of a population using such attributes as race, nationality, age, education, psychological traits, lifestyle characteristics, etc. The underlying assumption is that groups or market segments,which share certain attributes will react homogeneously to marketing efforts.

Forward Stock 1. (physical distribution definition) Inventory placed in the channel of distribution in advance of customer commitment. 2. (retailing definition) Merchandise carried on the selling floor, rather than in a reserve stockroom.

Foul-Weather Pricing A pricing strategy in which a company charges so little for its product that it is sold at no profit or, in extreme cases, production costs are not even met. This strategy is employed on the short-term in an effort to keep a company in business during times of economic crisis.

Franchise The privilege, often exclusive, granted to a distributor or dealer by a franchiser to sell the franchisor's products within a specified territory. A franchise is an example of a contractual vertical marketing system.

Franchising In general, franchising may be regarded as a vertical marketing system in which a manufacturer or service organisation confers upon an individual or firm the privilege of marketing a product or service. Thus, franchising is seen as a system or method of doing business in which the franchiser and franchisee have entered into a contractual relationship which involves clearly established rights and responsibilities. Franchise organisations take four basic forms: (1) those which are part of a limited distribution system for particular products, *e.g.*, automobile dealerships, gasoline stations; (2) wholesaler sponsored retail outlets, *e.g.*, certain drugstore and automobile parts stores; (3) wholesaler licensing systems, *e.g.*, soft drink bottles, beer distributors; and (4) retail outlets which carry the trade name of a nationally known organisation and which commonly provide a service, *e.g.*, fast food restaurants, car rental agencies. Automobile dealerships, gasoline service stations and soft-drink bottles account for roughly 75% of all franchise sales.

Free-Flow Pattern A store layout arrangement consisting of a series of circular, octagonal, oval or U-shaped fixture patterns, resulting in curving aisles characterised by a deliberate absence of uniformity.

Free-Form A store design used primarily in specialty stores or within the boutiques of larger stores that arranges fixtures and aisles in an asymmetrical pattern.

Free Goods Merchandise offered at no additional charge by a manufacturer or distributor to a reseller (usually a retailer) as a reward for placing a large order. Free goods are usually given in lieu of a special discount and are treated as price concessions by the Federal Trade Commission.

Free Merchandise A trade sales promotion technique in which an additional amount of the product is offered without additional cost as an incentive to purchase a minimum quantity. The incentive is typically offered for a limited period of time.

Free Sample A consumer sales promotion technique in which a regular or specially sized quantity of the product is given away without cost to prospective purchasers.

Free Standing Insert (FSI) 1. (sales promotion definition) A preprinted advertising page(s), commonly offering coupons or other promotional activities, that is inserted into a separate publication, such as a newspaper. 2. (advertising definition) Preprint advertising of one or more pages that is loosely inserted between the pages of a newspaper or magasine.

Free Trade Area The area of jurisdiction encompassing a group of countries that have agreed to abolish all internal barriers to trade between the member countries.

Free Trade Association An association of countries that agrees to reduce or eliminate the trade barriers which exist between them.

Freight Absorption A pricing policy in which the seller of goods absorbs some or all of the cost of shipping his products to their destination in an effort to maintain a competitive selling price in the local marketplace. Also called *freight equalisation*.

Freight Absorption Pricing A policy of pricing in which the seller picks up the tab for transportation. This is usually done in order to meet the delivered price of a local competitor.

Freight-All Kinds Rate (F.A.K.) A mixture of different products are delivered in a combination to a single or limited number of destinations. Rather than determine the classification and rate for each product, an average rate is applied for the total shipment. This simplifies paperwork associated with the bill of lading and freight bills.

Freight Classification All products transported by common carriers are grouped together into common freight classifications based upon the characteristic of the product that influences cost of handling and transport.

Freight Forwarder A transportation intermediary who consolidates the small shipments of a number of manufacturers into carload or truckload lots to take advantage of the lower rates offered by common carriers.

Frequent Shopper Programme A continuity incentive program offered by a retailer to reward customers and encourage repeat business. The reward is usually based on either purchase volume or number of store visits.

Friendship, Commerce and Navigation (F.C.N.) Treaties International agreements which, among a number of other things, cover a wide range of commercial matters such as marketing practices in the trading partner's country, agreements on duties and other taxes, foreign exchange, travel, communications, etc.

Fringe Market That segment of a firm's customers who are outside the firm's core market; *i.e.*, who patronize the firm on an occasional basis. See also *brand insistence for a definition of the hard-core market*.

Fringe Sizes The sizes that are either very large or very small, if offered at all, are offered in very limited depth because of the thin market demand for them. Some stores specialise in fringe sizes or out sizes *e.g.*, tall women's shops; petite size shops.

Fringe Stocks Those categories of merchandise from which a small percentage of sales come.

Full-Cost Approach to Cost Analysis A method of cost analysis in which all functional costs, including fixed and common costs, are allocated in some way to products, customers or other similar categories. This allows analysts and marketing managers to find the profitability of various customers, products, etc. by subtracting costs from sales. See also *contribution-margin approach to cost analysis* and *marketing cost analysis.*

Full Cost Pricing A relatively rigid pricing strategy in which all the variable and fixed costs of a product or service are covered by its sale price.

Full Demand A condition in the marketplace in which purchasers want and are willing to pay for all the products which are being produced.

Full Disclosure A practice in which all relevant data about a product is made available to the consumer so that an informed purchase decision can be made. Full disclosure is one of a number of consumer protections against deceptive practices.

Fulfilment The gathering of orders or offers from a sales promotion event and the process of completing the event and the process of completing the event by distributing items integral to the event such as premiums, rebates, bounce back offer or ordered merchandise.

Full-Cost Pricing An approach whereby prices are determined after all functional costs have been allocated.

Full-Function Wholesaler See *full-service wholesaler*

Full-Line Discount Store See *promotional department store*

Full-Line Forcing A trade practice in which a manufacturer forces wholesalers and retailers to buy his entire line of merchandise (including the less saleable items) if they are to sell any of his products.

Full-Line Pricing A pricing strategy which takes into consideration the way prices for individual products in a line relate to the prices of other products in the line. In general, an effort is made to present buyers with a logical pricing system, *e.g.*, General Motors prices its automobiles in a predictable manner from the least expensive Chevrolet to the most expensive Cadillac.

Full-Line Sales Organisation In this organization, each company or division salesperson sells all products to all accounts in geographic territory. This is an appropriate strategy when the product line is not large, is nontechnical and is sold through one channel of distribution. It is a lower cost strategy than specializing by product market or type of account.

Full-Line Strategy A marketing strategy in which a seller offers a wide variety of products for sale in an effort to broaden his customer base.

Full-Service (of Retailing) The offering of an adequate number of salespeople and sales supporting services to give customers the full range o expected services. It is usually compared to limited services, which implies some expected services are not offered—*e.g.,* credit.

Full Service Wholesaler A wholesaling middleman who, in addition to taking title to te goods he resells, often takes physcal possession of th emerchandise. Full-service wholesalers usually operate ware-houses and provide their customers with delivery services extend credit, and assist the customer with accounting, inventory, and marketing information.

Functional Account A functional account is one which indicates the purpose for which the expenditure was made. In marketing such accounts may include marketing research, sales and sales promotional activities, order processing, shiping, warehousing, bookkeeping, *etc.* Sometimes referred to as a marketing function account.

Functional Approach to Marketing An approach to the study of marketing in which such functions as sales, distribution, advertising, etc. are viewed as a key to understanding the marketing process. The investigator studies how each of these functions works and from these finding generalises about the lager marketing picture.

Functional Discount The discount given to middlemen or others who act in the capacity of performing distributive services that would otherwise have to be performed by the manufacturer itself. The discount sometimes prevails regardless of the quantities involved.

Functional Expense See *functional expense classification*

Functional Expense Classification A system of identifying the purpose of an expenditure by assigning it to a particular retail activity. The N.R.M.A. includes the following five major classifications to which expenses my be ascribed administration, occupancy, publicity, buying, and selling.

Functional Middleman A middleman who ordinarily assists directly in effecting a change in ownership but does not take title to the goods in which the middleman deals. The middleman specialises in the performance of a single marketing function or a limited number of such functions, one of which is usually related to the transfer of title.

Functional Need Any need of the consumer that is met by the practical application and use of a product or service without referring to style, image, etc.

Functional Obsolescence See *planned obsolescence*

Functional Organisation In a functionally organised company, the managers of each major function (such as marketing, production, research and development, and finance) report to the chief executive, who provides overall direction and coordination. Similarly, in a functionally organized marketing department, the managers of the major marketing functions (such as sales, advertising, marketing research and product planning) report to the marketing manager. Comment: the advantage of this form is that it provides specialisation by function, while coordination of functions is provided by the chief executive. The same can be said for the functional marketing department in which direction and coordination of marketing functions is provided by the marketing manager.

Functional Product Grouping The categorizing and displaying of merchandise by common end users.

Functional Theory of Attitudes A theory of attitudes based on the idea that attitudes develop to satisfy certain functions. *e.g.*, needs or goals, for the individual. According to this theory, attitudes reflect the underlying motives of the individual.

thus, the theory is sometimes referred to as a motivational approach to attitudes.

Furnishings (1) Those things in a store which are ot regarded as equipment of fixtures, e.g., carpeting, furniture, office appointments, etc. (2) In men's wear, furnishings includes ties, shirts, socks, underwear, sleepwear, robes, and accessories.

Future Dating A sales agreement whichsets the beginning of the discount and net periods for sometime in the future rather than a the time the goods are shipped. For example, terms of "2/10 net 30 as of November 1" for goods shipped in agust indicates that the discount and net periods begin on November 1.

G

Game A sales promotion device in which the participant competes for prizes by engaging in an activity which does not require skill, *e.g.,* winning numbers may be revealed on a rub-off card. Pure chance determines who wins. Some games have a continuity element, *i.e.,* they have been set up so as to encourage the participant to enter more than once. See also *contest* and *sweepstake.*

GATT See *General Agreement on Tariffs and Trade (GATT)*

General Advertising Advertising messages that do not contain direct response offers.

General Agreement on Tariffs and Trade (GATT) A multilateral trade treaty entered in force January 1, 1948 with 23 signatories which sets down reciprocal rights and obligations for member countries. GATT has as a principle goal the reduction of tariffs and the removal of trade barriers.

Gemstone A mineral found in nature suitable for use in jewelry due to such factors as beauty, clariy, rarity, etc. While some stones are far more valuable than others, there is less tendency today to divide them into precious and semi-precisous categories.

General Electric Strategic Planning Approach A company-wide approach to marketing planning which takes a number of factors (market growth, competition, market share, profitability margins, technology etc.) into account in order to set corporate strategies and objectives.

General Line Wholesaler A full-service wholesaler who carries one or two lines of merchandise in full assortments and who, for the most part, supplies single line retailers; *e.g.,* a general-line hardware wholesaler will have as his customers hardware stores.

General Merchandise Warehouse A form of public warehouse which may store any type of manufactured goods. See also *public warehouse.*

General Product Manager The executive who functions as the supervisor of a number of product managers and who, in addition is responsible for coordinating their plans and programs and for submission to the firm's marketing manager.

General Sales Manager This manager has overall responsibility for corporate, group, or division sales. Sales management at this level is concerned with developing sales policies, strategies and plans that support the overall marketing plan. In a small company the general sales manager may supervise all salespeople directly. As the number of salespeople increases, however, supervision of sales-people must be delegated to field sales managers. In a functionally organised company, the general sales manager reports to the marketing manager or the chief executive. In a divisionalised corporation, the general sales manager reports to the division marketing manager or to the division manager. In a divisionalised company with a centralised sales organisation, the general sales manager reports to the chief executive or to a group executive.

General Store A small, undepartmentalised version of the general merchandise store, this retail establishment is commonly found in rural areas and sells food, clothing, farm implements, garden supplies, hardware, and other highly utilitarian items.

Generic Advertising An approach to preparing advertising messages that concentrates on the customer benefits that apply to all brands in a product category, as opposed to benefits that are unique to specific brands.

Generic Market A market in which vendors offer substitute products which are different physically or conceptually. Markets are viewed broadly and from the customer's perspective. For example, there are several different ways of satisfying a customer's need for status. Vendors in the generic market aim to satisfy the customer's need (in this case, status) rather than focus on the differences between the individual products which will satisfy this need. Thus, quite different products may compete with each other in the same generic market. In the generic status market, for example, luxury cars compete with cruises, furs, jewelry etc. Each of these products will confer the desired status and so may be viewed by the customer as substitutes for each other. See also *product market and market.*

Generic Product (1) A product sold under a common name rather than a brand name. Generic products are merchandised in a "no frills" manner, given little advertising support, and are sold at a lower price than branded items, (2) In a broader sense, the generic product is not the item itself, but a concept which includes the expectations the buyer has with regard to the product, *i.e.*, the benefits the consumer sees the product embodying.

Gentlemen's Pricing A form of pricing generally found in the professions. For example, a physician may charge a flat $1,000 fee for performing an operation, making no effort to actually cost out the price in terms of hours worked, skill level employed etc.

Geocentrism A form of organisation, found in some multinational marketing firms, in which the marketing effort focuses on the whole world, rather than on any particular nation or region. No single national market is preferred over others. Employees, including management personnel, are hired from diverse backgrounds and nationalities.

Georeference Classification For analysis purposes, the data covering such things as sales, customers, product and demographics are often classified on a geographical basis. Distribution of such data by individual markets provides the geographical structure of demand that must be serviced. The most useful geographical classification structures for logistical modeling are customer point locations, country, standard metropolitan statistical area, economic trading area, ZIP code and grid structure.

Gift An item of value that is offered by the seller as an inducement to influence the consideration or purchase of a product or service.

Global Advertising The use of advertising appeals, messages, art, copy, photographs, stories, video and film segments on a global scale.

Global Brand A brand that is marketed according to the same strategic principles in every part of the world.

Global Corporation A stage of development of a company doing business outside the home country.

Global Marketing 1. (Global marketing definition) A marketing strategy that consciously addresses global customers, markets and competition in formulating a business strategy, (consumer behaviour definition) An approach to international strategy that argues for marketing a product in essentlally the same way everywhere in the world.

Global Marketing Information Systems A system designed to acquire, store, catalog, analyse and make available to decision makers information from global sources within and external to the firm for use as the basis for planning and decision making.

Global Retailing Any retailing activity that spans national boundaries.

Global Strategic Partnerships A linkage between two companies to jointly pursue a common goal on a global scale. They also are called strategic alliances and collaborative agreements.

Global Marketing See *international marketing*

Goals The definite mission of an organisation, *i.e.,* the achievements the organisation wishes to attain, the desired end of organisational activity. See also *objectives* and *advertising goals*.

Goals Down-Plans Up Planning A form of planning in which managers at the top of the organisational hierarchy set corporate goals and then communicate them down-ward to the various operating units within the organisation. These units develop plans for the achievement of the goals and communicate these plans upward for management's approval.

Goffman Model A view of consumer behaviour based on the sociology of Irving Goffman in which the consumer is seen as a role player and the goods he is shopping for are seen as props in a play. The buyer is thus viewed as a player in a drama of his own making.

Going-Rate Pricing A "collective wisdom" approach to pricing strategy in which a firm bases the prices of its products less on what it costs to make them and more on what their competitors are charging or on what the firm believes its customers may be willing to pay.

Good(s) A product that has tangible form,in contrast to services that are intangible.

Goods-Services Continuum A means of visualizing the distribution between goals and services. The continuum is graphically represented as a spectrum with pure goods at one end (a bottle of shampoo, for example) and a pure service at the other (a haircut, for example). As one moves along the continuum one moves from the tangible to the intangible.

Government Market That part of the industrial market which is in the public sector. Included are all levels of the federal, state and local government and their many branches, agencies and authorities.

Grade Labelling A system of identification that describes products by their quality, using agreed-on numbers or letters. The grade classes (standards) and the requirements for each are usually assigned by a government or trade group, and the actual scoring is sometimes done by inspectors. Grade labelling leads to product standardi-sation and ease of comparison by the buyer, often the purpose of the labelling.

Grading The sorting of goods into quality classifications, *e.g.*, meat, men's suits, and cotton are all graded according to predetermined quality standards.

Graphic-Rating Scale A scale in which individuals indicate their ratings of an attribute by placing a check at the appropriate point on a line that runs from one extreme of the attribute to the other.

Gravity Model A theory about the structure of market areas

The model states that the volume of purchases by consumers and the frequency of trips to the outlets are a function of the size of the store and the distance between the store and the origin of the shopping trip.

Gray Market Consumer and industrial products sold outside a manufacturer's authorised distribution channels. Unlike the black market, which is involved in illegal trade, the gray market is generally supplied by distributors or retailers who direct goods from their regular marketing channels to manufacturers outlets in a manner within the limits of the law. Gray market goods are sometimes called parallel imports.

Gray Market Good Merchandise that possesses a valid U.S. registered trademark and is made by a foreign manufacturer, but is imported into the United States without permission of the U.S. trademark owner.

Gridiron Pattern A store layout of fixtures and aisles in a repetitive or rectilinear pattern, best illustrated by a variety store or the grocery department in a typical supermarket. Secondary aisles run at right angles to aisles and each aisle is usually of the same width for its length.

Gross Additional Markup The original amount of additional markup taken before subtraction of any additional markup cancellations to determine net additional markup.

Gross Cost of Merchandise Sold The gross cost of merchandise handled less the closing inventory at cost. The gross cost of merchandise sold is subtracted from net sales to calculate maintained markup. Maintained markup is then adjusted by cash discounts and workroom costs to determine gross margin of profit.

Gross Domestic Product (GDP) 1. An estimate of the total national output of goods and services produced in a single country in a given time period and valued at market price. 2. GDP equals gross national product less net property income from abroad.

Gross Investment The total market value of all capital goods included in the gross national product in a given period.

Gross Margin The difference between the total cost of goods and their final selling price. Gross margin may be expressed as net sales less the cost of goods sold. Since markdowns, shortages, and discounts have been deducted in computing gross margin, the figure is not the same as maintained markup. Gross margin is often used synonymously with the term gross profit.

Gross Margin of Profit The difference between net sales and total cost of goods sold.

Gross Margin Return on Inventory Investment (GMRII) For each dollar invested in merchandise inventory, the equivalent dollars generated in gross margin. It is usually stated as the gross margin as a percentage of the average inventory investment at cost.

Gross Markdown The original amount of markdown taken before subtraction of any markdown cancellations to determine net markdown.

Gross National Product (GNP) The total value (at current market prices) of all goods and services produced by a nation over a specified period of time (commonly one year).

Gross Profit Total receipt less the cost of goods sold, but before selling and other operating expenses and income taxes have been deducted. Gross profit is often used synonymously with gross margin, but gross profit is more commonly used in the manufacturing sector, gross margin more commonly in retailing.

Gross Rating Point (GRP) A measure of the total amount of the advertising exposures produced by a specific media vehicle or a media schedule during a specific period of time. It is expressed in terms of the rating of a specific media vehicle (if only one is being used) or the sum of all the ratings of the vehicles included in a media schedule. It includes any audience duplication and is equal to the reach of a media schedule multiplied by the average frequency of the schedule.

Gross Sales Sales revenue before deductions have been made for returns and allowances, but after sales and excise taxes have been deducted.

Group Buying A form of buying in whicha number of non-competing stores consolidate orders for goods (usuallystaple merchandise) to secure a lower price through volume purchasing.

Group Product Manager This manager reports to the marketing manager and supervises several product managers and/or brand managers in companies, or divisions of companies in which there are more product managers and/or brand managers than the marketing manager can supervise directly.

Growth Stage That stage of the product life cycle during which demand for the product picks up momentum and competitive products are introduced into the marketplace. During the growth stage, production increases and profits rise until competition begins to drive down prices.

Growth Stage of Product Life Cycle The second stage of the product life cycle, during which sales are increasing at an increasing rate, profits are increasing, and competitors enter the market. Product differentiation takes place, and price competition begins. Industry profits usually taper off as the product category enters the third (mature) stage, during which sales increases come only at a declining rate and eventually cease.

Growth Stage The second stage in the product life cycle. In the growth stage, competition and competitive advertising increase rapidly. Personal selling focuses on getting additional outlets at first, and later on selling against the competition. Consumers are still flexible in their preferences at ths point and are willing to accept substitutes.

Guarantee A statement, either written or implied, by the seller of merchandise, in which assurances are made concerning the proper performance of the product and which stipulates the corrective measures which will be taken should it not perform properly.

H

Half Sizes Range of apparel sizes from 10½ to 26½ for women approximately 5'2" to 5 '4" haviga fuller figure than misses.

Hand Marking Merchandise is labeled or tagged by hand with price and other information written out in pencil, pen, or other writing instrument.

Making The choices or decisions made out of "habit" without much deliberation or product comparison.

Hard Goods As compared with soft goods, which have a textiles base, these goods mainly comprise hardware, home furnishings furniture and appliances. These goods are usually also durable goods.

Hard Sell Vigorous personal selling generally directed at the reluctant customer.

Harmonised Tariff System (HTS). This replaced the Brussels Nomenclature in January 1989 and incorporates a common classification system for all products.

Hart-Scott-Rodino Antitrust Improvement Act (1976) This act requires that mergers involving corporations of a certain size must be reported in advance to the enforcement agencies. It also permits state attorneys general to bring *parents patriae* suits on behalf of those injured by violations of the Sherman Antitrust Act.

Harvesting See *milking*

Harvesting Strategy The maximisation of short-run cash flow from a business in expectation of a deterioration of market share and eventual withdrawal from the market. The cash flow raised is directed toward other areas of business where it is needed.

Hazardous Substances Labelling Act(1960) See *Federal Hazardous Substances Labeling Act (1960).*

Headline The part of the written component of print advertising that is meant to help attract the reader's attention to the ad.

Head-on Positioning A market positioning strategy in which two products which are nearly identical compete with one another directly.

Health Care Marketing Marketing designed to influence the behaviour of target audiences in which the benefits would accrue to the target audience's physical and/or mental health. Comment: Health care marketing may be carried out by individuals, by hospitals or clinics or by national agencies such as the National Cancer Institute.

Heavy Equipment Products that are typically capital goods, normally purchased by end user customers. They are treated as an asset by the purchasing firm and depreciated for tax purposes. Examples are lathes, drilling machines and grinders.

Heavy Half That segment of the marketplace which represents numerically half of the consumers in the population, but which contains by a large majority most of a firm's actual customers.

Hedging In commodity marketing, a buying and selling practice in the futures market calculated to protect the purchaser against unfavourable price changes. Some commodities are purchased at current market prices and some are purchased on the commodity futures market at a speculative precise and some are purchased on the commodity futures market at a speculative price for delivery at a later time. The hedge lies in the purchaser's expectation that a change in one price will be accompanied by compensatory change in the other price.

Hedonic Goods Consumer goods whose attractiveness lies principally in that they give the purchaser pleasure.

Hedonistic Consumption A focus on the sensory pleasures or hedonic benefits provided by interaction with products or services.

Hendry Model A model representing the amount of switching among the brands in a product category. The model postulates that, for directly competing brands (*i.e.,* brands within the same market partition), the level of switching among those brands should be proportional to the product of their market shares. The exact level of switching (*i.e.,* the proportionality constant) is assumed to be the value that maximizes the entropy (*i.e.,* randomness or lack of information) in thus probabilistic system.

Herzberg, Frederick See *motive*

Heteogeneous Shopping Goods Shopping goods perceived by the customer as different in quality and suitability.For example, clothing and household furnishings are considered heterogeneous shopping goods. Style and quality play a significant role in the customer's decision to buy these and similar items. Price is of lesser significance. See also *shopping goods* and *homogeneous shopping goods.*

Hidden Buyer In purchasing, a person other than the purchasing agent who, through his power to specify the characteristics of a product, is the real buyer. Technicians, managers and others within an organisation may have the capacity to exert such influence.

Hidden Cost Any of the costs of doing business that cannot be recorded by an accountant and so do not show up on a firm's balance sheet or income statement. For example, the losses resulting from a customer's failure to reorder and cancellations of orders are considered hidden costs.

Hidden Service Sector Services which are to some extent concealed because they are provided by firms which are also manufacturers. For example, manufacturers of photocopiers also provide supplies and maintenance service.

Hierarchical Organisation A classic form of organisation which, during the 19th century, was adapted by business from centuries-old religious and military organisations. In this type of organisation, authority flows from the person in charge through various levels of supervision (called "chain of command" by the military). Conversely, information and requests for guidance and decisions travel upward through the same channels. Few, if any, modern business organisations follow this strict organisational structure. Rather, they delegate much decision making to lower levels of management. When top management needs to be involved, modern techniques for information processing enable top and lower levels of management to communicate quickly. Decisions are often made during discussions via telecommunications. Comment: Some business media continue to describe business organisations as if they operated in the outdated classical hierarchical manner. It is true that business organisation charts often follow the hierarchical pyramid design even though they operate in the less formal manner described above. The formal organisation chart shows the corporate management structure that is responsible to government and stockholders for fiduciary, fiscal and legal requirements. The line of authority from the top down enables top management to ensure that its legal and ethical policies are promulgated and followed.

Hierarchy of Effects Those stages (beginning with unawareness and ending with purchase of the product) through which consumers pass when responding to a firm's promotional efforts. In order, they are: awareness, knowledge, liking, preference, conviction, and purchase.

Hierarchy of Effects Model 1. A concept related to the manner in which advertising supposedly works; it is based on the premise that advertising moves individuals systematically through a series of psychological states such as awareness, interest, desire, conviction, and action. 2. An early model that depicted consumer purchasing as a series of stages including awareness, knowledge, liking, preference, conviction, and purchase.

Hierarchy of Merchandising Information The strategic placement of instore messages that lead the customers through the shopping and buying process beginning with the customers entering the store and ending with them looking at specific merchandise.

Hierarchy of Needs A theory proposed by Maslow (1943) concerning the specific order of the development of needs. He proposed that needs develop in an individual in a sequential order from lower to higher needs, ranging from physiological needs to safety needs (security, order) to belongingness and love needs. Then esteem needs (prestige, respect) and self-actualisation (self-fulfilment) follow. Higher order needs emerge as lower order ones are more or less satisfied.

High Income Countries Countries whose income per capita are high compared to the rest of the world.

High-Pressure Selling A selling approach in which the salesperson attempts to control the sales interaction and pressure the customer to make a purchase.

Hired Hand A salesperson who receives relatively little support or latitude from his or her sales manager. Hired hands tend to perform basically those tasks that are enumerated in the job description, as their managers perceive them as being unable or unwilling to take on additional responsibilities. Hide hands are the opposite of cadre salespeople.

Hit Rate The percentage of the desired number of outcomes received by a salesperson relative to the total activity level. For example, it is the number of sales as a percentage of the number of calls. It is also called *batting average* and *conversion rate*.

Home Country Orientation A marketing orientation in which a firm gives domestic business top priority, making little or no effort to developing markets overseas.

Home Improvement Centre A store category specialist combining the traditional hardware store and lumber yard.

Homemade Diversification Theorem A theorem that states that (in the absence of synergy) diversification by a firm is not valuable to shareholders because they can diversify their own portfolios more cheaply by purchasing shares of stocks in the market.

Homeostasis A state of physiological balance within the individual. For example, lack of water leads to the uncomfortable sensation of thirst. The individual seeks products, such as soft drinks, that reduce the ensuing tension to return to a state of physiological balance or homeostasis.

Homogeneous Shopping Goods Shopping goods perceived by the customer as basically the same. The customer is willing to substitute one brand for another and seeks the lowest price. Thus a slight price cut can significantly increase sales volume and price competition tends to be keen. See also *shopping goods* and *heterogeneous shopping goods*.

Horizontal Buy A purchase that is made from a direct competitor. For example, a west coast chemical company may buy a chemical compound from an east coast competitor because of a geographic supply and/or demand imbalance.

Horizontal Competition Competition between channel of distribution members at the same channel levels, *e.g.*, in retailing, department stores in head-to-head competition. Not to be confused with channel conflict.

Horizontal Cooperative Advertising An advertising partnership in which several retailers share the cost of a promotion.

Horizontal Cooperative Promotion Promotional efforts sponsored by two or more members of a distribution channel who are operating at the same level. For example, a number of manufacturers may cooperatively sponsor events in support of American participation in the Olympic Games.

Horizontal Diversification An effort to increase sales (primarily to current customers) through the introduction of products unrelated to the firm's existing line.

Horizontal Industrial Market A broad market for industrial goods—one which includes a number of industries. Products sold in horizontal markets have a relatively wide range of potential customers.

Horizontal Integration The ownership, achieved by acquisition or internal expansion of additional business units at the same channel of distribution level. Retail organisations often expand through horizontal integra-tion, either additing units or buying up other retail organisations.

Horizontal Merger The joining together or combination of companies in the same industry. The merger may be deemed illegal if it tends to reduce competition substantially.

Horizontal Price Fixing Resale price maintenance agreements between firms at the same level of the market, *e.g.*, collusive agreements between two or more manufa-cturers of the same product to fix prices at an artificially high level. Generally, horizontal price fixing has as its objective higher profits and/or the restriction of competition.

Horizontal Structure of the Sales Organisation A sales organisation may incorporate an internal company sales force or outside agents. When a company sales force is used, alternative approaches to sales organisation include: (1) geographical organisation; (2) organisation by type of product; (3) organisation by type of customer; and (4) organisation by selling function.

Host Country Orientation An overseas marketing orientation in which a firm's overseas subsidiaries are often managed by local people and are thus more responsive to the needs of the local consumer.

House Account A account, usually large, not assigned to a field salesperson, but handled directly by executives or home-office personnel.

House Agency An advertising agency owned or controlled by a single firm which commonly provides service only to that firm.

House Brand A private brand, usually associated with retailers.

House Publication An internally developed or produced magazine or brochure designed to communicate the views of the organisation to a selected audience without outside editorial restraints.

House-to-House Salesperson A salesperson who is primarily engaged in making sales direct to ultimate consumers in their homes.

Household According to the U.S. Bureau of the Census, a

household comprises "all persons who occupy a housing unit, that is, a house, an apartment or other groups of rooms or a single room that constitutes separate living quarters. A household includes the related family members and all the unrelated persons, if any, such as lodgers, foster children, wards, or employees who share the housing unit. A person living alone or a group of unrelated persons sharing the same housing unit as partners is also counted as a household." Quoted from the *Statistical Abstract of the U.S.*

Human Ecology The application of the concepts of plant and animal ecology to human collective life to seek knowledge about the structure of social systems and the way in which structures develop, paying attention to spatial configurations. It is the human population's adaption to the natural environment.

Hypermarket A European retailing development ("hypermarche" in France) which brings food and general merchandise together in a warehouse atmosphere. These stores include elements of the traditional discount operation as well as those of the supermarket and may be as large as 200,000 square feet. Merchandise carried is almost always high volume sellers, as the operation depends on moving very large quantities of goods to turn a profit. See also *superstore.*

Hypodermic Needle Model A largely discredited theory of mass communication which held that the mass media have a direct, immediate and powerful effect on the people receiving the media message. The people were seen as helpless victims whose attitudes and behaviour were influenced by the mass media masses, much as if they had been injected with a hypodermic needle. The theory was superseded first by the two-stop flow model and later by the multistep flow model. See also *two-step flow model* and *multi step flow model.*

Hypothesis A theory or proposition tentatively accepted to explain certain facts or relationships, make predictions about the future and to provide a basis for further investigation (in which case it is often, referred to as a working hypothesis). Researchers develop hypotheses from observation and intuition, then go on to test each hypothesis scientifically.

I

Iceberg Principle In the evolution of marketing performance, the iceberg principle states that much valuable information is not represented adequately in summary data—that such summary data, in fact, is only the tip of the iceberg and that only detailed figures will reveal the submerged information.

Id The part of the personality according to Freudian theory, that reflects the basic physiological and sexual drives (libido) of an individual demanding immediate gratification.

Idea Approach A technique used by a salesperson in the first few minutes of contact with a prospect. In this approach, the salesperson opens with a helpful new idea to interest the prospect. The idea should illustrate how the goods or services will increase the prospect's profits, productivity etc. See also *approach*.

Idea Generation That stage of the new product development cycle in which ideas are sought for new products. These ideas may be created in-house or sought from outsiders. This stage is often called concept generation rather than idea generation, because the new product is not a concept at this time. The activity of generation often follows some stated or implied strategic focus, and it precedes the concept evaluation stage.

Idea Marketing The application of marketing principles in an effort to promote ideas, issues, causes, etc. Idea marketing may be carried on by profit and nonprofit organisations.

Ideal Market Exposure The degree to which a product receives exposure to potential customers so that it is sufficiently available to meet customer needs without exceeding them.

Exceeding customer needs by providing additional exposure of the product is seen as adding unnecessarily to the total marketing cost of the product. See also *exposure*

Ideal Self Concept The knowledge, attitudes, and percep-tions people have about the self they would be like if they were. perfect or ideal.

Illegal Goods The sale of unlawful goods, *e.g.*, stolen property, certain drugs, firearms under certain circumstances etc.

Image Mental perceptions or impressions held by an individual about himself, about others or about products or services. How a customer sees himself and the way he fits into his environment influences his behaviour in the marketplace. See also *store image* and *self-image*.

Image Building Advertising and other promotional efforts intended to influen ce customers' perceptions of a firm. For example, a business may engage in activities which enhance its reputation for being socially responsible. See also *institutional advertising.*

Image Builder Pricing A practice generally found in retailing in which one product in a line is offered at a substantially higher price than the rest of the products in the line in an effort to enhance their image in the minds of consumers. For example, the Corvette helps stimulate sales for all the models in the Chevrolet line.

Image Marketing The application of marketing principles to the enhancement of the image of a person or organi-sation; *i.e.*, the alteration of the public's perception of the person or organisation.

Image Sell A type of advertising message which focuses on creating and conveying a particular image for the product or service being advertised. For example, the use of popular retired athletes in beer commercials is meant to convey an image of masculinity and success. See also *association advertising format*.

Imaginative Approach In advertising copy, an imaginative approach is one which concentrates on the possibilities for self-fulfilment and life-enrichment to be derived from the good or product.

For example, if you buy the toothpaste you'll get the fancy sports car and the pretty girl. Also called an *emotional approach*, it is calculated to take advantage of the customer's emotional buying motive. See also *emotional buying motive*.

Imitative Combiner A firm which uses the combined target market approach to market its goods to an already-established combination of sub-markets. The imitative combiner seeks to offer an improved marketing mix to the target market established by the innovative combiner. The products so developed tend to resemble or even duplicate the innovator's product. See also *combined target market approach* and *innovative combiner*.

Imitative Segmenter A segmenter which tries to offer an improved marketing mix to meet the needs of a target market already identified by an innovative segmenter. The products so developed tend to resemble or even duplicate the innovator's product. See also *segmenter* and *innovative segmenter*.

Imitative Strategy An imitative strategy relies on the designs of other companies in creating its designs. The imitative company also may base its accompanying product marketing strategy on the strategy of the market leader or pioneer. Imitative strategies frequently are used in the fashion goods, furniture, entertainment and food products industries.

Impact Evaluation In social marketing, the evaluation of programme outcomes in terms of original objectives. This is also known as outcome evaluation and summative evaluation.

Imperfect Competition 1. (economic definition) A market situation in which many sellers, each of whom has a relatively small market share, compete for consumer patronage. The term originated with English economist Joan Robinson in the 1930s. 2. (environments definition) The market conditions in which firms have some control, but not necessarily absolute control, over price, by such techniques as differentiating products and limiting supply. Monopoly, oligopoly, and monopolistic competition are examples of imperfect competition.

Implementation The stage in the strategic market planning process in which an action programme is designed to meet the strategic objective(s) using the available resources and given the existing constraints. The action programme is intended to be both a translation of a strategic plan into operational terms as well as a means by which the strategic performance may be monitored and controlled. The action plan has three major components: (1) *specific tasks*—what will be done including the specification of the marketing mix to be employed; (2) *time horizon*—when it will be done; and (3) *resource allocation and budgeting*—attaching a dollar figure to each income and expense-related activity and allocating capital funds.

Implicit Alternative An alternative answer to a question that is not expressed in the options.

Implicit Costs Those expenses in a business which are less obvious and accountable than explicit costs, but which may affect the overall profitability of the business. They may include the owner's salary (even if the actual money is not paid out) or the rental value of the building (even if it is owned by the business, since it is not being rented out to others).

Implicit Price Index (IPI) A relative measure of changes in the general price level of goods and services produced by an economy during a given time period.

Implied Warranty. A warranty (promise of performance) that is extended to the customer but unstated. It usually is assumed from common practice in the trade or suggested by statements made about the product by the seller.

Import (1) To bring or transport goods into a country especially for the purpose of sales. (2) An import is any item brought into a country.

Import Agent In international trade, a manufacturer's agent involved with the importation of foreign goods. The import agent sells similar products for several noncompeting foreign manufacturers in the domestic market and receives a commission on what is sold. See also *manufacturer's agent*.

Import Broker In international trade, an import broker is an agent middleman who brings buyers and sellers together for the purpose of selling foreign goods in a domestic market. Import brokers provide the domestic buyers of imported goods with information about the availability of such goods. They also provide potential importers with information about the needs of the domestic buyers. See also *agent middleman* and *export broker*.

Import Commission House A commission merchant involved in international trade, functioning to sell foreign goods in the domestic market. The import commission house handles goods shipped to them by foreign sellers, completes the sales, and sends the money to the seller. The import commission house is reimbursed for its services by means of a commission paid by the seller. See also *commission merchant*.

Import Licence An instrument of government control that regulates access to foreign exchange and the quantity and/or value of imports.

Importance-Performance Analysis A marketing research tool employed to identify strengths and weaknesses in a company's performance as they are perceived by customers or potential customers. Results are plotted on a two-dimensional grid in an effort to give marketing managers an indication of how their products are regarded in the marketplace.

Impulse Buying A purchase behaviour that is assumed to be made without prior planning or thought. Often, it is claimed, impulse buying involves an emotional reaction to the stimulus object (product, packaging, point-of-purchase display, or whatever) in addition to the simple acquisition act.

Impulse-Intercept Merchandise Merchandise purchased on impulse, when the customer happens to see it in the store,prior to which the customer had no perceived need.

Impulse Merchandise Items which, because of their immediate appeal to the customer, are purchased without prior planning or long consideration.

Impulse Product A convenience product (good or service) that is bought on the spur of the moment, without advance planning or serious consideration at the time, and often by the stimulus of point-of-sale promotion or observation.

Impulse Purchase (1) (consumer behaviour definition) A purchase typically made in-store with little or no decision making effort. (2) (retailing definition) An unplanned purchase by a customer.

In-Pack Premium A free gift or other item placed within the package of the item being promoted by the manufa-cturer. For example, the "prize in every package" inside each box of Cracker Jacks.

In-Store Coupon A certificate redeemable only at one specific retail store or chain. The Coupon is generally distributed through newspaper advertisements, flyers or within the store.

In-Store Marketing The marketing dollars spent inside the store in the form of store design, merchandising, visual displays, or in-store promotions.

In Supplier A firm currently supplying the company or currently on its approved vendor list.

In Transit. A condition that exists when merchandise has been shipped from the vendor and has not yet arrived at the buyer's receiving dock.

In-Transit Mixing. In transportation, a practice in rail shipping in which shippers are allowed to unload carload lots of goods at a warehouse, mix the goods into new carload lots, reload the cars and ship to their destination without incurring additional charges for the stopover privilege.

Incentive Pay Any compensation plan other than straight salary wherein the salesperson is given encouragement to sell more. Examples are straight commission (the strongest incentive); a salary plus a small percentage of net sales, etc.

Incentive Plan An event offering rewards or inducements to stimulate the salesforce or channel members to achieve predetermined sales, profit, distribution, or other goals.

Incentive Travel A form of sales promotional activity in which large companies reward their salespeople, agents, distributors, or dealers with trips to interesting places for attaining a specific objective, usually sales volume (or purchase commitments) in excess of some predetermined quota.

Incidence A percentage of the population or group that qualifies for inclusion in the sample using some criteria.

Incidence of Taxation The final resting place of the burden of the tax. The final resting place of the burden of the tax. The incidence may be on the person who originally pays the tax, or on someone else to whom the tax may be shifted.

Income A flow of money, goods, and benefits to a person or an organisation.

Income Differential The difference in income levels among people of various categories, such as different jobs, geographic areas, age classes, sexes, races, and the like.

Income Effect (1) (economic definition) The change in patterns of consumption for a product given consumers have an increase in real income. (DLS) (2) (Environments definition). The increase or decrease in a consumer's real income as a result of the change in the price of a good or service.

Income Maintenance The policies designed to raise or maintain the income levels of designated groups of individuals.

Income Segmentation The sub-division of a population on the basis of the earnings of each segment.

Income Sensitivity of Demand. The relationship between real increase in disposable personal income and the corresponding change in consumption.

Incremental Revenue The increase or decrease in revenue which results from the addition or subtraction of a unit of sales or from the advance or decline of price.

Incremental Sales Units of the product sold to retailers or consumers through a sales promotion effort over and above the amount that would have been sold in the absence of the promotional deal.

Incremental Technique A strategy used in budgeting for promotional purposes in which the current budget is based upon previous expenditures and upon the firm's expectations of future business. Depending on the planner's feelings, money is either added to or subtracted from the previous year's budget.

Incrementalism The notion that strategies are the outcome of a series of piecemeal and minor tactical decisions in response to problems and opportunities rather than through systematic, formal, prepared plans. Incrementalism holds that organisations are more reactive than proactive.

Independent Buying Office See *resident buying office*

Independent Carrier An owner-operator or individual trucker who provides line-haul service for others. Under current transportation regulations, an independent carrier can make business arrangements with common carriers, contract carriers, exempt carriers, and private carriers.

Independent Sector Collectively, all private nonprofit marketers.

Independent Store Typically owned and operated by an individual, family, or partnership, the independent store is not a part of a chain organisation or ownership group, although it may be a member of a voluntary chain. These retail outlets are often general stores or limited-line stores.

Index of Retail Saturation A technique normally used in larger areas to aid retailers' choice among possibilities for location of new outlets. It offers better insight into location possibilities than a simple descriptive analysis of market potential because it reflects both the demand side and the supply side; *i.e.*, the number of existing outlets in the area and the number and/or income of consumers.

Indexing A strategy employed to mitigate the effects of inflation by tying increases in wages, taxes, interest rates, etc. to changes in a price index; *i.e.*, as prices advance and retreat a variety of escalators are used to bring other aspect of the economy into line. For example, Social Security payments may be tied to fluctuations in the consumer price index.

Indirect Advertising An advertising programme designed to stimulate future buying decisions and sales over an extended period of time rather than an immediate purchase. The programme does so by emphasising the advantage of a product or service and suggesting that the consumer keep this in mind when the need for the product or service does arise. For example, much advertising by funeral homes is geared to having the firm's name in the consumer's mind at some future date when funeral services are required. Also called *indirect action advertising.*

Indirect Channel A channel whereby goods and services are sold indirectly from producer through independent middlemen to final users.

Indirect Channel of Distribution The movement of products from manufacturer through independent middlemen to the ultimate consumer or industrial user. The employment of middlemen in the channel of distribution leaves the producer with somewhat less control over distribution and with less contact with customers.

Indirect Cost Costs involved in doing business which cannot be directly related to a particular product or service or to a particular organisational unit. Included in this category are such expenses as the cost of heat and light, administrative expenses, building depreciation, etc. Also known as *common cost*. See also *overhead, fixed cost, variable cost, and direct cost.*

Indirect Denial A method used by sales-people to respond to prospect objections by denying the validity of the objection buy attempting to prospect objections by denying the validity of the objection but attempting to soften the response by first agreeing that the issue raised in the objection is important.

Indirect Export A method of exporting goods which involves the use of independent international marketing middlemen to enter the foreign market. These middlemen include the domestic-based export agent, cooperative international marketing organisations and the export management company. A firm interested in indirect marketing, may use any of these middlemen to reach the foreign market.

Indirect Exporting Sales to export intermediaries who in turn sell to overseas customers. The indirect exporter has no direct contact with overseas customers.

Indirect Promotion Those forms of sales promotion that are more impersonal than personal selling. For example, advertising, branding and packaging are all forms of indirect promotion.

Indirect Traceable Costs Costs that are not incurred solely for a particular activity but, through reasonably objective means, can be traced, in part, to the activity for which they are incurred.

Individual Brand A particular product offered for sale by its producer under a unique brand name, *i.e.,* none of the manufacturer's other products carry the same name.

Individual Offerings In a firm's product mix individual offerings are single products.

Industrial Advertising Advertising by producers of industrial goods or by providers of business services directed to purchasing agents or other industrial buyers.

Industrial Distributor Mainly a wholesaler of goods to producers and manufacturers rather than to retailers, the industrial distributor may provide his customers with a wide range of services including calls by salespersons, the extension of credit, the stocking of large assortments, delivery, etc. These establishments, depending on where they operate in the industry, are also known as mill supply houses, industrial supply houses, and general merchandise distributors. See also *wholesaler* and *general merchandise wholesaler*.

Industrial Goods Products whose end use is at the manufacturing levels, *i.e.,* those which will be in corporated into other products or which are used in making other products, Included are raw materials, machinery, tools, components, and supplies necessary in the manufacturing process.

Industrial Market The industrial market consists of all those organisations which are involved in production, manufacturing, providing services wholesaling, and retailing, together with the many levels of government and a wide variety of institutions; *i.e.,* all potential customers with the exception of individuals buying goods for themselves or their immediate families. Most products purchased in the industrial market are used to produce a commodity, manufacture a product, deliver a service, or are consumed in the day-to-day operation of the organisation. Also known as the business market. See also *producer market, government market* and *institutional market*.

Industrial Market Segmentation The process of separating an industrial market (business market) into groups of customers or prospects such that the members of each resulting group are more like the other members of that group than they are like members of other segments.

Industrial Marketing Those activities which result in the sale of goods or services at the organisational level of the marketplace; *i.e.,* at the production, manufacturing, wholesaling, institutional, governmental or retailing levels. Organisational consumers either incorporate the products they buy into other products, use them in the course of their operations or resell them.

Industrial Products Goods that are destined to be sold primarily for use in producing other goods or rendering services as contrasted with goods destined to be sold primarily to the ultimate consumer. They include accessory equipment; installations; component parts; maintenance, repair and operating items and supplies; raw materials; and fabricating materials. The distinguishing characteristic of industrial goods is the purpose for which they are to be used, *i.e.,* in carrying on business or industrial activities rather than for consumption by individual ultimate consumers or resale to them. The category also includes merchandise destined for use in carrying on various types of institutional enterprises. Relatively few goods are exclusively industrial products. The same article may, under one set of circumstances, be an industrial goods and under other conditions, a consumer good.

Industrial Purchasing The buying of goods and services at the business, industrial or institutional level.Most industrial purchasing is carried on by professionals skilled in negotiating prices and buying in large quantities. Also known as procurement. See also *buying.*

Industrial Salesperson A salesperson who is primarily responsible for making sales of goods and services to businesses and institutions such as hospitals

Industry A set of companies that vie for market share of a given product.

Industry Forecasting The practice of predicting sales

expectations for a class of products (such as shampoos) rather than a particular product (such as Prell shampoo). Industry forecasting is based on the amount of industry-wide marketing activity as well as the prevailing social and legal climate of the marketing area. The goal of industry forecasting is to predict the share of income that consumers are willing to spend on a product rather than save or spend elsewhere.

Inelastic Demand 1. A situation in which a cut in price yields such a small increase in quantity taken by the market that total revenue decreases. (2) A situation in which the percentage of quantity taken in the market "stretches" less than the percentage drop in price.

Inelastic Supply (1) A situation in which the quantity offered to the market increases less than proportionately to an increase in price. (2) A situation in which the percentage of goods offered to the market "stretches" less than the percentage increase in price.

Inelasticity The relative insensitivity of a product's sales volume to changes in price. A product which has inelastic demand does not motivate its marketer to cut the price, since sales revenue per unit of product decreases more rapidly than unit sales increase. This, however, is a relative concept. For example, a small change in the prices of gas heat will not significantly affect the market for natural gas, and the demand may be said to be inelastic. A major decrease in the price of natural gas, however, may cause consumers to switch to gas heat, use more of it, and thus increase demand. In the second case, the demand for natural gas may be said to be elastic

Inept Set In consumer behaviour, inept set refers to those specific brands which, for one reason or another, the buyer excludes from consideration when shopping a product category. See also *evoked set and inert set.*

Inert Set In consumer behaviour, inert set refers to those specific brands to which the buyer exhibits indifference when shopping a product category. See also *evoked set and inept set.*

Infant Industry An industry that justifies a national policy of protection from global competition on the grounds that it needs time to get established. Infant industry protection is always temporary.

Inferences The beliefs consumers form to represent relationships that are not explicit in the environment; inferences are largely influenced by prior knowledge in memory.

Inferior Goods The less expensive substitutes for products that consumers prefer.

Inferential Statistics Statistical tools used in marketing research in order to project the findings of a sample to a large population. Probability theory, inferential statistics (or inductive statistics as they are sometimes called), may be used to reduce random error.

Influence Strategy A means of communication used by a channel member's personnel in applying its power in specific channel relationships.

Influencer In industrial purchasing, the influencer, although he does not make the final buying decision, has input during the preliminary discussions regarding the transaction, generally on the strength of some technical expertise.

Infomercial The use of a programme-length time period to advertise products and services. This approach often includes a direct response offer to sell the advertised items directly to the public.

Informal Group The interpersonal and intergroup relationships that develop within a formal group or organisation. This might include cliques, "coffee-colleagues" or friendship circles. An informal group tends to form when the formal organisation fails to satisfy important needs of the members.

Information Control. A term applied to studies using questionnaires and concerning the amount and accuracy of the information that can be obtained from respondents.

Information Search An activity by which consumers gather product information and weigh alternatives. The search may be carried out internally, *i.e.,* by the consumer consulting his memory for relevant information collected in the past or it may be carried out externally, *i.e.*, through the examination of advertising, discussions with friends or salespeople, etc.

Information Utility The usefulness (or consumer satisfaction) derived primarily from adversiting and promotion efforts on the part of a marketer. For example, billboards along a highway have information utility when they inform the motorist of available services.

Informational Advertising Advertising that presents factual, usually verifiable, information about the product or product usage.

Informative Advertising A form of advertising which figures heavily in the pioneering stage of new product development and other situations in which the aim is to build primary demand. Informative advertising serves to tell customers about a new product, suggest new uses for a product, inform the market of a price change, explain how the product works, describe available services, correct false impressions, reduce consumers' fears, and to build a company image.

Infrastructure A term used in international marketing. Infrastructure refers to a country's essential facilities and services, such as its transportation and communication system or its banking and financial system, (*i.e.*, those facilities which make marketing activities in the country possible).

Initial Markup When expressed in dollars, initial markup is the difference between the cost price of merchandise and its first retail price. When expressed as a percentage, it is computed as the difference between cost price and first retail price divided by retail price. In both cases mark-down and stock shortages are not counted in the computation. Initial markup is sometimes referred to as original markup, initial markon, or markon.

Initiating Structure A leadership style wherein sales managers closely direct their sales personnel; clarify their roles for them; and plan, coordinate, problem solve, criticise and pressure them to perform. A sales manager using this leadership style tends to exhibit task-oriented behaviour.

Inner-Directed A person guided primarily by goals and ideals stemming from his/her own value system rather than by the opinions of others. Inner-directed people are often considered nonconformists by their peers. See also *other-directed.*

Inner-Directedness A system of values prevalent in production-oriented societies in which members of the society are taught specific value systems dependent on self-sufficiency and inner values. This was first developed by David Resummon in his monograph *The Lonely Crowd* and later adapted by Stanford Research Institute in its VALS programme.

Innovations In the product development process, innovations are changes in or additions to a firm's product line which the consumer will generally perceive as new. Innovations fall into two categories: (1) minor innovations—products the firm did not previously produce but which already existed in the marketplace and (2) major innovations—products which have not been produced before by any firm. See also *congruent innovation continuous innovation, dynamically continuous innovation* and *discontinuous innovation.*

Innovative Maturity A stage at the end of the product life cycle in which the product is either repositioned or modified to extend its life-span. Tactics employed include finding new uses for the product, encouraging more frequent use by current customers and attracting new customers by expanding the market for the product.

Innovative Segmenter A segmenter that seeks out new sub-markets, identifies unsatisfied needs and attempts to develop a marketing mix to reach the new segment. Innovative segmenters are often followed into the marketplace by a number of imitators seeking to utilise the newly identified market segment for their own products. See also *imitative segmenter* and *segmenter.*

Innovativeness (1) (product development definition) When applied to a buyer, the extent to which that person or firm is willing to accept the risks of early purchase of an innovation. (2) (consumer behaviour definition) A personality trait designed to account for the degree to which a consumer accepts and purchases new products and services.

Innovator In the diffusion process, the innovator is the first consumer to accept and adopt a new product, service, or idea. Innovators tend to be young, high in social and economic status, and willing to take considerable risk in adopting new trends and fashions. Also known as an *early acceptor*.

Input Evaluation Measure An objective measure of the amount of effort or resources expended by the sales force, including the number of sales calls; amount of time and time utilisation; expenses; and nonselling activities such as letters written, number of phone calls made and number of customer complaints received.

Input-Output Model A technique employed in an effort to measure and forecast fluctuations in supply and demand in the industrial market. The model is based on the relationship between industries in which the output of one is purchased by the other industries in the marketplace (goods and services becoming their input).

Inquiry A customer's request for additional information about a product or service. Comment: Inquiries are often generated through advertising in which a customer can request additional information by mailing a card or coupon.

Inquiry Test A method of testing the effectiveness of an advertising message and/or media vehicles based on the number of customer inquiries that can be directly attributed to the message by means of coupons attached to the ads or special telephone numbers or code numbers used in ads or commercials.

Inside Salesperson A salesperson who performs selling activities over the telephone at the employer's location. Comment: An inside salesperson typically answers questions and takes orders; however, there is a growing trend for an inside salesperson to actively solicit orders.

Inspection Buying In industrial buying, the practice of purchasing a product only after every item has been carefully examined. This method is used primarily for products that are not standardised and require inspection. For example, one-of-a-kind products such as cars and buildings must be inspected.

Installations These are non-portable major industrial products such as furnaces and assembly lines that are bought, installed and used to produce other goods or services. They are often grouped with accessory equipment to comprise capital goods. They also are called *heavy equipment.*

Installed Base The number of units of a durable product in use at the customers' premises. The term is used for equipment such as *computers* and *copiers.*

Installed Equipment Capital equipment which is generally fixed, long-lasting and expensive such as the plant machinery used to manufacture a firm's products. Installed equipment does not become a part of the finished product and is thus distinct from materials and components used in manufacture. Also referred to as *major equipment* and *installations.*

Installment Account The resulting charge account of a customer who has purchased on an installment-credit plan; *i.e.,* pays a down payment and specified amount per month including a service charge. The customer has the use of the merchandise during the life of the installment account.

Installment Credit A consumer credit arrangement between retailer and customer, generally implemented for the purchase of expensive durable goods. Unlike revolving credit, the installment plan usually involves formal contract which is secured by a down payment. The customer agrees to pay the balance at periodic intervals, each installment including interest and service charges which represent revenue for the retailer. Under this plan the store retains title to the merchandise until it is fully paid for, thus leaving the way open for repossession if it should be necessary.

Installment-Credit Plan A plan enabling consumers to pay their total purchase price (less down payment) in equal installment payments over a specified time period.

Installment Sale A sale of real or personal property for which a series of equal payments is made over a period of weeks or months.

Institutional Approach to Marketing An approach to the study of marketing in which attention is given to the various types or organisations involved in the marketing process (manufacturers and producers, wholesalers, retailers, etc.) in an effort to understand the marketing system.

Institutional Boundary A market area that is defined by governments (*e.g.*, tariffs, post office districts) or by firms in order to restrict spatial competition (*e.g.*, dealerships).

Institutional Market The institutional market consists of a wide variety of organisations, many of them non-profit, including schools, churches, hospitals, etc. The institutional market is a part of the larger industrial market. See also *industrial market, producer market* and *government market.*

Institutional Marketing The marketing of goods and services to the institutional market.

Institutional Signage The signage that describes the merchandising mission, customer service policies, and other messages on behalf of the retail institution.

Institutionalisation In social marketing, creating the conditions under which a behaviour-change programme is continued beyond its initial campaign. Comment: institutionalisation is of major concern to agencies funding social marketing programmes in developing countries that wish to terminate programme support but see the *effects continue.*

Instrumental Function of Attitudes A function of attitudes that provides the maximum benefits and the minimum costs to the individual. Instrumental attitudes are those that provide the individual with more rewards than punishments. These attitudes are usually based on attributes of the attitude object and thus the instrumental function is highly similar to Fishbein's learning theory of attitudes. It is also referred to as utilitarian function of attitudes or adjustive function of attitudes.

Intangibility of Services A concept which embodies the notion that most services are not tangible—that they have no physical properties, that they have no existence until they are performed.

Intangible Resources With reference to a business organisation, intangible resources include the firm's reputation in the marketplace, the relationship it maintains with customers, the quality level of its products or services etc

Integrated Development A process of combining diverse organisational talents and functional groups to support a new product's development. Also called cross-functional integration, integrated development requires regular, high-quality communication and problem solving among the different contributors to the new product development process.

Integrated Division This division contains both marketing and production functions, thereby providing the division manager coordination and control of the principal factors affecting profits.

Integrated Marketing A strategy in which all of a company's marketing efforts are handled by a single organisation, generally a large advertising agency (sometimes called a super agency). Those agencies are equipped to provide services such as direct mail, coupons and other promotions, publicity releases and public relations activities as well as traditional advertising.

Integrated Marketing Communications A planning process designed to assure that all brand contacts received by a customer or prospect for a product, service, or organisation are relevant to that person and consistent over time.

Integrated Service Provider A for-hire firm that performs a range of logistics service activities such as warehousing, transportation, and other functional activities that constitute a total service package. The majority of these firms customise the service package to meet individual customer needs.

Integration In business organisations, particularly large, complex firms, integration is the attempt to coordinate all the functions of the firm into a cohesive whole so that all functions and specialisations work toward the same goal. This effort is particularly important when timing and consistency are significant, as they are in marketing firms. Some larger organisations employ integrators whose primary function is to coordinate demand and supply, packaging programmes, and customer service functions. Integrators are expected to maintain the balance between production and sales, long-term and short term goals, and similar counterpoising influences while resolving interdepartmental conflicts.

Intensity of Distribution Intensity is said to be increased as the number of outlets (wholesale and retail) are increased.

Intensive Distribution A form of market coverage in which a product is distributed through all available wholesalers or retailers who stock and sell the product in a given market area.

Intensive Market Opportunities Opportunities in the marketplace which may be further developed by a company through more aggressive marketing activities. For example, a company may increase sales by persuading existing customers to buy more of the firm's product, by persuading current customers of competing products to switch to the firm's brand, by improving the distribution through such means as vertical integration etc.

Intercept Merchandise The merchandise that customers do not specifically go to a store to buy, but buy because the retailer intercepts them in the course of their store visit activities.

Interindustry Competition Competitive activity in the marketplace between large industries, particularly those which manufacture complementary products, *e.g.*, the textile and apparel industries.

Intermediate Customer A generic term for any buyer between the producer of the basic raw materials that are used to make the product and the ultimate consumer. Manufacturers, wholesalers, retailers, and other middlemen are all intermediate customers.

Intermodal Services In transportation, such coordinated services as piggyback and fishy back which combine two or more modes of transportation, *e.g.*, truck trailers on railroad flatcars.

Intermodal Transportation The movement of goods that combines two or more modes of transportation such as truck and rail to maximise the benefits of both modes while minimising their drawbacks. For example, the combination of rail and motor carriage utilises the flexibility of motor carriers and the low line-haul cost of rail.

Internal Data Marketing information derived from a firm's own internal records. Included are such accounting records as profit and loss statements and financial ratios, sales revenues and costs, inventory data, etc.

Internal Inventory Transfer In plant operations, the movement of semi-finished goods through the manufacturing process.

Internal Marketing Management strategies for employee development, particularly for those employees involved in selling. The intent of internal marketing is to improve the organisation's relations with its customers.

Internal Validity One criterion by which an experiment is evaluated; the criterion focuses on obtaining evidence demonstrating that the variation in the criterion variable was the result of exposure to the treatment or experimental variable.

International Advertising The advertising phenomenon that involves the transfer of advertising appeals, messages, art, copy, photographs, stores, video and firm segments (or spots) from one country to another.

International Channel of Distribution The structure of intercompany organisation units and extra company agents and dealers, wholesale and retail, through which a commodity, product, or service is marketed in international markets.

International Corporation Any early stage in the development of a global/transnational corporation. An international corporation may operate in many countries, but in does not have a global vision or strategy.

International Court of Justice .The principal judicial organ of the United Nations. It settles disputes between the sovereign nations of the world but not between private citizens.

International Department. That part of a firm charged with the conduct of foreign operations.

International Development Association (IDA) An affiliate of the International Bank for Reconstruction and Development formed in 1960 to help developing countries by extending financial aid on subsidised terms. It helps countries whose credit standing does not enable them to borrow from the bank, and it is prepared to finance a wide variety of projects.

International Marketing There are two basic forms of international marketing; (1) operations carried on in the home country, which produce goods to be exported and marketed in a foreign country; and (2) operations in foreign countries which produce goods in that country for sale there. Some foreign operations are wholly-owned subsidiaries of the parent company while others may be joint or licensed ventures or contract manufacturing operations.

International Newspaper Advertising and Marketing Executives (INAME) A professional association of advertising and marketing executives employed by daily newspapers. The goal of the association is to promote the use of advertising in daily newspapers, and it works to achieve this goal through the presentation of annual awards and the sponsorship of educational programmes. Its *News* is published ten times per year, its *Digest*, semiannually and its *Roster*, annually. INAME also publishes a semiannual *Sales and Idea Book*. INAME's headquarters are in Washington, D.C.

International Product Cycle A model developed by Professor Raymond Vernon that shows the relationship of production, consumption and trade over the life cycle of a product. Based on empirical data for the pre-1967 era, the model showed how the location of production shifted from the United States to other advanced countries and then to less developed countries.

International Retailing Retailing activity by an organisation that reaches across national boundaries.

International Trade Product Life Cycle A trade cycle model that suggests that many products go through a cycle in which high income, mass consumption countries are initially exporters, then lose their export markets and finally become importers of the product.

Interpersonal Factors Those influences or forces on the consumer due to other individuals within the individual's life space or sphere of activity. Wearing a tie when others are doing so would be an example, as would a person purchasing perfume to impress someone else.

Interstate Commerce Commission (ICC) (1887) The first independent regulatory agency established, the ICC is required to "foster the preservation and development of a national transportation system adequate to meet the needs of the commerce of the United States, of the postal service, and of the national defense."

Intertype Channel Conflict A form of distribution channel conflict which occurs when middlemen of different types (*e.g.*, specialty stores and department stores) attempt to impede the operations of one another in such a way as to create channel dissonance. See also *channel conflict*.

Intertype Competition The competition between different types of firms selling the same product. For example, automobile tires may be sold through discount stores; gasoline service stations; department stores; tire, battery, and accessory dealers; and independent garages.

Interurbia A strip of seemingly continuous urban-suburban population centres. For example, the East Coast of the United States may be considered an interurbia—a single population centre jining the cities of Washington, Baltimore, Philadeplphia, New York, and Boston, and including the suburban areas surrounding each city.

Inter-selling The process of selling between and among departments to facilitate large transactions and to make it more convenient for the customer to accessorise.

Interview In marketing research, a method of gathering data in which a questionnaire is administered to a respondent. Interviews may be conducted on a one-to-one, face-to-face basis, by telephone, by mail or by a respondent filling out a questionnaire by himself.

Interviewer Bias Distortion in the results of an interview due to the intentional or unintentional intervention of the interviewer.

Intraindustry Competition The rivalry among sellers of the same product or service to achieve such objectives as increasing sales, market share or profits.

In Transit Storage A facility for storing, transferring, or modifying shipments enroute to their final destination, often used for break-bulk or consolidation purposes.

Intrapreneurship The practice of entrepreneurship within a large firm. Intrapreneurship is a style of management thought to be independent, risk taking, innovative, daring and typical of the style used in successful start-up firms. In some situations intrapreneurship requires that the entrepreneurial unit be segregated or isolated from the other units, this permitting the unique style of management.

Intratype Competition The conflict (or competition) between firms of the same type—*e.g.*, a department store competes with another department store; a supermarket competes with another supermarket.

Intrinsic Reward A reward that comes from within the individual rather than externally. Practicing the piano for the sheer joy of learning and creating music rather than for a cash reward is an example.

Introductory Approach A technique used by a salesperson in the first few minutes of contact with a prospect. This approach features a letter of introduction, business card, or testimonial from someone known to the prospect as a means of gaining the prospect's trust and attention. See also *approach.*

Introductory Price Dealing A method of pricing used to attract customers to a new product. Prices are cut Temporarily during an introductory offer and raised again at the end of the introductory period. The set time period of the price cut distinguishes introductory price dealing from penetration pricing. Some competitors meet introductory price cuts in order to maintain customer loyalty to their products. Others prefer to ignore such dealing, especially if the introductory offer is neither too long nor too successful. See also *penetration pricing.*

Introductory Stage The beginning (or pioneering) stage in the product life cycle during which the marketing effort is directed toward introducing the product (rather than the specific brand) to the consuming public. Many products fail at this stage because they never capture the interest of the consumer. See also *fashion cycle and product life cycle (PLC).*

Introductory Stage of Product Life Cycle The first stage of the product life cycle. The new product is introduced to the market, sales are slow, promotion is usually heavy, costs are accumulated, profits are frequently negative and expectation is focused on determining when and if the product will soon enter the second (growth) stage of the cycle.

Invention A new device, process, etc., that has been created. The invention can be in either physical or conceptual form. Preexisting knowledge is combined in a new way to yield something that did not heretofore exist. It is not to be confused with a product innovation, which is an invention that has been converted by future management and process development into a marketable product. Invention is thought to require both engineering science and art, but scientific findings and artistic creations, alone, though they may be original, may not constitute inventions.

Invention Pricing Policy A pricing policy in which the company neither fixes a single price worldwide nor remains aloof from subsidiary pricing decisions, but strikes an intermediate position.

Inventory (1) The assets of a business other than those commonly referred to an "plant and equipment," *i.e.,* inventory includes raw materials, semi-finished goods or work-in progress, and finished goods to be either used internally or offered for sale. (2) A detailed, often descriptive list of goods held in stock for future sale.

Inventory Carrying Costs Those costs of doing business directly related to goods held in inventory, including warehousing, deterioration and obsolescence, theft and insurance charges.

Inventory Control The procedures used to ensure that desired inventory levels are maintained. Most procedures are based on either perpetual or periodic review.

Inventory Cushion The allowance in the inventory made for uncertainties in sales or deliveries, often added to the basic low stock to provide for conditions neither controllable nor accurately predictable.

Inventory Echeloning In logistics management, inventory echeloning is the practice of basing the number of inventory locations for an item on the basis of sales. In general, this means that high-volume goods will be stocked at a greater number of distribution centres within the marketing territory (including some in outlying areas), while low-volume goods will be stocked at fewer locations (perhaps even at a single, central location).

Inventory Management. Those activities calculated to insure that the proper stock levels are maintained at all times. Included in the inventory management function is the responsibility for the smooth flow of goods from producer to consumer. Functions include the estimation of such factors as customer demand, production capacity, lead times etc.

Inventory Overage The value of physical inventory in excess of the book value.

Inventory Policy A firm's standard practice regarding the level of inventory to be maintained. For example, it may be customary to hold a 60-or 90-day supply.

Intentory Profit Profits accrued on goods held in inventory during a period when the value of the goods increased.

Inventory Risk. The financial risk involved in carrying goods in inventory—because their value has decreased or because there is little demand for them.

Inventory Stock Shortage The value of the book inventory in excess of the actual physical inventory, often expressed as a percentage of net sales. It is the amount of theft, breakage, sales in excess of amounts charged customers, and errors in record keeping. It may be either clerical (caused by miscalculation), or physical (caused by misappropriation of goods).

Inventory Turnover (1). (physical distribution definition) The number of times average inventory is sold during a specified time period (usually one year). (2) (retailing definition) The number of times per year the retailer sells its average inventory.

Inverse Demand A condition opposite the normal demand pattern (in which demand decreases as prices increase), inverse demand is a condition in which, as prices increase, demand also increases. A condition of inverse demand often results in prestige pricing at the retail level.

Investment Any outlay of cash flow in the near term that is expected to generate cash inflows in future periods. Typically some or all of the cash outlay is capitalised on the balance sheet of the firm.

Investment Opportunity Chart A grid or matrix representation of opportunities available to a firm in the marketplace. The chart is a tool used for strategic planning.

Investment Strategy A strategy that specifies (1) the requirements for funds needed to achieve the competitive advantage, and (2) the outcomes expected from the allocation of these funds. The broad investment choices are build, defend, or harvest market position.

Invisible Assets Assets that are hard to copy, very time-consuming to develop, capable of many uses, and unattainable with money alone. Invisible assets are mainly embodied in factors such as the superior skills of people, corporate culture, advanced technical design and production skills, and mastery of the dominant technologies. These assets may be acquired through first-mover advantages, accumulated experience, continued investment in training and insightful nurturing of strengths.

Invoice A bill or statement, usually itemised, which is enclosed with a shipment of merchandise or mailed later by the seller. Information generally includes quantities shipped, prices of goods terms of sale, discount, method of shipment, and other particulars including total amount due the seller.

Involvement The degree of personal relevance a consumer perceives a product, brand, object or behaviour to have. High involvement products are seen as having important personal consequences or as useful for achieving important personal goals. Low involvement products are not linked to important consequences or goals.

Isolated Store A free-standing building having no other retail outlets in the immediate vicinity and generally located on a highway or back street.

Item A specific article of merchandise, often a best seller.

Item Merchandising The special planning and control effort employed to discover and take advantage of the sales opportunities afforded by items that are in greater consumer demand.

Item Pricing A method of setting prices which allows for deviaions from the standard mark on percentage. The retailer takes into consideration such factors as whether an item is a fast or slow mover, personal experience, the amount of risk involved, etc. to raise or lower the selling price.

J

Jewelery Articles of personal adornment made of either precious or non-recious materials. Included are necklaces, rings, earrings, pins, hais, etc.

Jobber Earlier, a dealer in odd lots or job lots; now, a middleman who buys from manufacturers (or importers) and sells to retailers; a wholesaler. (See also *supply house.*)

Job Description In any business establishment, a job description is a statement of what the employee holding that job is expected to do. It may outline specific tasks and should provide clear guidelines for the employee to follow. Job descriptions often include the kind of person who should be hired for the job, the training to be provided and the type of motivation that should be used by the employee's supervisors.

Job Evaluation A process in which jobs are compared with one another in an attempt to determine their relative rank, generally on the basis of job content.

Job Induction The informal orientation of a new employee which emphasises the responsibilities of the job and the role the new employee will play in the department. Usually performed by the department manager or other direct supervisor of the new employee. Includes expecta-tions, hours, schedule, hourly rate, pay schedule, etc.

Job Lot A broken lot, unbalanced assortment, or discontinued merchandise reduced in price for quick sale. Also called *odd lot.*

Joint Ownership Venture A form of joint venture in which foreign and domestic investors join to create a local business. Each firm shares in the ownership and control of the new firm. Some foreign governments require joint ownership as condition for entry into their markets. See also *joint venture.*

Joint Promotions A marketing effort, generally widely advertised, aimed at increasing sales. The cost of the promotion is shared by the two participating companies. Joint promotions are used to introduce new products or services or to revitalise those already established. They are commonly employed to push undifferentiated products or services, *e.g.*, airline tickets, soap, hosiery, hotels, etc.

Joint Venture In international marketing, a partnership arrangement in which a domestic company shares the ownership and control of production and marketing facilities with at least one foreign partner. Some production facilities are established in the host country, which distinguishes a joint venture from exporting. A joint venture also differs from a direct investment in that a partnership is established by a citizen of the host country. There are several types of joint venture, including licensing, contract manufacturing, management contracting and joint ownership ventures.

Joint Venturing A linkage between two companies in order to facilitate the supply and/or sale of products to a market or market segment. A joint venture arrangement might be set up between two or more companies in order to enter a new market (*e.g.*, a foreign market) or between two or more companies in the value chain as when the child of two corporate parents develops a new distribution or builds a supplying plant. Joint ventures can be informal sharing agreements or formal equity-sharing arrangements.

Junior Department Store Not as large as the traditional department store, the junior department store carries a relatively wide variety of merchandise in a departmenta-lised form of organisation. Prices are often moderate and major appliances and furniture are usually not Included in the merchandise offering.

K

Kanban Literally "visible record" in Japanese, kanban has become a more general concept applied to vendor-carrier-retailer relations. It facilitates the flow of merchandise from the manufacturer through the transportation system thus making it easier for the retailer to regulate inventory levels. Cooperation between all parties is central to the concept

Keep-out Pricing See *preemptive pricing*

Key Selling Price That price which is nearly dead center between the prices a store's customes regard as low and high. When a bell curve is drawn to represent a store's price range the key selling prices will be at the top of the curve.

Key Account A large account, usually generating more than a prespecified annual sales level, that receives special treatment from salespeople.

Key Items The items that are in the greatest consumer demand. They are also referred to as best sellers.

Key Resource A vendor whose past dealings with a retailer have been excellent and from whom the retailer has consistently bought a substantial portion of its merchandise.

Key Success Factors Those factors that are a necessary condition for success in a given market. That is, a company that does poorly on one of the factors critical to success in its market is certain to fail.

Knock-Off The copying of another manufacturer's fashion design, usually at a cheaper price point.

Knowledge Consumers' meanings or beliefs about products, brands, stores, etc., that are stored in memory.

L

Labour Intensive A product or an industry in which labour requirements are large relative to requirements for capital goods.

Labour Intensive Industry An industry which makes greater relative use of human labour than it does of machinery and automation. Labour costs in such industries are therefore relatively high. The construction and garment industries are examples of labour intensive industries.

Laissez Faire Leadership A leadership style wherein sales managers supervise their sales personnel minimally and thus have a low degree of active involvement with them. Using this sales management leadership style usually requires sales personnel to resort to their own devices to execute their job tasks.

Landed Cost Price The quoted or invoiced price of a commodity, plus any inbound transportation charges.

Lanham Trademark Act (1946) This act provides for the registration and protection of trademarks.

Late Majority In the diffusion process, the late majority includes those consumers in the mass market who are slow to purchase new products and services. Members of this group are likely to have below average incomes, relatively little social prestige and to be relatively unresponsive to innovation.

Latent Conflict The existence of antecedent conditions of other states of conflict.

Latent Demand A condition in the marketplace in which consumers have a desire for a product or service which is unmet, commonly because the product or service is as yet undeveloped.

Launch Control The process by which a management plans for and supervises the introduction of a new product; the product's progress is monitored against preestablished norms, variances are detected and corrections made such that the original goals set for the product are achieved.

Law of Comparative Advantage This law states that a country tends to export those economic goods in the production of which it has a comparative advantage and to import those economic goods in the production of which it has a comparative disadvantage. If a country has no comparative advantage, then it should tend to produce those products for which it has the least comparative disadvantage.

Law of Demand A law stating that as the price of a product is raised the demand for this product will diminish, *i.e.*, consumers purchase more goods at a low price than at a high price. Also known as the *law of dimini-shing demand.*

Law of Diminishing Return After a certain point has been reached, each successive application of a factor of production will add less to total output than before.

Law of Effect A technical term from learning theory in psychology often credited to Thorndike. Of the several responses made to the same situation, that which is accompanied or closely followed by satisfaction, other things being equal, will more likely be repeated and the connections learned. Those responses that are followed by punishment will be extinguished. For example, the consumer's probability of repeating purchase of a brand would increase if he/she were satisfied with the purchase and decrease if he/she were dissatisfied. However, whether rewards and punishment are essential for learning to occur is controversial in that many learning theorists claim that reinforcement is unnecessary.

Layout In retail stores, refers to the interior arrangement of departments and merchandise withindepartments, as well as space allocation for aisles counters, fixtures, etc.

Lead In sales, a lead is a possible new customer. A lead may be either a person or an organisation, but the salesperson has not yet determined whether the lead is really interested in the product or service. Once this has been determined, the lead becomes a prospect. See also *prospect* and *qualified prospect*.

Lead, Sales An inquiry or referral about an individual or organisation that is a potential customer.

Lead Time (1) In physical distribution, the elapsed time between placement of an order and the arrival of the goods. Also known as *order cycle time*. (2) In advertising, the elapsed time between the placement of an advertise-ment and its appearance in the media.

Leader Pricing A strategy in which the prices of certain items (called leaders or loss leaders) are established at levels so low that they yield little or no profit. The objective of this practice is to increase customer traffic flow and to create the general impression of store-wide low prices.

Leadership Substitute A non- supervisory source of direction, guidance, support and encouragement for salespeople. Examples of leadership substitutes include closely-knit, cohesive work groups; advisory and staff personnel; formalised and detailed job descriptions; quotas; sales force compensation plans; and expense plans. Use of leadership substitutes can provide direction and guidance to sales personnel in the absence of a sales manager and may afford a sales manager additional time to attend to particularly important supervisory duties.

Learning According to Hilgard, learning refers to more or less permanent change in behaviour that occurs as a result of practice. It is a process by which an activity originates or is changed through reacting to an encountered situation, but does not include those changes induced by maturation, generic response tendencies or temporary situations such as fatigue or drug influence. It includes such activities as the learning of facts and skills, brands, jingles, purchase behaviour, beliefs and attitudes.

Learning Curve A graphic representation of the fact that as production increases, unit costs decrease; *i.e.*, when a great many items are manufactured, each individual item will be cheaper because the manufacturer has learned to reduce expenses and to increase efficiency.

Learning Curve Pricing A pricing strategy in which a manufacturer reduces the price of his product as production increases and becomes more cost-efficient.

Learning Decay The fading of memory of a specific learned response. Because forgetting is a controversial issue among learning theorists—some claiming that nothing is ever forgotten—the terms decay of advertising effects or decay of a learned response are more accurate for the process of forgetting.

Legitimisation With reference to the introduction of new products into the marketplace, legitimisation refers to the process by which early triers of the product serve as examples for other consumers who may be somewhat less innovative.

Less-than-Carload Freight Rate (L.C.L.) A shipment which does not fill a railroad freight are and thus does not qualify for full-car rates. See also *carload freight rate* (C.L.).

Less-than-Truckload (L.T.L.) A small freight shipment typically less than 10,000 pounds transported by common carriers.

Letter of Credit A written instrument issued by a bank to a buyer of goods which is evidence of the buyer's good credit standing. The letter of credit is presented to the seller of the goods by the buyer, the seller delivers the goods to the buyer and collects his money from the bank which issued money from the bank which issued the letter of credit which, in turn, collects from the buyer. The letter of credit is useful in international trade where the buyer has been unable to establish a line of credit with the sellers of goods.

Letters to the Editor A newspaper section used to air public opinion. When used as publicity device, letters to the editor can help a company make known its position on various topics of community interest.

Level Expenditure Method A method of developing media advertising schedules in which each segment of the campaign is treated equally.

LEXIS An on-line database that indexes articles and casework related to legal matters.

Licensing (1) An agreement between the creator of a product or line of products and a manufacturer in which the creator (licensor) gives the manufacturer (licensee) permission to use his name in the marketing of a product in return for a royalty, usually computed as a percentage of sales. (2) A form of joint venture in which a domestic manufacturer seeks entry into a foreign market by granting a license in the foreign market permission to use a manufacturing process, trademark, trade secret, etc. in exchange for a royalty or fee. The partnership thus formed allows the domestic manufacturer entry to the host country market with minimum risk, since the licensee is providing the means of production. The licensee, on the other hand, gains access to a well known product or product line.

Life-Cycle Costs The costs of a durable good over its entire operating life. Comment: Life-cycle costs are often introduced to show that products with higher initial costs (*e.g.*, because they are built better) really have lower costs over their effective lives. (*e.g.*, because they need fewer repairs).

Lifestyle A distinctive mode of behaviour centered around activities, interests, opinions, attitudes and demographic characteristics distinguishing one segment of a population from another. In this view, one's lifestyle is seen as the sum of one's interactions with one's environment. Lifestyle studies are a component of the broader behavioural concept called psychographics.

Lifestyle Segmentation The division of a market into subgroups based on the way the members of each group live. Particular attention is given to the activities and interests of the members of each group.

Limited-Function Wholesaler The term applied to a variety of types of wholesalers that have placed emphasis upon reducing, eliminating, or modifying certain well-established functions ordinarily performed by regular wholesalers.

Limited-Line Store A retail outlet in some respects similar to the specialty store in that it carries a limited number of product lines but has considerable depth in the lines it carries. Limited-line stores are often known by the name of the product they sell, *e.g.,* shoe store, furrier, bakery, flower shop, etc. Also known as *limited assortment stores.*

Limited-Line Strategy A marketing strategy in which the number of products in a line is restricted.

Limited Problem Solving In consumer behaviour, limited problem solving is the effort taken to understand one's needs and how best to satisfy them at a particular point in time, particularly when many possible solutions are available and possible. See also *extensive problem solving.*

Limited-Service Advertising Agency An advertising agency that specialises on a particular function such as the development of advertising messages, media planning, or media buying.

Limited-Service Wholesaler A wholesaling middleman who, like his full-service counterpart, takes title to the goods he resells, but who provides fewer services in an effort to reduce costs. Also known as a *limited-function wholesaler.* Included under this term are the following enterprises: drop shipper, wagon distributor, cash-and-carry wholesaler, rack jobber, mail-order wholesaler, and producer's cooperative.

Line Authority The authority managers need to manae the people assigned to them in order to achieve the goals for themin order to achieve the goals for which they are held responsible by higher management. It generally encompasses the authority to hire, assign direct,reward, demote, and fire, although company policy may require that some of these actions have the approval of higher line managers or managers with functional authority.

Line-Haul Rate The transportation rate commonly charged by common carriers (motor carriers). There are three basic types of line-haul rate: class rate, exception rate, and commodity rate.

Line Manager An executive in a firm having a line organi-sation, *i.e.,* a direct line of responsibility and control from top to bottom. The line manager has direct responsibility for certain operations which represent the primary mission of the organisation.

Line Structure The extension of a line of products by its manufacturer beyond the range currently produced. For example, the extension may involve products at higher and/or lower prices or products at different levels of quality.

Linear Learning Model A brand choice model that views the probability of choosing a particular brand on the current choice occasion as linearly related to the consumer's probability for choosing that brand on the previous occasion. The particular linear function applied to the previous period's choice probability depends on whether the brand of interest was actually chosen last time (in which case the "acceptance operator" is applied) or not chosen last time (causing the "rejection operator" to be applied) Kuehn 1962) In this model, the consumer's probability of selecting a particular brand on the current choice occasion is affected by the entire sequence of previous choices—hence the term learning model is appropriate.

Liquid Assets Cash, money on deposit in checking and savings accounts which is not encumbered, stocks, bonds and other securities which are readily market-able etc.

List Price The list price may be at the point of production; *i.e.*, it may be the manufacturer's price to the distributor or retailer as represented on a list or in a catalog, but more often list price is meant to indicate the retail price suggested (and sometimes advertised) by the manufacturer before any discounts or other price reductions are made.

Live Rack A storage rack designed so product automatically flows forward to the desired selection position. The typical live rack contains roller conveyors and is constructed for rear loading. The rear of the rack is elevated; gravity causes the product to flow forward.

Living Standard A measure of the possession and distribution of the material goods among members of a society.

Loading As practiced by manufacturers, loading is the sale to wholesalers and retailers of more goods than they really need. Loading places the middleman in an overstocked inventory position.

Local Advertising Advertising sponsored by local businesses who provide products or services in the local market. When conducted by stores it is frequently called retail advertising despite the fact that some retailers are national advertisers.

Local Brand Goods marketed in a particular geographical region such as bread, beer etc.

Local Rate The price charged local advertisers for space and time in local advertising media. Traditionally, newspapers, radio and television stations have charged lower rates for local advertising than for national advertising.

Logistical Marketing Function Any marketing function which involves the transportation and physical distribution of goods and services. Logistical marketing functions include storage, assorting, assembling and related tasks. See also *marketing functions*.

Logistical Resource Planning (LRP) A formal plan for controlling and monitoring overall materials logistics process. Emphasis is placed on integrating the overall objectives of the enterprise with logistical requirements.

Logo Generally one or more letters worked into some distinctive typographic or calligraphic design. Logos are often in the form of initials (representing the name of a brand or company) but the logo of the Coca-Cola Company, which is entirely written out, is probably the most famous in the world. Also known as a logotype, a signature cut or a sig cut.

Longer Combination Vehicle (LCV) A truck tractor pulling two or more trailers that exceed standard length. LCVs are restricted to certain states and highways in the United States. Considerable debate exists regarding the safety and environmental impact of LCVs.

Loop Layout A type of store layout that provides a major customer aisle that begins at the entrance, loops through the store, usually in the shape of a circle, square, or rectangle and then returns the customer to the front of the store. It is also referred to as a racetrack layout.

Loss Leader A term used in retailing to describe an item which, in order to build store traffic, is priced so low that is does not yield a profit. Loss leaders are usually well-known high-demand products which will attract customers who will, in turn, buy other merchandise at regular prices. The term price leader is also used synonymously with loss leader, particularly in the food retailing business. See also *leader pricing*.

Loss Leader Pricing The featuring of items priced below cost or at relatively low prices to attract customers to the seller's place of business

Low-Ball Price The promotion of a product, usually by telephone, at a very low price calculated to lead a customer into a store. Upon arrival at the store the customer is informed by the salesperson that management will not allow him to sell the product at the promised price and attempts to pressure the customer into buying a more expensive item.

Low-Balling A negotiation strategy in which the salesperson agrees to a low price and later raises the price claiming that circumstances changed after agreeing on the price, but before the order was placed.

Low Income Countries Countries with the lowest income per capita compared with the rest of the world. Normally the bottom decile to bottom quartile are considered low income.

Low-Involvement Goods Merchandise purchased on a regular basis which is low in cost and familiar to the customer. Low-involvement goods require little thought and planning on the part of the buyer

Low-end Merchandising A retailing strategy in which stores are located in low rent areas and in whch the merchandise is presented with few amenities. Goods are often displayed on dump tables or in cartons and bin and little sales help is available. Low-end merchandisers depend largely on low prices to attract customers and to generate the high volume necessary to make a profit. These firms are sometimes called low-margin/high-turnover stores.

Low Involvement Hierarchy In the hierarchy of effects model, the order consists of acquiring information, leading to formation of positive attitudes and then to the behavioural act of purchase or trial. Under low involvement conditions, the process is reversed such that it is after purchase, if at all, that interest and attitudes emerge.

Luxury Goods Top-of-the-line merchandise in terms of price and quality.

M

Made-to-Measure Goods which are custom made, e.g., apparel cut and fitted to a particular individual or slip covers made for a particular piece of furniture.

Mail Order House A non-store retailing organisation whose business is generated through merchandise catalogs. Customers select goods from the company's catalog and mail or telephone in their order which is subsequently filled by mail or other delivery service.

Mail Order Retailing A form of selling in which personal contact and store operations have been eliminated. The retailer contacts potential customers through the use of direct mail, catalogs, television, radio, magazines, newspapers, etc. Merchandise is described in words and pictures, customers order by mail or telephone and orders are filled by the seller through the mail or via parcel services. See also *direct mail*.

Mail Order Wholesaler A limited service wholesaler who sells merchandise by direct mail to industrial organisations, institutions, and retailers. Orders are generated from catalogs. The wholesaler distributes to potential customers, and deliveries are made by the U.S. Postal Service or by private delivery services. Also known as catalog houses.

Mail Questionnaire A questionnaire administered by mail to designated respondents under an accompanying cover letter and its return, by mail, by the respondent to the research organisation.

Maintained Item A specific item that is continuously maintained in assortments.

Maintained Markup The difference between net sales and the cost of goods sold. The maintained markup figure (expressed as a percentage of net sales) does not reflect deductions for cash discounts and workroom costs, and represents the actual markup which was achieved for the selling period. See also *gross margin.*

Maintenances and Repair Services Business services aimed at keeping the plant and equipment in good operating condition or repairing inoperable equipment. They are usually available from the original equipment manufacturer, but in many industries specialised organisations perform this function as well. Examples are window cleaning and air conditioning system repairs.

Maintenance Marketing That form of marketing appropriate to a marketplace in a full-demand condition. Monitoring the market for changes in customer demand is of primary importance in maintenance marketing.

Make-Bulk Centre A central distribution point where small shipments of goods are consolidated into larger ones and then shipped to their ultimate destination.

Makegood The rescheduling of an ad or commercial by an advertising media operator when it has been incorrectly printed, broadcast or distributed or when unavoidably canceled or preempted.

Mall In shopping centre design, the mall is composed of pedestrian walkways which may be enclosed (and thus heated and air conditioned) or open to the sky. In larger centres, the mall provides access to the anchor stores as well as the inward-facing smaller shops. See also *shopping centre.*

Mall-type Shopping Centre A grouping of stores near the centre of a shopping centre plot with parking area surrounding the store concentration on all sides. All or most of the stores face a mall or pedestrian shopping area.

Management-by-Exception Leadership A leadership style wherein sales managers intervene only when their salespeople have failed to meet their performance standards (*e.g.*, a sales quota). If sales personnel are performing as expected, the sales manager will take no action.

Management Contracting A form of joint venture in which a domestic firm provides management expertise to a foreign company. The foreign company provides the capital investment. See also *joint venture.*

Managerial Marketing Marketing as it is conducted in large organisations. Involves formal planning, establishing objectives, developing strategies for their achievement and other highly rationalised courses of action designed to reach the firm's marketing goals.

Manufacturer An organisation which, through the use of materials, machinery, and labour, produces finished products. In retailing, a manufacturer may also be referred to as a vendor, supplier, or resource.

Manufacturer Wholesaling A practice in which a manufacturer assumes the duties commonly performed by a wholesaler or other middleman within the channel of distribution.

Manufacturer's Agent An agent middleman who represents a producer or manufacturer in what is usually an exclusive territory. The manufacturer's agent may sell the products of a number of non-competing clients simultaneously and may also carry an inventory of the products he sells. Manufacturer's agents have limited control over prices and terms of sale and act as salespersons calling on industrial customers and retailers. Sometimes called a manufacturer's representative, even though this term more accurately describes a salesperson employed by a manufacturer. Also known as a sole agent. See also *selling agent.*

Manufacturer's Branch Office A wholesaling establishment from which a producer or manufacturer conducts sales activities and which includes warehousing or other storage facilities from which merchandise may be shipped to customers. These establishments are sometimes known as *captive jobbers, distribution centres, captive wholesalers*, or *district offices* See also *manufacturer's sales office.*

Manufacturer's Brand Nationally advertised goods offered for sale by their producer or maker. Manufacturer's brands often carry a distinctive and widely recognised brand name or trademark. Also known as a *national brand.*

Manufacturer's Export Representative Combination export management firms often refer to themselves as manu-facturer's export representatives whether they act as export distributors or export commission representatives.

Manufacturer's Sales Office An establishment owned and operated by a producer or manufacturer from which sales are solicited by a permanent staff of salespeople employed by the company. Sales offices carry no inventory and thus operate like drop shippers in that they have no warehouse from which goods could be shipped to the customer. See also *manufacturer's branch office.*

Manufacturer's Salesperson A salesperson employed by a manufacturer to sell products at all levels of the market (to industrial buyers, wholeselers and retailers) but not to the ultimate consumer.

Manufacturer's Store Retail outlets operated by the manufacturer of a product, *e.g.,* automobile tires, for the purpose of selling the product and providing services to the customer. Also known as *producer outlets.* See also *factory outlet.*

Margin The difference between the selling price and total unit costs for an item.

Marginal Cost The amount of money expended to produce one additional unit of a product or service.

Marginal Profit Marginal profit may be calculated by subtracting the marginal cost from the marginal revenue. For example, if the marginal revenue (the amount of money accruing from the sale of one additional unit of a product or service) is $10, and the marginal cost (the amount of money expended to produce that one additional unit of the product or service) is $9, the marginal profit is $1. On the other hand, if the marginal cost is higher than the marginal revenue, it may not be profitable to produce the extra unit of the product or service. For example, if the marginal cost is $11 and the marginal revenue is $10, the producer will lose $1 in producing an extra unit.

Marginal Propensity to Consume The fraction of each extra dollar that consumers will spend on consumption, given an extra dollar or real income.

Marginal Propensity to Save The fraction of each extra dollar that consumers will save, given an extra dollar or real income.

Marginal Revenue The amount of money accruing from the sale of one additional unit of a product or service.

Marginal Unit The last unit, *i.e.*, that unit whose acquisition or loss is under consideration.

Marginal Utility The amount of satisfaction a consumer receives from the acquisition and use of one more unit of a product.

Markdown Control Any system ensuring that every markdown taken is accounted for, so that book retail inventory may be kept in line with the actual physical inventory.

Markdown Ratio In retailing, a measure of the operating efficiency of a particular department and/or entire firm. The dollar value of all markdowns and allowances is divided by net sales in each department, according to the following formula:

$$\text{Markdown \%} = \frac{\text{\$ markdowns} + \text{\$ allowances}}{\text{\$ net sales}}$$

For example, if a retailer had originally priced ten blouses at $30 each, sold four of them at the original price, marked down the remaining six blouses to $20 and sold four more of them and gave an allowance of $5 on one of the originally priced blouses, the markdown ratio would be computed as follows:

$$\text{Markdown \%} = \frac{(\$10 \text{ markdown} \times 6) + \$5 \text{ allowance}}{(\$30 \times 4) + (\$20 \times 4)}$$

$$= \frac{\$65}{\$200}$$

$$= .325$$

The result is then multiplied by 100, which gives us a total markdown ratio of 32.5%.

Market (1) The physical place where goods and services are bought and sold, *e.g.*, a farmer's market where growers sell their produce to the public. (2) The physical place where a substantial number of suppliers have established their businesses in an effort to make themselves readily available to retail buyers, *e.g.*, the garment centre in New York City where hundreds of apparel manufacturers maintain showrooms. (3) The aggregate demand for certain products or services, *i.e.*, all the actual or potential customers who have the means to purchase the product or service and who actually have access to it should they make a decision to buy.

Market Analysis The collection and evaluation of data on the potential markets for a firm's products and/or services in an attempt to determine which segments may offer opportunities for profitable entry and expansion. Market analysis encompasses much of what is regarded as marketing research with an emphasis on demographic, geographic and socio-economic market segmentation.

Market Attractiveness-Competitive Position Matrix In this matrix, each business unit or product is classified jointly by market attractiveness and the strength of the competitive position. The market attractiveness-competitive position matrix is a multifactor portfolio model developed jointly by McKinsey and General Electric (GE) with each dimension of the matrix being based on mutiple factors. It is sometimes called a nine-block matrix because each of the two dimensions is divided into three levels.

Market Basket Pricing A pricing straegy most commonly found in supermarkets in which some items (generally those about which the consumer is most price-conscious) are priced low to create the impression of a bargain. Other less familiar items are then given a high compensating markup.

Market Build-up Method A forecasting technique in which information from a number of market segments is gathered, separately analysed and then added together to form a more or less complete picture of the marketing environment for the purpose of forecasting sales.

Market Coverage The number of available outlets in a given line of retail or wholesale trade, relative to a saturation level, that are selling a manufacturer's brand in a given market area. Manufacturers typically follow one of three forms of market coverage: exclusive distribution, intensive distribution or selective distribution.

Market Defense The strategic moves that attempt to minimise or deter threatening actions by existing or potential competitors. Strategic moves can deter all or some of the prospective challengers by making the profit prospects so unattractive and risky that market share gains are not worth pursuing. Deterrence strategies include the following; (1) signaling intentions to defend, (2) foreclosing avenues for attack by building barriers to entry or mobility, (3) increasing entry costs or investments and (4) reducing market attractiveness by lowering prices. If challengers cannot be deterred, then the purpose of market defense is to contain challengers' moves and minimise the damage.

Market Demand The total volume of a given product or service bought by a specific group of customers in a specified market area, during a specific time period.

Market Development A strategy in which a firm develops new markets for its products or in which the firm develops alternative uses for its products. The objective is to increase sales.

Market Economy An economic system in which, at least theoretically, free enterprise is the operating principle, *i.e.,* one in which the forces of supply and demand are given free reign to determine the allocation of resources.

Market Evolution The market (or industry) life cycles describe the evolution of the market. These cycles have a similar shape to the product life cycle and similarly, have a number of distinct stages: (1) *embryonic*—the product class and industry definitions are virtually synonymous, diffusion rates rare gradual and there is considerable uncertainty about the product; (2) *growth* the industry structure develops, the introduction of new product classes becomes easier as consumers become more knowledgeable, and the channels facilitate the marketing of new product classes established; and (3) *maturity*—an established infrastructure facilitates rapid introduction and diffusion of new product variants or product classes, competitors jockey for position, and older products have to make adjustments to protect their declining position.

Market Factor A variable in the marketing environment which may affect demand for a product or service. For example, the number of teenagers will a affect the sale of phonograph records, or high interest rates will affect the sale of new homes.

Market Factor Analysis Market factors are variables in the marketing environment. When market factors can be correlated with sales trends, the resulting analysis may be used to forecast future sales. See also *direct derivation* and *correlation analysis*.

Market Factor Index When a number of market factors are taken together, analysed, and expressed in relation to a base number, a market factor index has been created. Such an index is used in the projection of future sales trends.

Market Fit In product marketing, market fit refers to the degree to which a new product is suited to a company's present market, i.e., the degree to which the new product is likely to appeal to the company's existing customers.

Market Fragmentation The emergence of new market segments with distinct needs and requirements out of previously homogenous segments. These new segments limit the usefulness of mass marketing and erode brand loyalty.

Market Grid A device employed in market segmentation studies in which a total market is subdivided in an effort to more precisely target potential customers. The information is frequently presented in the form of a grid. See also *Boston Consulting Group Matrix*.

Market Growth Rate The annual growth or decline of a market, either at preset or as forecast. The market growth rate is most often expressed as a percentage. In the growth/share matrix, the market growth rate represents the vertical axis of the graph. See also **Boston Consulting Group Matrix**.

Market Index A mathematical expression that combines two or more market factors into a numerical index, typically by forming a linear combination of the factors in which the weights assigned each factor reflect their relative importance in affecting demand for a product or products.

Market Manager Within an organisation, a person assigned responsibility for overseeing all functional activities (*e.g.*, manufacturing, pricing, service) that relate to a particular market (customer group or product application). The market manager is to a market what a product manager is to a product, and delineating their respective roles in industrial firms is difficult.

Market Minimum The rate of sales for a product or service which would be achieved without any demand stimulating expenditures such as advertising or promotion.

Market News Specific information about conditions in the marketplace having àn immediate bearing on the conduct of business, *e.g.*, news of a crop failure quickly effects commodity traders.

Market Opportunity Analysis The analysis and evaluation of probable future situations by a variety of techniques to identify market opportunities that a company can profitably cultivate. It is part of the strategic analysis of the company's strengths, weaknesses, opportunities, and threats.

Market Opportunity Index The use of relevant criteria by a company to rank future o opportunities that have been identified and facilitate the selection of the most promising opportunities.

Market Penetration Pricing A market strategy in which goods are priced low enough to have immediate wide appeal in the marketplace. The object of market penetration pricing is to quickly capture a significant share of the market.

Market Penetration Strategy A move by management to increase its market share held by current products in currently serviced markets. Market share may be increased by some combination of (1) attracting users of competitive brands, (2) persuading current users to increase usage, or (3) attracting nonusers of the product category.

Market Period In the marketing process, that period from the time a product is manufactured (or a commodity is produced) until the time it is sold. During this period costs are fixed and the amount of product does not vary. Price will be determined by current demand.

Market Planning The process by which a firm identifies its customers and determines their needs. Market planning is a part of the marketing planning effort together with such activities as sales forecasting, sales planning, and promotion budgeting. Included in market planning are such factors as product development, quality control, packaging, shipping, pricing, advertising, sales force management, and customer service. See also *marketing planning.*

Market Positioning Positioning refers to the customer's perceptions of the place a product or brand occupies in a market segment. In some markets, a position is achieved by associating the benefits of a brand with the needs or life style of the segments. More often, positioning involves the differentiation of the company's offering from the competition by making or implying a comparison in terms of specific attributes.

Market Positioning Those efforts aimed at establishing a product or service in a particular niche or segment of the marketplace. Market positioning strategy usually includes those promotional activities which differentiate the product from competitors and which vividly establish the product's image in the minds of potential customers. Also known as *positioning, product positioning*, or target positioning. See also *target market and brand position.*

Market Potential Represents both the realised and unrealised total "capacity to buy" existing in a market or segment of a market. The calculation includes all the goods or services offered by all the sellers competing in the particular market over a specific period of time. See also *sales potential* and *market share.*

Market Price A price determined by supply and demand in the marketplace. Prices for farm products are almost always set in this way.

Market Pricing The determination of selling price for a product or service by the unrestricted forces of supply and demand. The seller has little or no control over the price his goods or services will fetch in the marketplace.

Market Research The systematic gathering, recording and analysing of data with respect to a particular market, where market refers to a specific customer group in a specific geographic area.

Market Rollout The introduction of a new product into a market sequentially. The rollout may be by geographical areas, by applications or uses, or by individual customers. Over time, depending on the speed of the rollout, the entire market is covered.

Market Segment A subdivision of a population (commonly ultimate consumers), the members of which share similar identifiable characteristics, *e.g.*, age, wealth, style, education level, marital status, sexual orientation, etc. A firm may develop different marketing programmes for each segment of its target market.

Market Segmentation The subdivision of a population (frequently ultimate consumers) into smaller parts or demand segments, having similar characteristics. These smaller parts will, presumably, exhibit homogenous responses to various marketing programmes. See also *differentiated marketing*.

Market Share The part of a total market controlled by one firm. It is expressed as the firm's sales or the sales of a particular product or line of products, in relation to total industry sales and in commonly computed as a percentage. Also known as *brand share*. See also *market potential* and *sales potential*.

Market Share Analysis An analysis of a firm's sales which takes into account the activities of a firm's competitors and views the company as a participant in the general market-place. Market share analysis is a more precise measure of performance than sales volume analysis.

Market Share Objective A benchmark which represents that portion of a market a company wishes to capture.

Market Stretching A strategy employed in marketing products which have reached the maturity stage in their life cycle. Sales are maintained at present levels or at times, expanded through such means as technical improvement and more effective marketing research.

Market Target Decision Analysis A system used to identify target markets for goods and services through an analysis of the various segments which marke-up the total market. Frequently the information is presented in the form of a grid to facilitate decision making.

Market Targeting Those strategic decision-making activities which precede both the selection of a target market and the market positioning of a product. Market targeting enables the organisation to focus its resources on the achievement of specific goals. Making a choice between targeting the total market or limiting market efforts to one or more specific segments is a significant market targeting activity. Also known as *target marketing*. See also *target market*.

Market Test A controlled experiment, done in a limited but carefully selected sector of the marketplace, whose aim is to predict the sales or profit consequences, either in absolute or relative terms, of one or more proposed marketing actions.

Market Testing A marketing research technique in which a new product or service is introduced, usually in a limited, carefully selected geographic area (a test. market), in an effort to predict its performance in the marketplace. Market testing also provides management with the opportunity to correct production problems before a total market commitment has been made. Also called test marketing and product testing.

Market Value The prevailing price at which a product can be expected to sell in a given market. See also *value* and *price*.

Marketer All organisations and individuals engaged in business may be regarded as marketers in that they are all, in one way or another, selling something to somebody. In addition, many nonbusiness organisations engage in what must be regarded as marketing activities and thus must be classified as marketers.

Marketing Broadly constructed, marketing is a part of an economic process concerned with the supply of and demand for goods, services, and ideas in the society at large. It includes those activities which facilitate the exchange of goods and services as they move from production to the industrial user or ultimate consumer.

Marketing-as-Usual Approach to Shortages An approach to actual or anticipated shortages of the raw materials required for production. When companies feel they cannot produce enough goods to meet customer demand, they may assume that such shortages are temporary and continue to produce the same quantities of their products and sell to the same customers. The firm adopting this approach continues to spend the same amount on advertising, sales force, marketing research, etc., as it did prior to the shortage. Minor changes may be made in the advertising message and prices may rise somewhat to cover cost increases, but other marketing factors remain unchanged.

Marketing Audit A systematic, comprehensive evaluation of a firm's marketing, philosophy, objectives, and strategy with a view toward implementing corrective action if deemed appropriate. The audit may be applied to on-going marketing programs (a control audit) in an effort to determine their effectiveness or to completed programmes (a review audit) in an effort to evaluate their results.

Marketing Budget A financial plan, often based on projected sales (or past sales), used as a basis for allocating money to cover marketing costs over a period in the future. The marketing budget includes projected costs for administration and materials, marketing research, advertising and sales promotion and other marketing functions. In many respects, the marketing budget is a projected income statement for the particular marketing functions in question.

Marketing Channel A set of institutions necessary to transfer the title to goods and to move goods from the point of production to the point of consumption and as such, which consists of all the institutions and all the marketing activities in the marketing process.

Marketing Communication All those messages transmitted from sender to receiver which involve the buyer-seller relationship. In addition to formal promotional messages, informal nonsystematic communication such as word-of-mouth is also included.

Marketing Company Era A stage in the evolution of marketing (from roughly the mid-1960s to the present) during which marketing departments took on dominant roles in many manufacturing organisations.

Marketing Conduct A legal view of marketers' decisions on marketing mix variables and the process by which they make these decisions.

Marketing Cost Analysis An analysis of the firm's marketing operations in terms of the cost of such activities as selling, advertising, transportation, storage, delivery, etc. An effort is then made to correlate these tools with the profitability of various products, customer groups, territories, etc. The objective of the analysis is to determine the efficiency of the firm's marketing efforts. See also *contribution-margin approach to cost analysis and full-cost approach to cost analysis.*

Marketing Department Era A stage in the evolution of marketing during which the marketing department in a firm, although still subordinate to production and sales, is beginning to influence the development of the company marketing programme.

Marketing Dynamics Changes in a firm's marketing mix determined by changes in the external environment. Most marketing dynamics are controllable by the organisation as contrasted to environmental dynamics which are largely out of the firm's control.

Marketing Environment That complex of legal, political, economic and social influences which surrounds a firm and affects its marketing activities. A firm may be seen as having two distinct marketing environments: (1) an internal, or micro-environment over which it has a degree of control, and (2) an external, or macro-environment which is largely beyond its control.

Marketing Ethics Those standards, values, moral principles, etc.

which govern the marketer's behaviour in the marketplace.

Marketing Functions Those activities which form the basis for marketing. They include product and planning development, financing, pricing, promotion (including advertising and personal selling), transportation, storage, distribution etc. Marketing research, which is sometimes regarded as a support function, may also be included. Marketing functions are also known as marketing variables and marketing instruments.

Marketing Geography The field of study that analyses the spatial characteristics of marketing activities: the consumers and the distribution network.

Marketing Information System (MIS) A marketing information system is a complex of persons, procedures, and equipment which, in concert, collect information relevant to marketing decision-making. It is more broadly based than marketing research in that the system gathers data from within the firm as well as externally in the marketing environment. The system provides for the evaluation of the collected data to determine its usefulness to the executives responsible for planning the firm's marketing strategy. See also *decision support system (DSS)*.

Marketing Institutions The organisations which make up the marketing system. Marketing institutions include manufacturers and producers, middlemen (wholesalers, retailers, etc.), and a wide variety of facilitating organisations such as trucking firms, railroads, warehouse facilities, advertising agencies, etc.

Marketing Intelligence System The network of outside information sources through which marketing executives collect data useful in making marketing decisions.

Marketing Manager, Corporate Level Executive Some large divisionalised companies have a corporate marketing vice president who performs a staff role designated by the corporate chief executive officer. In general, the principal role is to view marketing problems and opportunities from a broader perspective than that of division management. It may also include specific functions such as providing marketing counsel to corporate management, monitoring divisional marketing performance, critiquing divisional marketing plans, evaluating potential acquisitions, assisting with or directing the corporate strategic planning function, searching for new product and business opportunities outside of present division charters, assisting with setting research and development priorities, and administering the corporate advertising and/or corporate image programmes. This position usually reports to the corporate chief executive.

Marketing Manager Organisation System A company organisation for product management in which a number of areas including product planning, advertising and sales promotion report to a single manager.

Marketing Mix Those marketing variables (such as product planning, pricing, promotion, and distribution channel selection) which when blended together form a marketing strategy designed to satisfy the firm's customers.

Marketing Mix Models The determination of an optimal marketing mix is often aided by models that take into account the market response to the various marketing mix elements and their interactions. These models include econometric market response models to the marketing mix variables of the firm (and its competitors) as well as specialised models such as Advisor and Brabdaud, microsimulation models, various optimisation models, and customised applications of the analytic hierarchy process and other resource allocation models.

Marketing (Only) Division This division contains the usual marketing functions, including sales, but its products are supplied by a centralised production operation that supplies two or more marketing divisions. When standardised products can be mass produced by a centralised facility, economies of scale are the usual result.

Marketing Organisation An organisational arrangement of formal and informal relationships which form a system through which marketing personnel execute a firm's marketing plans.

Marketing Plan The formal written document which puts the decisions reached during the marketing planning process into action. The marketing plan sets forth those activities which will carry for ward the firm's marketing programme and which will enable the firm to reach its ultimate goals.

Marketing Programme The overall plan maintained by a firm which blends all its strategic plans. The marketing programme is the responsibility of the entire firm, not just one division. When the various plans are quite different, there is little concern for how they all fit together. When they are similar, however, the same sales force may have to carry out several plans. Consideration is always given to the way each plan competes for the firm's limited financial resources. See also *strategic planning*.

Marketing Public Relations Publicity activities intended to encourage product purchase and consumer satisfaction.

Marketing Research The systematic collection of information from sources outside the business or research organisation. Gathered data is subsequently analysed to determine its usefulness in marketing decision-making. In 1986 the American Marketing Association further elaborated on the definition: "Marketing research is the function which links the consumer, customer, and public to the marketer through information—information used to identify and define marketing opportunities and problems; generate, refine, and evaluate marketing actions; monitor marketing performance; and improve understanding of marketing as a process.

Marketing Services Sometimes called customer services, this is an all-inclusive term that covers different sets of functions for different companies. Historically it has included some or all of the functions needed to service channel intermediaries and/or end customers, such as inventory planning and control; order processing, shipping, and delivery information; product installation, maintenance, repair, replacement and warranty administration; and answering customer inquiries. Organisationally most of these services are provided by functional departments other than marketing. They may or may not be coordinated by a marketing service manager or customer service manager reporting to the marketing manager. Comment: While the above named services are basic to providing marketing services to channels of distribution and customers, another use of the term applies to a centralised department that provides in house services to company divisions.

Marketing Services Department A unit in a multi-division company that performs marketing functions for divisions that can be performed better or at less cost when carried out centrally. Although the functions of this unit may vary by company, they may include some or all of the following: media planning, coordination of media buying, sales promotion planning and counselling, providing sales promotion materials, package design, control of advertising production costs, advertising research, creative services and advertising claims substantiation. For small divisions with limited personnel, the marketing services department may serve as their advertising, sales promotion, product publicity or marketing research department.

Marketing Services Director This person manages the marketing services department and may report to a corporate executive, group executive or to the manager of a major division. Irrespective of the reporting level, this manager provides the services for all divisions that require them.

Marketing Strategy The logical, comprehensive plan of action through which a firm intends to reach its objectives in the marketplace. Marketing strategy is primarily concerned with the implementation of company policy and with those marketing activities through which the company's goals are to be achieved.

Marketplace In its broadest context marketplace refers to the marketing environment. For a more restricted definition. See *market*

Markup Percentage The difference between cost and retail, expressed either as a percentage of cost or commonly, as a percentage of retail.

Markup Table A tabulation giving markup percentages on cost price with the corresponding markup percentage on retail price.

Mass Market The mass market does not include "everyone." East organisation selling to the mass market targets a large and widely dispersed (but clearly defined) group of consumers who are its potential customers. See also *mass marketing.*

Mass Merchandising The retailing, on a very large scale, of goods (largely staples) at prices lower than those commonly found in department and specialty stores. Mass merchandising is characterised by: (1) an emphasis on products whose market is not highly segmented, (2) customers who are willing to sacrifice sales assistance and store services in return for lower prices, (3) high volume and a rapid stock turnover rate, and (4) a very highly competitive marketplace.

Mass Promotion Sales promotion activities concentrated at a particular time, *e.g.,* Christmas season.

Matching Concept In accounting, the matching of costs and revenue in an effort to relate expenses to the income they helped to produce; *i.e.,* to determine a firm's net income for a given period, usually one year.

Materialism The evaluation of the self in terms of how much is owned or how much can be consumed. The importance that people attach to worldly possessions.

Materials Management Logistic activities concerned with the movement of production materials from their place of origin to the site of manufacture and with the movement of semi-finished products within the manufacturing facility.

Materials Requirement Planning (MRP) A technique used in production management to control inventory and plan production steps. The goal of MRP is to provide the correct materials for production at the correct time, while avoiding unnecessary stockpiling. Computer programmes are used to determine when materials are needed, when they should be ordered and when they should be delivered.

Matrix Organisation A type of business organisation in which functional managers are often responsible for activities such as advertising and other functions which require special expertise for all products, while product (or brand) managers are responsible for marketing their particular products, brands, or product lines. These roles may sometimes overlap and even conflict.

Maturity Stage That stage of the product life cycle in which demand levels off and profits begin to decline. Levels of competition have increased to the point where a shake-out is taking place in the market. See also *product life cycle (PLC)* and *retail life cycle*.

Maturity Stage of Product Life Cycle The third Stage of the product life cycle, in which initial rapid growth is over and sales level off (though there may be intermitted surges and declines over the years before final decline sets in). During the maturity stage price competition becomes very strong, similar products are made available by competition, the adoption process is mostly over and profits fall.

Maximum Operating Stock The largest quantity of inventory that should ever be on hand during normal operating conditions, usually at the stock keeping unit level. It consists of merchandise to sell during the buying period, the cushion and the basic low stock.

Maximum System of Stock Control The system of setting, for each item of staple merchandise carried, an amount large enough to take care of probable demands of customers and of reordering, periodically, the difference between the actual stock and the maximum set.

McGuire-Keogh Fair Trade Enabling Act (1952) This act declared that exemption of resale price maintenance agreements from antitrust laws as provided under the Miller-Tydings Resale Price Maintenance Act would be extended to non-signer agreements (whereby all dealers are bound to the contract if only one signs) in states that have non-signer clauses in their fair trade statutes.

Means Ends Chain A simple knowledge structure that organises consumers' product knowledge by linking product attributes to the more abstract consequences and finally to high-level consumer values.

Measurement A rule for assigning numbers to objects to represent quantities of attributes.

Media Buying The advertising agency function that involves negotiating with the salespeople of various advertising media in order to obtain needed time and space for advertising agency clients at the most favourable prices.

Media Buying Service An organisation that specialises in buying media time and space for advertisers Some media buying services also engage in media planning activities for their clients.

Media Representative A person or a company that specialises in selling space or time in advertising vehicles to advertisers and advertising agencies.

Media Schedule A specific Schedule showing the media vehicles (including dates, positions in the publication or time of day and size of ad space or duration of commercials) to be used during an advertising campaign.

Media Selection Strategy Strategy employed in choosing the appropriate advertising media. An effort is made to choose media which will effectively reach the target audience and to establish a schedule appropriate to the advertising goals.

Media Vehicle A specific newspaper, magazine, radio station, television programme, outdoor advertising location, edition of Yellow Pages, etc., that can be employed to carry advertisements or commercials. For example, The *New Yorker Magazine* is a media vehicle in the magazine category of advertising media.

Megamarketing Defined by Philip Kotler (Kellog Graduate School of Management, Northwestern University) as "the strategically coordinated application of economic, psychological, political and public relations skills to gain the cooperation of a number of parties in order to enter and/or operate in a given market." Kotler adds power and public relations to the four Ps of the marketing mix.

Memorandum Purchase and Dating This indicates that merchandise shipped to a buyer is returnable within a specified period of time. Payment for goods kept longer or sold need not be made until this time, though legal title usually transfers at the time of shipment.

Memorandum Terms A special form of indcfinite future dating under which the title of the merchandise passes to the buyer and the buyer assumes all risk of ownership.

Mercantile Credit Credit at the trade level, *i.e.,* credit extended by manufacturers or wholesalers to other channel members such as retailers. Such credit avoids the need for COD shipments or for limiting business to a cash-and-carry basis.

Mercantile Trade Credit The credit one businessperson extends to another when selling goods on time for resale or commercial use.

Mercantilism A set of economic policies designed to give a country an advantage by developing a favourable balance of trade, encouraging agriculture and manufacturing, creating a merchant marine, and establishing foreign trading monopolies.

Merchandise Budget A statement prepared by management containing planned dollar commitments for all the components of the merchandise plan (sales, reductions, stocks, margins, and purchases) for a seasonal period.

Merchandise Classification A subdivision of a selling department; a dissection of a department's inventory, purchase, and/or sales figures for the purpose of closer control.

Merchandise Control The determination and direction of merchandising activities, both in terms of dollars (dollar control) and in terms of units (unit merchandiser control).

Merchandise Cost The billed cost of merchandise less any applicable trade discounts or quantity discounts, plus inbound transportation costs if paid by the purchaser.

Merchandise Line A group of products closely related because they are intended for the same end use, are sold to the same customer group, or fall within a given price range.

Merchandise Management The analysis, planning, acquisition, promotion and control of merchandise sold by a retailer.

Merchandise Mix The breadth and depth of the merchandise inventory carried by retail establishments.

Merchandise Plan A plan, generally for department stores, for a six-month period, by months, in which the chief elements enter into gross profit. The essential are sales, markdowns, retail stocks at the first of each month, purchases, and markup percentages. Inventory short-ages, cash discounts and alteration costs may also be budgeted.

Merchandising The planning involved in marketing the right merchandise at the right place at the right time in the right quantity at the right price. More specifically, it is the buying and selling of appropriate goods coupled with the accurate targeting of consumers for the ultimate purpose of making a profit, or more simply, matching the goods to market requirements.

Merchant Middleman A middleman who buys the goods outright and takes title to them.

Merchant Wholesalers The wholesalers who take title to the products they sell.

Mere Exposure Effect The repeated exposure to an object resulting in a more positive attitude toward the object, the mere exposure to the object is believed to produce the more positive attitude.

Merger The joining together of two or more independent business organisations into a single entity.

Message Words and symbols (in a written or oral form) which constitute an intelligible communication. In marketing, messages are frequently transmitted through the media, *i.e.*, radio, television, newspapers, magazines, etc. See also *advertising message*.

Message Argument A statement of the customer benefit and the specific product performance characteristic that delivers that benefit.

Micro-Environment The set of forces close to an organisation that have direct impact on its ability to serve its customers. The microenvironment includes channel member organisations, competitors, customer markets, publics, and the capabilities of the organisation itself.

Micro-Marketing Marketing as seen from its narrow perspective, *i.e.*, at the level of individual sellers and buyers.

Micro-Segmentation A strategy employed in industrial marketing in which market potential for products or services is established by gathering information about the characteristics of potential customers, often through the personal experience of salespeople.

Middleman A broad term applied to individuals or firms who act as marketing intermediaries between producers and manufacturers on the one hand and the end user on the other. They may be wholesaling middlemen (which includes wholesalers, agents and brokers) or they may be retailers. Middlemen perform a number of functions which facilitate the transfer of goods in the distribution system. See also *wholesaling middleman, wholesaler, agent middleman*, and *retailer*.

Military Buying The purchase of goods and services by the Defence Department largely through the Defence Logistics Agency, the General Services Administration and the three military departments: Army, Navy and Air Force.

Milking A strategy in which a company prices an established product above the level which would ordinarily be justified by production costs and competitive conditions in the marketplace. Companies employing this strategy are cashing in on consumer brand loyalty in an effort to increase short-term profits. Sometimes called harvesting.

Miller-Tydings Act (1937) Federal legislation which permitted state governments to enact fair trade or resale price maintenance laws. The Act was declared unconstitutional by the U.S. Supreme Court in 1951, and the McGuire Act (1952) reinstated the legality of the nonsigner clause. See also *resale price maintenance*.

Minimum and Maximum System of Stock Control A system whereby for each item of staple merchandise carried, a minimum quantity of inventory is established which, when reached, indicates a need to reorder. Maximum stock consists of the minimum and the predetermined reorder quantity.

Minimum Charge In most transportation tariffs, the minimum charge is the lowest price at which a carrier will accept a shipment for delivery. A minimum charge reflects the fixed cost component of the transportation carrier's cost of doing business and is often used as an incentive to encourage the shipper to consolidate multiple shipments.

Minimum Order The smallest unit of sales permitted by a manufacturer or wholesaler. It may be expressed in units, as a dollar amount or, sometimes, as a weight.

MIS See *marketing Information System (MIS)* and *management information system (MIS)*

Mismarketing Failed Marketing efforts generally as a result of faulty information and poor decision making.

Misredemption The improper claiming of price savings, premiums, prizes, or other sales promotion rewards by not following the stated rules, after the specified time period or by persons not eligible for the incentive.

Mission Identity The company perceived by its customers in terms of its goals. Sometimes referred to as company image, mission identity is more accurately the sense of purpose which keeps a firm on track.

Mission Statement A detailed statement of the goals and objectives of an organisation calculated to provide the members of the organisation with a sense of direction.

Missionary Salesperson A manufacturer's representative who assists the middlemen customers of the firm (usually wholesalers and retailers) by demonstrating the manufacturer's products to salespersons and customers, arranging displays, planning advertising programmes and other promotions, etc. The missionary salesperson does not usually engage directly in selling activities. In the health-care field, these sales representatives are called *retailers*.

Mixed Brand Strategy A marketing strategy in which a manufacturer produces a number of similar products under different brand names or in which a middleman or retailer sells products under different brand names, or in which a middleman or retailer sells products under dealer or generic names as well as under manufacturer names.

Mixed Bundling The practice of offering for sale two or more products or services either at individual prices or for "bundle" is usually less than the sum of the individual prices.

Mixed Merchandising See *scrambled merchandising.*

Mixed-Use Development (MXD) The shopping centres that have various types of non-retail uses such as office towers, hotels, residential complexes, civic centres and convention complexes on top of or attached to the shopping area.

Model (1) In management science, a set of variables and their interrelationships designed to represent a real system or process. Such models are developed by management scientists (also called *operations researchers*) in order to gain insight into the problem, control over the problem or the ability to predict the outcome of the problem. In marketing, models are used for forecasting new product sales (where no historical data is available), site selection, sales-call planning, media mix, and budgeting. (2) A sample, usually handmade, which serves as the prototype for a manufactured product. (3) A person who wears clothes for the purpose of displaying them.

Model Stock Approach to Space Allocation A method of determining space allocation for departments in a retail store. It is based upon an analysis of an ideal stock necessary to achieve projected sales volume, of how much stock should be displayed versus how much should be kept in reserve space, of how much physical space will be required to display the merchandise, and of how much physical space will be needed for any service requirements.

Model Stock List An assortment of fashion merchandise indicating in very general terms (product lines, colours and size distribution) what should be carried in a particular merchandise category.

Model Stock Plan An outline of the composition of an ideal stock in terms of general characteristics or assortment factors, usually with optimum quantities indicated in an amount that reflects balance in relation to expected sales.

Model System The part of a decision support system that includes all the routines that allow the user to manipulate the data so as to conduct the kind of analysis the individual desires.

Modified Break—Even Analysis A form of break-even analysis in which the level of demand for a product is analysed at various levels in an effort to determine the price-quantity mix which would maximise profits. Such analysis recognises that profit does not necessarily increase as quantity sold increases, as increased sales are frequently the result of lowered prices.

Modified Rebuy An industrial buying situation in which some adjustments have been made in the specifications or price of the product to be ordered, thus making the process somewhat more complex than a straight rebuy. See also *new task buying* and *straight rebuy.*

Monitoring Skills The skills used by marketing managers to develop and manage a system of controls and provide feedback on the results of marketing activities. These controls may be annual-plan controls, profitability controls, and/or strategic controls. See also *allocating skills, organising skills* and *interacting skills.*

Monopolist A business organisation operating in a competition-free environment.

Monopoly 1. (environments definition) A market situation where one firm a markets all the goods or services and can influence price. 2. (economic definition) The complete control of an economic good for which there is no substitute.

Monopsonist A buyer operating in a market in which there are no other buyers.

Monopsony A market condition in which there is only one buyer.

Montage Format A form of advertising found in the print media and on television in which a number of pictures or images are juxtaposed in such a way that an overall impression is created in the mind of the viewer.

Mores The cultural norms that specify behaviour of vital importance to society and embody its basic moral values. The prohibition against bigamy or child abandonment in some cultures are examples. Mores often are codified into law such that legal as well as social sanctions can be applied to assure confirmity. In comparison, folkways are cultural norms that specify behaviour not vital to the welfare of the groups and the means of enforcement are not clearly defined (according to Krench, Crutchfield and Ballachov). For example, folkways specify that a student shall wear specifically defined clothes on campus. If the student does not, the student may be considered a boor or a nerd, but this nonconfirmity is not regarded as having important consequences for the group. The punishment for nonconfirmity is informal, mild and variable.

Most Favoured Nation (MFN) Principle The principle whereby each country agrees to extend all countries the most favourable terms that it negotiates with any country.

Motivation The positive or negative needs, goals, desires, and forces that impel an individual toward or away from certain actions, activities, objects or conditions. It is the needs and wants of the individual, the driving force, guided by cognitions, behind the behaviour to purchase, approach or avoid products and ideas and things.

Motivation Research A segment of marketing research in which the principles of behavioural science are applied to marketing problems in an attempt to explain why consumers behave in the marketplace as they do. Motivation research is primarily concerned with people's feelings and attitudes and how they affect the individual's buying behaviour. Sometimes abbreviated MR.

Moving Average In time series analysis, the moving average is the basis upon which predictions are made contingent upon the average outcomes of experiences over two or more recent time periods. Moving average for sales, for example, assumes that the sales figures for the next period will be the average of the sales figures for a given number of previous time periods. Thus, if a firm's cigarette sales for four previous months were 6,000, 5,000 7,000 and 7,500 cartons, respectively, the four-month moving average would be the sum of the sales (25,500) divided by 4, or 6,375 cartons.

Multiattribute Attitude Models These models are designed to predict attitudes toward objects (such as brands) based on consumers' evaluations of product attributes or expected consequences

Multiattribute Models of Attitudes The several theories of attitudes, such as Fishbein's learning theory of attitudes, with the basic assumption that attitudes are based upon the individual's perceptions of the attributes of the choice alternatives. These models usually include the idea that the individual assigns importance weights to each attribute and arrives at an overall evaluation on the basis of these weighted attributes

Multibusiness Organisation This is a corporation engaged in more than one class of business. Each business may be organised as a division of the corporation or as a subsidiary company. Comment: Organisationally, there may be no difference in the way a division and a subsidiary are viewed by corporate management even though the subsidiary is a separate legal entity controlled by the parent corporation through majority ownership or full ownership.

Multichotomous Question A fixed alternative question containing three or more alternatives in which respondents are asked to choose the alternative that most closely corresponds to their position on the subject.

Multidimensional Scaling (MS) A marketing research technique in which the perceptions and attitudes of respondents are geometrically represented. The information presented in this manner is subsequently analysed in an effort to aid managers in solving marketing problems, *e.g.*, determining how consumers perceive a brand or product category.

Multidomestic Strategy A strategy that enables individual subsidiaries of a multinational firm to compete independently in different domestic markets. The multi-national headquarters coordinates financial controls and some marketing policy, and may centralise some R&D and component production. Each subsidiary behaves like a strategic business unit that is expected to contribute earnings and growth proportionate to the market opportunity.

Multilevel Selling 1. A sales approach that involves using company employees at multiple levels in the firm's hierarchy to call on similar levels in the account. For example, the Vice President of Sales would call on the Vice President of Purchasing. 2. A strategy used by direct selling companies to have independent agents serve as distributors and resell merchandise to other agents who eventually make sales to consumers.

Multinational Corporation (MNC) A firm which conducts a significant proportion of its business in two or more countries and which almost always has a direct investment in the countries in which it operates. Multinational corporations typically perform their functions in global context.

Multinational Marketing Marketing efforts in more than one foreign country which may include the operation of production and distribution facilities and the employment of local labour and management personnel.

Multinational Marketing Information System (MMIS) A system which organises and analyses data from within the multinational corporation and from its various marketing environments and then presents the organisation's managers with the information they need to make marketing decisions. The overall system generally has a separate subsystem for each country in which the corporation operates.

Multiple Basing-Point Pricing System In a multiple basing-point pricing system, several locations are designated as basing points. The choice of a basing point is the point that yields the lowest delivered cost to the buyer.

Multiple Branding A marketing strategy in which a firm gives each item in a line of products a separate brand name as, for example, a large cereal manufacturer may market several dry breakfast foods under different brand names as part of an effort to reach various segments of the market and to dominate supermarket shelf space.

Multiple Channels The use of a combination of channels in selling a product or service to reach different and isolated target markets with different demands for service outputs.

Multiple Correlation In statistical analysis, the comparison of the effect of several independent variables on a single dependent variable. Each independent variable is carefully weighted to determine its effect.

Multiple-Line Representative A salesperson carrying the lines of several manufacturers.

Multiple Packaging The packaging together of two or more items (men's underwear, cans of beer, packages of chewing gum etc.) as a means of encouraging multiple purchases on the part of the consumer.

Multiple Pricing (1) The practice of offering more than one unit at a given price, *e.g.*, 3 for $1, with the intention of (a) creating the impression that the goods are being sold at a bargain price, thus (b) increasing the number sold per transaction. (2) The term is also applied to the practice frequently found in supermarkets of inadvertently marking an item with two or more prices.

Multiple Purchasing The strategy of dividing annual purchasing requirements of a good or service among more than one supplier. This is done to create a more competitive environment among suppliers and to reduce the buying firm's dependence on a single source of supply. This is also called multiple sourcing.

Multiple Purpose Trip A key concept in central place theory that argues that consumers prefer to visit more than one store per trip, generating positive externalities for neighbouring stores.

Multiple-Unit Packaging The practice of putting two or more finished packages of a product into a larger packaged unit (such as six-pack of soda). The new wrap may vary from a band to a larger completely closed container. Multiple packaging may be temporary, related to a promotional programme.

Multiple-Unit Pricing 1. (retailing definition) The combination of several like products as a unit of one, involving at least a slightly different markup than is obtained when the items are sold separately. 2. (pricing definition) The practice of pricing several items as a single unit.

Multiple-Zone Pricing System In a multiple-zone pricing system, delivered prices are uniform within two or more zones.

Multiplicative Competitive Interaction (MCI) Model An attraction model for explaining and predicting market share. In an MCI model each brand's attractiveness is modeled as a multiplicative function of some explanatory variables (*e.g.*, brand attributes). Nakanishi and Cooper (1974) show how such a nonlinear model can be estimated by least squares regression techniques.

Multistage Pricing A planning strategy in which a broad price policy is developed by integrating a series of individual pricing decisions into a coherent price framework for the firm. A number of steps are taken in sequence beginning with the selection of a target market and ending with the formulation of a specific price.

Multistep Flow Model A theory of mass communication which supersedes both the hypodermic needle model and the two-step flow model. The theory maintains that there are a variety of ways in which messages can flow from the mass media to the audience. In some cases, mass media may have a direct effect on its audience, as in the hypodermic needle model. In other cases, mass media messages may flow to opinion leaders and then to the general public, as in the two step flow model. In yet other cases, however, message may flow through a series of opinion leaders and involve more than two steps. The model also takes into account the diversified sources of information available to opinion leaders as well as the selective processes used by the audience to filter the messages they receive.

Multiunit Establishment One of two or more establishments in the same general kind of business operated by the same firm. It is sometimes referred to as a chain store.

Mutual Delivry System A parcel delivery service formed by a number of retailers which picks up, sorts, and delivers customer purchases. Each member of the system shares in its ownership and in the expenses it generates.

N

NAB See *Newspaper Advertising Bureau (NAB)*

NACDS See *National Association of Chain Drug Stres (NACDS)*

NACS See *National Association of Convenience Stores (NACS)* or *National Association of College Stores (NACS)*

National Account A prospect or customer with locations in several sales territories that are sold, using a coordinated national strategy rather than strategies that focus on specific locations. A national account with an international scope is referred to as a global account.

National Account Manager An account executive responsible for coordinating the sales effort directed toward a national account.

National Account Marketing A marketing strategy in which a firm's largest and most important national customers are given special attention in recognition of the volume of business they provide. These clients frequently are served by a specially dedicated sales force which is responsible for finding and maintaining these accounts. Also known as *key account marketing* and *major account marketing.*

National Advertising Advertising sponsored on a national or regional basis, generally by manufacturers or producers. Also known as *general advertising.*

National Advertising Review Board (NARB) An advertising industry self-regulating organisation created by the Council of Better Business Bureaus and three industry trade groups in 1971. The NARB screens national advertising for deceptive practices and hears appeals of complaints brought by the public to the National Advertising Division (NAD).

National Brand A brand that is marketed throughout a national market. It contrasts with regional brand and local brand. It usually is advertised and usually is owned by a manufacturer, though neither is necessary for the definition because Kmart's brands, for example, are obviously national, even international.

National Character The values, beliefs and personality characteristics that describe the people of a country in general terms.

National Environmental Policy Act (NEPA) (1969) The act in which Congress applied at the national level an across-the-board policy of environmental protection for the federal government and all its agencies. Environmental quality under the NEPA has become a major factor in agency decision making.

National Rate The price charged national advertisers for space and time in local advertising media. Traditionally, newspapers, radio and television stations have charged higher rates for national advertising than for local advertising.

Natural Classification of Expenses An accounting practice in which expenses are grouped into classes based on the kinds of expenses involved, *e.g.*, rent, salaries, supplies, raw materials, taxes, interest etc. rather than on the function of the expenditure, *e.g.*, the costs of operating a particular department. Also known as *ledger expenses or object-of-expenditure costs.*

Natural Trading Area That geographic area which contains the customers who patronise a firm. Natural trading areas seldom have clearly defined boundaries—customers simply thin out as distance increases.

Need Satisfaction Selling A type of customised sales presentation in which the salesperson first identifies the prospective customer's needs and then tries to offer a solution that satisfies those needs.

Negotiated Contract A contract to buy goods or services in which the buyer and seller negotiate its specific terms. Negotiated contracts are frequently employed instead of competitive bidding when there is a sole supplier and thus no competition in the marketplace.

Negotiation The process of trying to find mutually agreeable terms in an exchange situation. Negotiation leads either to mutually acceptable terms (agreement) or a decision not to transact (disagreement).

Neighbourhood Shopping Centre A small shopping centre, often arranged on the strip plan, which serves its surrounding community—typically persons living within five minutes of drive time. Neighbourhood centres are frequently anchored by a supermarket or variety store and may include service retailers (beauty shops, card shops etc.) and stores selling convenience goods (drug stores etc.). Sometimes called strip shopping centres as they usually stretch out along a well-traveled street or highway.

Net Cost See *cost of goods purchased*

Net Cost of Delivered Purchases See *cost of goods purchased*

Net Investment Gross investment minus allowances for capital consumption.

Net National Product (NNP) Gross national product less capital consumption allowance, *i.e.,* depreciation on capital goods plus capital goods destroyed or damaged plus depreciation on minor capital goods.

Net Operating Income Net sales less net cost of goods sold less operating expenses.

Net Present Value In accounting, a means of taking into accounting the value of money to be expended in an investment project. Net present value or, as it is sometimes called, "discounted cash flow" expresses in terms of current value outlays and inflows which will occur in the future as the project is developed.

Net Profit Gross Margin (or in manufacturing terminology, gross profit) less all the costs of running the business. Such costs include the cost of sales, operating expenses such as payroll, advertising, insurance and (according to the American Institute of Certified Public Accountants' *Business Information Guide*) income taxes. The term net profit is frequently used synonymously with operating profit, net operating profit, net operating income, and net income.

Net Sales Sales revenue after returns, allowances, discounts, cancellations and taxes (sales and excise) have been deducted for the accounting period. Net sales represents the actual sales dollars the company will receive.

New Product A term relative to one's position in the marketplace. To customers, a product is new if it is perceived as significantly different from other available products. For manufacturers, distributors, and retailers a new product is one never before produced or sold. New products range from the truly unique and innovative to those which are merely modifications or copies of existing merchandise.

New Product Failure A new product that does not meet the objectives of its developers. Depending on what those objectives are, a profitable new product can be a failure and an unprofitable new product can be a success.

New Product Planning Process Those stages through which a product passes in the developmental process. Included are idea generation and screning, analysis and evaluation, product development and production, branding, test marketing and positioning, and finally, full scale marketing and production. To be effective the new product process must be made sensitive to the needs of the marketplace.

New Product Screening Checklist A form used in the systematic evaluation of ideas for new products. Such factors as marketability and growth potential are included for consideration.

New Product Strategy The goals a product is expected to achieve in a market. A product's strategy supports and complements the overall marketing strategy. Some products are used to introduce or pioneer new technologies while others are expected to balance current market offerings in terms of product price, product format, style and features.

New Task Buying A form of industrial buying in which the purchasing officer must buy a new product or service. New task buying requires greater attention to detail than rebuying and often involves more than one person. see also *straight rebury* and *modified rebury.*

New Unsought Goods Products offering new ideas and applications of which the consumer is not at all aware. The marketing of such goods requires informative promotion so that potential customers will accept and seek out the product. See also *unsought goods.*

Niche Marketing A marketing strategy in which a manufacturer or supplier identifies a narrow market segment in which he believes he can successfully compete with his product or service. Products and services may be created specifically to fill these perceived niches.

No Frills Product See *generic product*

Nominal Credit Terms The terms applied to the date on which full payment of the account is due. For vendors that bill customers on a monthly basis, full payment is usually due by tenth day after billing.

Nominal Scale A measurement in which numbers are assigned to attributes of objects or classes of objects solely for the purpose of identifying the objects.

Non-business Organisation Although imprecise, the term non-business is generally taken to mean non-profit or not-for-profit and thus includes a very wide variety of organisations such as schools, cultural institutions, charities, fraternal organisations, health care delivery organisations etc.

Non-durable Goods Tangible products generally having a lifespan of three years or less. Most nondurable goods are consumed close to the time at which they are purchased.

Non-goods Service A category of consumer service in which no tangible product is offered for sale or rental, *e.g.*, hairdressing, medical care, etc.

Non-personal Retailing A form of selling in which the customer does not visit a store and in which there is no face-to-face contact between seller and buyer. There are three principal types of nonpersonal retailing: (1) catalog retailing, (2) mail order retailing and (3) vending machine retailing.

Non-price Competition Competition in the marketplace based on factors other than price. A firm may emphasise service, terms of sale, delivery, attractive packaging, extensive promotion or the product's reputation in an effort to 'gain a competitive advantage.

Non-probability Sample A sample that relies on personal judgement somewhere in the element selection process and therefore prohibits estimating the probability that any population element will be included in the sample.

Non-probability Sampling A method of selecting a sample for marketing research in which the judgement (and possible bias) of the researcher enters into the selection process. The three major types of non-probability samples are the convenience sample, the judgement sample and the quota sample. Nonprobability sampling is sometimes preferred by market researchers over probability sampling when special expertise is an important characteristic of the sample group. This sampling method may also be desirable when budget and/or time constraints are a factor. However, the results of research using nonprobability samples contain many unknowns and such results must be regarded with caution when used to draw conclusions about the total population. See also probability sampling.

Non-profit Marketer An individual or organisation conducting nonprofit marketing.

Non-profit Marketing Conducted by organisations which operate on a not-for-profit basis. Such marketing is almost always concerned with services and ideas rather than with physical products and may include a wide variety of political, social and religious activities. See also nonbusiness organisation.

Non-selling Area The floor space, other than selling area, used in the conduct of business in a store building or in remote service or warehouse buildings, including entrances, show windows, vertical transportation facilities, offices, air conditioning systems, alteration rooms, work rooms, repair shops, receiving and marking rooms. and stock rooms.

Non-selling Department Any department of a store engaged in work other than direct selling of merchandise—*e.g.*, receiving department.

Non-store Retailing A form of retailing in which a traditional store building is not involved, *i.e.*, in which the retailer and customer transact their business through such means as: (1) direct mail, (2) door-to-door sales, (3) in-home or party-plan selling, (4) telephone sales, (5) catalog sales, (6) interactive television, or (7) vending machines.

Non-tariff Barriers Government policies and laws, other than tariffs, which restrict international trade. Nontariff barriers include local content laws (such as the Japanese restriction on U.S. paperboard which does not comply with Japanese paperboard standards), export subsidies, safety and health standards, import quotas, government purchasing rules and border taxes. See also *tariff*.

Non-traceable Common Costs Those expenses in a business which cannot be assigned to a particular function, *e.g.*, executive salaries, interest payments, etc.

Nonverbal Communications The non-spoken forms of expression communicating thought and emotions including body language, space between the communicators, speech and appearance.

Normal Margin Retailer Offers merchandise at prices comparable to those found at other stores at the same market level. The normal margin retailer has chosen not to complete by attempting to undersell the competition.

Notes Payable In accounting, current liabilities to banks and other lending institutions payable on a specific date.

Nutritional Labelling The practice of indicating on the packages of food products the nutritional value of the product (in particular, the proportion of the U.S. recommended daily allowances supplied by a specified quantity of the product) and the specific ingredients contained within the product.

O

Objective A goal, either long or short range, that a retailer or other business attempts to achieve. A retailer's objectives may include sales, profit, image, etc. The objectives of a retail establishment are periodically reevaluated during the *retail oudit*.

Objective-and-task Budgeting An advertising budget method in which advertising expenditures are determined on the basis of a specific audit of the resources needed to achieve the specific objectives and tasks outlined in the advertiser's media plan.

Objectives The intermediate benchmarks or reference points which an organisation must reach as it pursues its goals. Objectives may be regarded as forming a ladder by which an organisation may achieve its mission. See also *goals, advertising objectives* and *marketing objectives*.

Observation A marketing research technique frequently used in retailing in which primary data is collected by watching individuals, *e.g.*, store customers, either directly or with cameras in order to record the subjects' shopping behaviour and buying habits.

Observation Error A nonsampling error that arises because inaccurate information is secured from the sample elements or because errors are introduced in the processing of the data or in reporting the findings.

Obsolescence The act or process of a product's becoming out-of-date, discarded, no longer in use. The rejection is for some reason other than being worn out or inoperable. It may apply to an individual item or to all of the items in a given class or group. The active verb form, less widely acceptable, is to obsolete or to make obsolete.

Odd-Even Pricing A form of psychological pricing that suggests buyers are more sensitive to certain ending digits. Odd price refers to a price ending in an odd number (*e.g.*, 1, 3, 5, 7, 9), or to a price just under a round number (*e.g.*, $0.89, $3.99, $44.98). Even price refers to a price ending in a whole number or in tenths (*e.g.*, $0.50, $5.00, $8.10, $75.00).

Odd-Line Pricing A method of ascribing prices ending in odd numbers, especially five, seven or nine, to convey the impression of a lower price. For example, a retailer using odd-line pricing would charge $10.99 rather than $11.00 to convey the idea of a bargain. Also known as odd-value pricing, penny pricing, odd-cent pricing, odd-ending pricing and odd-even pricing. See also *even-line pricing*.

Odd Lot Dealing with broken lots or unbalanced assortments reduced in price for quick turnover.

Odd Price A price ending in an odd number (such as 57 cents or 63 cents), or a price just under some round number (such as $98 instead of $100).

Off-Price Retailing The selling at retail of merchandise, often carrying status or premium labels, at less than "regular" prices. In contrast to discount retailing (where the discounter pays the same price for his merchandise as everyone else and sells it for less than traditional retailers) off-price retailers buy merchandise at cut-rate prices and pass the savings along to their customers. In addition, expenses are kept low by limiting advertising expenditures, turning stock over quickly, and other cost-cutting techniques.

Off-Price Shopping Centre A shopping centre specialising in off-price retail tenants such as T.J. Maxx or Burlington Coat Factory.

Off-Retail Percentage The markdown as a percentage of the original price. For example, an item originally retails for $10 and is marked down to $5; the off-retail percentage is 50%.

On Order When the retailer has ordered merchandise and it has not been received, it is considered to be on order and thus a commitment against a planned purchase figure. Thus, the open-to-buy figure is affected by the amount of the on order dollars.

On-pack Premium A free gift or other item attached to the outside of a package. The premium acts as an incentive to purchase the merchandise offered for sale. The two items may be held together by a band of paper or tape or by plastic film. Also called *a banded premium or a package band.*

On-Percentage The result of multiplying together the complements of a given series of discount percentages. To find the net merchandise price, the list price is multiplied by the on-percentage.

One-Level Channel A marketing channel in which there is only one intermediary, commonly a retailer, between the producer and the consumer.

One Price Policy A policy in which prices are fixed and uniform for all customers buying essentially the same amounts of merchandise. Such a policy precludes bargaining or negotiation.

One Price Retailer A store that offers all merchandise at a fixed price, the same to all customers, as opposed to bargaining or negotiating a price.

Open Account (1) A policy under which a vendor extends interest-free credit to his customers on a short term basis. Commonly bills are payable in full at the end of 30 days. The practice of recording such transactions in a ledger gave rise to the popular term "on the books." (2) Any credit account in which there remains a balance to be paid.

Open Bid An offer to perform a service or to supply goods submitted to a buyer and announced openly so that all bidders know the price submitted.

Open-Code Dating A system used on food products to include the last day on which they may be sold. Open-codes are understandable to customers and thus aid them in making judgements regarding the freshness of the merchandise.

Open Dating The practice of putting onto a product information that reveals the date beyond which it should no longer be sold or used. This applies primarily to perishable products, those that lose some important attribute over time while awaiting sale in the channel between maker and user. Open dating is common to certain industries (for example, dairy products and pharmaceuticals) and is sometimes mandated by law.

Open Order A order sent by a store to a market representative to be placed with whatever vendor the latter finds can best fill it. In department store buying, it is the authority granted to a resident buyer to purchase merchandise required by the store.

Open Rate The highest rate charged for space or time by an advertising vehicle.

Open-to-buy Report A statement of existing or expected relations between dollar inventory and sales, used to calculate open-to-buy amounts.

Operant Conditioning The process of altering the probability of a behaviour being emitted by changing the consequences of the behaviour.

Operational Buying Motives Consumer motives based on how the product being considered for purchase functions, *e.g.*, an automobile may be chosen for purchase on the basis of its performance. See also *motive*.

Operational Definition A definition of a construct that describes the operations to be carried out in order for the construct to be measured empirically.

Opinion Approach A technique used by salespersons in the first few minutes of contact with a prospect. The salesperson shows the product to the prospect and asks for his opinion. This focuses attention on the product and directly involves the prospect in the presentation. See also *approach*.

Opinion Leader A person whose opinions are widely respected (especially within a reference group), who is often a trend-setter and who influences the purchase decisions of others.

Opportunistic Pricing A strategy in which a company raises the prices for its products or services during a time of shortage in an effort to take advantage of increased demand on the part of the consumer.

Opportunity Cost The cost incurred when one alternative must be chosen over another. If marketing alternative A is chosen over alternative B, then the opportunity cost of alternative A is the benefit lost by not pursuing alternative B. Another view of opportunity costs is that they may more accurately be regarded as foregone profits.

Opportunity Forecast A form of business forecast in which an effort is made to predict future conditions in the marketplace which might present opportunities for new products, the reduction in production costs, or the avoidance of changes in the marketing environment which might prove detrimental to the organisation.

Optional Product Pricing A pricing strategy applied to products which are offered to the public with a number of options, *e.g.*, automobiles with their nearly limitless list of optional equipment. Decisions are made regarding which items are to be included in the price of the core product and which are to be offered as options at additional cost to the buyer. Optional products may be priced to generate a profit or priced to act as enticements to purchase the core product.

Options Pricing Models A class of models designed to calculate the value of an option. Comment: The empirical adequacy of these models is an unresolved issue in financial economics.

Order Entry The order entry phase is the beginning phase of the order cycle process. Order entry refers to the process of actually entering an order into the seller's order processing system. This may be done by a sales person writing an order, a customer ordering by phone, a telemarketing solicitation, or by the buyer's computer communicating directly with the seller's computer, as in an electronic data interchange (EDI) system.

Order Processing The system of the firm that generally refers to the way orders are recorded by the firm and how this information is used to provide customer service and manage various functional elements of the business. It includes the management of the order entry process as well as the information flows that surround and support the order fulfillment objectives of the firm.

Order Processing Costs Those costs associated with handling merchandise, processing order forms, generating invoices and shipping bills, maintaining credit records, etc.

Order Register A form or computerised record of orders placed with vendors. It includes the date of each order, the name of the vendor, the total amount of each order, the month in which shipment is to be made, the amount to be delivered each month, and a serial number.

Order-Shipping-Billing Cycle This describes the paper work or information cycle of the order processing system.

Order-Taker A salesperson involved in the routine clerical and sales functions of taking customers' orders for goods and services. Most retail salespeople are regarded as inside order-takers as most of their customers are already inclined to make a purchase. Outside order-takers include salespeople who call on customers, note the merchandise they need, and turn in the order. Little or no creative selling is involved.

Ordering Costs All those costs of doing business which directly relate to the ordering of goods and services including operating expenses associated with the order and receiving departments.

Ordinal Scale A measurement in which numbers are assigned to attributes of objects or classes of object to reflects the order (for example, more than, greater than) of the objects.

Organisation Chart A visual representation of an organisation structure. It identifies the organisation unit and portrays each position in relation to others. Positions are usually represented by squares or rectangles (although circles or ovals are sometimes used) that contain the position title; they may show the name of the incumbent as well. Each position is connected by a solid line running to the immediate supervisor and to positions supervised, if any. Broken or dotted lines may be used to show other than line relationships (*e.g.*, advisory or functional).

Comment: Some managers eschew organisation charts because they like open and informal relationships among persons of different rank. They believe that an organisation chart is inhibiting in this respect. Others believe it is the manager's style and not the organisation chart that determines the degree of open and informal relationships. They see the organisation chart as a useful device for assisting employees in understanding the organisation and their role in it.

Organisation Marketing Generally an effort on the part of non-profit organisations to sell their objectives and goals and/or to solicit contributions. Included are mutual benefit organisations (unions, fraternal organisations, political parties, etc.), service organisations (charities, schools and colleges, etc.), and government organisations (the military, police and fire departments, etc.).

Organisational Consumer Organisational consumers include manufacturers, wholesalers and distributors, retailers, and government agencies and non-profit organisations. They use the products they buy to make other products, to maintain the organisation's operations, or to be offered for resale.

Organisation Market This market consists of industrial markets, reseller markets and government markets. Industrial buyers buy goods and services to aid them in producing other goods and services (derived demand). Resellers buy goods and services to resell them as a profit. Government agencies buy goods and services to carry out mandated governmental functions.

Organised Market A group of traders operating under recognised rules in buying and selling a single commodity or relate commodities; a commodity exchange.

Organising Skills The skills used by marketing managers to specify and structure the relationships among marketing personnel within the firm, both formal and informal.

Original Equipment Manufacturer (OEM) This organisation purchases industrial goods in order to incorporate them into other products that are sold in the industrial market (business market) or ultimate consumer market. For example, IBM, acting as an OEM, buys microprocessors for its personal computers from Intel.

Original Retail The first price at which merchandise is offered for sale, accounted for as the retail value of receipts.

OSMA See *Overseas Sales and Marketing Association of America (OSMA)*

Other-directedness A mode of confirmity to the culture in which one draws values and beliefs from the peer group rather than from the family group. Tradition-directedness, inner-directedness, and other-directedness are part of the conceptualisation of David Riesman in his monograph the Lonely Crowd.

Out-of-Stock Cost The estimated profits lost as the result to insufficient quantities of inventory on hand to meet customer demand. Customers and sales are lost through a stock-out.

Output Evaluation Measure An objective measure of sales force performance including number of orders average size of orders; number of cancelled orders; and number of active, new, lost, overdue, and prospective accounts.

Out Sizes The sizes that are either very large or very small and, if offered at all, are offered in very limited depth because of the thin market demand for them. Some stores specialise in fringe sizes or out sizes—*e.g.*, tall women's shops, petite size shops.

Overfull Demand A condition in the marketplace in which demand for a product exceeds the capacity of the suppliers to produce it.

Overhead Those business costs other than direct labour (the wages of the workers actually making a product or delivering a service) and direct materials (the actual components incorporated into the product). Overhead includes the wages of support personnel, fringe benefits paid to all workers, handling and shipping expenses, etc. Unlike fixed costs, overhead expenses are directly related to production levels and sales volume.

Overrun Production In excess of that which had been originally scheduled.

Overseas Sales and Marketing Association of America (OSMA) A professional association of firms engaged in export management and trading, OSMA sets professional standards and acts as a clearing house for international contacts. Its headquarters are in Oak Park, Illinois. OSMA publishes a monthly Newsletter and an annual Directory.

Overseas Sales Branch In direct export, the overseas sales branch is a branch or subsidiary of the exporting firm, located in the host country. This allows the exporter greater exposure and control in the foreign market and also avoids total reliance upon a domestic-based export department employing an independent, international, marketing middleman. See also *direct export*.

Overstored A condition in the marketplace in which there are more stores in an area than can operate profitably.

Owned-Goods Service A firm or department of a store which repairs or improves existing products already belonging to the customer. For example, upholstery shops, clock repair shops, or shoe repair shops. Often these shops or departments also sell auxiliary goods at retail such as shoe polish, upholstery sprays, etc.

Ownership Utility The utility (or value or satisfaction) added to a product or service when it is in the possession of the right person at the right time. Also called possession utility.

P

Pack (1) A container or carring case in which something is stored for convenience and ease of carrying. Often used as a ombining form, as in six-pack, snak-pak, etc. (2) To pack is to fill a bag or box wit items, as occurs at the check-out point in a supermarket. (3) To pack is also to put merchandise (particularly food) into can, boxes and other ontainers for preservation or sale.

Package A wrapper or container in which a product is stored and sold. In addition to protecting the product, the package also provides space for labels, instructions and other useful information.

Package-based Premium A gift or other special offer advertised on a strip wrapped around the package of the product being promoted. The gift may be free or offered at a reduced price to purchasers of the product.

Package Delivery Service A transportation service offering that requires packages to confirm to specified size and weight restrictions. The packages may be moved by ground or air transportation, within a variety of delivery schedules. Prominent package delivery service carriers include Federal Express (FedEx), United Parcel Service (UPS) and the U.S. Postal Service.

Parallel Pricing The practice of following the pricing practices of other organisations, particularly competitors.

Party Selling 1. A direct selling approach that involves demonstrating and selling products to a group of consumers attending a party at a neighbour's or friend's house. 2. A practice in which salespeople arrange to have a party in a home, at which merchandise is demonstrated to a group of the host's or hostess' friends.

Pass-along Readers The members of the audience of a print media vehicle who do not subscribe to the publication but obtain their copies from people who do subscribe. They are also called secondary readers in contrast to subscribers, who are called *primary readers*.

Pass Up Method. A method used by salespeople to respond to a prospect objection by letting the prospect talk, acknowledging that the concern was heard, and then moving on to another topic without trying to resolve the concern.

Pass-through Rate The number or percentage of sales promotion incentives offered to wholesalers or retailers by manufacturers that are extended to consumers by those channel members.

Patent A government grant of protection to an inventor which confers exclusive rights of manufacture and sale of an invention for a fixed period of time. In order to be patentable an invention must generally be novel and useful.

Patronage Motive The reason, whether rational or emotional, for which a customer (either an individual or an organisation) chooses to patronise one establishment rather than another.

Payback The amount of money a new product must earn (calculated as net income before depreciation but after taxes) to recover the initial investment made in its development.

Payout Budgeting An advertising budget method in which advertising expenses are treated as part of the investment required to establish a new product.

Penetrated Market The total number of persons who are already customers for a product or service.

Penetration Pricing A strategy in which a new product is introduced into the marketplace at a lower than usual price in an effort to rapidly penetrate the market and build sales volume. Sometimes called impact pricing, as the strategy is also calculated to increase consumer awareness of the product.

Per Capita Income A nation's total income divided by the number of persons in its population. Cross national product is a popular, but technically incorrect, surrogate for total income.

Perceived Quality The amount of quality buyers believe a product or service has. Perceived quality is usually based on some information or cues about the product, *e.g.*, its price, brand name or country of origin.

Perceived Role Ambiguity The degree to which a salesperson feels he or she does not have the information necessary to perform the job adequately. The salesperson may be uncertain about what some role set members expect of him or her in certain situations, how he or she should go about satisfying those expectations or how his or her performance will be evaluated and rewarded.

Perceived Role Overload The degree to which a salesperson believes that he or she has more to accomplish than is possible given the time available.

Perceived-Value Pricing A strategy in which the prize of a product or service is based upon the buyer's perception of its value rather than on the seller's cost of production.

Percent-of-sales Budgeting An advertising budget method in which advertising expenses are established as a fixed percentage of past, current or future sales levels.

Percent of Sales Method of Promotional Budgeting A method of computing a promotional budget in which the amount allocated is based upon a percentage of previous or projected sales.

Perceptual Mapping A marketing research tool in which a number of factors such as product attributes, customer preferences and particular brands are plotted on a chart on the basis of computer analysis. Since various factors tend to form clusters, it is possible for marketers to distinguish between various competing brands and to spot open niches in the marketplace.

Perfect Competition A market condition so rare as to be largely theoretical, perfect competition entails: (1) so many sellers and buyers that no one party can control prices; (2) buyers and sellers who are familiar with the market and who can quickly react to changes in the supply and demand situation; (3) a product or commodity which is highly substitutable; and (4) the existence of relatively few barriers to parties entering and leaving the market. Conditions approaching perfect competition are sometimes encountered in the trade in agricultural commodities. Also known as pure competition or free competition.

Performance Index A quantitative measure of the relation-ship between standards that have been set by a firm and the firm's actual performance. In a sales performance index, for example, the actual sales are divided by the expected sales (for a particular area, sales representative, or product, etc.) and multiplied by 100.

$$\text{Sales Performance Index} = \frac{\$\ \text{Actual sales}}{\text{Expected sales}} \times 100$$

Performance Monitoring Research Research, generally in the form of interviews or questionnaires, employed to monitor a particular marketing programme and to provide the marketing manager with the feedback required to evaluate the firm's marketing activities.

Periodic Inventory System An inventory system in which orders are placed at scheduled intervals (*e.g.,* first day of month) but the amount of product ordered will be variable.

Peripheral Route to Persuasion One of two types of cognitive processes by which persuasion occurs. In the peripheral route, the consumer does not focus on the product message in an ad but on other stimuli such as attractive or well-known celebrities or popular music. The presence of these other stimuli may change the consumer's beliefs and attitudes about the product.

Perishability of Services A concept which suggests that services, by their very nature, have a limited life span, *i.e.,* that services left unperformed cannot be stored and used at some future time.

Perpetual Inventory System A stock control system that is designed to keep continuous track of all additions and deletions to inventory.

Person Marketing In an effort to cultivate the attention, interest and preference of a target market for a person (rather than goods or services), person marketing consists of activities such as press conferences, media coverage, public appearances, etc. These activities are generally undertaken to create, maintain, or alter attitudes and/or behaviour toward particular persons. Both political candidate marketing and celebrity marketing are forms of person marketing.

Personal Consumption Expenditure The aggregate amount spent each year by consumers to buy goods and services from the marketplace.

Personal Disposable Income Current money income less all taxes and money spent for the purchase of necessities.

Personal Income For statistical purposes, the U.S. Bureau of the Census includes the following money income: wages and salaries, self-employment income (including losses), Social Security and Supplemental Security Income, public assistance (except non-cash benefits), interest, dividends, rents, royalties, veterans' payments, unemployment compensation, workers' compensation and both public and private income from pensions. Personal income does not include capital gains (or losses).

Personal Relationships in Organisational Buying Personal relationships in business marketing have a strong influence on organisational buying behaviour. Positive or negative relationships between members of the buying and selling organisations often represent the deciding factor in supplier's choice.

Personal Selling A sales technique which frequently involves face-to-face contact between seller and customer, but which may also be conducted by telephone. Includes wholesale and contact sales in which the salesperson initiates the contact by making a call on the customer, as well as retail selling, in which the customer initiates the contact by entering a store and approaching the salesperson.

Persuasive Impact The level of influence a form of communication has upon consumers. Television has a high degree of persuasive impact because it reaches more than one of the senses.

Phantom Freight Freight charges sometimes encountered when shipping rates are based geographically as in basing-point pricing. It is not uncommon that some customers pay rates in excess of those actually incurred by the shipper while others pay less.

Phony List Price A list price designed solely to be shown to the customers as evidence that the price has been discounted from list. Customers who are unduly impressed by the size of the supposed discount may end up paying more than the actual market price. This practice is banned by the Wheeler-Lea Amendment. See also *list price.*

Physical Distribution (PD) Although the flow of raw materials to the producer may be regarded as a part of physical distribution, the process is more commonly seen as beginning with the completed manufactured product as it enters the appropriate marketing channels and moves through various transportation and storage stages to its final consumption. See also *distribution.*

Physical Distribution Management Logistic activities concerned with the movement of completed products from point of manufacture to consumer.

Physical Distribution Manger This manager (increasingly referred to as logistics manager) plans the flow of materials in a manufacturing organisation (beginning with raw materials and ending with delivery of finished products to channel intermediaries or end customers) and coordinates the work of departments involved in the process, such as procurement, transportation, manufacturing, finance, legal and marketing. In the more limited marketing sense, physical distribution management is concerned with the efficient movement of finished product from the end of the production line to customers. This is usually a staff position, reporting to corporate or division management, with the functional authority needed to coordinate the execution of distribution plans by functional departments so as to provide good customer service at acceptable cost.

Physical Inventory An inventory determined by actual count and evidenced by a listing of quantity, weight or measure. It is usually compiled in dollars as well as units.

Physical Obsolescence With regard to manufactured products, a broken down or worn out state generally reached through normal wear and tear.

Piecemeal Processing A cognitive process in which an individual considers each piece of information separately in order to arrive at an evaluation. This type of processing is fairly effortful and is based on the assumption that each piece of information has some subjective value and that the individual somehow combines the pieces of information to determine the overall value. Information Processing Theory approaches traditionally assume this type of processing. Piecemeal processing is an alternative to category-based processing.

Piggyback Marketing An arrangement whereby one manufacturer obtains distribution of products through another's distribution channels.

Pioneer Selling Selling a new and different product, service or idea. In this situation, it is often difficult for salespeople to establish a need in the buyer's mind.

Pioneering Innovativeness A strategy of trying to be the first to market new types of products. The highest order of innovativeness (others are adapting, emulating, and imitating), it is often based on technical breakthroughs.

Pioneering Stage A nonspecific period early in the life cycle of a new type of product during which the pioneers are trying to build primary demand for the product type more than secondary demand for their particular brands.

Place Marketing Marketing designed to influence target audiences to behave in some positive manner with respect to the products or services associated with a specific place. Comment: Attempts by an individual or organisation to educate target audiences or change their attitudes about a place are not marketing.

Planned Buying vs. Unplanned Buying Planned buying is purchasing activity undertaken with a problem previously recognised and a buying intention previously formed. Most organisational buying is planned buying. Unplanned buying is buying activity that occurs as a result of exposure to an advertisement or a salesperson's visit. Trial of new supplies or consumable supplies may begin as unplanned buying.

Planned Economy 1. (economic definition) An economy in which a governmental authority decides what, when, and how much is to be produced and distributed. 2. (environments definition) An economy in which a central authority makes economic decisions, as contrasted with a market economy.

Planned Stock The dollar amount of merchandise a buyer desires to have on hand at a given time in a certain department, merchandise classification, price line or other control unit.

Planned Urban Development A totally conceived and supervised community including housing, retail, and business activity.

Planning The process of establishing the goals of an organisation and projecting the most effective means of accomplishing them. Planning attempts to anticipate the needs of the organisation both in the near and distant future. Planning may be shortrange or long-range. Short-range plans are developed for those situations likely to occur month by month, weekly or daily. They may be covered by procedures, practices, rules, etc. A firm's budget is a common form of short-range plan. Long-range plans, on the other hand, are developed for upto several years and involve the long-term goals of the organisation, often expressed in a statement of purpose. The firm's objectives and policies are designed to accommodate long-range planning. See also *marketing planning, management by objectives (MBO), tactical planning* and *strategic planning*.

Plus-One Dialing A technique used in studies employing telephone interviews in which a single randomly determined digit is added to numbers selected from the telephone directory.

Point of Diminishing Return That point at which total production begins to increase at a decreasing rate with successive applications of inputs.

Point of Negative Return That point at which total production decreases absolutely with successive applications of inputs.

Point-of-purchase Advertising Advertising usually in the form of window and/or interior displays in establishments where a product is sold to the ultimate consumer.

Point-of-Purchase Display In retailing, an interior display of merchandise at the register, check-out counter or other point-of-sale designed to attract the customer's attention at a place closely associated with purchase decisions and to stimulate impulse buying. Display materials are frequently supplied by the vendor.

Point-of-Purchase Promotion See *point-of-purchase display.*

Point-of-Sale (POS) In retailing, that area of the store or department where the sale is consumated, *i.e.,* where the customer pays for and receives the merchandise. This is often the location of point-of-purchase displays and other promotions. Also called the *point-of-purchase.* See also *point-of-sale (POS) perpetual inventory control system.*

Point-of-Sale (POS) Perpetual Inventory Control System In retailing, an automated system in which the store's cash registers are linked to computer processing systems. The cash register is actually a point-of-sale terminal. The register controls and records all sales (cash, charge, COD, layaway etc.) at the point-of-sale. The terminal issues sales checks, prints transaction records and feeds information about each transaction into the data bank of the computer. For example, in the National Cash Register (NCR) 280 Retail System, the automated equipment handles marketing, checkout and data recording functions. Merchandise is ticketed with coloured bar code tags which are read with wand readers at the check-out counter. The computer accumulates sales transaction information on magnetic tape for daily input into the computer's memory bank or storage system. Also called an *electronic cash register* (ECR), or *shortened to point-of-sale* (POS) in common usage.

Point of Sale Transfer Payment for retail purchases by using an electronic funds transfer card.

Poison Prevention Packaging Act (1970) Federal legislation which required manufacturers to use safety packaging on products containing substances deemed harmful to children.

Polarity of Retail Trade A trend in retailing that indicates that the predominant retailing institutions are on one hand (pole) mass distribution outlets and, on the other hand (pole), specialty, single-line, boutique type retail institutions.

Political Candidate Marketing A form of person marketing in which activities are undertaken to create, maintain or alter attitudes and/or behaviour toward a person seeking elective office. In recent years, political candidate marketing has be political candidate marketing has become a major industry and area of specialisation as office seekers hire an increasing number of advertising professionals to assist in their campaigns. See also *person marketing* and *celebrity marketing*.

Political Marketing Marketing designed to influence target audiences to vote for a particular person, party, or proposition. Attempts by an individual or organisation only to educate or change attitudes are not political marketing.

Polycentric Orientation The unconscious bias or belief that it is necessary to adopt totally to local culture and practice. It is a host country orientation in management.

Pool Car Shipment A mode of rail shipment in which two or more companies combine their goods in order to take advantage of carload freight rates.

Pooled Buying The practice of independent merchants informally pooling their orders.

POP See *point-of-sale (POS)* and *point-of-sale (POS) perpetual inventory control system*.

Population In marketing research, the entire group under observation by the researcher and about which he will draw conclusions. The terms universe and sample set are frequently used synonymously with population. See also *sampling*.

Portfolio 1. (advertising definition) A collection of the best creative work done by an art director or copywriter, used in job interviews to demonstrate the individual's talent, skill and experience. 2. (product development definition) A set of things that are developed and/or marketed in relationship to each other. It most often is applied to that group of projects currently active in a research laboratory, but may apply to all new projects underway.

Positions Analysis The analysis of existing products including the manufacturing programme of the present company and of the subsidiaries, analysis of competitors' market shares, a technical and economic evaluation of all products in comparison with competitors' products, assessment of manufacturing capacity.

assessment of sales capacity in the field and in the home organisation, appraisal of product knowledge within the group, analysis of custom duties and tariffs and some study of innovations to be expected in the future.

Position Description A written description that helps the incumbent of a position know what is expected of him or her. It includes the organisational unit, position title, purpose of the position, reporting relationships, duties and responsibilities and authority (if any).

Positioning Advertising A form of advertising in which a segment of the market is targeted and the product or service presented in a way which specifically appeals to that segment. Consideration may also be given to the product's position as it relates to competing products in the marketplace.

Possession Utility The increased usefulness created by marketing through making it possible for a consumer to own, use, and consume a product. It is also called ownership utility.

Postage Stamp Pricing A method of setting uniform delivered prices throughout the national market by charging equal freight costs regardless of actual distance shipped. In this respect, it resembles letter postage. Also known as uniform geographic pricing and uniform delivered pricing.

Post-exchange A retail store operated by the armed forces primarily for the convenience of military base personnel and their families. It is also called a *PX*.

Postindustrial Society A concept referring to the next stage in our societal evolution in which the production of knowledge will be our major activity and most of the employment opportunities will be in the service sector.

Postpone Method A method used by salespeople to respond to prospect objections by asking permission to address the prospect's concerns at a later time.

Postpurchase Behaviour The final stage in the consumer adoption process, postpurchase behaviour includes such activities as continued evaluation of the product, the use and maintenance of the product and the decision whether or not to repurchase the product in the future.

Post-Purchase Evaluation The evaluation of a product or service after consumption. This may involve remorse as well as the feeling of satisfaction or dissatisfaction.

Poverty Level The poverty level is based solely on money income and updated every year to reflect changes in the consumer price index; it reflects the consumption requirements of families based on their size and composition. It is used to classify families as being above or below the poverty level.

Predatory Pricing The setting of prices at a level so low as to drive competitors out of business. Much predatory pricing is illegal under the provisions of the Clayton and Sherman Acts. Also known as *put-out pricing* and *extinction pricing.*

Preemptive Marketing The advertising of a product or service before it is actually available in the marketplace in an effort to forestall the purchase of a competitor's product.

Preemptive Pricing A strategy in which price levels are set so low that makers of competitive products are discouraged from entering the marketplace. Also known as keep-out pricing and stay-out pricing.

Premarking The price marking by the manufacturer or other supplier before good are shipped to a retail store. It is also called prepricing.

Premium Merchandise employed as a sales promotion device, *e.g.*, it may be used as an incentive to encourage customers to make a purchase or to reward sales people for increased productivity. The essential appeal of premiums is that the recipient feels he is getting something for nothing.

Premium Pricing The setting of prices at a level above that commonly found in the marketplace in an effort to indicate that the product is of a premium quality. Similar to prestige pricing.

Prepaid Rate A transportation charge that is paid before a shipment is delivered, usually by the shipper or seller.

Preprint An advertisement printed at the retailer's expense and distributed as a free standing insert with a newspaper.

Preprint Advertising Any advertising material printed ahead of a publication's regular press run, often on a printing press other than the regular publication press. The preprint advertising is inserted into the publication during its regular printing and binding process. Preprint advertising includes a variety of approaches, including multipage inserts, free standing inserts, reply cards and reply envelopes, and ads printed on paper stock that is different from the paper stock on which the publication is printed.

Preretailing The practice of determining prices and placing them on a copy of the purchase order at the time that goods are bought (orders placed).

Presentation, Sale The core of the personal selling process in which the sales-person transmits the information about the product and attempts to persuade the prospect to become a customer.

Presold Market Purchasers who exist before a product or service is available in the marketplace.

Press Release Publicity in the form of a written communication of commercially significant news (usually of 300 words or less) distributed to the communications media. Press releases generally identify the source of the information and carry a release date.

Prestige Pricing In retailing, the setting of prices at artificially high levels on certain items in an effort to attract customers who identify high prices with high quality and status. Also known as *symbolic pricing*.

Pretesting The testing of the potential communication effectiveness of advertising messages before they are exposed to audiences as part of a regular media schedule. Advertisers often expose versions of advertising messages that are under development to small samples of audience members to examine the extent to which the intended message is likely to be conveyed.

Price The price of goods and services is that amount of money (or other valuable consideration such as time, goods, votes, etc.) for which they may be purchased. Asking price is a representation of the value the seller places on the product offered for sale; selling price is that amount actually exchanged when the sale is consumated and includes provision for discounts, shipping charges, credit charges, allowances, etc. See also *value and cost.*

Price Agreement Plan A central buying arrangement in which the buyer for a chain of stores arranges prices, colours, sizes, styles and assortments of merchandise as well as the terms of shipping. The manager of the individual store can order from the pre-selected assortment as needed. Also called *a catalog plan.*

Price Awareness The degree to which buyers are knowledgeable of the prices of alternative products and services that they are interested in buying.

Price Bundling The practice of offering two or more products or services for sale at one price.

Price Ceiling That maximum price level beyond which customers will not longer make purchases.

Price Code A symbol or code placed on a price ticket or bin ticket to indicate the cost price of an item.

Price Competition A marketing strategy frequently employed as a means of gaining or maintaining a competitive advantage. Typically, a firm may reduce prices in an effort to attract new customers or as a response to the price reductions of a competitor. Some organizations, such as discount stores, engage as a matter of policy in price competition on a permanent basis.

Price Consciousness The degree to which buyers are sensitive to differences in price between alternative choices. Generally, a price-conscious person seeks to minimise the price paid for an item.

Price Controls Government mandated ceilings on the prices a firm may charge for its products. Firms which fail to abide by the guidelines are subject to penalties.

Price Cutting A selling strategy, usually encountered at the retail level, in which merchandise or services are offered at prices below those recommended by the vendor or at levels which are recognised by the general pubic to be lower than "regular retail."

Price-Demand Curve Response Function See *response function*

Price-Demand Elasticity See *elasticity of demand*

Price Discrimination The practice of charging different buyers different prices for the same quantity and quality of products or services.

Price Fixing The practice of two or more sellers agreeing on the price to charge for similar products or services.

Price Floor The minimum price level below which a firm can no longer realise a profit.

Price Guarantee (1) An incentive offered by the vendor to the buyer (wholesaler or retailer) who buys well in advance of the season and who places a large order. The vendor promises to reimburse the retailer for any losses resulting from decline in market price of the goods between the date of the purchase and the start of the normal selling season. (2) A promise made by a vendor to a wholesaler or retailer to reimburse the difference between the planned selling price and the actual selling price if the reseller is unable to trade the goods as planned. Also known as a *price protection rebate* or a *vendor paid markdown*.

Price Guideline A suggested target for price levels directed at marketers by government officials.

Price Leader (1) That company in any industry which, apparently without collusion, is the first to make price changes. Because the price leader is often the largest company in the industry, smaller companies tend to fall in line.

Price Leadership The practice in an industry of recognising and adopting the price established by one or more members of the industry.

Price Level Discount A discount from list price offered on particular items to avoid reprinting the entire price list. Customers are advised that certain products carry an additional percentage discount.

Price Lining A retail pricing strategy in which merchandise is offered for sale at a limited number of predetermined price points. For example, a store may offer men's shirts at $18, $26, and $35 in an effort to (1) simplify the buying process, and (2) present the customer with a manageable number of choices.

Price Maintenance The determination by the manufacturer of the price at which an identified item shall be resold by wholesalers and/or retailers.

Price-Minus Pricing A method used to determine the price of a product or service by first estimating the price at which that product or service might achieve a particular share of the market or goal volume, and then proceeding to develop the product or service to be profitable at that price.

Price Pack Products offered at a reduced price to the consumer, commonly in the form of a banded pack in which (1) two items are offered for the price of one or (2) two products (for example, shaving cream and a razor) are sold together.

Price Promotions A practice found at both the wholesale and retail levels in which prices on some items are reduced for a short period to stimulate sales. These promotions may be simple price reductions or may be in the form of allowances, discounts, free goods, premiums etc.

Price-Quality Association A theory which holds that consumers equate high prices with high quality goods and low prices with low quality goods. See also *prestige pricing*.

Price-Quality Relationship The degree to which product or service quality coveries with price.

Price Reducers Devices employed to reduce the actual selling price of a product. Includes various discounts and allowances, free service, rebates, trading stamps etc.

Price Shading A pricing policy in which discounts are offered by a manufacturer to wholesalers and retailers or by salespeople to the consumer. Price shading is used as a means of increasing demand for the product without changing the list or book price.

Price Stability A condition in the marketplace in which price competition between firms is kept to a minimum, usually as the result of the price leadership provided by one or more large firms in an industry (automobiles, steel, etc.).

Price Structure A price structure includes the time and conditions of payment, the nature of discounts to be allowed the buyer, and where and when title is to be taken by the buyer.

Price Variable A part of the marketing mix concerned with establishing product prices. It is a variable in that it is one of the components in the mix which can be altered as conditions warrant.

Price War A fiercely competitive situation in which competing firms drastically lower their prices in an attempt to undersell each other in order to attract each other's customers. Price wars sometimes result in one or more participants being forced out of business.

Pricing Any of a variety of methods used to determine the price at which goods will be sold. These methods include demand-oriented pricing, flexible rate pricing and gross margin pricing, etc.

Pricing above the Market A policy of setting prices above those of the competition so as to convey an image of superior product quality or prestige and to differentiate the product in the minds of potential customers.

Pricing at the Market A policy of setting prices at approximately the same level as one's competition, thus minimising the use of price as a competitive factor.

Pricing below the Market A policy of setting prices below those of the competition in an effort to maximise the use of price as a competitive factor. This strategy may also be an alternative to expensive promotional efforts.

Pricing Objectives Those considerations which precede the establishment of pricing policies. Pricing objectives are the comprehensive goals which the firm expects to achieve in the long run. Included may be the maximising of sales or profits, the achievement of a predetermined return on investment, an increase in market share, maintenance of a status quo with respect to price competition, etc. See also *pricing strategy and pricing policies.*

Pricing Policies Those considerations which follow the establishment of a firm's pricing objectives. Pricing policies provide marketing decision makers with predetermined guidelines to be employed in pricing individual products or services. See also *pricing strategy* and *pricing objectives.*

Pricing Strategy A component of a firm's overall marketing strategy. Pricing strategy, *i.e.*, the establishment of a realistic price framework, is crucial in determining a company's competitive position in the market-place.

Primary Advertising An approach to the advertising message that emphasises the basis attributes of the product category. This approach is usually employed by trade associations in an attempt to build demand for all the competing brands in the product category and to enhance the image of the industry involved.

Primary Buying Motive The motive that induces an individual to buy a certain kind or general class of article or service, as opposed to the selection of brands within a class.

Primary Demand Consumer demand for a class or type of product rather than for a particular brand; *e.g.*, the demand for jeans in general as opposed to the demand for levi's jeans. Also known as *generic demand.*

Primary Groups Those reference groups to which an individual belongs which exert a strong influence on his attitudes and behaviour. The most significant primary groups for most individuals are the family and the peers with whom they frequently associate.

Primary Needs Among the basic motivations which cause individual consumers to make purchase decisions, primary needs are those which derive from basic physiological factors such as thirst, hunger, the need for shelter, etc. Primary needs are universal and neither determined nor limited by cultural factors. See also *needs, Maslow's hierarchy,* and *secondary needs.*

Prime Contractor The business awarded the contract on a large and complex job which commonly necessitates the subcontracting of various parts of the job to other businesses.

Private Buying Office See *resident buying office*

Private Nonprofit Marketer A nonprofit marketer incorporated privately. Comment: Nonprofit marketers collectively have been defined as the third sector or the independent sector.

Private Sector The economic activities that are outside the so-called public sector, or those activities that are independent of government control. They are usually, but not exclusively, carried on for profit.

Private Warehouse A storage facility operated by the user. It has the advantage of total user control, important when items needing special treatment (such as chemicals and pharmaceuticals) are being stored or when storage volume is large and handling volume is constant. See also *public warehouse* and *contract warehouse.*

Prizes The reward structure of cash and/or merchandise offered in a contest, game, or sweepstakes sales promotion

Proactive Pricing The managerial practice of deliberately analysing the factors that influence prices before setting prices. Normally, a proactive pricer establishes specific objectives to be accomplished by the prices and then proceeds in the development of specific prices.

Proactive Selling A sales effort in which customers are actually pursued by a firm's sales force. See also *reactive selling.*

Probability Sample A sample in which each population element has a known, non-zero chance of being included in the sample.

Probability Sampling In marketing research, probability sampling is a method of selecting a representative subset of the total population to study so that each member has a known and equal chance of being selected. There are three basic types of probability samples: The random sample. The stratified random sample, and the area (or cluster) sample. In each type of probability sample the members of a given group are selected through an objective process without the interference of judgements made on the part of the researcher. See also *nonprobability sampling.*

Problem Recognition, in Organisational Buying The recognition that the current product or service can be replaced by a better product or service or that a cheaper way to operate exists. It is followed by a search for information and evaluation of whether new purchases are justified. Problem recognition may be stimulated internally (by a value analysis or audit, for example) or externally (by exposure to an advertisement or by a salesperson's visit).

Producer Market The producer market includes a wide variety of organisations which purchase goods to be (1) incorporated into other goods, (2) used to produce other goods, or (3) consumed in the day-to-day operations of the organisation. The producer market is a part of the larger industrial market. See also *industrial market, government market* and *institutional market.*

Producer Price Index A monthly price index of about 2,800 commodities prepared by the U.S. Bureau of Labour Statistics, formerly known as the *wholesale price index.*

Producers' Cooperative Marketing A type of cooperative marketing that primarily involves the sale of products of the membership. It may perform only an assembly or brokerage function, but in some cases, notably milk marketing and citrus fruits, it extends into processing and distribution of the members' output.

Product Advertising Advertising whose objective is the stimulation of demand for a specific product or service. It may seek an immediate response on the part of the customer, in which case it is termed direct-action advertising or it may seek a response at some time in the future, in which case it is termed indirect action advertising. Also known as brand advertising. See also *institutional advertising.*

Product Approach A method used by sales people to approach prospects in which salespeople demonstrate the product features and benefits as they walk up to the prospects.

Product Augmentation A strategy employed in marketing products which have reached the maturity stage in their life cycle. The life of a product may be extended by enhancing the way it is presented (more attractive packaging etc.), by augmenting it with services (repairs, etc.) or by superficially changing it periodically as in the woman's ready-to-wear industry.

Product Class A group of products that are homogeneous or generally considered as substitutes for each other. The class is considered as narrow or broad depending on how substitutable the various products are. For example, a narrow product class of breakfast meats might be bacon, ham and sausage. A broad class would include all other meat and meat substitutes even occasionally sold for breakfast use.

Product Deletion The withdrawal of a product from a company's line of products, generally because it is no longer profitable. Also called product pruning.

Product Depth In terms of product mix, product depth refers to the number of items in each product line offered for sale. In retailing, assortment depth is a measure or description of the quantity of each item available in the assortment of goods. An assortment containing an item in great quantities and many sizes is said to be "deep."

Product Design Models Optimal product design models are often based on consumers' perceptions and preferences data and have typically been formulated in the context of multidimensional scaling methods or conjoint analysis. In the latter case, simulation and various optimisation programmes have been used.

Product Design Simplification A marketing strategy in which a product's design is simplified in an effort to reduce manufacturing costs and increase profits. Generally, the consumer will perceive no difference in such a redesigned product.

Product Differentiation A marketing strategy in which an effort is made to clearly distinguish one product from another with particular attention to features the customer might regard as superior to those of competing products. Product differentiation may be subjective, *i.e.* it may exist largely in terms of appearance or it may be objective, *i.e.*, there may be significant physical differences between products which affect quality, safety, etc.

Product Division of Authority In marketing management, a form of organisation in which line authority is organised to correspond to the lines of products being manufactured. This arrangement is most common in large first making a highly diversified line of products.

Product Driven A company orientation in which products are developed and produced with little regard for the wants and needs of the customer,

Product Form The physical shape or nature of a good or the sequential steps in a service. Form is provided by one or more technologies and yields benefits to the user; for example, many technologies are used to make a front-wheel drive form of an automobile. Products of the same form make up a group within a product class (*e.g.,* all front-wheel drive automobiles). Differences in form of service separate discount stock brokers and full-service stock brokers.

Product Introduction The first stage of the product life cycle, during which the new item is announced to the market and offered for sale. Most methods of market testing are considered pre-introduction, but many marketers call the market rollout an introduction because of the commitment implied in the method. If successful during the introduction, the new product enters the second (growth) stage.

Product Item A particular product having enough distinctive attributes to be easily distinguished from other products in a line. For stock keeping purposes, product items frequently are assigned a unique identifying number. See also *stock keeping unit (SKU).*

Product Liability The legal responsibility of a manufacturer or seller of a product to pay damages to parties injured through the use of the product when it has proven to be defective or unsafely designed.

Product Life Cycle (PLC) The product life cycle is a series of stages through which a product or service passes as it evolves in the market-place. Four stages are readily identifiable:

(1) introduction of the product, (2) its growth, i.e., the extent of demand for the product, (3) market maturity, (4) the ultimate saturation of the market by the product (or its failure to capture a market) and its eventual decline.

Product Line A group of products closely related by some factors such as physical characteristic, price, end-use, etc. In retailing, various lines make up what is known as variety. Variety, in turn, is a component of the merchan-dise assortment.

Product Line Marketing A strategy in which two or more products are marketed by a firm under a common (and frequently respected) brand name. Product line marketing enables a company to expand its product lines and to develop coordinated advertising campaigns. See also *brand marketing*.

Product Line Pricing A pricing strategy in which a firm's entire line of products and their interrelationships are considered when prices are set for individual products.

Product Management Organisation Product managers or brand managers are responsible for developing marketing plans, coordinating implementation of the plans by the functional departments, and monitoring performance of their assigned products. Product managers report to the marketing manager unless there are large numbers of them in which case they report to an intervening level of supervision such as the group product manager or category manager. The terms *product management* and *product manager* are interchangeable with *brand management and brand manager*. Comment: The advantage of this form of organisation is that each product receives the full attention of one person responsible for its success.

Product Manager An executive who functions as the head of the product team responsible for the planning and development of a particular product, product line, or brand. The product manager (or brand manager as he is sometimes called) oversees the development of a competetive strategy, coordinates all aspects of planning and directs advertising and promotional efforts on behalf of the product. The product manager is, in many respects, the marketing manager for his particular product.

Product Manager System A middle management system employed by firms marketing a relatively large number of distinct products. Each product has a manager who is totally involved in the development and marketing of the product from its conception through its commercialisation. Such a system is meant to ensure that each product in the marketing mix receives adequate attention.

Product Management Those business activities concerned with the development of new products or brands, their introduction into the marketplace, and their management through the product life cycle. See also *product manager*.

Product Market A market in which vendors offer similar products which may be considered substitutes for each other. These products may be either physically or conceptually similar and are regarded comparable in satisfying consumer needs. For example, all luxury automobiles would be considered part of the same product market, since they may substitute for each other in satisfying customers' needs for transportation, luxury and status. See also *generic market* and *market*.

Product Mix The aggregate of products offered for sale by a firm. The product mix may be measured in breadth (*i.e.*, the number of product lines carried), or in depth (*i.e.*, the assortment of sizes, types, colours and styles within each product line). The consistency of a company's product mix depends on how the various lines relate to one another in terms of distribution requirements, ultimate end use, etc.

Product Modification The altering of a current product so as to make it more appealing to the marketplace. This contrasts with creating a line extension and with repositioning a current product, both of which can be used to achieve the same purpose.

Product Planning A term of many meanings, but generally it is used to designate a staff position charged with part or all of the task of managing product innovation within an organisation. In some firms, it also includes acquisition of products or processes.

Product Planning Manager In a functionally organised department (with no product managers), the product planning manager represents the marketing manager in contacts with functional units within and outside the marketing department with respect to product line planning, development of new products, improvement of existing products, and pruning the product line. The product planning manager reports to the marketing manager and assists this executive with the development of overall product strategy. Comment: This position usually is not present in a product functions listed above are the responsibility of product managers or category managers, except for new product development, which is usually assigned to a new product manager.

Product Portfolio Concept A strategic marketing tool in which a firm views the products it produces as part of a larger product mix and then treats the various product mixes (or divisions within the company) as though they were parts of a stock portfolio. These units are evaluated in terms of profitability and are either given support or are sold off just as stocks with a poor return on investment are sold off. The portfolio approach to marketing management is somewhat limited in that it takes a short-run view of product performance.

Product Positioning (1) The way consumers, users, buyers and others view competitive brands or types of products. As determined by a market research techniques, the various products are plotted onto maps, using product attributes as dimensions. This use of product positioning is perceptual, not necessarily valid as based on measured product attributes. Historically, the competitive product positionings were based on sales rank in the market, but this limited perception has long since given way to the full range of product assessments, including psychological ones. (2) For new products, product positioning means how the innovator firm decides to compare the new item to its predecessors. For the new item, the mental slates of persons in the market place are blank; this is the only chance the innovator will have to make a first impression. Later, after the introduction is over, the earlier definition of positioning will take over, as persons make their own positioning decisions. (3) For both new and established products, a product's positioning may be combined with a target segment to integrate the marketing tool decisions.

Product Profoliferation A charge sometimes leveled against organisations for marketing so many new products that economic resources are wasted; the consumer becomes confused and mistakes are made in the purchase of products.

Product Quality (1) The measure of any particular attribute a product has (what flavour, how much, how lasting). (2) The measure of the intended customer's reactions to that attribute, how it is liked, its affect. On manufactured goods, the quality assessment is most often made on the quality of the product's physical features as created by the manufacturing process; the judgements are made by managers using proprietary standards. (3) Product quality may also be related to price, in which any particular lower-price item might be said to have good quality for the money; this use equates product quality with product value.

Product Recall The call back of products because of defects, imperfections or other shortcomings. Agencies such as the Consumer Products Safety Commission or the Federal Trade Commission may compel a producer to recall a product when it violates safety or other regulations.

Product Screening A stage in the new product planning process during which product proposals which are deemed unsuitable are weeded out and dropped from further consideration.

Product Segmentation In industrial marketing, the subdivision of a market on the basis of product specifications which meet the requirements of the purchaser.

Product Symbolism The sum total of what a product means to the consumer and what the consumer experiences in purchasing and using it.

Product Trade Life Cycle An empirical cycle that recognises the relationship between production, consumption, trade, and the product life cycle for certain countries at certain times in history. The model shows how product of mature products with stabilised technologies has relocated from the U.S. to the developing to the less developed countries of the world as companies takes advantage of lower wage and other factor costs in various parts of the world.

Product Transformation This occurs when the same physical product ends up serving a different function or use than that for which it was originally designed or created.

Product Use Test One of several key evaluation steps in the product development process. This involves giving a prototype or pilot plant product to persons or firms in the intended target market and asking them to use it for a time and report their reactions to it. The purposes of a product use test are (1) to see if the item developed by the organisation has the attributes prescribed for it, (2) to learn whether it satisfies the market needs that were identified during the ideation process, and (3) to disclose information about how and by whom the item is used.

Product Variables Those aspects of a product which are subject to change such as colour, size, price, operating cost, reliability, availability, brand name, packaging, etc. Product variables are marketing mix variables in that they are controllable by the organisation. They are unlike variables in the marketing environment which are largely out of the control of the firm.

Product Width In terms of product mix, product width (or breadth) refers to the number of product lines offered for sale. In retailing, assortment width refers to the number of different categories or classifications available in a store or department without reference to the quantity available in any one style. An assortment is said to be wide (or broad) when a large variety of different items is available within a classification.

Production 1. (economic definition) The addition of utilities to goods or the rendering of services of possessing utility. 2. (marketing definition) The creation of form utility, *i.e.*, all activities used to change the appearance or composition of a good or service with the intent of making it more attractive to potential and actual users.

Production Era A time period in the United States during which firms emphasised manufacturing or producing products, usually at the expense of marketing strategy.

Production Era of Marketing A stage in the evolution of marketing (during the Industrial Revolution) characterised by a high level of competition. Manufacturers concentrated their efforts on producing goods and moving them to their customers as efficiently as possible. Little consideration was given to the wants and needs of the consumer.

Production Fit In product marketing, production fit refers to the degree of compatibility of a new product with the firm's existing machinery of production.

Production Function The technical relationship, given a state of technical knowledge, relating to the amount of output capable of being produced by different sets of specified inputs.

Production Orientation A business philosophy that emphasises the output of products, usually at the expense of marketing strategy.

Productivity As a marketing concept, a measurement of the efficiency of a producer, generally expressed in terms of the number of man hours expended per unit of production. The concept may also be applied to such factors as capital or land.

Productivity Sales Goal An objective for a salesperson based on the salesperson's efficiency assessed by dividing outputs by inputs such as sales per call.

Professional Advertising (1) Advertising by professionals, such as lawyers, physicians, dentists etc., (2) Advertising by manufacturers or distributors of products whose success in the marketplace depends on the acceptance and approval of professionals. The message is directed to the professional in the hope that he will recommend or specify the particular product. For example, physicians are encouraged to prescribe particular drugs, engineers to specify particular building materials, etc.

Professional Pricing A pricing strategy employed by professionals (lawyers, architects, etc.) in which services are rendered for a flat, predetermined fee rather than calculated on an hourly basis.

Professional Services Marketing The marketing of advisory services offered by licensed or accredited individuals or organisations.

Profit Although profit may be regarded in a general sense as the abstract goal of a business or profession, in its marketing context it is generally taken to mean total revenue less all costs and expenses. Profit is commonly qualified by another term such as gross or net, thus making the concept more precise.

Profit and Loss Statement An accounting statement of net profit (or net loss) based on the firm's revenues less expenses and losses for a specific period of time. Also called an income statement, operating statement or statement of operations.

Profit-Oriented Audit An evaluation of a marketing plan in terms of the expenses and revenues generated by that plan. See also *marketing audit*.

Profit Target Analysis A method used to calculate the volume of sales needed to pay for all costs (both fixed and variable) of operation and return a predetermined profit. Similar to a break-even analysis, except that fixed costs include a predetermined level of profit. That level of profit represents a targeted return on investment, often required by the firm's management. See also *break even analysis*.

Profit-Volume Ratio The dollar contribution per unit divided by the unit price. The profit-volume ratio indicates the rate at which fixed costs are recovered and after the break-even point has been reached, the rate at which profits are earned as sales volume increases.

Promotion Marketing Association of America (PMAA) A New York based association of promotion service companies, sales incentive organisations and related businesses. PMAA's membership also includes manufacturers of premium merchandise, consultants and advertising agencies as associate members. The association studies and promote premium usage and co-sponsors both the New York Premium Show and the National Premium Show.

Promotion Mix The selected combination of advertising, publicity, sales promotion and personal selling used to communicate with, inform and sell goods to the consumer. The elements may be varied to arrive at the most effective and cost-effective programme.

Promotion Models Models to estimate the effect of a promotion (*e.g.*, temporary price change, etc.) include models based on market response functions or a combination of empirical data with management subjective judgement as in BRANDAID. Promotion models often are stochastic and based on behavioural assumptions regarding retailers and consumers. Many of these models decompose the value of the promotion into components such as increased loyalty among current customers, attraction of deal prone switchers etc. Inventory control-based promotion models have also been proposed, incorporating the inventory carrying costs of consumers and retailers. The increased availability and popularity of scanner data have focused attention on promotion models.

Promotion Planning Those activities which lead to the development of a firm's comprehensive promotional plan including the formulation of objectives, budgeting, and the development of an appropriate promotional mix.

Promotional Department Store A discount store which, due to its size and merchandise mix (both hard and soft lines), approximates a department store. Promotional department stores operate at lower gross margins than traditional department stores because of their relatively low- rent locations, lack of amenities, and minimal service. They are, however, often as profitable as other types of stores in their price class. Also called full-line discount stores.

Promotional Package The collection of sales promotion materials and offers developed by the seller to influence retailers, wholesalers or salespeople to support a particular promotional theme.

Promotional Price A reduced price offered on a temporary basis to promote specific merchandise.

Promotional Stock A retailer's stock of goods offered at an unusually attractive price in order to obtain volume trade. It generally represents special purchases from vendors.

Proof-of-Purchase Some element of the product or package used as evidence that the consumer has purchased the product. Common proofs-of-purchase are labels, boxtops, ingredient listings, etc.

Proprietary Store An establishment selling the same merchandise as a drug store, except that prescriptions are not filled and sold.

Protection Department The operating unit of a retail store that is responsible for protecting the merchandise or other assets from pilferage (internal or external). Those working in the department may be store employees or outside people. It is sometimes referred to as a loss prevention department or function.

Protection in Transit In shipping,the function performed by a product's package, *i.e.,* protection from damage

Prototype The first physical form or service description of a new product, still in rough or tentative mode. Occasionally a prototype may precede research and development if making it is easy (*e.g.,* cake mixes). With complex products, there may be component prototype as well as one finished prototypes. On services, the prototype is simply the first full description of how the service will work and comes from the systems design or development function.

Proximo Dating This specifies the date in the following month on which payment must be made in order to take the cash discount—*e.g.,* terms of "2%, 10th proximo, net 60 days, " meaning that the bill must be paid prior to the tenth day of the month following purchase in order to take the discount, but that a credit period of 60 days from the first of the month is allowed.

Psychoanalytic Theory A psychological theory developed by Sigmund Freud that emphasises unconscious motivation.

Psychological Buying Motive Consumer motives which have their roots in social or psychological needs. Products such as expensive automobiles and jewellery are frequently purchased to satisfy psychological needs, which are the time motivating factors. See also *motive.*

Psychological Pricing A pricing strategy most commonly found in retailing in which an effort is made to generate an emotional response on the part of the consumer through one of a number of tactics. See *leader pricing, odd-line pricing, even-line pricing, prestige pricing and customary price* for examples of psychological pricing.

Public Market A wholesale or retail market primarily for foodstuffs, supervised or administered by a municipality that rents space or stalls to dealers. It is also called a municipal market or a community market.

Public Nonprofit Marketer A nonprofit marketer that is a unit of a national, state, or local government.

Public Opinion The consensus view of a population on a topic.

Public Policy A course of action pursued by the government pertaining to people as a whole on which laws rest.

Public Sector Those marketing activities that are carried out by government agencies for public service rather than for profit.

Public Service Advertising Advertising designed to serve the general public on a nonprofit basis. Such advertising is generally meant to inform the public or to encourage or discourage certain behaviour, *e.g.*, campaigns against drunk driving. Not a synonym for institutional advertising.

Public Warehouse An independently owned storage facility serving a variety of users. The public warehouseman does not own or take title to the goods stored. The user of the facility is charged on the basis of cost per unit and the storage arrangements are made on a month-to-month basis. Other services such as receiving, packing and invoicing may be available at additional cost. See also *private warehouse* and *contract warehouse*.

Publicity Unpaid, nonpersonal public notice in the print or electronic media (usually in the form of news stories) which may stimulate the sales of a product or service, or enhance the reputation of a person. A firm may attempt to plant favourable stories in the media via news releases which convey commercially significant information about the company, its products, or its role in the community.

Publicity Plan A company's overall plan for nonpaid, nonpersonal promotional activities. Includes the objectives, rationale, evaluation of the programme, and the media used. See also publicity.

Publics 1. (Legislation definition) Groups of people with common interest in a specific area, domain, topic or organisation. 2. (sales promotion definition). Those groups that have an actual or possible interest in or impact on the company's efforts to achieve its goals.

Purchase Act In general the act of buying a product or service. More specifically, in the consumer adoption process the purchase act follows the evaluation and trial stages of the process.

Purchase Contract A written agreement between the buying and supplying organisations that specifies the terms of the transaction: product specifications, price, payment schedule, delivery terms, penalties and the like. It differs from the purchase order in that it is generally written by and signed by both parties.

Purchase Decision, in Organisational Buying That phase of the organisation's buying process in which alternative offers of suppliers are evaluated and a selection of one (or more) supplier is made.

Purchase Intention A decision plan to buy a particular product or brand created through a choice/decision process.

Purchaser The person who actually buys a product or service. The purchaser may be a buyer at the industrial level or a customer at the consumer level.

Purchase Order A (generally standard) document that is issued by a purchasing organisation to a supplier requesting items in the quantities, price, item and other terms agreed upon.

Purchasing A generic term used to describe a title, a function or process by which a firm acquires the factors necessary to produce and distribute goods and services.

Purchasing Agent A professional buyer employed by governmental, industrial or institutional organisations charged with the responsibility for procuring equipment and supplies for use in the organisation.

Purchasing Department The organisational unit responsible for learning the needs of operating units, locating and selecting supplier(s), negotiating price and other pertinent terms, and following up to ensure delivery.

Purchasing Power Parity An economic principle stating that a change in the relationship between price levels in two countries will require an adjustment in the currency exchange rate to offset the price level differences.

Purely Competitive Market Structure See *perfect competition*

Push Marketing Strategy See *push strategy*

Push Money Bonus money paid as an incentive to push specially designated products. Push money is generally paid by a manufacturer to the salespersons employed by wholesalers and retailers and may also take the form of prices such as appliances and vacation trips. Also called prize money.

Push only Allowance See *push money (PM)*

Push or Pull Distribution Strategy A plan for increasing the market penetration of a product. "Push" refers to intense personal selling on the part of sales personnel representing the vendor. Dealers are encouraged to stock and push the product. "Pull" (also called forced distribution) refers to direct appeals to the ultimate consumers, encouraging them to ask their dealers to stock the item.

Push Strategy A marketing distribution strategy in which a firm's promotional efforts are directed toward members of the channel of distribution, *e.g.*, wholesalers, distributors and retailers who are motivated (*i.e.*, pushed) through such devices as advertising allowances and discounts to stock and sell the firm's products. See also *pull strategy*.

Pushing Strategy See *push strategy*

Put-out Pricing See *predatory pricing*

Q

Quality Check A form of merchandise checking done in the receiving department in which the condition of the arriving merchandise is determined.

Quantity Check A form of merchandise checking done in the receiving department in which correctness of quantity received is verified.

Quality Control An activity which includes the monitoring of products as they are produced in an effort to measure their quality, the comparison of the product to an established standard and all subsequent efforts to maintain that standard.

Quality of Life A sense of well being about a person's or society's way of life and life style, often estimated by social indicators. The governing factors include income, wealth, safety, recreation facilities, education, health, aesthetics, leisure time and the like.

Quantity Discount A reduction in price offered by the seller of goods as an inducement to the buyer to purchase large quantities.

Quantity Price Discount See *quantity discount*

Question Approach A technique used by a salesperson in the first few minutes of contact with a prospect. In this approach, the salesperson gives the prospect an interesting fact about the product or service phrased as a question. This question is intended to stimulate the prospect's participation in the sales presentation. See also *approach.*

Questionnaire A data-gathering instrument (usually a printed form) used to collect information from respondents. Generally one of three methods is employed: (1) personal interview, (2) telephone interview or (3) mail survey.

Quick Response A strategy in which a manufacturer or service industry makes an effort to supply its customers with products or services in the precise quantities required at exactly the right time. In the U.S. quick response operations are sometimes found in the soft goods industry where an attempt is made to shorten the cycle time in the textile maker/apparel manufacturer/ retailer pipe line. See also *kanban* and *just-in-time (JIT) system*.

Quota A fixed amount which is used as a goal, e., a dollar figure fixed as the sales goal for a salesperson.

Quota-Bonus Compensation A plan that involves a basic salary and commissions paid on sales in excess of a predetermined quota.

Quota Bonus Plan For Salespeople, a compensation plan in which a base salary is paid without regard to productivity, but which also includes a bonus when a fixed quota of sales is exceeded.

R

Rack A floor stand sed as an interior display for holding and/ or showing merchandise. Utilizes shelves, hooks, or pockets.

Rack Jobber A limited-service wholesaler who sells specialised merchandise, *e.g.*, books, pantyhose, records, sun glasses, etc. to supermarkets, drug stores and other self-service retailers. The store provides the counter or floor space and the jobber sets up racks, stores merchandise, marks prices and maintains stock levels through periodic calls. The rack jobber is a consignment wholesaler in that he is paid only for goods actually sold by the retailer who, in turn, keeps a percentage of the profit. Also known as service merchandisers.

Random Sampling In marketing research, a method of selecting a representative subset of the total population in which each member of the population has a known and equal chance of being included in the sample group. The members are selected on an objective basis, such as every tenth name on a list. Random sampling is one form of probability sampling.

Randomised Response Model An interviewing technique in which potentially embarrassing and relatively innocuous questions are paired and the question the respondent answers is randomly determined.

Range The maximum distance a consumer is ordinarily willing to travel for a good or service; as such it determines the outer limit of a store's trade area or market area.

Rate 1. (advertising definition) The cost of a unit of space or time in an advertising media vehicle. 2. (physical distribution definition) A charge usually expressed in dollar terms for the performance of some transportation or distribution service.

Rate Card A printed listing of the charges associated with different amounts of time or space, different placements in the vehicle and other conditions of sales. Often rate cards serve as the starting point for negotiation in the fashion of the sticker on the window of a new car.

Rate Differential The difference between the local advertising and national advertising rates charged by a local advertising vehicle.

Rate of Return Pricing A method of determining prices by adding a markup that will produce a predetermined return on investment.

Rate Regulation The process by which rates are administered. In a highly regulated economy, this could include extensive rules and policies on pricing and related services. Regulation occurs at the federal, state and local levels.

Rating The percentage of the total potential audience who are exposed to a particular media vehicle. In television, a rating is the number of households with their television sets tuned to a particular programme for a specified length of time divided by the total number of households that have television. In print media, ratings are computed using survey data about actual readership rather than information about circulation.

Ratio Scale A measurement in which the numbers assigned to the attributes of the objects have a natural or absolute zero and that therefore allow the comparison of absolute magnitudes of the objects.

Rational Appeals 1. (consumer behaviour definition) The concept of rational or irrational appeals does not exist in modern consumer behaviour thinking but rather this is a term carried over from economics. From the point of view of the consumer, all behaviour is rational although it may not appear so to the observer. 2. (industrial definition) Claims that attempt to show that a specific product will yield certain functional benefits. Rational appeals form the core of most organisational sales massages while more emotional appeals, addressing self-image, life style and the like, are more often used to position, products in the consumer marketplace.

Rational Buying Motive Any factor affecting a consumer's decision to buy merchandise or services which is based on logic, reason and careful thought. See also *motive* and *emotional buying motive.*

Rationalisation An ego defense in which unattainable goals are perceived to be undesirable (sour grapes) and those that are attainable are perceived to be remarkably adequate (sweet lemons).

Rationing A system of allocating goods and services that are in short supply, other than by price, to prevent prices from rising to unreasonable levels and prevent inequitable distribution. It is often used in periods of emergency.

Raw Materials Materials in their unprocessed natural state (*e.g.*, iron ore), or in a semi-finished state (*e.g.*, pig iron), used in the production of other goods. Raw materials may be produced (such as cotton, grain, and livestock), or they may be extracted (such as lumber, ore or fish).

Reach The number of readers or viewers who are exposed to a medium, *e.g.*, radio, television, magazines, newspapers, at least one in a given period of time. Reach is a term commonly used in advertising to describe the breadth of coverage of a single advertisement, a series of a advertisements, or an entire advertising campaign. Also known as *media coverage.*

Reactive Selling A sales effort in which customers are allowed to take the initiative in seeking out a vendor. See also *proactive selling.*

Real Income Income (whether that of an individual, group or country) expressed in terms of purchasing power rather than dollars. Real income is a useful concept when incomes are compared over time and price levels have changed, e.g., price increases between 1970 and 1980 reduced the value of dollar increases in salaries during that period by about half.

Rebate A reduction in price granted the buyer of goods (wholesaler, retailer, or consumer) by the manufacturer or producer of the goods for the purpose of encouraging sales. The rebate is generally made as a cash refund sent to the buyer after the transaction has been completed at the regular price. Also known as a *money refund offer*.

Recall Loss A type of error caused by a respondent forgetting that an event happened.

Recall Test A test of advertising effectiveness in which a sample of members of the audience are contacted at a specific time after exposure to a media vehicle and asked to recall advertising messages they remember seeing and/or hearing in the media vehicle. It is called *unaided recall* if there is no prompting with elements of the ads or commercials being examined. With prompting, the results are called *aided recall*.

Receipt of Goods Dating An invoice agreement specifying that the discount period allowed by the seller to the buyer does not begin until the goods are actually received by the buyer.

Recession A turning point in a business cycle characterised by dropping production and increasing unemployment.

Reciprocity An arrangement commonly found in industrial purchasing in which two organisations buy each other's products. Simple reciprocity (sometimes called innocent reciprocity) in which there is no effort on the part of one firm to dominate another, may degenerate into coercive reciprocity if one firm attempts to force a subordinate firm to purchase its products.

Redemption Rate The number or percentage of sales promotion offers that are acted on by consumers or retailers out of the total number possible.

Redemption Store An establishment operated by a trading stamp company redeeming stamps for merchandise.

Redlining The arbitrary exclusion of certain classes of customers, often those from poor neighbourhoods, from such economic activities as borrowing money or getting real estate mortgages.

Reduced-Price Pack A package conspicuously market with a price lower than regular retail.

Reference Group Those persons from whom an individual derives his values, standards, tastes, etc. and on whom the individual molds his attitudes and behaviour; *i.e.,* a group that forms a basis of comparison for the individual. A person need not belong to a group nor have direct contact with it for it to serve as a reference group. In fact, certain groups exert a negative influence in that an individual, in an attempt to avoid identification with the group, avoids certain kinds of behaviour.

Reference Price The price that buyers use to compare the offered price of a product or service. The reference price may be a price in a buyer's memory, or it may be the price of an alternative product.

Referral A lead for a prospect given to the salesperson by an existing customer.

Referral Approach A technique used by a salesperson in the first few minutes of contact with a prospect. In this approach, the salesperson mentions the name of someone known to the prospect who has referred the salesperson to him as someone who might be interested in the good or service being sold. See also *approach.*

Referral Lead See *chain prospecting*

Referral Sample A form of non-probability sample in which the research is done in waves, *i.e.,* the first stage of the research uncovers other organisations or individuals who may be sampled in a second wave. Also called a snowball sample.

Refund 1. (pricing definition) A return of the amount paid for an item. 2. (sales promotion definition) An offer made by the seller to return a certain amount of money to the purchaser when the product is purchased alone or in combination with some other product.

Refusal-to-Sell The right of a seller to refuse to sell merchandise to another party, *e.g.,* a wholesaler or retailer, because that party fails to meet his standards or qualifications.

Regional Cooperation Groups An association of two or more countries cooperating in one or more joint ventures. Each country contributes to the financing of the project and agrees to buy a percentage of the project's output.

Regional Edition The subdivision of a national magazine's circulation into geographic regions, so that advertisers can purchase only the portion of the publication's circulation that applies to their immediate needs. A region can be a group of neighbouring states, a single state, or in some instances, regions within specific states. A demographic edition operates on the same principle, except that the subdivisions are based on various demographic characteristics of the publication's circulation.

Regional Shopping Centre The largest of the shopping centres, usually anchored by one or more full-line department stores and complemented by as many as 150 or more smaller retail stores and related businesses. Most regional centres have a gross leasable area of 4,00,000 square feet or more—centres having over 7,50,000 square feet are regarded as super-regional and are generally anchored by three or more department stores. Most regionals centres need a surrounding population of at least 1,50,000 to operate profitably. Their radous of attraction is in the 10-15 mile range. See also *shopping centre*.

Regression Analysis In causal research, regression analysis is the attempt to project the future levels of one unknown variable, such as sales, on the basis of forecasts for one or more known variables, such as disposable personal income. Variables are selected on the basis of whether a relationship between them has been observed in the past.

Regularly Unsought Goods Products that are regularly needed by consumers, but which they will not extend themselves to find. For example, gravestones, insurance and encyclopedias are all regularly unsought goods. This class of goods requires extensive promotion. See also *unsought goods*.

Regulation The efforts by governmental units to create and enforce conditions that specify acceptable business practice.

Reilly's Law A model used in trade area analysis to define the relative ability of two cities to attract customers from the area between them.

Reilly's Law of Retail Gravitation A theory concerning the relative pull of two competing shopping areas on potential customers residing between them. Proposes that customers will be drawn from the intermediate town at or close to the point of equal probability, approximately in direct proportion to the populations of the two shopping areas and in direct proportion to the squares of the distance between the town and the two shopping areas.

Reinforcement Advertising Advertising which assures the purchaser of a product that the has made a wise choice if norms him on ways in which he may derive the most satisfaction from his choice.

Relationship Marketing Marketing with the conscious aim to develop and manage long-term and/or trusting relationships with customers, distributors, suppliers, or other parties in the marketing environment.

Relationship Value The bonds, both actual and perceptual, that are created between the customer, the marketer, and the brand by a specific sales promotion event.

Relative Advantage In new product development, relative advantage is the degree to which the product is viewed by potential customers to be superior to all the products available for sale in the marketplace.

Relative Market Share The share of the market held by a firm or product as compared to the market shares of competitors.

Relative Precision A degree of precision desired in an estimate of a parameter is expressed relative to the level of the estimate of the parameter.

Relevant Market In strategic planning, a market selected as best corresponding to a firm's own purposes. The relevant market offers opportunities for the firm to obtain its objectives given its available resources. The relevant market selected should be bigger than the firm's current market, thus allowing for expansion. It should not, however, be so large that the firm would be unable to become a significant competitor in the new market. For example, a small manufacturer of children's clothing that distributes its goods locally may have the production and/or marketing capability to expand to a national market. However, worldwide distribution may be considerably beyond the company's grasp. See also *market* and *strategic planning*.

Reliability In marketing research, reliability is the accuracy with which data portrays reality, particularly when a sample group is studied in order to make generalisations about to total population. See also *sampling*

Remarking The practice of remarking merchandise due to price changes, lost or multiplated tickets or customer returns.

Remerchandising A strategy to improve the salability of a product while leaving the product itself unchanged. Changes are made instead in the accompanying services (such as standardisation of product quality, improvement of product service, and the provision of promotional guarantees). Packaging may also be modified in design, cost and size of package. Branding, the broadening of price points, and an increase in the variety of styles offered may also be used to increase the market share of the product.

Reminder Advertising A form of competitive advertising calculated to keep a product service, industry, viewpoint, etc. in the public eye. It reinforces previous promotional efforts and, in the case of products, is generally used at the maturity stage in the product life cycle. Sometimes called retentive advertising.

Rented Goods Service (1) A category of consumer service in which a product is rented or leased for a specified period, *e.g.*, automobile rentals. (2) In retailing, a service firm or department in a store renting products at a fee to customers for their temporary use, *e.g.*, the rental of rug shampooing equipment by supermarkets.

Reorder Point (ROP) The pre-established minimum inventory levels at which additional orders should be placed for a particular item so as to avoid going into an out-of-stock position. Also known as *threshold-point ordering*.

Reorder Unit The unit in which an item is reordered, the exact amount depending on trade practices—*e.g.*, dozen, gross, nearest hundred weight or foot.

Repeat Sale The subsequent sale of a product after the initial purchase. The level of repeat sales for a product is often used as a measure of customer satisfaction—the higher the level of repeat sales, the more satisfied customers are.

Replacement Level Fertility A total fertility rate of 2,120 or 2.12 births per 1,000 women. It is the rate at which a population reaches zero population growth.

Replacement Sale A sale that takes place when a product becomes physically or economically obsolete. The timing of replacement is influenced by a customer's business prospects, its cash flow, product alternatives in the market, as well as the seller's financing terms and sales efforts.

Repositioning A marketing strategy designed to increase the consumption of an already existing product by changing its target market. For example, the product may be repositioned to appeal to a larger or faster-growing market segment. Brands, too, may require repositioning. Shifting customer preferences and/or a competitor's incursions into the brand's original market may leave a company's brand with diminished demand and a smaller share of the market. In order to capture a new target market and increase sales, a company will select a new group of consumers to whom it gears its advertising and other promotional activities. As with the original selection of a target market, the new target group is selected on the basis of the number of potential customers in the group, their average purchase rate of similar products, the quality and quantity of competitors in the segment, and the pricing structure of the brands in the new segment. See also *market positioning*

Repurchase Rate The volume of purchase and the amount of time that typically occur between consumer or retailer purchasing occasions for a specific product.

Request for Proposal (RFP) A request issued by a potential buyer desiring bids from several potential vendors for a product or service satisfying specifications describing the buyer's needs.

Request for Quotation (RFQ) A document transmitted to a potential supplier requesting price and delivery terms on a specific item or set of items. A supplier responds to an RFQ with a quotation.

Resale Price Maintenance Laws Federal and state statutes permitting agreements between a supplier and a retailer that state that the latter should not resell commodities below a specified minimum price.

Research and development (R&D) The function of working through various sciences and technologies to design new products. This usually involves some basic research for creating new technologies and some applied research for converting those basic discoveries (and others) into specific new products. The applied (or developmental) phase begins after new product concepts have been screened and desirable attributes set up for them. It ends when scientific personnel deliver to manufacturing the necessary process specifications and finished product specifications. R&D departments also have many other duties not so directly related to new products.

Research Design The formal model or plan for the conduct of a research study. The research design usually states the hypothesis to be tested, the research method to be employed and the manner in which the collected data is to be analysed.

Research Process A sequence of steps in the design and implementation of a research study, including problem formulation, determination of sources of information and research design, determination of data collection method and design of data collection forms, design of the sample and collection of the data, analysis and interpretation of the data, and the research report.

Reseller Market Those marketing intermediaries such as wholesalers, distributors and retailers who buy finished goods for the purpose of reselling them. Resellers generally do not significantly alter the goods they sell nor do they incorporate them into other products.

Reservation Price The highest price a buyer is willing to pay for a product or service.

Resident Buyer A market representative employed in a resident buying office which, in turn, acts as an agent for its clients and member stores. The resident buyer is often a specialist, buying in a particular segment of the market. Once the merchandise has been purchased the resident buyer, unlike the store buyer, has no further merchandising responsibilities, *i.e.*, he or she does not have to resell the merchandise as does the retailer.

Resident Buying Office A purchasing agent located in a a national or international market centre whose representatives shop the market daily in order to provide their clients or member stores with information and to select and buy merchandise for them. Buying offices are either independent (the salaried office and the commission buying office) or store-owned (the private office, the cooperative office, and the corporate office). The resident buyer-client relationship is most commonly found in the apparel industry.

Residual Market Value The image-enhancing communication about the product or service that remains with the consumer after the sales promotion event is over.

Resource Allocation Models Models for guiding the allocation of marketing resources. Mathematical programming, decision calculus models, and the analytic hierarchy process are often used.

Resource Rating The evaluation of resources through the statistical measurement and rating of vendors according to their respective contributions to store volume and profits and quality or dependability of service.

Response (1) In communications, the response to a message is the reaction on the part of the receiver (2) In consumer behaviour, the individual reaction to environmental cues.

Responsibility In organisations, responsibility defines the job to be done by an individual, including the measurement of the individual's performance The responsibilities of any given job are generally defined in the job description, as is the degree of power or authority associated with that position.

Restraint of Trade An act or agreement which is calculated to limit the free exercise of commercial competition. Restraint of trade often takes the form of monopolies, attempts by one or more parties to control prices or levels of production, or other restraints on free trade to the detriment of the public.

Retail According Theory A theory of retail institutional change that suggests that retail institutions go from outlets with wide assortments to specialised narrow line store merchants and then back again to the more general wide assortment institution. It is also referred to as the general-specific-general theory.

Retail Cooperative A voluntary association of independent retailers who jointly own and operate their own wholesale facilities and/or who act together as a buying club in order to achieve the economies of large scale purchasing. The member stores often display a common emblem or logo and carry, in addition to nationally recognised brands, their own distributor brands. Also known as a *retailer-owned cooperative, retailer-sponsored cooperative*, and a *retailer's cooperative chain*. See also *voluntary chain and consumer cooperative.*

Retail Etablishment A single or separate place of business principally engaged in the performance of marketing functions, where in or out sales are made primarily to ultimate consumers.

Retail Inventory Method of Accounting A type of accounting system whereby the closing inventory at cost is determined by the average relationship between cost and retail value of all goods available for sale during the period.

Retail Life Cycle A theory which attempts to describe the evolution of a retail store from its inception to its decline. The theory maintains that a retail establishment passes through four identifiable stages: (1) innovation, (2) accelerated development, (3) maturity, and (4) decline. In the innovation stage, the store (or type of store) is new and must be introduced to customers in hopes that it will attract a following. If the store or concept catches on, it enters a period of rapid growth (accelerated development) in which other retailers imitate or adopt the store's concept and seek to attract the same target customers. The store itself may experience rapid growth in sales and popularity. As competitors enter the market by using the same or similar strategies, the market eventually approaches saturation and growth slows. The store enters the maturity stage. Once growth has significantly decreased or even ceased, the decline stage follows. This is comparable to the product life cycle. See also *product life cycle (PLC)* and *wheel of retailing theory.*

Retail Marketing A concept in which sales goals are set on the basis of market potential with increased attention to the behaviour of the consumer. While merchandising has lines and departments as its point of focus, *i.e.,* what is selling, retail marketing is more concerned with who is buying what and the underlying reasons for this behaviour.

Retail Price Index See *Consumer Price Index (CPI)*

Retail Price Maintenance See *resale price maintenance*

Retail Reductions The total of mark-downs, discounts to employees and other classes of customers and stock shortages.

Retail Salesperson A salesperson employed by a retailer who is involved in selling goods and services to the ultimate consumer in retail stores.

Retail Store A place of business (establishment) open to and frequented by the general public, and in which sales are made primarily to ultimate consumers, usually in small quantities, from merchandise inventories stored and displayed on the premises.

Retail Structure The spatial distribution of retail stores and store types, including the composition of groupings of stores, spacing and relationship to market.

Retail Transaction A sale made to an ultimate consumer. Such sales are retail transactions regardless of how the outlet describes itself, *e.g.,* a wholesaler making sales to the ultimate consumer is engaged in a retail transaction.

Retailer A merchant intermediary (either an individual or a firm) engaged in selling goods or services to the ultimate consumer. The term is sometimes restricted to enterprises which generate one half of their total income from such sales.

Retailer Coupon A coupon, usually of the "cents-off" variety, distributed by a retailer through advertisements. Since the objective of the promotion is to build customer traffic the coupon is redeemable only in the store running the promotion. See also *coupon*.

Retailer Sponsored Cooperative A form of contractual vertical marketing system that is an example of backward integration. Independent retailers organise contractually to form a cooperative that gives them greater market power in dealing with suppliers.

Retailer's Cooperative Chair See *retail cooperative*

Retailer's Handling Charge A sum of money above the face value of a coupon paid by the manufacturer to the retailer as a fee for accepting and initially processing manufacturer-originated coupons.

Retailing That business activity concerned with the selling of goods and/or services to the ultimate consumer for his personal or household use. Retailing activities are commonly conducted in stores, but telephone and mail-order sales, automatic merchandising, in-home selling and street vending are all forms of retailing and represent the final step in the marketing process.

Retailing Cooperative See *retail cooperative*

Retailing Cycle See *retail life cycle*

Retailing Mix A retail store's particular combination of controllable variables that give it its distinct image and position in the marketplace. These variables include product, price, promotions, place, operating policy, buying, human resources, service, etc. See also *marketing mix*.

Retailing the Invoice (1). The practice of writing the unit selling prices on vendors' invoices that serves as the buyer's authorisation. (2). It also refers to extensions of price-quality relationships to ascertain total retail value for purposes of the retail inventory method of accounting.

Return on Assets (ROA) A measure of the profitability of a business which compares the net profit (after taxes) to the assets of the business used to generate that net profit.

$$\text{ROA} = \frac{\text{Net profit}}{\text{Assets used}}$$

The result then multiplied by 100. See also *return on investment (ROI).*

Return on Investment (ROI) A measure of the profitability of a business which compares the net profit to the amount of money needed to operate the business and, by extension, create that profit.

$$\text{ROI} = \frac{\text{Net profit}}{\text{Amount of investment}}$$

Return on Investment Price A selling price which will generate a predetermined margin of profit which represents a desired return on investment.

Return to Stock When a customer returns merchandise to the store for an exchange, credit, or money-back, this process of placing the merchandise into stock again is accompanied by a transaction to return to stock so that the item and the dollar amount are added back to inventory levels.

Returns and Allowances from Suppliers The sum of purchased goods returned to the supplier and unplanned reductions in purchase price. This represents a reduction in the cost of purchased items or total purchases. It is also referred to as purchase returns and allowances.

Returns and Allowances to Customers The dollar sum of goods returned to the store and of reductions in price allowed customers by the store. It is deducted from gross sales to get net sales It is also referred to as sales returns and allowances.

Returns Goods Bought or sent back to the vendor by the customer. The vendor may exchange the merchandise for the customer, give a cash refund, or credit the customer's account. The term applies equally to goods returned by consumers to retail establishments and to goods returned by retailers to manufacturers or whole-salers. Returns are generated by such factors as delay in delivery, defective goods, customer dissatisfaction, etc.

Reverse Marketing A proactive, market-oriented approach to procurement.

Reverse Reciprocity. A selling arrangement in which two organisations agree to sell their scarce products to one another.

Risk Aversion Pricing A pricing strategy aimed at the elimination (or at least the reduction) of risk and uncertainty in the marketing environment through the careful analysis of all available marketing intelligence. The basis of the strategy is the development of clearly stated price policies aimed at maximizing profits.

Risk Taking One of the facilitating marketing functions. Risk taking includes handling the uncertainties that are part of the marketing process and exposing oneself and one's firm to the chance of loss or failure. See also facilitating marketing functions.

Roadrailer A transportation innovation that allows a truck chassis to be outfitted with a set of rail trucks (wheels) that allows that truck to be used directly on the rails. This provides significant intermodal flexibility and service improvement.

Role Set The set of people who have a vested interest in how the salesperson performs the job. These people include the individual's immediate superior, other executives in the firms, purchasing agents and other members of customers' organisations and the salesperson's family. They all try to influence the salesperson's behaviour, either formally through organisational policies, operating procedures, training programmes and the like or informally through social pressures, rewards and sanctions.

Roll Out The extension of the physical distribution and promotion of a product to a wider geographical area. Thus a firm marketing its products regionally may seek a national market. The firm is then said to have "rolled out" to a national distribution.

Routine Consumer Decision Making In consumer behaviour

decisions which require little deliberation and planning because of the routine nature of the purchase. Goods involved are generally low-cost and carry no perceived risk to the consumer.

Rule For Maximising Profit A method to calculate a firm's optimum output so that the marginal cost is just less that equal to the marginal revenue. Total cost and total revenue may also be used to calculate the optimum output. See also *profit maximisation.*

Rule of Reason 1. (economic definition) A principle for determining the legality of business practices. Illegality is determined by evidence concerning the country, competitors, and consumers. 2. (legislation definition) A standard applied to the Sherman Antitrust Act that interprets it to prohibit only "unreasonable restraints of trade" rather than every restraint of trade. The courts have not consistently defined the term "unreasonable."

Run Paper (ROP) A newspaper advertisement placed at the publisher's discretion rather than positioned by the advertiser. Charged at the ordinary position rate. For other print media, this agreement is referred to as run of publication.

Run of Time Scedule (ROS) Television and radio commercials scheduled and broadcast at the discretion of the station. Also called run-of-day (ROD) and run-of-day (ROD) and run-of-week (ROW) scheduling, whichever is applicable to the specific agreement.

S

Safety Stock Merchandise Inventory used as a safety cushion for cycle stock so the retailer won't run out of stock if demand exceeds the sales forecast.

Salaried Buying Office An independent resident buying office which is paid a fixed fee (either a percentage of sales or a flat fee) on an annual contractual basis by the stores it represents.

Salaried Office See *resident buying office*

Salary Compensation paid periodically to a salesperson, independent of performance.

Salary Plan See *straight salary*

Salary Plus Commission A compensation system in which the employee receives a straight salary plus a percentage of his total sales during a specific period.

Saleable Sample A regular or specially sized quantity of the product offered at a low price to induce trial.

Sales Agent See *selling agent*

Sales Analysis The actual examination of a firm's sales results, generally in terms of territory, product classification, type of customer, cost of sales, order size or other measure. A primary objective of sales analysis is to detect marketing problems before they become acute and to facilitate the marketing management function.

Sales Branch The local office of a manufacturer which provides services similar to those of a merchant whole-saler, i.e..

stocks merchandise, fills orders, makes deliveries, etc. Office may also provide space for the local sales force.

Sales Budget The portion of a firm's total marketing budget allocated for sales force training, compensation, travel, entertainment expenses and the costs of sales force administration.

Sales Compensation Money paid to salespeople. May be in the form of straight commission, salary or a combination of the two.

Sales Demonstration An aspect of the sales presentation that provides a sensory appeal to show how the product works and what benefits it offers to the customer.

Sales Development A selling plan designed to develop new customers

Sales Era of Marketing A stage in the evolution of marketing (following the production era) during which the roles of advertising and the sales force were expanded in an effort to create consumer demand for products. No genuine effort was made to determine the consumer's needs before goods were produced.

Sales Expense Budget A budget which allocates expenditures relating to personal selling activities. Included are salaries, commissions, incentives and expense account charges as well as the cost of managing the sales operation. Such activities as sales meetings are also included. See also *budget*.

Sales Force A term generally applied to a firm's field sales organisation, *i.e.*, those salespersons and their immediate supervisors who have direct contact with customers and who perform the selling function.

Sales Force Compensation A financial reward or inventive programme based on salesperson's performance and tenure. A major purpose of any sales force compensation programme is to motivate or influence the sales force to do what management wants, in the way they want it done, and within the desired time. The three major methods of compensating salespeople are (1) straight salary plan, (2) straight commission plan, and (3) combination compensation plan consisting of a combination of salary and incentive pay in the form of commissions bonuses or both.

Sales Force Indoctrination The initial phase of sales training which covers knowledge of the company, its products, policies, and promotional support. Indoctrination also may encompass knowledge of the marketing environment and the competition. Finally, sales force indoctrination covers fundamental selling skills, and the principles of time and territory management (where applicable). See also *sales training*.

Sales Force Management Audit A periodic and in-depth review of the adequacy of a firm's sales management process. It is conducted to identify current and potential strengths, weaknesses and problems at all levels of the sales organisation.

Sales Forecast The level of sales anticipated for a particular period expressed either in dollars or in units. The forecast is a subjective estimate of future demand for goods or services.

Sales Job Satisfaction A feeling (positive or negative) that a salesperson has about his or her work situation. This includes all of the characteristics of the job itself that salespeople find rewarding, fulfilling, satisfying or frustrating and unsatisfying.

Sales Management Those management efforts directed toward the development of a sales force (recruiting, selecting, and training) and its maintenance (planning, supervision and motivation) which, taken together, will provide the firm with salespersons who are able to achieve the dollar volume necessary for profitable operation.

Sales Management Development Training That stage in sales sales personnel are taught to perfect their selling skills and prepare to become sales managers. Sales management development training focuses on developing administrative, decision-making and leadership skills. See also *sales training*.

Sales Manager A line marketing executive responsible for directing sales force activity. Principal duties fall into six major areas: recruitment, selection, training, planning, supervision and motivation. The sales manager may set levels of compensation for the members of his sales force and, in some organisations, may also have such broad responsibilities as planning and developing advertising and sales promotion programmes, developing positive customer relations, etc. See also *advertising sales manager* and *department manager*.

Sales Objectives A clear statement of the tasks to be performed by the salespeople in a firm. Objectives may be expressed in terms of total sales in dollars or units, as increases over past results or in number of sales calls completed, etc. See also *sales quota*.

Sales Organisation Specialised by Market Organisation, different salespeople specialise in the sale of the product line to different markets, such as *consumer, institutional* and *industrial markets*. They may report to the same supervisor or there may be separate sales organisations for each market. Specialisation may be an each market. Specialisation may be an appropriate strategy when market knowledge is more important than product knowledge. Sales costs are higher than for a full-line strategy because two or more salespeople travel over the same geographic area and more supervisors are needed if there is more than one sales force.

Sales Presentation That stage in the selling process during which the salesperson presents the product, service or idea, explains its benefits, and attempts to convince the prospect to accept the promises being made and to make a purchase.

Sales Promotion In retailing, sales promotion includes advertising, visual merchadising (display), public relations (including publicity), special events, and the selling efforts of the store's sales people. In large department stores there is generally a separate division for sales promotion.

Sales Promotion Calendar A planing device used to schedule special promotioal events and to coordinate them with holidays, national observances, seasons,e tc.

Sales Promotion in Organisational Buying Those activities other than advertising and personal selling aimed at stimulating product sales. Some of the components of sales promotion are trade shows, premiums, incentives, give-aways and specialty advertising (in which a firm's name may be printed on a calendar, for example).

Sales Promotion Manager The individual within a firm responsible for filling the gaps between the sales and advertising managers and handling the firm's diversified sales promotion activities. In some organisations, sales promotion managers are responsible to the sales manager, while in others they are responsible to the marketing manager.

Sales Report A report submitted by salespeople that tells management what is happening in the field. Most managers expect salespeople to report competitive activities, reactions of customers to company policies and products, as well as any other information management should know. In addition, sales reports can provide records for evaluating sales force performance. Sales reports often include such information the number of calls made, orders taken, miles travelled, days worked, new prospects called on, and new accounts sold.

Sales Representative Generally applied to a salesperson who sells a manufacturer's product in a particular territory. Sometimes called manufacturer's representatives, these salespeople may sell to industrial customers, wholesalers and retailers or, in some cases, to the ultimate consumer.

Sales Retail The final sales price at retail, i.e., the original retail price less discounts and allowances, shrinkage and markdowns.

Sales-Results Test An effort to measure the impact on sales of a particular advertisement or advertising campaign.

Sales Revenue The total income derived from sales for a given period.

Sales Skill Level An individual's level of sales-related knowledge or proficiency at carrying out the specific tasks necessary to perform a sales job. Sales skills are proficiency levels that can change rapidly with learning and experience.

Sales Staff See *sales force*

Sales Training A company's systematic programme of training sales personnel. The objective of such a programme is to increase sales and reduce costs by maximising the effectiveness and efficiency of the sales force. The company must first identify and analyse its needs and objectives. This allows priorities to be established and specific programmes to be set in motion. The company must also determine the type of learning required, the specific training time allowed and the training methods to be employed. Each of these elements varies considerably from company to company, depending on the nature of the product or service being sold and related factors. In most companies, training and development includes initial indoctrination and training of sales employees (or trainees), advanced training on an ongoing basis and management development training (for potential sales managers). Trainers may be drawn from sales management, staff training personnel, experienced salespeople or outside specialists. Training may take place within the firm itself, in the field or at outside locations (such as college campuses, hotel seminars etc.).

Salesperson A broad term which includes a variety of order-takers, sales employees at both the wholesale and retail levels of the market, manufacturer's represen-tatives and sales engineers, missionary salespeople and detailers, etc.

Salesperson Motivation The amount of effort the salesperson desires to expend on each activity or task associated with the job. Job tasks include calling on potential new accounts, developing sales presentations, filling out reports, etc.

Salesperson Role The set of activities or behaviours that are to be performed by any person occupying the position by any person occupying the position of salesperson in a firm.

Salient Beliefs Those beliefs that are activated from memory in a situation to influence comprehension or decision making.

Sample 1. (marketing research definition) The selection of a subset of elements from a larger group of objects. 2. (sales promotion definition) A small portion of a product that is made available to prospective purchasers to demonstrate the product's value or use and to encourage future purchase.

Sample Size The number of people, companies or other units surveyed in marketing research.

Sample Survey A cross-sectional study in which the sample is selected to be representative of the target population and in which the emphasis is on the generation of summary statistics such as averages and percentages.

Sampling (1) In marketing research, sampling is the process of selecting a representative subset of a total population for obtaining data useful in the study of the whole population. The subset is known as the sample. Inferences about the characteristics of the population as a whole are drawn from the characteristics of the sample. The total population is known as a *universe.* The study of the characteristics and attitudes of the sample are meant to decrease the time and costs involved in studying the total universe and may actually be more accurate. All marketing research samples fall into one of two major classes: probability samples and non-probability samples. Probability samples are those that are selected randomly, so that each member of the total population has an equal and quantifiable chance of being selected. In non-probability samples, the judgement of the researcher enters into the selection process. See also *non-probability sampling probability sampling, random sampling and stratified sampling.* (2) In sales promotion, sampling is the distribution of a product to a consumer free of charge in an effort to encourage trial use of the product and bolster consumer demand. Samples may be placed with channel inter-mediaries, or given directly to end users, as is often done in direct mail marketing.

Sampling Control A term applied to studies relying on questionnaires that concerns the researcher's dual abilities to direct the inquiry to a designated respondent and to secure the desired cooperation from the respondent.

Sampling Form A list of sampling units from which a sample will be drawn; the list could consist of geographic areas, institutions, individuals, or other units.

Sampling Plan The design of marketing research which specifies the composition of the sampling unit, sample size, and sampling procedure (probability or non-probability). See also *sampling.*

Sampling Principle The concept that if a small number of units (otherwise known as the *sample*) is chosen at random from the total population or universe being studied, the sample will tend to have the same characteristics, and in the same proportion, as the universe. See also *sampling*.

Sampling Unit The segment of the total population that is to be sampled in marketing research.

Scanner 1. (marketing research definition) An electronic device that automatically reads imprinted Universal Product Codes as the product is pulled across the scanner, looks up the price in an attached computer, and instantly prints the price of the item on the cash register tape. 2. (sales promotion definition) An electronic device that records retail purchase data (prices, brands, product sizes, etc.) at the point of sale by means of reading the universal product code.

Scenario A narrative sketch, description of possible developments or outline of a conceivable state of affairs at some future period. It is designed to focus attention on future causal processes and decision ponts.

Sealed Bid Pricing A pricing strategy in which a firm sets the prices for its products on the basis of what it anticipates its competitors will bid.

Seasonal Merchandise Goods closely identified with a particular season or holiday, *e.g.*, Christmas decorations, bathing suits, antifreese, etc. Seasonal merchandise commonly has a short sales life.

Seasonal Variations The regular changes occurring in the production or sales of products due to such factors as climate, vacations, holidays and customs.

Secondary Trade Zone The geographic area of secondary importance in terms of customer sales, typically generating about 20 percent or so of a store's sales.

Security An operating unit that is responsible for protecting merchandise and other assets from pilferage (internal or external). Those working in security may be employees or outside agency people.

Segmentation Descriptors In market segmentation studies, the descriptors are the individual units of analysis within each segment. For example, if the segment is a demographic characteristic such as race, the descriptors would be white, black, oriental, etc.

Segmentation Pricing A strategy in which prices are set at different levels for different segments of the population. This legal form of price discrimination is commonly found in the airline industry (where different classes of service are provided for different segments of the traveling public) and in other industries where costs do not decline greatly when consumption or use declines.

Selective Advertising An approach to developing advertising messages that seeks to present the unique or differentiating characteristics of a particular brand of product or service.

Selective Demand The market demand for a particular brand of merchandise as opposed to demand for the total class of products. For example, demand for Levi's jeans as opposed to demand for jeans in general. See also *primary demand.*

Selective Distribution A marketing strategy standing between exclusive distribution on the one hand and intensive distribution on the other. Manufacturers engaging in selective distribution restrict the number of middlemen and retailers who resell their product in a particular area in order to better control both the degree of exposure and the cost of distributing the product. Also called selective selling.

Selective Perception The ability of individuals to filter out certain sensory data or stimuli, while retaining others. Marketers have learned that consumers tend to notice only a portion of the stimuli to which they are exposed (selective exposure) to selectively interpret the information they do receive (selective distortion), and remember only those perceptions that seem relevant to their own lives or current needs (selective retention). Consumers are also more likely to perceive stimuli they anticipate and those that show a major change in price, quality or design. Marketers have devised various methods of over-coming selective perception, such as increasing the frequency with which advertising messages are repeated, creating unusual and attention grabbing ads, varying the format of the ads run for any given product, etc. Some markets have also experimented with the use of subliminal perception to reach consumers below the level of their conscious perception. See *perception, subliminal perception* and *thresholds of perception*.

Self-Concept 1. (consumer behaviour definition) The ideas, attitudes, and perceptions people have about themselves. 2. (consumer behaviour definition) The image one has of oneself. Research indicates that the self-concept is a relatively important variable in how a person judges and evaluates other persons or products. For example, the person with a self concept of "upwardly mobile urban professional" may well prefer and purchase a different model or brand of automobile than the individual with a self concept of a middle-aged dowager.

Self-Image The mental picture an individual has of himself and the way he imagines others perceive him. Self-image, also called self-concept, includes characteristics, traits, possessions, role, behaviour, etc., but emphasis is on the way these things are perceived rather than on the things themselves. An individual's idel self or ideal self-image, is the person the individual would like to be or the end to which the individual is striving. An individual's others-self-concept is the way the individual thinks others perceive him. The problem for the marketer is to determine which concept of self will prompt the purchase of the product or service and how best to appeal to that concept. See also *motivation research*.

Self-Liquidator A gift, premium or other reward offered to consumers by the seller at the seller's net cost, generally including postage, handling and taxes.

Self-Selection A form of retail selling in which the customer is required to select the item he wants from the array of merchandise available on the selling floor and to then take the item to a salesperson who will complete the transaction. Cash registers are usually placed strategically around the store rather than concentrated at the exit as they are in self-service outlets. See also *self-service*.

Self-Service A form of retail selling in which merchandise is displayed so that the customer can make a selection without the aid of a salesperson. The customer then takes his purchases to a checkout point (usually near the exit of the store) where a cashier completes the transaction.

Self-Service Retailing A retailoperation in which merchandise is displayed so that the customer can make a selection without the aid of a salesperson. Customer usually takes purchases to a checkout station and pays a cashier. Common in discout and supermarket operations.

Seller's Market An economic situation in which there is a shortage of goods and services so that demand exceeds supply. This situation favours sellers and gives them considerable power in the marketplace. It also tends to push prices upward. A company may create a seller's market intentionally by keeping production low so that prices and apparent desirability of the product remain high.

Selling In a general sense, selling is simply he offering of goods or services for sale—thus, to be "in sales" is to be a professional salesperson. In a more restricted sense, selling may be regarded as a marketing function whose object is to arouse demand for a product on the part of potential customers. This may be a creative endeavour which includes advertising and other forms of promotion or it may be more mundane, *e.g.*, the order-taking which so often passes for selling at the retail level.

Selling Against the Brand One is selling against the brand when artificially high prices are maintained on certain categories of merchandise in an effort to increase sales on some other merchandise. This tactic is sometimes employed by retailers in an effort to sell private label merchandise at the expense of manufacturer's brands.

Selling Agent An agent middleman who sells all the products of his client manufacturer under a contractual agreement, but who does not take title to the merchandise. He may also provide his client with market information for the extensive territory he covers. The selling agent has considerable authority with regard to prices, credit, delivery dates, and other terms of sale, and, in fact, is virtually in charge of the selling activities of the firm. See also *manufacturer's agent*.

Selling Price The actual price the customer pays at the time the transaction is completed.

Selling Process A series of steps taken by a salesperson engaged in selling activities. These include prospecting, the preapproach and approach, the sales presentation, and finally the closing. Follow-up activities are sometimes included as a part of the selling process.

Sell-through Analysis A comparison between actual and planned sales to determine whether early markdowns are required or whether more merchandise is needed to satisfy demand.

Semi-Manufactured Goods Products which have required manufacturing (plate glass, insulation, textile fabrics, etc.) but which will be incorporated into another product.

Send Transaction A sales at retail which is to be delivered, or sent, to the customer

Served Market The business develops, manufactures and markets products appropriate to a selected segment of the market. It should be noted that the market for which the product is developed (called the qualified market) and the market that is targeted in marketing efforts will often not overlap precisely. The overlap between the qualified market and the target market represents the served. market.

Service Approach A technique used by a salesperson in the first few minutes of contact with a prospect. The salesperson promises to relieve the prospect of some work or responsibility through the product or service being sold. See also *approach*.

Service Business Business organisations that sell services rather than tangible products.

Service Retailing Service retailling organisations sell services rather than tangible products.

Service Quality An area of study that has developed to define and describe how services can be delivered in such manner as to satisfy the recipient. High quality service is defined as delivery of service that meets or exceeds customers' expectations.

Service Salesperson A salesperson concerned with such matters as delivery and installation and whose responsibilities generally begin after the sale has been consummated.

Service Wholesaler See *full-service wholesaler*

Services Although services may sometimes be included in broad marketing definitions of the term product they are for the most part separately identifiable intangible activities or benefits. Services are just as real as physical products and may, in fact, be closely tied to the sale of a product (for example, service contracts on appliances), but they are essentially different in that services do not entail the permanent ownership of any tangible object on the part of the buyer. Services may be offered for sale (for example, carpet cleaning) or may be provided free (for example, repair services under warranty).

Services Marketing Those activities which facilitate the sale or delivery of a service. Included are those services offered for profit by private concerns, those provided by government agencies, and those furnished by non-profit organisations. See also *marketing* and *services.*

Share of Audience The proportion of sets in use that are tuned to a particular radio station, television station or cable television channel during a given time period. It is computed by dividing the rating by the sets in use.

Share of the Market A share of the market is that portion of the available business held by a store in a paticular trading area.

Shared Services Common carriers, a combined captive sales force, or public warehousing are among those services which may be shared by two or more marketers at the same time. These services may be provided by one of the cooperating firms or by a third party.

Shelf Stock In a complex distribution system, inventory occurs at the plant and at field locations. Shelf stock refers to inventory that has been accumulated for display at the point of final sale.

Shelf Talker A printed card or other sign used in retail stores to call attention to a shelved product. It commonly is attached to the shelves or railings of display cases.

Shippers' Cooperative A nonprofit organisation that pools members' shipments so that they can be moved at low carload or truckload rates instead of the more expensive LCL or LTL rates.

Shopkeeper See *merchant* and *retailer*

Shopping Centre A cluster of stores and related facilities (community rooms, restaurants, automobile service areas, parking lots, etc.) which have been planned and developed to serve a particular trading area. Shopping centres are managed as a unit and the component stores generally observe uniform operating hours. They are located on convenient access roads and are surrounded by large parking lots. Most centres include one or more large anchor magnet store designed to attract customers. The largest shopping centres are called *regionals*; the smaller centres are called *community* or *neighbourhood shopping centres.*

Shopping Goods Merchandise purchased by the consumer only after considerable effort has been made to comparison shop. Shopping goods are often expensive products, *e.g.*, automobiles and major appliances, in which price and quality comparisons are of primary importance. They may also be products in which appearance or style comparisons are of greater significance, e.g., clothing.

Shop-at-Home-Retailing Selling merchandise or a service in the customer's home at the customer's invitation e.g.,carpet and furniture cleaning.

Shopping Goods Stores Most large department stores, discount stores, and supermarkets may be regarded as shopping goods stores, *i.e.*, stores which have such breadth of assortment in their merchandise offerings that the customer may compare prices, styles and quality.

Shopping Product A product as a better dress or hair treatment for which the consumer is willing to spend considerable times and effort in gathering information on price, quality and other attributes. Several retail outlets are customerily visited. Comparison of product attributes and complex decision processes are common.

Short Delivery A discrepancy in the amount of goods delivered, the number being less than shown on the purchase order or invoice.

Simulated Test Market A form of market testing in which consumers are exposed to new products and to their claims in staged advertising and purchase situation. Output of the test is an early forecast of sales and/or market share, based on mathematical forecasting models, management assumptions, and input of specific measurements from the simulation.

Simulated Test Marketing Test marketing done by firms in shopping malls or consumers' homes as a prelude to a full-scale marketing test for the product.

Single-Line Retailer See *limited-line store*

Single Price Policy/Store The offering of all goods at a single price—*e.g.,* everything for $ 5, or $ 10, etc. It is not to be confused with one price policy.

Single Product Stratecty A manufacturing strategy in which a decision is made to produce a single product or a single product with a limited number of options.

Single Target Market Approach A method of market segmentation in which one homogeneous group is selected as the target market and one marketing mix is used to market the product. See also *market segmentation.*

Single-Zone Pricing The practice of setting one price for all buyers regardless of their distance from the seller.

Situation Analysis The systematic collection and study of past and present data to identify trends, forces and conditions with the potential to influence the performance of the business and the choice of appropriate strategies. The situation analysis is the foundation of the strategic planning process. The situation analysis includes an examination of both the internal factors (to identify strengths and weaknesses) and external factors (to identify opportunities and threats). It is often referred to by the acronym SWOT.

Size Scale A chart of the proper quantity of an item to order in each size.

Skimming Price Policy A method of pricing that attempts to first reach those willing to buy at a high price before marketing to more price-sensitive customers.

Slotting Allowance 1. (retailing definition) A fee paid by a vendor for space in a retail store. 2. (sales promotion definition) The fee a manufacturer pays to a retailer in order to get distribution for a new product. It covers the costs of making room for the product in the warehouse and on the store shelf, reprogramming the computer system to recognise the product's UPC code and including the product in the retailer's inventory system.

Small Group Theory A set of conceptualisations and hypotheses relating to the behaviour of individuals within a small group of psychologically interrelated individuals. It is the study of the influence of others in a small group of interdependent individuals on the beliefs, attitudes and behaviour of the individual.

Small Order Problem Orders for merchandise which are so small that the transaction does not yield a profit.

Social Advertising The advertising designed to educate or motivate target audiences to undertake socially desirable actions.

Social Audit A systematic assessment and report of some domain of a company's activities that have social impact; thus, it is an assessment of social performance.

Social Channel A personal communications channel consisting of neighbours, friends, family members and associates talking to potential customers. Also known as *word-of-mouth influence*.

Social Character A term coined David Riesman to describe values and behavioural characteristics of people in various stages of cultural development.

Social Consciousness Marketing managers' concern for meeting social purposes, pursuing social benefits and adhering to social criteria as compared with achieving the sales, profit and other wealth-producing goals of capitalism. Social actions are often taken at the expense of immediate profits.

Social Costs When calculating the cost of doing business social costs are those incurred by society in the form of damager to the environment, increases in illness, etc. Social costs are viewed in much the same way as private costs in determining the total costs of a business.

Social Marketing The application of marketing strategies concepts, and techniques to the promotion of social ideas or programs. The effort may be designed to propagate a particular idea (*e.g.*, that freedom and democracy are synonymous), to encourage a particular form of behaviour (*e.g.*, one should vote in an election), or to support a particular non-profit organisation (*e.g.*, The League of Women Voters). See also *societal marketing concept*.

Social Marketing Perspective The orientation or perspective that focuses on social purposes and reflects on whether or not a company should market a good or a service as compared to whether or not it can do so economically.

Social Marketing Report A report on those marketing activities that have social impact, usually in the form of disclosures to relevant publics, overall rating schemes, or internal performance review.

Social Mobility The ability of the individuals to climb above or slip below, the social class or position in society into which he or she was originally reared. Social mobility can be increased through education, occupation or fortuitous circumstances.

Social Profits The benefits which accrue from the operations of non-profit organisations, *e.g.*, health care, police protection, education, etc.

Social Responsibility A concept embodying the notion that business has an obligation to society to operate in the public interest.

Social Responsibility of Marketing The obligation of marketing organisations to do no harm to the social environment and wherever possible, to use their skills and resources to enhance that environment. Comment: Social responsibility of marketing also is called *societal marketing*. This term is frequently confused with social marketing.

Societal Forces In the marketing context, societal forces are social pressures and influences which affect the operation of the marketplace. They include changes in demographics, alteration of lifestyles, modification of expectations, etc.

Societal Marketing Concept A marketing management orientation in which the interests of society at large are taken into consideration when new products and services are planned. Primary among these concepts are the conservation of resources and the preservation of the environment. Societal Marketing may be adopted as a strategy for one of two reasons: (1) a company may feel that socially responsible behaviour attracts customers and avoids government regulation, or (2) a company may act responsibly for the simple reason that it is the proper thing to do.

Sorting A function performed by intermediaries in order to bridge the discrepancy between the assortment of goods and services generated by the producer and the assortment demanded by the consumer. This function includes four distinct processes: accumulation, allocation, assorting and sorting out.

Sorting Out A sorting process that breaks down a heterogeneous supply into separate stocks that are relatively homogeneous.

Sorting Process The combined processes of assembling, allocation, grading and assorting in the channel of distribution. The sorting process serves to bring homogeneous groups of products together for economical handling and shipping early in the distribution process and, later, to break the inventories down into increasingly smaller quantities on their way to the ultimate consumer. Also called regrouping activities. See also *discrepancy of quantity and discrepancy of assortment*, both of which are overcome by the sorting process.

Sound Bite The basic element of a broadcast news story, consisting of a news maker speaking on camera in 10 to 20 second blocks.

Source Marking The price marking of merchandise (generally destined for retail sale) at the point of production. Products so marked are said to be pre-priced.

Span of Control The number of people that one supervisor will be able to deal with effectively. The concept is based on both personal limits and the demands of various supervisory assignments. The span of control varies inversely with the level of difficulty of the supervisory task.

Special Event A sales promotion programme comprising a number of sales promotion techniques built around a seasonal, cultural, sporting, musical event or other activity.

Special Event Pricing A form of promotional pricing in which a sale is advertised, often in connection with some event such as a holiday. The objective of special event pricing is to bring inventories into line with demand or to raise cash.

Specialty Advertising The placement of advertising messages on a wide variety of items of interest to the target market such as calendars, coffee cups, pens, hats, note paper, paper weights, T-shirts, watches, etc. In contrast to premiums, specialty advertising items are usually given to members of the audience.

Specialty Department Store A large store with a department store format that focuses primarily on apparel and soft home goods.

Specialty Distributed Coupon The coupons distributed through nontraditional media, such as the back of cash register tapes, egg cartons, shopping bags, pizza boxes, etc.

Specialty Goods Merchandise well known to the consumer because of its high quality, brand identification, uniqueness or other specific characteristic. Shoppers will often make a special effort to find this merchandise and are unlikely to accept substitutes. Price is seldom the deciding factor in the purchase of specialty goods.

Specialty Product A product that has unique attributes or other characteristics that make it singularly important to the buyer. Multiple-store searching, reliance on brand, and absence of extensive product comparisons are the rule. Cigarettes, deodorants and specialized insurance policies are examples.

Specialty Store A retail enterprise carrying a product mix narrower than a department store and broader than a single-line store. The specialty store has a clearly defined market segment as its target, *i.e.*, buyers who seek a wide variety of unique merchandise. Specialty stores generally offer wide assortments within their product lines, trained salespeople, credit, delivery services and other amenities.

Specialty Wholesaler A highly specialised full-service wholesaler, or middleman, who carries a narrow range of products which are offered to carefully targeted customers. Services provided are similar to those offered by general merchandise wholesalers. The specialty wholesaler may deal in a single product, *e.g.*, frozen foods, while his general merchandise counterpart would carry a complete line of groceries.

Specifications Exact descriptions of goods. Specifications are commonly used when purchasing is carried on by bidding.

Spot Market The market for immediate delivery or, in the interbank market, for delivery within two business days of the transaction.

Spot Sale The sale or purchase of a commodity for immediate delivery, often on a cash basis.

Spurious Correlation A condition that arises when there is no relationship between two variables but the analyst concludes that a relationship exists.

Stability A technique for assessing the reliability of a measure by measuring the same objects or individuals at two different points in time and then correlating the scores; the procedure is known as test-retest reliability assessment.

Staff Authority This includes two types of authority—advisory and functional. Advisory is implied authority based on the staff person's experience for expertise. A staff person with advisory authority cannot order something done but can recommend that it be done in a certain way. Functional authority is the authority held by functional managers (*e.g.*, finance and personal) to issue orders to people not under their direct (line) supervision; however, this authority encompasses only those functions designated by the chief executive.

Staff Manager An executive in a firm's staff organisation, *i.e.*, in that part of the firm responsible for providing line managers with special services and support activities.

Stake Holder One of a group of publics with which a company must be concerned. Key stakeholders include consumers, employees, stockholders, suppliers and others who have some relationship with the organisation.

Standard Industrial Classification (SLC) A scheme developed by the U.S. Office of Management and Budget for classifying business establishments by the type of economic activity in which they are engaged. Established in the 1930s, the SIC code is updated every fifteen years. Categories for goods producing industries tend to be broken down in detail while service businesses tend to be lumped together in general categories.

Standard International Trade Classification A numeric-based commodity code for products moving by air transportation. It was developed by the United Nations and is used by U.S. air carriers.

Standard Package In some trades, custom or law has stipulated one or several package sizes that the goods are customarily sold in. Bread and sodas are typical, though few product categories today adhere only to the standard sizes.

Standard Test Market A market in which companies sell their products through normal distribution channels when testing these products or the marketing efforts supporting these products.

Standardise To make or bring to an established or uniform size, weight, quality level, etc. Some products may be standardised in conformance with specifications recognised on an industry-wide basis. See also *grading*.

Standing Order An arrangement with a vendor to make shipments periodically in specified quantities in which the vendor may be authorised to ship a certain quantity each month or week for a set period.

Staple Good A convenience product such as sugar or potatoes that is bought often and consumed routinely. Staples often offer little differentiation and are sold importantly on the basis of price. These sometimes are called commodity products, but industrial products can be commodities, too.

Staple Merchandise The merchandise for which a fairly active demand continues over a period of years and which the retailer finds necessary to carry continually in stock.

Staple Scale A self-report technique for attitude measurement in which the respondents are asked to indicate how accurately each of a number of statements describes the object of interest.

Staple Stock List The list of items that are to be carried regularly in stock.

Startling-Statement Approach A technique used by a salesperson in the first few minutes of contact with a prospect. A startling statement of facts known about the prospect's needs or problems is used to attract attention to the sales presentation. See also *approach*

Statistical Demand Analysis A method of developing a sales forecast that attempts to determine the relationship between sales and the important factors affecting sales, typically using regression analysis, and the use of that relationship to forecast sales for the future.

Statistical Efficiency A measure used to compare sampling plans; one sampling plan is said to be superior (more statistically efficient) than another if, for the same size sample, it produces a smaller standard error of estimate.

Status Quo Pricing A strategy in which prices are maintained at the level charged in the mature stage of the product life cycle. This practice tends to avoid price wars with competitors.

Stimulus Response Sales Approach A sales presentation method that emphasises the importance of saying the right things at the right time by means of a well-prepared sales presentation (stimulus) in order to elicit the desired response (sale).

Stock Balance This balance is concerned with planning and controlling merchandise investment so that it is balanced with expected sales. The three perspectives from which one can view stock balance are (1) stock width (breadth), (2) stock support (depth), and (3) total dollars invested in stock.

Stock Control The activity of regulating inventory levels so that stock-on-hand is properly balanced between market demand on the one hand and production capacity on the other.

Stock Depth The number of units in individual merchandise items needed to meet sales of each assortment factor.

Stock or Inventory Control A system or approach to the management of material that is received, stored, and distributed within the firm and between the firm and its vendors or customers.

Stock-Out An out-of-stock condition with regard to a particular item, *i.e.,* insufficient quantity was ordered to meet demand.

Stock Rotation A term used in inventory management to describe the process of moving stock to ensure freshness and shelf life of inventory.

Stock Sales Ratio The ratio between the stock on hand at the beginning or end of a period and the sales for that period. It is determined by dividing stock, preferably at the beginning of the period, usually monthly, by sales. It is distinguished from inventory turnover or stock turnover, which are ratios or averages for a period of time, usually annually.

Stock Shortage This includes all unexplained or unrecorded shrinkages in the value of merchandise available for sale. It is the amount by which a physical inventory is short of a book inventory figure.

Stock Spotting In warehousing, a practice by which manufactured goods or other commodities are warehoused near the customer rather than at the point of production in an effort to reduce delivery time and transportation costs.

Stock Turnover A financial ratio commonly calculated for one year which is determined by dividing net sales (in dollars) by average inventory at selling prices (in dollars). Stock turnover rate is the number of times the average inventory has been sold and replaced in a given period. Also called *inventory turnover.*

$$\text{Stock turnover} = \frac{\$\ \text{Net sales}}{\$\ \text{Average inventory at selling price}}$$

Store Audit A data collection method employed in retailing to track the performance of particular brands or products in a specific time frame. Store audits commonly *conform* to the following formula.

Inventory on hand + new purchases (less returns) = stock available for sale—present inventory = consumer sales.

Store Layout The interior retail store arrangement of departments or groupings of merchandise. It should be organised to provide for ease of customer movement through the store and to provide for maximum exposure and attractive display of merchandise.

Store Loyalty 1. (consumer behaviour definition). The degree to which a consumer consistently patronises the same store when shopping for particular types of products. 2. (retailing definition) A condition in which a customer regularly patronises a specific retailer.

Storyline Format A form of advertising in which a story unfolds which features the products or in some way relates its history to some present day useful purpose.

Storytelling A questionnaire method of data collection relying on a picture stimulus such as a cartoon, photograph or drawing, about which the subject is asked to tell a story.

Straight Commission For salespeople, straight commission payment means that they receive a fixed percentage of their total sales as their sole compensation. See also *commission.*

Straight Commission Plan A sales force compensation plan that uses commissions as the sole basis for pay. A commission is payment for achieving a given level of performance. Salespeople are paid for results. Usually, commission payments are based on the salesperson's dollar or unit sales volume. However, they may be based on the profitability of sales so as to motivate the sales force to expend effort on the most profitable products or customers.

Straight Extension Strategy A strategy employed in international trade in which a company exports the same products that it manufactures for the domestic market. No attempt is made to alter them to meet the requirements of foreign markets.

Straight Salary A method of payment in which an individual is paid on a fixed rate basis and at regular intervals, independent of productivity considerations.

Strategic Intent An ambitious organisational goal that is not proportional to current resources and capabilities and remains stable over time. To ensure long-term success, management envisions a desired leadership position and then establishes the criterion that the organisation will use to chart its progress. The concept encompasses an active management process that includes focusing the organisation's attention on the essence of winning; motivating people by communicating the value of the target; leaving room for individual and team contributions; sustaining enthusiasm by providing new operational definitions as circumstances change; and using intent consistently to guide resource allocations.

Strategic Marketing A marketing posture in which an effort is made to make a company more customer oriented by forging a stronger link between marketing functions and strategic planning functions. Generally, marketing activities such as marketing research and new product development are given a larger share of the organisations budget.

Strategic Market Planning The planning process that yields decisions in how a business unit can best compete in the markets it elects to serve. Strategic market decisions are based on assessments of product market and pertain to the basis for advantage in the market. The plan that is the output of the process serves as a blueprint for the development of the skills and resources of a business unit and specifies the results to be expected. In many companies these are called strategic business plans.

Strategic Planning The consideration of current decision alternatives in light of their probable consequences over time. The practice of strategic planning incorporates four distinguishing features: (1) an external orientation; (2) a process for formulating strategies; (3) methods for analysis of strategic situations and alternatives; and (4) a commitment to action.

Strategic Sales Programme A programme that organises and plans the company's overall personal selling efforts and integrates these with the other elements of the firm's marketing strategy. The strategic sales programme should take into account the environmental factors faced by the firm.

Strip Shopping Centre A shopping centre configuration in which the stores are arranged in a straight line along a street or highway. The line of stores is usually set back enough to allow for a covered pedestrian walkway and for automobile parking between the street and the row of shops.

Stripped-Down Price A product, frequently an automobile, may be advertised at a particularly low price. Once at the showroom the customer discovers that the car offered at the low price is stripped-down, *i.e.,* is lacking in many of the amenities most consumers desire in a new car.

Strip-type Shopping Centre A shopping centre in which stores are aligned along a thoroughfare, usually set back some distance from the street to permit front parking.

Stub Control A perpetual inventory system of unit control in which sales information is obtained from stubs of price tickets rather than from sales checks, scanning of bar codes or other sources.

Subliminal Advertising Advertising messages that are supposedly disguised so that they are not able to be overtly seen and/or heard yet are nevertheless effective in persuading members of the audience. There is no scientific evidence to indicate that this approach effective communication and, if there were convincing evidence of effectiveness, the approach would likely be prohibited as a deceptive business practice.

Submissive Selling Style A selling style often used by excellent socialisers who like to spend time talking about non-business activities. These salespeople usually are reluctant to obtain commitments from prospects.

Suboptimisation A condition in an organisation in which at least one component is operating at a level lower than its very best.

Substantiation An FTC requirement that advertisers have a reasonable basis for their advertising claims.

Substitute Substitutes-in-kind are products that look alike and represent the same application of a distinct technology to the provision of a distinct set of customer functions. Substitutes-in-use are products that have shared functionality based on the customer's perceptions of all the ways in which their needs can be satisfied in a given usage or application situation. The attractiveness of a substitute product depends on (1) its initial price, (2) customer switching costs, (3) post purchase costs of operation, and (4) the additional benefits the customer perceives and values.

Substitute Method of Forecasting In forecasting the potential sales of new products, the substitute method may be used to predict the upper limit on potential sales of the new product. Researchers examine and analyse the sales of products which the new one may displace. The resultant figures must then be modified to include customer preferences at various price points and the availability of other substitutes in the marketplace. The substitute method may be used to forecast new product sales in both the consumer and the industrial markets.

Substitute Products The products that are viewed by the user as alternatives for other products. The substitution is rarely perfect, and varies from time to time depending on price, availability, etc.

Suggested Retail A recommended list price submitted by a manufacturer or other vendor to a retailer.

Suggestion Selling A sales technique in which the sales-person recommends to the customer related merchandise, such as seasonal items, thus encouraging additional purchases.

Summated Rating A self-report technique for attitude measurement in which subjects are asked to indicate their degree of agreement or disagreement with each of a number of statements; a subject's attitude score is the total obtained by summing the scale values assigned to each category checked.

Superette A grocery stores in which much of the merchandise is arranged for self-service, but in which counter service is still available. Superettes stand between supermarkets and convenience stores.

Superficial Discounting. See *psychological discounting.*

Supermarket A large retail store specialising in groceries, produce, meat, dairy products and a wide variety of non-food items. Supermarkets operate on self-service basis with customers paying at a central checkout. These stores are characterised by high unit volume, low unit prices and a broad assortment of merchandise.

Super Regional Shopping Centre One of several standard classes of shopping centres recognised by The Urban Land Institute. It provides for extensive variety of general merchandise, apparel, furniture, and home furnishings. Typically, it has three or more full-line department stores of more than 1,00,000 square feet each and total store area of centre may be about 6,00,000 square feet to more than 15,00,000 square feet.

Superstation A television station in a particular city that sends its signal via satellite to subscribing cable television stations anywhere in the world. Television station WGN In Chicago is an example of such a superstation. The cable system disseminates the signal to its subscribers.

Superstore A large retail establishment combining many of the features of the supermarket with those of the discount store. Superstores often have 25,000 to 30,000 square feet of floor space and carry food and non-food general merchandise in a ratio of approximately 70% to 30%. These stores carry from 3 to 4 times the number of products found in the conventional supermarket out of which the superstore evolved. Superstores are geared to meet all the routine needs of the customer in one stop.

Super Warehouse A store at least twice the size of the typical supermarket operating on a high-volume, low overhead basis. The super warehouse is a hybrid, being partly a no-frills warehouse outlet, but, at the same time, stocking much of the merchandise found in a traditional supermarket. Goods are often displayed in cartons and the customer is expected to pack and carry his own groceries.

Supplement A special, preprinted section of a newspaper or magasine that is then inserted durings the regular printing process for the publication. Supplements usually contain both editorial matter and ads. Supplements inserted in a variety of newspapers (often appearing on Sunday) are called *syndicated supplements.*

Supplier Management The process whereby industrial buyers make suggestions about the suppliers' policies, procedures, and strategies to improve the quality of products and services furnished.

Supplies Business or industrial goods treated as expense items which are not incorporated into a finished product. Most supplies fit into one of three categories: (1) maintenance items such as cleaning materials and paint; (2) repair items such as glass and pipe; and (3) operating items such as paper and fuel. The three categories are sometimes known by the acronym MRO.

Supply 1. (economic definition) A schedule of the amounts of a good that would be offered for sale at all possible prices at any one instance of time. 2. (business definition) The number of units of a product that will be put on the market over a period of time.

Supply House A middleman selling industrial goods to manufacturers or other business or institutional users. Generally, this is a distributor, wholesaler or jobber.

Support Salespeople A sales-person generally not directly involved in order-getting, i.e., is more concerned with the technical details of the product being offered for sale. Detailers and technical salespeople as well as parasalespeople (trainees, etc.) are all employed in a support role.

Supportive Service In marketing, any auxiliary benefit or service which makes the product more attractive to the customer. Supportive services contribute to the firm's overall marketing effort. For example, the extension of credit is a supportive service which facilitates the selling process. Warranties, guarantees, installation, and initial free service contracts are also supportive services which may encourage customers to select one product over another. Also known as *supporting activities*. See also *service*.

Surplus Store A store which sells, along with other goods of non-governmental origin, merchandise which has been declared surplus by an agency of the U.S. Government, *e.g.*, clothing and equipment no longer of use to the armed forces.

Survey. A method of gathering primary data from a sample of the population using such techniques as face-to-face and telephone interviews and mail surveys (self-administered questionnaires). The survey method is commonly used to determine the knowledge, attitudes, and beliefs of particular segments of the population.

Sustainable Competitive Advantage A sustainable competitive advantage exists when a firm is implementing a value-creating strategy not simultaneously being implemented by any current or potential competitors and when these other competitors are unable to duplicate the benefits of this strategy. The sustainability of a competitive advantage depends upon the possibility of competitive duplication. Invisible assets may allow a firm to sustain a competitive advantage.

Swap Market A meeting place where people gather to exchange goods, generally personal or household articles for which they no longer have a need. Early swap markets did not involve the exchange of money, but soon evolved into more conventional retail operations like the flea market

Switch Trading A mechanism that can be applied to barter or countertrade. A professional switch trade, switch trading house or bank steps into a simple barter arrangement, clearing arrangement or countertrade arrangement when one of the parties is not willing to accept all the goods or the clearing credits in a transaction. The switching mechanism provides a secondary market for counter or bartered goods and credits.

Swing Shop Generally found in department stores, a swing shop is an area wheretrend-setting merchandise is featured. It takes its name from the idea that the area can quickly swing from one look to another as fashions change.

Symbolic Interaction A sociological theory that focuses on the formation of self through interactions with other people. The meaning attached to products is a function of the interaction of the self and others to the object.

Symbiotic Marketing A strategy in which two or more firms enter into a venture jointly, *e.g.*, the marketing of European automobiles in the U.S. through already established dealerships for American cars.

Syncratic Decision Making A pattern of decision making within a family in which most decisions are made jointly by both spouses.

Systematic Sample A probability sample in which every *k*th element in the population is designated for inclusion in the sample after a random start.

System Selling In personal selling, a team effort built around a master salesperson and a team of less experienced salespeople. The technique is calculated to overwhelm the prospect and to systematically answer his objections.

T

T-Account In accounting, a method of expressign the effect of certaintransactiosn in teh from of a T (a horizontal cross bar combined with a vertical line separatign debits on the left from credits on the right).

Tactical Planning Short-term business planning, particularly when focused on the implementation of the organisation's long-term strategic goals. See *strategic planning*.

Take-over The process by which a firm or group of investors acquires control of a corporation via merger or a tender offer. The empirical evidence suggests that both the shareholders of the acquired firm and the bidding firm or group gain in the transaction on average—although the major portion of the gain goes to the target firm's stockholders.

Tally Card A form on which a sales-person records each transacton. The form is sometimes printed on an envelope into which the tally (the next days starting amount of money) may be placed.

Target Market For retail organisations, the target market includes those perons whom it would most like to attract as customers and toward whom it directs its marketing strategy.

Target Market Identification The process of using income, demographic and life style characteristics of a market and census information for small areas to identify the most favourable locations.

Target Pricing A pricing strategy in which the selling price of a product is determined by adding a sum to the fixed cost of the product to achieve a predetermined profit margin.

Target Return Pricing A method of pricing that attempts to cover all costs and achieve a target return.

Tariff A tax levied against imported products. The actual amount of the tax is referred to as the duty or customs duty. There are two forms of tariff: (1) revenue tariffs which raise money and (2) protective tariffs which are meant to protect domestic producers or manufacturers by excluding foreign competitors to raise the price of the imported goods to a competitive level.

Tariff System The system of duties applied to goods and services from foreign countries. It may be a single rate of duty for each item applicable to all countries or groups of countries or two or more rates applicable to different countries or groups of countries.

Task Force In new product development, a group drawn from a number of functional departments within the firm which is responsible for seeing that the development of the new product is given coordinated and sufficient support. Members of task force generally perform these duties in addition to their regular assignments.

Team Selling The practice of involving a group of people familiar with the view-points and concerns of key decision makers of the customer's organisation to sell and service a major account. Comment: This is especially prevalent in the sale of complex industrial products, where a particular salesperson cannot be an expert on all aspects of the purchase process.

Technical Salesperson An industrial salesperson whose principal duties are those of the technical consultant. Technical salespeople, who often possess special knowledge and skills, are commonly called upon to provide assistance to purchasers of complex equipment such as computers.

Technological Forces Those technical developments in a society which influence the way people live and which determine what they desire and which, in turn, affect the activities of marketers who supply these wants and needs.

Technological Forecasting The prediction of innovations and advances in a particular technology. Both exploratory research methods and normative research methods are used, the former to project future developments based on the past and the latter to focus more on planning and planned technological innovation.

Technological Mapping The gathering and analysis of information about the direction and timing of possible competitive technological developments.

Telemarketing A term commonly employed to describe two distinct forms of marketing: (1) Sales of products and services via the telephone in what AT&T calls the "marriage of telecommunications technology and direct marketing techniques." Telemarketing is conducted at both the industrial and consumer levels of the marketplace. (2) Sales of products and services via an interactive system or two-way television, *i.e.,* electronic in home or in-office systems which employ cable television, telephone lines, data banks, etc. See also *electronic direct marketing.*

Telephone Interview A telephone conversation between a representative of the research organisation, the interviewer and a respondent or interviewee.

Telephone Retailing Selling by telephone at the retail level, *i.e.,* to the ultimate consumer. It may be employed to canvass potential customers or customers may be encouraged by other advertising, *e.g.,* print, radio, or television, to call by telephone to place an order. See also *telemarketing* and *teleshopping.*

Telephone Selling Selling that involves interacting with customers using a telephone.

Teleshopping The use of the telephone by customers to order merchandise or services they have seen in print advertising, heard about on the radio or seen on television. Teleshoping is frequently facilitated through the use of toll-free numbers for inbound calls. See also *tele-marketing* and *telephone retailing.*

Terms of Purchase The conditions in a purchase agreement with a vendor that include the type(s) of discounts available and responsibility for transportation costs.

Terms of Sale The conditions governing a sale as set forth by the seller. Terms include amount of discount (if any), payment period date of delivery, point of transfer of title to the merchandise, allocation of transportation costs, and any other specific obligations and conditions.

Territorial Allocation The rights given to the wholesaler or retailer (by the manufacturer) to sell the manufacturer's product or brand in a defined geographic area that is, at least to some extent, removed, isolated or protected from other wholesalers and retailers also selling the manufacturer's items.

Tertiary Trade Zone The outermost ring of a trade area. It includes customers who only occasionally shop at a store or shopping centre. It is also known as *fringe trade area.*

Test Market The trading area selected to test a company's new or modified product, service or promotion.

Test Marketing One form of market testing. It usually involves actually marketing a new product in one or several cities. The effort totally representative of what the firm intends to do later upon national marketing (or regional market rollout). Various aspects of the marketing plan may be tested (*e.g.*, advertising expenditure levels or, less often, product form variants), by using several pairs of cities. Output is a mix of learning, especially a sales and profit forecast. In some areas, test marketing is currently being stretched to include scanner market testing, in which the marketing activity is less than total, but the term is best confined to the full-scale activity.

Third World Distribution A term used by manufacturers to refer to such nontraditional retail institutions as discounters, promotional department stores and off-price merchants.

Tie-in Products Products sold together as a package either literally (as razor and shaving cream may be packaged together) or as a deal (as cosmetic products are frequently sold, the purchase of one being contingent on the purchase of another). Some tie-in arrangements (for example, camera film being tied-in with film processing by the same company) have been found to be in restraint of trade and thus illegal.

Time Rate of Demand The quantity of product that the market will absorb at a particular price per period of time.

Time Series Analysis A sales forecasting technique in which the analysis is based on the firm's performance over past time. An effort is made to discover patterns of activity which can be used to forecast sales volume in the future.

Token Order The placing of a small order with the possibility of a larger one in the future.

Top-Down Planning A managerial system in which planning is conducted by top management.

Total Cost (TC) 1. (economic definition) The sum of total fixed cost and total variable cost for a given level of output. 2. (physical distribution definition) In a physical distribution system, total cost includes all the costs of transportation, warehousing, order processing, packaging etc.

Total Cost of Goods Sold The gross cost of goods sold plus alteration room and workroom net cost, if any, less each discount earned on purchases.

Total Costs The sum of a firm's fixed and variable expenses.

Total Fertility Rate The number of births that 1,000 women would have in their lifetimes if at each year of age, they experienced birthrates occurring in the specified year.

Total Physical Distribution Concept A management strategy in which all distribution functions in an organisation are fully integrated, generally accomplished by making the distribution department the equal of the marketing and production departments. The objective of the total physical distribution concept is to minimise distribution costs while maintaining adequate customer service.

Total Revenue The price per unit multiplied by sales volume and summed over all products and services.

Traceable Common Costs Those expenses in a business which can be assigned to a particular activity despite the fact they they are not immediately apparent. For example, the costs related to production space in a plant may be determined by calculating the square footage given over to that activity and then subtracting that amount from the plant's total (the costs for which are known).

Tractor-Trailer The power unit and the van of a motor truck. This term usually refers to the two units that are commonly used for over-the-road surface transportation.

Trade Advertising Advertising by the producers of products or the providers of services directed to customers other than the ultimate consumer, *i.e.,* wholesalers, distributors, middlemen, retailers etc. The objective is to widen the distribution of the product or service.

Trade Allowance A short-term special offer, made by marketers to channel members as an incentive to stock, feature or in some way participate in the cooperative promotion of a product.

Trade Area 1. (geography definition) A geographical area containing the customers of a particular firm or group of firms for specific goods or services. 2. (retailing definition) A geographic sector containing potential customers for a particular retailer or shopping centre.

Trade Association A nonprofit voluntary organisation of businesses having common interests. The association sponsors research, promotes educational programmes, attempts to form public opinion and to influence the passage of legislation which might affect members.

Trade Balance A sub-balance of a country's balance of payments showing the relationship between total exports and total imports for a given period of time.

Trade Coupon A coupon that may only be redeemed at a particular store or group of stores.

Trade Credit Credit offered by manufacturers and wholesalers to their customers on a short-term basis.

Trade Deficit A condition in international trade in which the value of a country's imports is in excess of the value of it's exports.

Trade Discount A reduction is price granted by manufacturers to middlemen (including, at times, retailers) to compensate them for performing some marketing functions which would ordinarily have been the responsibility of the producer. These functions may include storage of merchandise, transportation, processing, selling, etc. Trade discounts are calculated independently of quantity discounts and are not dependent on the terms of sale stated on the invoice. Also known as a functional discount. See also *allowance, promotional allowance*, and *discount*.

Trade-in Allowance A price reduction granted by a seller to a customer in the form of a credit for traded-in equipment. The list price is unaffected but the buyer pays less as a result of the allowance.

Trade Industry In industrial marketing, trade industries are made up of organisations like wholesalers and retailers who, for the most part, purchase for resale to others or for use in conducting their business.

Trade Name A name used to designate a particular business organisation, *i.e.*, the firm together with its reputation and accrued goodwill. Trade names may or may not be exclusive. The term trade name is not applied to individual products which often carry the firm's trademark. Sometimes known as the commercial name. See also *brand name, trademark* and *brand*.

Trade Premium A prize, usually merchandise, given by jobbers' retailers for their cooperation in achieving sales.

Trade Quota In international trade, a quota which imposes a specific limit on the amount of goods which may be imported into a country.

Trade Sales Promotion Short-term non-recurrent effort whose object is an increased buying response on the part of wholesalers and retailers. These efforts commonly take the form of buying allowances, free goods, cooperative advertising money, push money, sales contests, etc.

Trade Salesperson A salesperson whose primary responsibility is promotional, *i.e.*, helping customers to promote the company's products at the wholesale or retail level by setting up displays, stocking shelves, providing demonstrations etc. Trade sales-people write orders, but are, for the most part, concerned with maintaining good relations with established customers.

Trade Show A gathering of manufacturers or wholesalers in a particular industry (housewares, food, electronics etc.) for the purpose of exhibiting their wares. Trade shows are commonly held in exhibition centres or hotels and give buyers (at the retail level) an opportunity to see many lines of merchandise in one place and to form an opinion as to what is available in the market.

Trade Surplus A condition in international trade in which the value of a country's exports is in excess of the value of its imports.

Trading Across A practice in which a firm (such as a store), in an effort to broaden its customer base or to reposition itself in the marketplace, alters its marketing strategy in a way calculated to appeal to a new market segment. In trading across, the firm is seeking to attract a customer on the same economic level as the original segment, but whose life-style, demographics or psychographics are somewhat different. See also *trading down* and *trading up*.

Trading Area In a general sense a firm's trading area is that geographic zone containing the people who are likely to purchase the firm's goods or services. The term is most commonly applied to retailing where it refers to that area from which a store or shopping centre attracts most of its customers.

Trading Company Companies organised to do business in foreign countries (or, for example, in Japan where they operate within the country), the trading company is involved in all aspects of buying, accumulating, transporting, distributing and selling goods.

Trading Down A practice in which a firm (most commonly a store), in an effort to broaden its customer base or to reposition itself in the market-place, alters its marketing strategy. Generally it would reduce prices and/or lower the quality level of its products. It may also promote itself in a way calculated to appeal to customers of a lower socioeconomic level.

Trading Stamps Printed stamps given to customers by retailers as a continuity premium for shopping in the store. Stamps are pasted into books and redeemed for merchandise offered by the trading stamp company or for their value in cash. Trading stamps are regarded as a form of non-price competition.

Trading Up (1) A practice in which a firm (frequently a store), in an effort to attract customers of a higher socio-economic level, alters its marketing strategy. Goods of higher quality may be produced or offered for sale at generally higher prices than before and the firm may promote itself in a manner calculated to attract more affluent customers. (2) A salesperson is said to be trading up (or selling up) when he or she encourages the customers to buy more expensive merchandise.

Traffic and Motor Vehicle Safety Act (1966) See *National Traffic and Motor Vehicle Safety Act (1966)*

Traffic and Safety Act (1958) See *National Traffic and Safety Act (1958)*.

Traffic (Customer) When applied to retailing, this refers to those people who frequent the store (or the shopping area) within a particular period of time. Traffic may be heavy, light or medium.

Traffic Item A consumer product in demand and with high replacement frequency that regularly brings traffic to a store or department.

Traffic Management In a narrow industrial sense traffic management means buying transportation service for the purpose of shipping goods. This includes such functions as the determination of freight charges, application of tariff regulations, freight consolidation etc. In a broader marketing sense, traffic management is concerned with the transportation and warehousing of goods in the distribution chain. Efficiency of movement and cost reduction are primary goals of traffic managers.

Transaction An individual act of reciprocal giving and receiving (involving either money or barter) in the exchange process. A transaction nearly always involves the transfer of ownership of some product or the transfer of the use of some service from one party to another. See also *exchange*.

Transaction Code The unique identifying number that defines the specific data being transmitted via an electronic data interchange transaction. Numbers are assigned to various types of document transactions such as purchase orders, warehouse shipping orders and motor carrier shipment information.

Transaction Value The subjectively weighted difference between the buyer's reference price and the actual price to be paid.

Transactions Cost Analysis An approach to analysing the economics of vertical relationships. The basic premise is that firms will internalise those activities they are able to perform at lower cost and will rely on the market for those activities for which other providers have an advantage. The costs of transactions are determined by the frequency with which they recur, the environmental uncertainty surrounding them and the specificity of the assets they require.

Transactional Marketing Function Any marketing function which involves the transfer of ownership of either goods or services between parties. Transactional marketing functions include buying, selling, risk assumption and related tasks. They overlap somewhat with facilitating marketing functions. See also *marketing functions*.

Transfer (Interdepartmental Merchandise) An intrafirm transaction accounting for the movement of merchandise from one selling department or location to another, which is a transfer-in for the department or other selling unit receiving the goods and a transfer-out for the department or location sending the goods.

Transfer Price Intracompany charges made for goods transferred from one division to another or for goods shipped to foreign subsidiaries.

Transfer Pricing. The pricing of goods and services that are sold to controlled entities of the same organisations, *e.g.*, movements of goods and services within a multi-national or global corporation.

Transformational Advertising. The advertising that associates product usage with certain feelings, images or meanings that then transform the experience of using the product. For example, a transformational ad could make the experience of using a product warmer or more exciting.

Transit Privileges In transportation, the privilege offered a shipper by a shipping company (usually a rail-road) or unloading goods in transit for future processing (*e.g.*, wheat to be milled into flour) then reloaded and delivered to their destination without incurring additional charges. Also known as processing in transit or milling in transit.

Transit Rate A rate that allows the through shipment of goods to be interrupted for intermediate processing. Even though the goods are stopped enroute to the ultimate destination, a through rate is charged similar to a rate that would be charged if the goods had not stopped enroute to their ultimate destination.

Transit Time The period of time a carrier (railroad, trucker etc.) has possession of a shipment.

Transnational Corporation A stage of development of the global/transnational corporation.

Transportation Mode A specific class of related carriers such as truck, rail, air or water. It is a generic class of transportation carrier.

Travelling Salesperson A firm's travelling representative who covers a particular region or territory soliciting orders for the firm's products. Also called a commercial traveller or travelling sales representative.

Trend Analysis The use of analytical techniques, such as time series analysis, to discern trends.

Trend Extension A method of forecasting sales for existing products. Since such products have a record of previous sales data, market forecasters simply project past sales performance into the future.

Trend Extrapolation The projection of patterns identified in data about the past into the future.

Trial A psychological term denoting the number of a practice run, such as a 5-trial learning experience or a series of repetitions of a learning experience. It is also used to imply a sampling of a product before repurchase.

Trial Sampling In sales promotion, the encouraging of product trial by the consumer through the giving of free samples.

Truck Wholesaler A limited-service wholesaler who operates his business from a truck from which he sells and delivers merchandise and collects payment. Truck wholesalers carry a limited line of goods, *e.g.,* bread or dairy products and generally serve retail outlets, industrial facilities or institutions. Known also as truck jobbers, wagon distributors and merchandise deliverers.

Truth-in-Lending Act (1968) See *Consumer Credit Protection Act (1968)*

Truth-in-Packaging Act (1966) See *Fair Packaging and Labeling Act (1966)*

Turnkey Operation A business arrangement involving a buyer, a prime contractor, a number of subcontractors and a product. The prime contractor pulls all the sub-contractors together, manufactures the product and, finally, delivers it to the buyer. Thus it is said that the buyer, to achieve his needs, simply turns a key and it is accomplished.

Two Column Tariff A system of tariffs in which the initial single column of duties is supplemented by a second column of duties that shows reduced rates agreed through tariff negotiations with other countries.

Two-Step Flow Model A theory of mass communication which held that both mass media and opinion lenders influenced behaviour. In this two-step process, information was seen to flow from the mass media to the opinion leaders who then influenced the general population. The theory has now been superseded by the multistep flow model. See also *hypodermic needle model* and *multi-step flow model.*

Two Step Flow of Communication The belief that the process of influence of communications material is not directly from the communicator to the audience or interpreters, but rather influence is a two step process from the mass communications, such as advertising, to the opinion leader in the group and from the opinion leader to the other individuals.

Twofers Two items being sold for the price of one.

Tying Agreement An agreement in which a manufacturer requires a dealer or middleman to purchase certain goods in order to purchase certain other goods or in which the manufacturer requires that the dealer not sell competing goods. In return, the dealer may be granted exclusive rights to sales of the manufacturer's products in a specified territory.

Type Face Anyone of a wide variety of systematically designed styles or patterns used to present letters of the alphabet, numbers, and punctuation marks. A font is a particular point size and style variation (such as italic) with a given type face.

U

Ultimate Consumer The ultimate consumer is the end user—the person buying goods or services for personal use or for use in the home. In retailing, the term is commonly taken to mean the store's customers. Also known as the *final consumer*.

Umbrella Pricing A strategy in which a large firm maintains the prices of its products at a level higher than necessary in an effort to protect smaller competitors from ruinous competition. Umbrella pricing is the opposite of predatory pricing.

Unaided Recall A method of testing a consumer's ability to remember an advertisement and, hence, a means of determining the ad's effectiveness. Subjects are asked to identify advertisements they have recently seen or heard but are given no stimulus to aid their memory, *i.e.,* they are not shown the actual ads and are not given any other hints or clues.

Unbundling Prices A pricing policy in which customers (usually at retail) are permitted to choose certain services on an optimal basis. Prices are unbundled in the sense that a single price is no longer quoted for a product/service package.

Unchanging List Price List prices that remain the same for extended periods of time, despite the fact that both add-ones and discounts may affect the actual selling price of the goods. See also *list price*.

Uncontrollable Factors Those elements in the marketing environment which are out of the control of the organisation, e.g., shifts in the economy, government regulations, international politics, etc.

Underprivileged Family A family in a social class that does not have enough money to purchase the necessities, *i.e.*, shelter clothing and transportation, appropriate for its class status. An underprivileged family is not able to acquire what is expected for its class status and usually is defined as having at least 15 per cent lower income than the median for the social class.

Undifferentiated Marketing A marketing strategy in which one or more products are offered for sale to the total market, i.e., no attempt is made to address individual market segments. Undifferentiated marketing, which is usually applied to staple products (gasoline, sugar, salt, etc.), focuses on those characteristics which are common to large numbers of customers. It is a simpler and cheaper strategy to execute than differentiated marketing.

Undifferentiated Oligopoly An oligopoly that produces and markets standardised products—*e.g.*, cement or paperboard boxes.

Uneven Exchange An exchange of goods made by a customer when the value of the new goods received is different from that of the goods returned.

Unfair Trade Practices Acts State laws intended to discourage predatory pricing by wholesalers and retailers. In general the acts prohibit the reselling of goods for less than their purchase price (except in the case of legitimate clearance sale merchandise) and, in addition, may require a minimum markup of, for example, 6%. In some states these laws apply to all products, in others, to certain categories of products, *e.g.*, alcoholic beverages, groceries, etc. Also known as *minimum markup laws*.

Uniform Communications System (UCS) A communication standard adopted by the food industry for electronic transmission of information between buyer and seller.

Uniform Freight Classification A system that allows the grouping of related products into specific rate categories. These ratings are based on handling characteristics, bulk, value, and perishability of the product. These ratings are used as the basis for a standardised rates for classes of products.

Unique Selling Proposition (USP) The unique selling proposition was the brainchild of Rosser Reeves, co-founder of the Ted Bates advertising agency. He explained the concept in his 1961 book *Reality in Advertising*. Essentially, Reeves advocated using research to verify the truthfulness of advertising claims and to then launch hard-hitting campaigns based on the unique properties of the product. The unique selling proposition is a promise made in a highly competitive and convincing manner which positions the product clearly in the minds of the consumer.

Unit Control The control of stock in terms of merchandise units rather than in terms of dollar value.

Unit Load A shipment that contains multiple units but moves as a single entity. For example, shipments that are palletised or slipsheeted or containerised are unit load shipments.

Unit Packing Packing merchandise in selling units (by the manufacturer) so it can be sold from sample and delivered to the customer without repacking at the store.

Unit Pricing The practice of pricing merchandise (groceries, meats, etc.) relative to a common denominator such as price per pound, price per quart, price per dozen, etc. The label displaying unit pricing will also display the price for the package as a whole.

Unitary Price Elasticity A special situation in which a cut in price increases quantity just enough that total revenue remains unchanged.

United Nations (UN) An international organisation founded in 1945 of countries whose mission is to promote the cause of peace, prosperity and human rights for all people.

United Nations Conference on Trade and Development (UNCTAD) An organisation set up by the United Nations to assist the less developed nations. It seeks to accelerate the growth rate of the less developed countries (LDCs) to not less than 5 percent per annum.

Unitising The consolidations of a number of boxes or packages into one load, frequently stacked on a pallet to facilitate movement.

Universal Product Code (UPC) Adopted by food industry in 1973, the UPC is a classification system in which each product (and each size, flavour, colour etc.) is assigned a ten-digit number. The numbers are premarked on the package by the manufacture in the form of a bar code (thick and thin vertical lines) over the ten corresponding Arabic numerals. The bar code is readable by an optical scanner at the checkout counter and the information it contains is transmitted to a computer. It is the computer which contains the prices not the UPC and it is the computer which controls the cash register.

Universe In marketing research, the universe is the total population to be studied, whether by census or by sampling.

Unplanned Business District A group of retail establishments which have grown up together without benefit of formal planning. Central business districts, *i.e.,* down towns, are examples of unplanned business districts.

Unplanned Centre A cluster of retail stores within the city in which there is a structured internal pattern of locations, achieved by the independent decisions of stores operating within the land market.

Unprotected Consumers Those groups of consumers relatively unable to defend their rights in the marketplace and for whom sufficient protective legislation has not been written. Children, the elderly, the poor and the infirm are regarded as unprotected consumers. See also *consumer laws* and *consumer advocate.*

Unsought Goods Merchandise which the customer: (1) does not know about, (2) feels is not a good value, or (3) does not believe he needs.

Unstructured Questionnaire A questionnaire in which the number of questions is limited and in which the interviewer is allowed to vary the wording and sequence of the questions. The interviewer is also allowed some latitude in probing the subject for additional information. See also *structured* *questionnaire* and *questionnaire.*

Unwholesome Demand The desire for goods, services and activities that are deemed to reduce individual and social welfare. Comment: Examples include the desire for illegal drugs, excessive amounts of alcoholic beverages and driving at excessive speeds.

Urban Population Persons living in places of 2,500 or more inhabitants incorporated as cities, villages, boroughs or areas designated as such by the Census, with some exceptions.

Urbanised Area An area consisting of a central city or core together with contiguous, closely settled territories that have a combined total population of at least 50,000.

Uruguay Round The multilateral negotiations between the member countries of GATT that were held in Uruguay from the mid-1980s to 1993.

Usage Rate Segmentation A method of market segmentation based on the rate at which consumers buy and use products. Typically, usage rate segmentation divides the market into heavy, light and non-users. Data is gathered by research firms (such as W.R. Simmons Associates in their annual *Study of Media and Markets*), usually through the use of a selected group of consumers who records daily purchases in a diary. The data is then analysed by product category and the terms "heavy, light and non-users" defined for that category. See also *market segmentation.*

Useless Quality A level of quality built into a product in excess of that required by the consumer

Use Up Rate The volume or length of time required by a consumer to move from one purchase occasion to another.

V

Valuation Account In accounting, a contra account is one which accumulates subtractios from another account, so as to establish the net valuation of the other account. for example an accumulated depreciation account would be a contra account for machinery. Also called a valuation account.

Value Value is that inherent worth which is possessed by a product or service. It is generally expressed in terms of its price, *i.e.,* in money terms or as credit or as other goods and services. See also *price* and *cost*.

Value Added The increase in the worth of a product as a result of the activities it passes through in the producton/distribution chain.

Value Added Tax (VAT) A tax levied on the increased worth of goods at each level of the production/distribution process represented by the difference between the cost of goods at the beginning of one stage in the process and the price of the goods at the end. Thus, a retailer would be taxed on the difference between the wholesale price of goods and their retail price

Value Added By Marketing The increase in the worth of a product as a result of the activities it passes through in the distribution chain. It may be computed as the value of sales, less the cost of goods sold, less the cost of supplies, energy, and all other activities involved in the marketing of the product.

Value Analysis An effort made by the purchasers of products, parts, and materials to examine the quality level of their acquisitions and to reduce costs to the lowest possible level.

Value Based Pricing A price setting process based on the value the product provides to the customer.

Value-Expressive Function of Attitudes A function of attitudes that allows the individual to express his or her self-concept. The value-expressive function is served by attitudes that demonstrate one's self -image to others. It is one of the functions of attitudes proposed by the functional theory of attitudes.

Value-in-Exchange The amount of money or goods actually paid for a product or service.

Value-in-Use Pricing A method of setting prices in which an attempt is made to capture a portion of what a customer would save by buying a firm's product.

Variable Cost An operating expense that changes as sales volume changes, e.g., delivery costs.

Variable Cost, Average The sum of all variable costs, *i.e.,* those costs that vary directly with the number of units produced and marketed, divided by the number of units currently produced.

Variable Cost, Total The sum of all costs directly incurred by production and marketing of a given number of units.

Variable Import Levies The import charges levied when the prices of imported products would undercut those of domestic products. The effect of these levies would be to raise the price of imported products to the domestic level.

Variable Leader Pricing Leader pricing is a strategy in which certain items are offered for sale at prices so low that they yield little or no profit. Variable leader pricing is a strategy commonly found in the supermarket industry in which the leader items are frequently changed, often on a weekly basis.

Variable Price Policy A policy most commonly found at retail in which prices are not fixed, *i.e.,* one in which the seller may alter price to make a deal or in which the buyer may try to negotiate more favourable terms. Variable prices are used primarily where the customer realises that list prices are merely the starting point in reaching a final price as in the automobile industry.

Variety Seeking The choice of an alternative in order to experience diversity or variety in consumption over time. For example, someone may eat a Butterfinger candy bar for a snack one day, but choose a Baby Ruth candy bar the next day specifically to get something different.

Vendor An individual or business (manufacturer, importer, jobber, agent, wholesaler etc.) who sells goods to other businesses. Commonly known as a *supplier* and in the *retail trade,* as a *resource.*

Vendor Analysis An examination of how well a particular supplier performs. Included in the analysis are matters of price (are they competitive, are terms reasonable), matters of reliability (is merchandise of high quality, are deliveries on time) and resale considerations (how much can merchandise be marked up, what percentage will have to be marked down).

Venture Team A group of specialists within a firm brought together for the specific purpose of planning, developing, and introducing into the marketplace a new product. Venture teams are usually disbanded when their assignment has been completed. See also *product planning committee.*

Vertical Cooperative Advertising Advertising in which the retailer and other previous marketing channel members (*e.g.,* manufacturers or wholesalers) share the cost.

Vertical Industrial Market A narrow market for industrial goods but one in which nearly every organisation is a potential customer.

Vertical Integration The ownership achieved by merger or internal expansion, of the marketing channel intermediaries connecting the manufacturer/producer with the consumer. Vertical integration may be accomplished through forward integration (the manufacturer may own his own distribution network and retail outlets) or through backward integration (in which the retailer controls his sources of supply). Sometimes referred to as a corporate distribution system. See also *dual distribution*.

Vertical Market A situation in which an industrial product is used by only one or a very few industry or trade groups. The market is narrow but deep in the sense that most prospective customers in the industry may need the article.

Vertical Marketing System (VMS) Large, centrally managed industrial organisations in which two or more levels of the market (manufacturing, wholesaling, retailing) are controlled by a dominant member of the channel. The system may be organised in one of three ways: (1) administered vertical marketing system, (2) corporate vertical marketing system and (3) contractual vertical marketing system. Vertical marketing systems have as their objective the achievement of operating economies resulting from greater size, increased efficiency achieved through closer control, economies achieved through the elimination of duplicated activities, and increased bargaining power resulting from large-scale operations.

Vertical Price-Fixing A conspiracy among marketers at different levels of the channel to set prices for a product.

Vidale-Wolfe Model An econometric model that represents the rate of change of sales as function of the rate of advertising spending. The lagged effect of advertising is incorporated using a sales-decay term. (Vidale and Wolfe 1957). The model allows the effect of advertising to have different rise versus decay rates.

Visual Merchandising A strategy frequently used in retailing for the in-store presentation of merchandise so that it would be shown to its greatest advantage. Visual merchandising, which includes traditional display techniques, increasingly involves planning store layout, decor, and activities which appeal to other senses, such as music. The object of these efforts is to increase the sale of merchandise. See also *display*.

Volume Zone The range of prices covering middle-priced merchandise which is aimed at customers who are moderately budget conscious but who tend to buy also of merchandise oif theyfindit affordable. See also *price zone.*

Voluntary Group A contractual vertical marketing system in which a wholesaler bands together its independent retail customers into a voluntary group. A complete range of services is offered to retail members including centralised advertising and promotion, store location and store layout, training, financing and accounting.

Voluntary Chain A wholelsaler-sponsored voluntary association of independnet retailiers. Teh member stores buy all or most of their merchandise fro thc sponsoring whole-saler who, in turn, provides certain management services such as, accounting systems, display direction, standardised merchandise packages, central data proessing, etc. members of voluntary chains often display common identifyng names or logos. see also *retail cooperative and consumer cooperative.*

Voluntary Inter-Industry Communications Standard (VICS) A communications standard adopted by the mass merchandising industry for electronic transmission of information between buyer and seller.

W

Wagon Distributor A wholesaler whose inventory of merchandise is carried on trucks that are operated by driver sales people. The retailer's requirements for merchandise are determined at the time of the sales call and orders are filled immediately from the stock carried on the truck. It is a somewhat archaic team.

Walk-outs Persons wholeave a store without making a purchase because of prices, lack of merchandise, etc.

Wall Display An interior display made up of posters and/or actual mechndise hung from the walls of the store. Used to attract the customer's attention and promote the sale of particular merchandise.

Want Book 1. The information collected by retail salespeople to record out-of-stock or requested merchandise. 2. A notebook in which store employees record the names for items called for by customers but are not in stock.

Want Slip A slip on which the salesperson records customer requests for items that cannot be supplied from stock.

Warehouse A commercial establishment in which large quantities of goods may be stored. See also *public warehouse, contract warehouse* and *private warehouse.*

Warehouse, Bonded A warehouse that is bonded to insure the owners of the stored goods against loss.

Warehouse, Chain Store A establishment that is operated by a retail multiunit or organisation primarily for the purpose of assembling and distributing goods and performing other wholesale functions for the stores of such an organisation.

Warehouse, Contract A facility where the user of the warehouse contracts with a third party for some mix of labour, management, and materials handling capability over a specified contract period. The contract period usually exceeds one year.

Warehouse, Field A warehouse facility used to store and transfer merchandise enroute from manufacturing location to other channel members.

Warehouse, Private A private or corporate, warehouse is a facility that is operated by the buyer or the seller of the product. It may be used to store raw materials in anticipation of production, work in process or finished goods awaiting shipment to the buyer.

Warehouse, Public 1. (physical distribution definition) A for-hire facility that is available to any business requiring storage or handling of goods. The public warehouse usually operates on a monthly contract and charges for storage plus a handling fee for receiving goods and moving goods out of storage. 2. (retailing definition) A storage facility generally privately owned that does not take title to the goods it handles. It may issue receipts that can be used as security for loans.

Warehouse Receipts The receipts that every public warehouse issues to depositors for goods, placed to storage.

Warehouse Retailing A form of high-volume, low overhead mass merchandising characterised by facilities lacking traditional amenities, few customer services and isolated low rent buildings. Merchandise (especially food appliances, and furniture) is sold at prices below regular retail in these facilities reminiscent of warehouses.

Warehouse Store A large discount retailer that offers merchandise in a no-frills or warehouse type of environment.

Warranty An assurance given by the manufacturer of a product as to the quality and performance of the product and a statement relating the conditions under which the product will be replaced or repaired should it prove to be defective. A warranty may be expressed, *i.e.,* it may be represented verbally or in writing or it may be implied, *i.e.*, that there is a general understanding that the product is safe and in proper operating condition. See also *guarantee*.

Wearout A condition of inattention and possible irritation that occurs after an audience or target market has encountered a specific advertisement too many times.

Webb-Pomerene Association Organisations jointly owned, maintained, or supported by competing U.S. manufacturers especially and exclusively for export trade. Special legislation gives them qualified exemption from antitrust laws.

Weber's Law This states that product purchasers and users are more interested in the relative differences between products than in the absolute characteristics of products standing alone.

Weeks' Supply Method of Stock Planning A method of stock planning whereby one plans for a certain number of weeks' supply. In utilising this method, it is assumed that the same stock turnover can be maintained throughout the selling season; thus, inventory carried is in direct proportion to expected sales.

Wheel of Retailing Theory A theory of retail institutional change propounded by Malcom P. McNair (Harvard Business School) in which retail innovators are seen as beginning the growth cycle as low status, low margin, low price operators. A period follows during which facilities become more elaborate, costs increase, and higher margins are required to survive. As the innovative retail institution thus matures, the cycle begins again with the next low margin innovator. The complete cycle is one turn of the wheel.

Wheeler-Lea Amendment (1938) An amendment to the Federal Trade Commission Act (1914) which provides the FTC with the authority to protect consumers from unfair trade practices (particularly those involving deceptive advertising) in cases where it is not possible to prove that competition being injured.

White Goods 1. Large kitchen appliances. 2. Sheets and other bedding items.

Whole Market Method A marketing approach which is geared to the entire range of potential customers and which neither recognises nor attempts to appeal to the differences between various segments. See also *mass marketing* and *market segmentation.*

Wholesale Club A general merchandise wholesaler and/or retailer that offers a limited merchandise assortment with little service at low prices and sells only to club member ultimate consumers and member trade people. It is sometimes called a warehouse club.

Wholesale Establishment A recognisable place of business that is primarily engaged in performing marketing functions, including the functions of exchange on the wholesale level of distribution.

Wholesale Market Centre A concentration of vendors' sales offices or display rooms in one place, usually a city or an area within city. Sometimes it is identified by a concentration of production facilities, as well as sales offices.

Wholesale Merchant An establishment primarily engaged in buying and selling merchandise in the domestic market and performing the principal wholesale functions.

Wholesale Price Index (WPI) A relative measure maintained by the U.S. government of average price changes in commodities sold in wholesale markets in the United States.

Wholesale Transaction A non retail sale including sales by manufacturers to middlemen and retailers, sales by manufacturers to other manufacturers, sale from farmers to processors, governments sales, etc.

Wholesaler A term applied to a category of wholesaling middleman primarily engaged in buying merchandise from a producer and selling it to an industrial user, institutional user, or retailer, but seldom, to the ultimate consumer. The wholesaler ordinarily takes title to and possession of the goods he sells. Wholesalers fall into two broad categories: (1) the full-service or full-function wholesaler who performs a number of function including assembly, warehousing, breaking bulk, selling, delivery, credit extension, etc. (2) the limited service or limited-function wholesaler who performs fewer service functions than his full-service counterpart. Wholesalers are sometimes called merchant wholesalers, jobbers, and distributors.

Wholesaler's Salesperson A sales representative of a wholesale firm who calls on retail (and sometimes manufacturer) customers.

Wholesaler Sponsored Cooperative A form of contractual vertical marketing system that is an example of forward integration. Retailers achieve vertical system advantages by affiliating with a sponsoring wholesaler.

Wholesaling Those marketing transactions which involve the sale of goods to retailers, other wholesalers, and to business, institutions and industrial users for the purpose of (1) resale, (2) use in performing the organisation's basic function, or (3) incorporation into another product. Wholesaling's most important function is breaking bulk, i.e., providing buyers with manageable lots of the merchandise the wholesaler has bought in large quantities.

Wholesaling Middleman A term generally applied to a number of marketing intermediaries. which includes wholesaler, agent, broker, manufacturer's branch and sales office, and certain cooperative organisations. Wholesaling middlemen are also known as marketing middlemen and merchant middlemen.

Wholly-Owned Subsidiary A separate firm, owned and completely controlled by a parent company.

Will-Call The products ordered by customers in advance of the time delivery is desired.

Women in Advertising and Marketing (WAM) An association of women in advertising and marketing. WAM serves as a network by promoting professional contact between its members. It publishes a quarterly *Membership Directory*, as well as a quarterly newsletter. WAM also maintains a Job Bank and a Speakers Bureau. The association's headquarters are in Washington. D.C.

Women's Direct Responses Group (WDRG) An association of women professionally involved in direct marketing. The association serves as network and information centre for its membership. WDRG also maintains a career talent bank and sponsors summer internship programmes. It publishes a quarterly *Newsletter* and an annual *Membership Roster*. The association's headquarters are located in New York City.

Word-of-Mouth Communication Communication via the spoken word on a person-to-person basis. Although not strictly speaking a form of advertising it can be crucially important in the success or failure of certain business endeavours, as, for example, the success of a motion picture.

Word Association A questionnaire containing a list of words to which respondents are instructed to reply with the first word that comes to mind.

Workable Competition An economic model of a market in which competition is less than perfect, but adequate enough to give buyers genuine alternatives.

Workload Analysis Procedure for determining the total amount of sales effort required to cover each sales territory after considering the sales potential and the number of accounts to be served. Comment: The number of sales calls to be made on each, the duration of each sales call, and the estimated amount of non-selling and travel time are explicitly considered.

Workroom A service department such as apparel alterations, drapery manufacture, furniture polishing and repair, or carpet, workroom.

World Corporation Organisation A form of decentralised organisational structure applicable to certain multinational firms. In a world corporation organisation the world is viewed as the firm's area of operations and no single national market draws greater attention than that merited by its size. Markets, techniques, ideas, personnel, processes, and products are drawn from the entire area of operations. Divisions for each of the national territories operate side by side as equals, rather than as part of a hierarchical scheme.

Y

Yield Management The practice of pricing to maximise the amount of revenue received per unit sold. It is commonly associated with the pricing practices of airlines, hotels, and other sellers of "perishable" products.

Young Contemporary Customer A category of retail customer with a strong interest in clothes, but not really a fashon pace-setter. These young people are extremely peer conscous and, although they may be fashion advanced, they are not trend-setters.

Youth Market The segment of the population aged 14–24.

Youth Research Institute of New York (YRINY) A New York based organisation which surveys the teenage, college and young adult market.

Youths Size ranges in teenage apparel for males in even numbers usually ranging from 1 through 18 or 20.

Z

Zero-based Budgeting A method of determining the budget for a store or other business which requires each department or sales area to justify each item on its expense budget. Past history is not considered justification for any expenditure.

Zero Defects A condition in which a production unit makes every product without defect. It is usually only a theory or a reference point, but it is actually sought in such categories as aerospace, serums, U.S. mint and others.

Zero Order Model A probabilistic model in which the probability of occurrence of any given outcome at a particular point in time does not depend on any previous outcomes of the process. Models of this kind are often used to represent brand choice behaviour or media exposure patterns (Lilien and Kotler 1983). Evidence that this simple zero order assumption for brand choice behaviour cannot be rejected, given empirical choice patterns, has been provided by Bass, Givon, Kalwani Reibstein and Wright (1984).

Zone of Rate Freedom (ZORF) A zone within which a carrier can raise or lower rates without regulatory or other administrative action.

Zone Pricing A strategy in which a manufacturer charges all customers in the same geographic zone a uniform delivered price without regard to individual transportation charges.

Zoning 1. (retailing definition) The regulation of the construction and use of buildings in certain areas of a municipality. 2 (sales definition). A method for scheduling sales calls that divides a territory into areas or zones.